BUSINESS ENGLISH FOR INDUSTRY AND THE PROFESSIONS

BUSINESS ENGLISH FOR INDUSTRY AND THE PROFESSIONS

Mary P. Cullinan
California State University, Hayward

The Dryden Press
Chicago New York Philadelphia San Francisco Montreal Toronto
London Sydney Tokyo Mexico City Rio de Janeiro Madrid

Acquisitions Editor: Mary Fischer
Developmental Editor: Rebecca Ryan
Project Editor: Karen Vertovec
Design Supervisor: Jeanne Calabrese
Production Manager: Mary Jarvis
Director of Editing, Design, and Production: Jane Perkins

Text Designer: Barbara Gibson
Cover Design: Vargas/Williams Design
Copy Editor: Joan Torkildson
Compositor: Modern Typographers of Florida, Inc.
Text Type: 10/12 Palatino

Library of Congress Cataloging-in-Publication Data
Cullinan, Mary.
    Business English for industry and the professions.

    Includes index.
    1. English language—Rhetoric. 2. English language—
Business English. 3. English language—Grammar—
1950–   . I. Title.
PE1479.B87C84 1987   808'.066651   86-6359
ISBN 0-03-008149-1

Printed in the United States of America
789-066-987654321

Address orders:
383 Madison Avenue
New York, NY 10017

Address editorial correspondence:
One Salt Creek Lane
Hinsdale, IL 60521

The Dryden Press
Holt, Rinehart and Winston
Saunders College Publishing

The Dryden Press Series in Business Communication

CONTENTS

PART THREE/Writing Grammatically   165

PART FOUR/Punctuating Sentences   243

PART FIVE/Learning Mechanics   307

PART SIX/Editing   351

TO THE INSTRUCTOR

METHOD AND ORGANIZATION

Business English for Industry and the Professions is designed to allow you and your students maximum flexibility. You will be able to adapt the information and materials to a variety of classroom situations and teaching methods, while your students will be able to pace themselves according to their individual writing levels.

Most business English texts focus principally on grammar and mechanics; business communication texts examine techniques for creating successful letters, memos, and resumes. Many students, however, do not get an opportunity to relate the exercises in their business English text to the practical problems of the workplace; yet they are not prepared to apply the sophisticated communication strategies of business communication texts without a grasp of basic grammar and punctuation.

Business English for Industry and the Professions is useful for students at many levels of writing competence. The text is organized so that students move from recognizing parts of speech to constructing sentences to working on grammar, punctuation, and mechanics. Throughout these chapters, moreover, students are writing and revising business-related sentences, paragraphs, and documents.

In the last two sections of this text, students apply this wide range of writing principles to effectively organizing, writing, and rewriting business materials.

Because writing is not a linear process, *Business English for Industry and the Professions* is designed so that students will be exposed to examples of business writing even in the earliest chapters. By the time students reach the section on business materials, they will already understand many of the principles underlying a good letter and memo.

Further, because learning to write requires more than memorizing principles, *Business English for Industry and the Professions* emphasizes practical applications. Students using this text will not be simply memorizing rules and filling in the blanks: they will be writing and revising sentences, paragraphs, letters, and memos much as they will have to in their jobs.

You and your students, in fact, may find it useful to go back and forth through this text rather than study it chapter by chapter. If some of your students already understand basic grammar, you can encourage them to spend a few days on Part One and then begin working on more advanced chapters. If your whole class has a good background in writing fundamentals, you may want to use the first chapters as reference and work primarily on the central and final sections.

FEATURES

Several features of *Business English for Industry and the Professions* encourage this type of individualized study:

- Pre-Tests that can be administered the first day of class to help you gauge each student's competence
- Pre-Tests at the beginning of each part that enable students to test their knowledge before they begin studying the section
- Objectives at the beginning of each part and chapter that summarize the students' goals
- Self-Check Tests that students may use to chart their progress by checking their answers at the back of the book
- Checklists at the end of each chapter that help students review the main points and key terms of the chapter
- References to other pages that provide more detailed information on a subject
- Review Tests at the end of each part that help students review what they have learned
- Chapter Reviews, Chapter Tests, and Exercises that provide a wide variety of materials for homework and in-class writing
- Exercises for Experts that will challenge ambitious students
- Cartoons that demonstrate common writing errors as well as provide a humorous touch to the writing process
- Readings for Resourceful Writers at the beginning of each part that serve as humorous commentary on an aspect of the upcoming chapters and provide springboards for in-class discussion and exercises.

TEACHER'S SUPPORT PACKAGE

The *Teacher's Edition and Test Bank* of *Business English for Industry and the Professions* comes in a three-ring binder, so you can remove pages to reproduce for students or add materials of your own. You may also choose to use one of our sample lesson plans. The answers to tests, Exercises for Experts, and Self-Check Tests are filled in for easy reference. The *Test Bank* is coordinated with each chapter of the text.

The writing classes you teach can be the key to your students' success in any field they enter. Your task is a difficult one, but a good text will make your work easier and more effective. We are sure that this practical, comprehensive, and readable text will be a valuable asset for you and your students.

ACKNOWLEDGMENTS

I want to thank the many people who have contributed their professional expertise and creative talents to *Business English for Industry and the Professions*. I am particularly grateful to the reviewers who shared their excellent suggestions and valuable criticisms at every stage of the book's development: Jane Bergman, St. Louis Community College; John R. Cole, the University of Akron; Peggy Cole, Arapahoe Community College; Doris D. Engerrand, Georgia College; Ruth Keller, Indiana Vocational Technical College; Shelby Kipplen, Michael J. Owens Technological College; Nancy Martinez, University of New Mexico-Valencia; Gil Storms, Miami University in Ohio; John Vaitkus, Waterbury State Technical College; and Dorothy Williamson, York Technical College.

My thanks go to the staff of The Dryden Press as well—particularly Joan Resler, Mary Fischer, Becky Ryan, and Karen Vertovec. I want to extend my appreciation, also, to Ford Button, who transformed my ideas into his wonderful cartoons.

Mary P. Cullinan
Hayward, California
October 1986

TO THE READER: WHY LEARN TO WRITE MORE EFFECTIVELY?

Technology, automation, and computerization are basic components of our modern world. Our lives have been altered as carbon paper was replaced by copying machines and as typewriters were replaced by word processors. Now home computers are everyday items, not figments of a science fiction writer's imagination.

Memorizing multiplication tables may seem useless to readers equipped with the latest in hand calculators and computer software. Learning grammar and punctuation may seem equally senseless, equally outdated. But is it?

Some computer programs can tell you if you have misspelled a word. Programs may scan your writing for a verb or pronoun error. But computers cannot know what you are trying to say. No machine can tell you that your memo to the bank president is wordy and confusing or that your job application letter is ineffective.

A computer, of course, is no better than the information fed into it. Without a sense of the way language works, you will find communication in a computerized world even more difficult than it was in the bad old days of carbon paper. In fact, the pressures of today's business world make fast, efficient communication even more vital to success. Language is the key to logic, to decision making—in fact, to communication. And, without written and spoken communication, our wonderful automated world would grind to a halt.

Since access to computers is not an excuse for avoiding basic writing skills, many businesspeople develop other excellent excuses. Some insist their secretaries "take care of all that." Others claim they do their communicating on the telephone or in meetings: they never need to write. Still others maintain they are successful the way they are—and cite a salary to prove it.

The truth is that almost everyone would like to be more comfortable with the written word. Most people want to write easily and confidently. Hardly anyone can rely solely on phone calls and meetings: almost all important transactions and decisions are put in writing. And most businesspeople know that a facility for writing a timely memo or letter can only be an asset to their careers and even their personal lives.

This book is geared for people who want to be successful in today's world. It is a practical text and workbook for writers who want results. You will find that the communications skills you acquire through studying this text will help you throughout your business career—in fact, throughout your life.

HOW TO USE
THIS BOOK

The opening sections of *Business English for Industry and the Professions* look suspiciously like an English grammar book—and there certainly are similarities. But this book is meant to be practical, to help you with writing situations you will encounter every day. While learning to recognize and use the basic elements of a sentence, you will also be learning to evaluate and create effective pieces of business writing. And you will be learning to overcome the pitfalls most people experience while writing business letters and memos.

If you are one of the lucky people who have a working grasp of grammar and punctuation, the first sections of this book will be a quick review. If you have forgotten the principles of grammar, you will have to take these chapters more slowly.

You can then go to the chapters on editing strategies, which stress ways of sharpening, modifying, and organizing your business writing to achieve the best possible results. The final section, on developing common business materials, provides techniques for creating persuasive, effective memos, resumes, and letters.

Writing, as you probably already know, requires performing several tasks at the same time. As you check your writing for spelling and comma errors, you will soon learn to look for confusing sentences, poor organization, and appropriate tone. When working on overcoming wordiness, you will learn about being persuasive and about constructing strong sentences.

Here are some tips for using this book effectively:

1. Take the Pre-Test at the beginning of each part. Afterward, check your answers in the back of the book to see how much you already know about the material.

2. Read the Objectives at the beginning of each part and chapter to determine your goals before studying the material.

3. Take the Self-Check Tests as you read through the material. They will help you make sure you have grasped each major idea. Do not look at the answers until you have worked on the tests! If you make errors on a Self-Check Test, you should study the material again.

4. Use the Checklist at the end of each chapter as a quick summary of major ideas and key terms in the chapter.

5. Flip ahead to later chapters if you want more information on a subject. Often, we will tell you what pages might be helpful.

6. Use the Glossary for definitions or examples of grammatical terms.

7. Take the Review Tests at the end of each part to review what you have learned.

8. Study the examples of business materials that appear throughout the book and particularly in the last part. They provide you with models of good and bad memos, resumes, and letters.

9. Before starting a writing assignment, check the Index for a list of the business materials we have used as examples. Under *memos,* for instance, you will find a listing for memos throughout the text.

The many examples in this book will help you gain an understanding of what to avoid and what to work on in your own writing. From now on, you will find yourself reading newspapers and magazines—as well as letters and memos—with a better sense of what the writers are doing both right and wrong.

Reading with a critical eye will help your own writing improve and develop. But, of course, you will have to continue writing in order to write effectively. This book offers hundreds of opportunities for writing, rewriting, and editing business materials. As you work on these memos, resumes, and letters, you will find the words, sentences, and paragraphs coming more easily.

And more and more often, you will find your writing is bringing you the results you want.

BUSINESS ENGLISH FOR INDUSTRY AND THE PROFESSIONS

PRE-TEST I
GRAMMAR, PUNCTUATION, MECHANICS, WORD CHOICE

_____
Name

I. **Cross out the wrong word choice in the following sentences and write the correct choice in the blank. (20 points)**

1. Please let us know by (March 15/March 15th) if you can attend the meeting.   _____

2. If Mr. Woodrow arrives before noon, ask him to speak to Jan or (I/me).   _____

3. Each of the new employees (has/have) been given a tour of the plant.   _____

4. (It's/Its) been nearly a decade since the last strike.   _____

5. The clerical staff and the technical employees will not be (effected/affected) by the change in policy.   _____

6. Every day for a year, Mona Simpson has (swum/swam) across the lake before going to work.   _____

7. (Has/Have) Mr. Parker and Ms. Hill been informed of the error?   _____

8. (Who/Whom) have you asked to the meeting?   _____

9. The programmers are not (all together/altogether) certain about the client's requirements.   _____

10. Neither James nor (I/myself) have been nominated for the position.   _____

11. (300/Three hundred) employees have been given an extended vacation until July.   _____

12. At the end of the report (appear/appears) three recommendations   _____

13. With every purchase, the customer receives a (complimentary/complementary) calculator.   _____

14. (Us/We) managers are working on a five-year plan to present to the board of directors.   _____

15. We hope you will return the items immediately if (they're/their) damaged.   _____

16. When we reach a (decision/decision,) I will call you.   _____

17. Paul has selected Jane and (I/me).   _____

18. The recipe includes these (ingredients;/ingredients:) flour, sugar, and butter.   _____

19. He enjoys playing (baseball/baseball,) and jogging.   _____

20. I will design the new (system;/system,) Philip will
    work as my assistant.   _____

**II. Underline the subjects in the following sentences. Do not
     underline articles or other modifiers. Then write the subjects in
     the blanks. (5 points)**

1. Until this afternoon, Roger had been planning a trip

   to Naples.   _____

2. This company and its subsidiaries are undergoing   _____

   some changes in management structure.   _____

3. When do you plan to return to work?   _____

4. Each of the terminals has been damaged.   _____

5. Karen Lowry will make an appointment for you.   _____

**III. Underline the helping verbs and main verbs in the following
      sentences. Then write the verbs in the blanks. (5 points)**

1. The personnel director has evaluated your application. _____

2. We will start the project at the end of April.   _____

3. Did you revise the report?   _____

4. Mary Todd has organized the material and outlined _____

   the proposal.   _____

5. The meeting lasted only an hour.   _____

PRE-TEST II

Proofread the following letter for errors in punctuation, mechanics, and grammar. Cross out each error and write the correct form above the error. (15 points)

539 Seminole ~~ave.~~ *Avenue*

Berkeley, CA 94704

January 1~~,~~19xx

single space

Mr. Wilson Reade, General Manager

Handy Supply Company

2398 Brande ~~road~~ *R*

San Francisco, ~~Ca~~ *A* 94745

Dear Mr. Reade, ~~:~~

I am applying for the part-time secretarial position advertised in the Wall Street Journal on December 1. I bel~~ei~~ve *ie* my education and skills qualifi~~es~~ me for *qualify* the position.

As you can see from my enclosed resume~~,~~ I am finishing my B.S. degree from Foster College. I will graduate in June with a double major in Management and Finance.

While attending school~~,~~ I ~~have~~ worked for several large retail company'~~s~~ such *companies* as yours. My skills include us~~e~~ing a word processor and a ten-key adding machine.

I would be very interested in meeting with you next week to discuss my qualifications. I will call ~~you're~~ office on January 5 to see if we can set up an *your* interve~~iw~~. *ie*

Sincerely ~~Y~~ours, *y*

Jan Miller

RECOGNIZING PARTS OF SPEECH

FAMOUS FIRST DRAFTS: FOLK MEDICINE
Writing Hint: Avoid Jargon

An apple a day keeps the doctor away.

Source: Ford Button

Reading for Resourceful Writers

The Case of the Missing Office Worker: A Dialogue with Eight Characters (soon to be a major mini-series)

Characters

Nora Noun: Competent business manager. Concerned with people, places, things, and ideas.

Herb Verb: Nora's associate. A man of action in the company.

Al Adjective: Nora's co-worker. Works in publicity, describing the company to clients. Often appears with Nora at business functions.

Alice Adverb: Herb's assistant and admirer. She often follows him around the office.

Connie Conjunction: Acts as company liaison. Links departments.

Peter ("Preppie") Preposition: Young intern. Often acts as leader of a group. Management thinks he's someone who is going places.

Hector Interjection: Very enthusiastic new employee.

Paula Pronoun: Assistant manager. Acts as stand-in for Nora Noun.

Setting: Company lounge

NORA NOUN: Where is *Paula*? Has *Paula* disappeared? Her *desk* is empty! Her *purse* is gone.

HECTOR INTERJECTION: *Oh! Heavens!*

NORA NOUN: I've checked the *hallway*, the *cafeteria*.

CONNIE CONJUNCTION: *And* the parking lot?

HERB VERB: *Run! Try* the parking lot. *Call* security. *Ask* for help.

ALICE ADVERB: Run *quickly!* Start *now!*

CONNIE CONJUNCTION: She's gone, *but* why would she leave?

PREPPIE PREPOSITION: Did you look *in* the library? *Near* the year-end reports? *Beside* the filing cabinets?

AL ADJECTIVE: *That messy, dreary* library! *Beautiful* Paula wouldn't be in *that horrible* place.

HECTOR INTERJECTION: *Ugh!*

NORA NOUN: The *company* needs *Paula*. Her *assistance*, her *skill*—

HERB VERB: *Have* you *telephoned* the police?

ALICE ADVERB: Call *immediately!*

PAULA PRONOUN (appearing at the door): Here *I* am. Thank *you* for *your* concern. Now *I* know *you* need *me*—and *I* need *you*.

HERB VERB: What *happened?* We *missed* you!

PAULA PRONOUN: *I* couldn't bear being a stand-in any more. *I* wanted a life of *my* own.

PREPPIE PREPOSITION: You wanted a life *without* Nora?

CONNIE CONJUNCTION: You wanted a life without Nora *or* Herb?

PAULA PRONOUN: Now *I* see *we* are all important here. *You* need *me* as much as *I* need *you*.

NORA NOUN: This *business* needs each of us, *Paula*. You've taught us a *lesson* this *morning*.

AL ADJECTIVE: A *valuable* lesson, Paula.

(Curtain)

PART ONE OBJECTIVE: To recognize the eight parts of speech when they appear in sentences.

Just as a good mechanic knows the parts of an engine, a good writer knows the ingredients of a sentence. In these first chapters, you will work on recognizing these ingredients, the eight parts of speech, so you will be able to use them effectively.

In the Reading for Resourceful Writers that you have just read, the eight parts of speech appear as characters. The part of speech that each character represents is italicized in his or her lines. Before completing the Part One Pre-Test on page 8, go back through the Reading and see if you are familiar with the eight "characters." You will be seeing a lot of them in the next eight chapters!

PART ONE PRE-TEST

Read the following paragraphs and answer the questions that follow.

> George began his job at ARMCO after he had worked as a technician for ten years. His new job requires more hours, but the increased pay and exciting work keep his morale high.
>
> "Oh, I cannot spend enough time with my family," he says, "but they completely understand the situation. In two years I will cut my hours at the plant and stay at home on Saturdays."

1. Go back through the paragraphs and look for every noun. Now list all the nouns you found. (Hint: There are more than 15.)

2. Now list all the helping verbs in the preceding paragraphs.

3. List all the *main* verbs.

4. List all the adjectives.

5. List all the adverbs.

6. List all the prepositions.

7. List all the conjunctions.

8. List all the pronouns.

9. List all the interjections.

When you have answered the questions to the best of your ability, check your answers at end of text.

Don't worry if you had trouble with this exercise. Just start working on Chapter 1. When you have studied these first eight chapters, try this exercise again. It will be much easier!

VERBS

OBJECTIVES: To recognize verbs and verb phrases in sentences; to distinguish between main verbs and helping verbs; to recognize false verbs.

Do you know which words in the following sentences are verbs?

Mr. Lawton helped the new employee.
Larry's new system simplified the sale.
Marie works for an account executive.
Charles has started the ad campaign.

If you chose *helped, simplified, works,* and *has started,* you already know something about verbs. To test whether a word is a verb, you can usually put *I, you, he, it, they,* or *who* in front of it:

I helped
they simplified
it works
he has started

Self-Check Test 1-1

Put a check after the following words if they can be used as verbs. If you are unsure, use the test just described. (Check your answers at end of text.)

sits   _____

hoped   _____

nervous   _____

wrote   _____

carefully   _____

attractive   _____

performs   _____

conclude   _____

determines   _____

manager   _____

VERBS MAY INDICATE ACTION

Most verbs show action in a sentence. Verbs like *run, write, hit, jump,* and *decide* show action: Jerry *hit* the desk. Other verbs, like *think, decide,* and *understand,* show internal action: I *understand* the equation.

VERBS MAY INDICATE STATES OF BEING

Verbs like *be, seem, feel,* and *appear* are called **LINKING VERBS**. (Terms in boldface are defined in the Glossary.) These verbs link one part of a sentence (the **SUBJECT**) with another part (the **COMPLEMENT**). We will study these more in later chapters.

> subject   verb   complement
> The [room] [appeared] [empty.]

> subject verb   complement
> [Thomas] [is] an [accountant.]

> subject   verb complement
> [I]   [feel] [absurd.]

VERBS INDICATE TIME

The form of a verb depends on the time the action in the sentence takes place. In fact, another method for locating verbs is to alter the time of the sentence: the words that change will be verbs.

For example, if you want to pick out the verb in the sentence *Joel enjoys skiing,* change the sentence to the past: *Joel enjoyed skiing.* The word that changes is the verb.

The time of the verb is called the **TENSE**. The tense indicates past, present, or future action:

> I *danced.* [past tense]
> I *dance.* [present tense]
> I *will dance.* [future tense]
> I *wrote.* [past tense]
> I *write.* [present tense]
> I *will write.* [future tense]

Self-Check Test 1-2

Rewrite the following sentences by changing the word *today* to *yesterday* and making any other necessary changes. Then underline the verbs in your sentences. (See end of text for answers.)

> Example: We ski on Mount Bear today.
> We <u>skied</u> on Mount Bear yesterday.

1. Today Kathryn wants to meet with James and Peter.

2. Today is the best choice for a holiday.

3. Sam and Marjorie decide on their wedding date today.

4. Today Henry is unsure about his schedule.

5. Helen looks very tired today.

Verbs also have a variety of tenses that allow us to indicate time more precisely than past, present, or future. For example, we can show ongoing action: Joan *is completing* the project right now. [present progressive tense]

Or we can indicate precisely *when* an action was completed in the past: Maureen had finished the report by 5:00 p.m. [past perfect tense]

We will discuss these tenses in detail in Chapter 15 (pp. 174–178).

MAIN VERBS

If a verb is formed from more than one word, we have a **VERB PHRASE**. A verb phrase is made up of both a main verb and one or more helping verbs. The main verb is the core of the action:

> I *am revising* the letter. [*Am revising* is the verb phrase; *revising* is the main verb.]
> The committee *will issue* a memorandum. [*Will issue* is the verb phrase; *issue* is the main verb.]
> The alteration *has been approved*. [*Has been approved* is the verb phrase; *issue* is the main verb.]

Self-Check Test 1-3

Underline the main verbs in the following sentences. (See end of text for answers.)

1. Jean was hoping for a raise.

2. The committee has encountered resistance from employees.

3. Our deadline has been changed to Friday.

4. Mr. Mason, our accountant, will deliver the package.

5. The negotiations have ended the dispute.

HELPING VERBS

Helping (or *auxiliary*) verbs provide more information about the main verb. If you use *will* before a main verb, for instance, you indicate a future event: Helen *will look* tired tomorrow. *You should eat breakfast* means something different from *You must eat* breakfast or *You did eat breakfast.*

Helping verbs are important for a number of reasons, so you should be able to recognize them. Most of them are forms of the verbs *have, do,* and *be.*

Common Helping Verbs

have, has, had, will have
am, is, are, will, will be, has been, had been, were, was
do, does, did
might, might have, shall, should, should have, would, would have, could, could have
must, must have, may, may have

With a main verb and this collection of helping verbs, you can create many variations in meaning.

I *worked* all night.
I *have worked* all night.
I *have been working* all night.
I *should have worked* all night.
I *should have been working* all night.
I *could work* all night.
I *could have worked* all night.
I *must work* all night.
I *might work* all night.
I *may work* all night.
I *will work* all night.

Self-Check Test 1-4

Put one line under the helping verbs and two lines under the main verbs in the following sentences. (See end of text for answers.)

1. Gloria has begun the meeting.

2. Laurie and I will orient the new employees.

3. Mrs. Calhoun should have arrived at noon.

4. We must have taken a wrong turn.

5. Peter has not played guitar for three years.

6. The new building will open in September.

7. Inez could have returned to the office.

8. Mr. Freeman may have discovered an answer to the problem.

9. I did not notice any changes in the office.

10. Shirley should know the way to the restaurant.

FALSE VERBS

Some words look like verbs but actually function as nouns or other parts of the sentence. These words, called **VERBALS**, come in three forms: **GERUNDS, INFINITIVES**, and **PARTICIPLES**. We will discuss these words more fully in later chapters; for now, however, watch particularly for words that look like verbs but do not indicate any action.

> I *am writing* to Mr. Keynes. [*Am writing* indicates action, so it is a verb phrase; *writing* is the main verb.]
> The *writing* has been smudged. [*Writing* acts as a **NOUN**; *has been smudged* is the verb.]
> The man *writing* to us is from Germany. [*Writing* is part of a group of words describing *man; is* is the verb.]
> Harold is learning *to write*. [*Is learning* is the verb; *to write* acts as a noun, not a verb.]

Once again, check whether a word is a verb by putting *I, he, you, we, they,* or *who* in front of it. You cannot write *He to speak* or *We answering*.

A word ending in *-ing* cannot function as a verb by itself: it needs a helping verb. You would not say *He deciding*, for example, but you may say *He is deciding* or *He has been deciding*. By itself, *deciding* is not a verb.

Self-Check Test 1-5

Underline the helping verbs and main verbs in the following sentences. (See end of text for answers.)

1. Gerald has sold 15 swimming pools this week.

2. Leasing a car can be less expensive than buying one.

3. He wants to win the writing award with a minimum effort.

4. Tim must have changed his plan to meet with us.

5. Lauren plans to edit the marketing report this afternoon.

QUESTIONS

So far we have looked only at sentences that make a statement. Questions often require a different format. Note the difference between

> Sally has bought a magazine.

and

> Has Sally bought a magazine?

In the question, the helping verb is separated from the main verb. Despite this separation, you should still be able to recognize both parts of the verbs.

Self-Check Test 1-6

Change the following sentences into questions; then underline the helping verbs and the main verbs in the questions. (See end of text for answers.)

> Example: Phil is going to the dentist.
> Is Phil going to the dentist?

1. Patricia was hoping for a more experienced assistant.

2. The Hoppers will be arriving at the usual time.

3. The committee should establish a new policy.

4. Mike could know the results of the election.

5. Harry Thorne should evaluate the candidates.

MULTIPLE VERBS

Some sentences have more than one verb. Be sure to check each sentence thoroughly.

> Rosemary *has painted* the house and *planted* a garden.
> We *ordered* the supplies, *received* the wrong items, and *sent* them back to the vendor.
> *Have* you *considered* the options and *revised* the report?
> William *has read* the letter, and Joanne *has answered* it.

Self-Check Test 1-7

Underline the helping verbs and main verbs in the following sentences. (Check end of text for answers.)

1. After dinner, we helped Martin with the chores and then went to the movies.

2. Will you join us at the restaurant, or will you meet us at the Frasers' party?

3. Jill must either stay after work to finish some typing or come in very early tomorrow morning.

4. Roger Grogan disagreed with the proposal, but Alice May supported it.

5. Please fill out the forms, check them over, and give them to Wanda on Tuesday.

Checklist for Chapter 1

1. Verbs indicate action or states of being.
2. Verbs may have *I, he, you, it, they,* or *who* in front of them.
3. The time of the verb is called the *tense.*
4. A verb phrase has one or more helping verbs as well as a main verb.
5. In a question, the helping verb is often separated from the main verb.
6. False verbs, or verbals, are formed from verbs but act as nouns or other parts of sentences.
7. Sentences may have more than one verb.

Verb Review

Read the following paragraph.

This report addresses the problems with our new simplified contracts. Analysts have thoroughly surveyed our customers and have found both positive and negative reactions. I have summarized these in the opening section of the report, listed further findings of the analysts in the second section, and outlined my recommendations in the conclusion.

Now go through the paragraph again and look for verbs.
List the helping verbs you found.

List the main verbs you found.

Check your answers at end of text.

**Chapter Test
1-1**

I. Put one line under the helping verbs in the following sentences. Put two lines under the main verbs.

1. Have you met Mr. Pine?

2. Gerry considered my recommendations before the last meeting.

3. Were any of you waiting for Robert?

4. Sarah and Lorraine will attend the convention and write a report about it.

5. Did she consider the financial aspect of the plan?

II. Turn the following sentences into questions; then put one line under the main verb and two lines under the helping verb in the question.

1. Barbara will be delivering a speech on new marketing techniques.

2. The war is having an effect on the price of gold.

3. The division manager has recommended a programming course for all of us.

4. Philip would be unhappy if we did not invite him.

5. Sharon has told us about your discovery.

III. Change the word *yesterday* to *tomorrow* in the following sentences and make necessary changes in the verbs.

1. Yesterday we came to a decision regarding the export problem.

2. Yesterday was a turning point for our company.

3. Holly White met with the committee yesterday.

4. Did you hire those attorneys yesterday?

5. Did Tara enjoy playing golf in Wellesley yesterday?

Chapter Test 1-2

I. **In the following memo, put one line under the helping verbs, two lines under the main verbs.**

To: Department Heads

From: Jack Marks

Subject: Visitors from China

Date: June 3, 19xx

On Tuesday, June 15, five managers from a Chinese textile company will tour our plant and have lunch with us. John Lee, production supervisor, has agreed to act as translator. You will meet these men, share ideas, and learn about their company and country.

If you are not available for lunch on that day, you should leave a message with Cathy Smithers, my secretary.

Date: Tuesday, June 15

Time: Noon

Place: Second floor cafeteria

II. **Fill in the blanks with an appropriate main or helping verb. Then indicate whether you have added a main verb or helping verb by putting *M* or *H* in the blank after each sentence.**

Example: I have *read* the report. _M_

1. The Potomac River, over 285 miles long, _____ from Cumberland, Maryland, to the Chesapeake Bay. _____

2. Tomorrow morning I _____ recommend John for the
position.   ____

3. Please _____ me when you have a complete proposal.   ____

4. Have you _____ a title for your speech?   ____

5. Karen should _____ revised the article by noon.   ____

6. The foreign legion, a French volunteer army, has been
_____ in many movies and novels.   ____

7. I will _____ to Idaho in June when this job is over.   ____

8. The Hendersons must _____ a place to stay in London for
the summer.   ____

9. I will never _____ the trip from Orland, California, to Fort
Wayne, Indiana.   ____

10. _____ Harold bring the television to the conference room? ____

Exercise for Experts

Write sentences using each of the following main verbs *and* a helping verb. Try to use a variety of helping verbs. Remember to change the spelling of the main verb if necessary. Look up any unfamiliar words in a dictionary.

After writing the sentences, underline the main verbs and helping verbs.

Example: [delay] Jonathan Brown <u>has delayed</u> his decision.

elevate	receive
accelerate	circumvent
negotiate	intensify
incite	delegate
bewilder	liquefy

1.

2.

3.

4.

5.

6.

7.

8.

9.

10.

CHAPTER 2

NOUNS

OBJECTIVE: To recognize common, proper, and collective nouns in sentences.

Do you know which words in the following sentences are nouns?

Sharon showed the employees some slides of the new products from Italy.

If you selected *Sharon, employees, slides, products,* and *Italy,* you already know something about nouns.

COMMON NOUNS

Nouns are words that give names to people, animals, places, things, and ideas. *Common* nouns refer to a general class, not to one item in particular. Many common nouns can be preceded by *the, a,* or *an.*

Nouns	Not Nouns
(the) girl	naturally
(a) student	and
(an) elephant	surprised
(a) need	write
(the) individuals	over
(an) association	toward
(a) country	never

Self-Check Test 2-1

Put a check after the following words if they can be used as nouns. (See end of text for answers.)

surprise	_____	radiator	_____
soon	_____	parade	_____
leader	_____	softly	_____
horse	_____	for	_____
detail	_____	analysis	_____

Not all common nouns may be preceded by *the, an,* or *a.* This technique is just a way to check for some nouns. In the following sentences, for example, the underlined words are nouns:

> We are studying botany.
>
> Samuels discussed capitalism in this article.

Some nouns are easily recognized because their endings identify them as nouns. Words ending in *-ment, -ness, -tion, -hood, -sion, -age, -ism,* and *-acy,* for example, are often nouns:

commandment	transmission
kindness	courage
information	socialism
falsehood	privacy

You can be sure a word is a noun, however, only by looking at its function in a sentence. A noun *names* something in a sentence.

Self-Check Test 2-2

Underline the nouns in the following sentences. (See answers at end of text.)

1. The man is giving a seminar on stress.

2. I hope you have seen the film on radiation.

3. Please lend me your radio and lamp.

4. This index is filled with typographical errors.

5. As I am going to visit the company in an hour, I am checking some regulations.

6. The partition is too high; privacy is less important than fresh air.

7. We will try to rewrite the contracts with the added information by next month.

8. The message from our president was very clear.

9. Laziness has infected the entire staff.

10. The ratio of clerks to managers has been altered.

PROPER NOUNS

Proper nouns name specific people, places, and things: names of streets, towns, cities, countries, continents, individual people, companies, brands of products, and so on. Proper nouns are capitalized. (See Chapter 27 for more on capitalizing nouns.)

COMMON NOUN	PROPER NOUN
girl	Kate Miller
country	France
dog	Rover
car	Buick
cookie	Oreo
company	King Lighting Company
day	Sunday

Self-Check Test 2-3

Replace the nouns in parentheses with appropriate proper nouns. (See end of text for suggested answers.)

Example: Give (the woman) <u>Mrs. Scott</u> the key.

1. Please help (the student) _____ with his homework.

2. Last summer we visited (city) _____ for a week.

3. We are enrolling in (college course) _____ next fall.

4. Pete is going to work for (corporation) _____.

5. My sister always shops in (department store) _____.

NOUNS MAY BE SINGULAR OR PLURAL

A noun may name one item (singular) or two or more items (plural). For many nouns, you simply add *s* to make a plural.

SINGULAR	PLURAL
boy	boys
book	books
coin	coins
pillow	pillows

Other nouns require *es* in the plural. (See Chapter 26 for more on spelling plurals.)

SINGULAR	PLURAL	INCORRECT FORM
couch	couches	couchs
branch	branches	branchs
pass	passes	passs

Hint: If you can't pronounce the plural noun, you may well have formed the plural incorrectly.

When nouns end in *y*, you often have to change the *y* to *i* before you add *es*.

SINGULAR	PLURAL	INCORRECT FORM
country	countries	~~countrys~~
dairy	dairies	~~dairys~~
enemy	enemies	~~enemys~~

False Friends

We see some words so often that we think we know how to use them. Yet these common words may have unusual forms that can take us by surprise. We call these words "false friends." Some plurals can be false friends. Be careful!

Some words change irregularly.

SINGULAR	PLURAL
child	children
goose	geese
mouse	mice

And some nouns remain the same in both forms.

SINGULAR	PLURAL
sheep	sheep
fish	fish

Some nouns are always singular.

SINGULAR	PLURAL
honesty	—
sincerity	—
research	—
information	—

Some nouns are always plural.

SINGULAR	PLURAL
—	scissors
—	trousers
—	pliers

Check your dictionary if you are unsure about a plural form. (Most dictionaries mention only irregular forms; if the plural is made by adding *s*, it probably will not appear in the dictionary.)

Self-Check Test 2-4

Change the nouns in parentheses to their plural forms. (Check your dictionary or end of text for answers.)

Example: Has the quarterback completed the (pass) <u>passes</u>?

1. When will the (secretary) _____ return for lunch?

2. Will the patient's (foot) _____ be bandaged until Friday?

3. The (man) _____ in the restaurant paid the bill.

4. The (knife) _____ will be used for boning the chickens.

5. The dentist will examine my (tooth) _____ this morning.

NOUNS SHOW OWNERSHIP

When used with a possessive apostrophe, nouns are used to show ownership.

> *Joe's* book
> The *woman's* automobile.
> A *company's* profits

For more information on possessive nouns, see Chapter 25.

COLLECTIVE NOUNS NAME GROUPS

Some singular nouns indicate more than one member. A company, for example, usually refers to two or more people, but *company* is still a singular noun. These nouns that refer to groups are called collective nouns. Usually these nouns are singular even though they indicate more than one person, place, or thing.

> The committee has changed its agenda.

Some Collective Nouns

family	government
series	corporation
committee	university
team	group
army	battalion

Naturally, if you have more than one army, team, and so on, the collective noun becomes plural:

> The army marched through France. [one army]
> The armies marched through France. [more than one army]

You have probably already noticed that some words can be used as nouns in one sentence and as verbs in another.

> I *run* a mile every morning. [*run* as verb]
> The *run* is over five miles long. [*run* as noun]
> Jean and Sam *surprise* their children on Christmas. [*surprise* as verb]
> The new car was a real *surprise*. [*surprise* as noun]

We will see that many words function as several parts of speech in different sentences. To determine whether a word is a noun or a verb, you can apply some of the tests described in this chapter and in Chapter 1. You can also look for the function of the word in the sentence; we will discuss these functions at length in Part Two.

Self-Check Test 2-5

In the following sentences, the italicized words are used as verbs. Write new sentences using the words as nouns. You may change the topics of the sentences. (See end of text for suggested sentences.)

> Example: I will *research* the problem. [verb]
> My research is nearly complete. [noun]

1. These snakes *bite,* but they are not poisonous.

2. This summer John will *climb* Mount Whitney.

3. The marketing committee *handles* problems of this kind.

4. Gail will *sample* the finished lasagna.

5. Please *control* the situation.

GERUNDS AND INFINITIVES

As we mentioned in Chapter 1, some verb forms act as nouns. Gerunds and infinitives may look like verbs, so check to see how they are used in a sentence. Gerunds end in *ing:*

WRITING HINT: AVOID CLICHÉS
What Mike Wrote   *What Lynn Thought*

Revision: Remember to speak firmly to management so you can explore all the options in the contract.

Source: Ford Button

> *Financing* this project could be difficult. [*Financing* is a noun.]

Infinitives are formed with *to* and either the basic form or the past form of a verb.

> *To speak* before a crowd is his ambition. [*To speak* acts as a noun.]
> *To have paid* his debts was his only regret. [*To have paid* acts as a noun.]

Self-Check Test 2-6

Put one line under the main verbs and helping verbs in the following sentences. Put two lines under the gerunds and infinitives. (See answers at end of text.)

1. Gerald hopes to begin his job in April.

2. Raising rents has been prohibited for six months.

3. Now that Christmas is here, flying first class to Newark costs only $50.

4. Mr. Morton is renting a cabin near Mount Whitney, since he loves to ski.

5. The company has asked Phyllis to transfer to Chicago.

Checklist for Chapter 2

1. Nouns name people, animals, places, things, and ideas.
2. Many nouns may be preceded by *the, an,* or *a.*
3. Common nouns refer to a general class of items.
4. Proper nouns name a specific person, animal, place, thing, or idea. Proper nouns are capitalized.
5. Nouns are either singular or plural.
6. A collective noun is a singular noun that includes more than one member.
7. Many words function as either nouns or verbs.
8. Gerunds and infinitives are verb forms that may act as nouns.

Noun Review

Reread the paragraph that you worked on at the end of Chapter 1.

> This report addresses the problems with our new simplified contracts. Analysts have thoroughly surveyed our customers and have found both positive and negative reactions. I have summarized these in the opening section of the report, listed further findings of the analysts in the second section, and outlined my recommendations in the conclusion.

Now list all the words that are used as nouns in the paragraph.

Chapter Test 2-1

I. **Put a line under each noun in the following sentences.**

1. The river is filled with sailboats.

2. A committee will meet next week.

3. The problem is not severe, but it is a nuisance.

4. When will the examinations be completed?

5. Harold will post fliers about the upcoming race.

II. **Replace the proper nouns in parentheses with common nouns. You may have to add *the, an,* or *a.***

    Example: (Joe) The man won the race.

1. (Ms. Hodges) _____ will supervise the production of the new toys.

2. (February) _____ is almost over.

3. The (Almond Joy) _____ is delicious.

4. (Dr. Hardy) _____ took my temperature.

5. The (Chevrolet) _____ needs an oil change.

III. **In the following sentences, change the nouns in parentheses to their plural forms.**

1. The (emergency) _____ will be over by tomorrow.

2. The red (leaf) _____ fell to the ground.

3. The real (hero) _____ remained invisible.

4. Henry gave the young (woman) _____ some tea.

5. The (sheep) _____ ran across the field.

Chapter Test 2-2

I. **Underline the common and proper nouns in the following paragraph.**

    Our costs have been rising, James. To remain solvent, PRT

    Company cannot offer any increases in salaries until June.

    We hope you will stay with this company; you are a good

    and loyal employee. Please remember that the salaries we

    pay are competitive and our benefits are outstanding.

II. Write a sentence using each of the following words as nouns.

Example: [desk] *The desk is too small for Jack.*

1. [ship]

2. [fashion]

3. [machinery]

4. [tour]

5. [tunnel]

6. [circle]

7. [garden]

8. [contest]

9. [corporation]

10. [push]

Exercise for Experts

I. Write two sentences for each of the following words. In the first, use the word as part of a verb phrase. In the second, use the word as a noun. Look up any unfamiliar words.

Example: [solving] My instructor is solving the algebra problem.
Solving computer problems is his job.

1. [annotating]

2. [duplicating]

3. [incorporating]

4. [deciphering]

5. [assimilating]

II. Some words that we have taken from foreign languages have unusual plurals. Use your dictionary to check for the plural forms of the following words. Then use the plural forms in sentences.

1. [cactus]

2. [bacterium]

3. [alumnus]

4. [phenomenon]

5. [radius]

CHAPTER 3

PRONOUNS

OBJECTIVE: To recognize personal, demonstrative, interrogative, reflexive and indefinite pronouns in sentences.

Do you recognize the pronouns in the following sentences?

> Give him a chance for success.
> Who was unable to attend?
> Is this the answer to your question?
> Everyone is invited to Jim's house.

You should have chosen *him, who, this, your,* and *everyone.*

PRONOUNS ACT AS STAND-INS

In Chapter 2, we saw that nouns name people, places, things, and so on. Most pronouns have one simple function: they act as stand-ins or replacements for nouns.

> The *project* [noun] is complete.
> *It* [pronoun replacing *project*] is complete.
> *George* [noun] will hire the accountants [noun].
> *He* [pronoun replacing *George*] will hire *them* [pronoun replacing *the accountants*].

As stand-ins, pronouns are very valuable. What would life be like without pronouns? We would have to *name* things all the time. Try writing without pronouns and see what happens:

> Jane gave the dog the dog's dinner in Jane's own dish.

> The author of this memo will telephone the reader of this memo so the author and the reader can discuss the new program when the new program is under way.

Self-Check Test 3-1

Put a check after each of the following words that can be used as stand-ins for nouns. (See end of text for answers.)

house _____	John _____	this _____
surely _____	why _____	I _____
it _____	soon _____	corporate _____
he _____	the _____	our _____

PERSONAL PRONOUNS

There are several types of pronouns. Personal pronouns may be the most familiar to you, since we use them in so many sentences as substitutes for common and proper nouns.

Personal Pronouns							
Singular						**Plural**	
I	you	he	she	it	who	we	they
me		him	her		whom	us	them
mine	yours	his	hers	its	whose	ours	theirs
my	your		her			our	their

Personal pronouns have several characteristics.

1. **Number:** Personal pronouns may be singular or plural.

2. **Gender:** Personal pronouns may be masculine, feminine, or neuter. (*Neuter* means simply that a word is not masculine or feminine.) Most nouns are neuter, but some singular nouns, like *woman, uncle, girlfriend, brother,* and *boy,* are masculine or feminine, so you have to be more careful with them. We do not distinguish the gender of plural nouns: *they* can take the place of *mothers, journals, giraffes, governments*—of any plural noun.

3. **Person:** Personal pronouns may be in the first, second, or third person. First person refers to the speaker; second person refers to the reader or listener; and third person refers to the people, places, or things being talked about.

FIRST PERSON	**SECOND PERSON**	**THIRD PERSON**	
I	you	he	who
me	your	him	whom
my	yours	his	whose
mine		she	they
we		her	them
us		hers	their
our		it	theirs
ours		its	

4. **Case:** Personal pronouns may be in the subjective, objective, or possessive **CASE;** that is, the pronoun will change its form according to its function in a sentence. (See Chapter 18 for more detail on pronoun case.)

    We will be examining pronoun characteristics in greater detail in Part Three. At this point, however, you should realize simply that a pronoun should have the same number, gender, and person as the noun it is replacing.

    man: singular, masculine, third person
    pronoun choices: *he, him*

    sister: singular, feminine, third person
    pronoun choices: *she, her*

magazines: plural, neuter, third person
pronoun choices: *they, them*

COLLECTIVE NOUNS

Do you remember the collective nouns we discussed in Chapter 2? Usually you will be using a collective noun as a unit, so you will replace the noun with a singular pronoun:

> When the team came onto the field, we cheered for *it*.

If you want to emphasize the individual members of the group, however, you may replace the collective noun with a plural pronoun.

> The play began as the audience took *their* seats.

Note the difference between the following:

> The board of directors has decided to appoint its new chairperson. [The board is acting as a unit.]

and

> The board of directors always argue endlessly among themselves. [The board members are acting as independent people.]

Self-Check Test 3-2

Replace the noun in parentheses with an appropriate pronoun. (Check answers at end of text.)

> Example: (The girl) <u>She</u> plays soccer.

1. (Greg and Larry) _____ are writing a manual.

2. (The committee) _____ is developing a new fiscal policy.

3. (The vases) _____ cost over $1,000.

4. (The country) _____ has declared war on France.

5. (My father) _____ will build a sailboat this summer.

DEMONSTRATIVE PRONOUNS

We have four demonstrative pronouns: *this, that, these,* and *those.* The word *demonstrative* means *to show.* Demonstrative pronouns show or point things out: *Those* are my file folders.

Demonstrative Pronouns	
Singular	**Plural**
this	these
that	those

Demonstrative pronouns must agree in number with the noun to which they refer.

> This is Gerry's fishing poles. [incorrect]
> These are Gerry's fishing poles. [correct]

Note 1: Remember that these pronouns, like personal pronouns, should refer specifically to nouns: do not use demonstrative pronouns to refer to some vague idea in a previous sentence. See Chapter 17 for more on pronoun reference.

Note 2: Demonstrative pronouns become **ADJECTIVES** if they are followed by a noun: *That horse* is hungry. [*That* is a demonstrative adjective.] See Chapter 4 for more on adjectives.

Self-Check Test 3-3

Replace the nouns in parentheses with appropriate demonstrative pronouns. (See end of text for answers.)

1. Those employees began work in June; _____ will begin in August.

2. I keep the book here because _____ is my favorite novel.

3. Those forms are illegible, so I assumed you wanted _____.

4. Barbara bought a new scarf since _____ is ruined.

5. Steve has two Camaros; _____ are his only hobbies.

INTERROGATIVE PRONOUNS

Their title should help you to remember these pronouns: interrogative pronouns help us to interrogate or ask questions.

Interrogative Pronouns
who, whom, whose, which, and *what*
Who will attend the party?
Whom is she going to hire?
Whose handkerchief is on the floor?
Which of these hats is Mary's?
What are you looking for?

(Note: If these pronouns do not appear in a question, they are not interrogative pronouns.)

We will discuss *who* and *whom* at greater length in Chapter 18 (pp. 209–210). Right now, simply learn to recognize them as interrogative pronouns if they appear in questions.

Self-Check Test 3-4

Underline the interrogative pronouns in the following sentences. (See answers at end of text.)

1. Whose hat did you bring home?

2. Which of these dogs has had its shots?

3. Who is their favorite movie star?

4. What are you going to do about our problem?

5. Whom did you choose for the award?

REFLEXIVE AND INTENSIVE PRONOUNS

Reflexive and intensive pronouns end in *-self* or *-selves*.

myself	yourself	herself
ourselves	yourselves	himself
		itself
		themselves

These pronouns have only two functions. (1) They may *reflect* back to a noun or another pronoun:

I saw *myself* in the mirror.
Winthrop heard *himself* on tape.

(2) They may *emphasize* a noun or pronoun:

They are going to the party; I *myself* am staying home.
Harold told me that she is a supervisor; Harold *himself*
is a vice-president.

Note: *Hisself, theirselves,* and *theirself* are not acceptable words. Do not use them!

INDEFINITE PRONOUNS

Indefinite pronouns, as their name implies, refer to a nonspecific person or group. Because these pronouns are nonspecific, they are often followed by a phrase giving more information about them:

Each *of the men* will give a presentation.
Neither *of my sisters* brought a notepad.

These pronouns do not replace a noun in a sentence; they have no definite reference.

Some indefinite pronouns are plural, but most of them are singular. A few indefinite pronouns may be singular or plural depending on the nouns to which they refer. (See Chapter 17 for more on pronoun agreement.)

Some Indefinite Pronouns

Singular		Plural	Singular/Plural
anybody	neither	both	all
anyone	nobody	few	any
anything	no one	many	more
each	one	others	most
either	somebody	several	none
everybody	someone		some
everyone	something		
everything			

Self-Check Test 3-5

In the following sentences, the pronouns are underlined. Put a *P* over the personal pronouns, a *D* over the demonstrative pronouns, *INT* over the interrogative pronouns, *R/I* over the reflexive/intensive pronouns, and *IND* over the indefinite pronouns. (See end of text for answers.)

               INT   P
Example: Which of the following entrées have you chosen for dinner?

1. Each of us will be going home for Christmas.

2. What are you planning to do about this?

3. Everyone here is planning a presentation on these questions.

4. Who do I think will be nominated?

5. Which of these manuals is being used by the sales representatives when they speak to clients?

6. Nobody understands these instructions; maybe we should rewrite them ourselves.

7. Those desks are on sale, but <u>we</u> can probably find a better price from <u>someone</u> <u>we</u> know.

8. <u>This</u> is the crucial issue: should <u>we</u> liquidate our resources?

9. Have <u>you</u> and <u>he</u> considered the options available to <u>us</u>?

10. <u>Neither</u> of the secretaries has given <u>them</u> information concerning <u>their</u> new copier.

Checklist for Chapter 3

1. Personal and demonstrative pronouns replace nouns.
2. Personal pronouns should be the same gender, number, and person as the nouns they replace.
3. *This, these, that,* and *those* are demonstrative pronouns when they take the place of nouns. Demonstrative pronouns must agree in number with the nouns to which they refer.
4. *Who, whom, whose, which,* and *what* are interrogative pronouns. They are used to introduce questions.
5. Reflexive and intensive pronouns end in *-self* or *-selves*. They are used to intensify or reflect back to a noun or another pronoun.
6. *Anyone, everyone, each, neither, either,* and so on are called indefinite pronouns because they refer to a nonspecific individual or group.

Pronoun Review

Underline the pronouns in the following paragraph.

The report addresses the problems with our new simplified contracts. Analysts have thoroughly surveyed our customers and have found both positive and negative reactions. I have summarized these in the opening section of the report, listed further findings of the analysts in the second section, and outlined my recommendations in the conclusion.

List the personal pronouns that you found.

(continued)

List the demonstrative pronouns.

List the indefinite pronouns.

List the interrogative pronouns.

Check your answers at end of text.

**Chapter Test
3-1**

I. Underline the pronouns in the following sentences. Put a *P* over the personal pronouns, a *D* over the demonstrative pronouns, *INT* over the interrogative pronouns, *R/I* over the reflexive/intensive pronouns, and *IND* over the indefinite pronouns.

INT   P

Example: <u>Which</u> dessert do <u>you</u> want?

1. Henry spoke quietly to her when he got back from the meeting.

2. Whose raincoat did she take off the rack?

3. Who brought the beer to the party?

4. If you have my new adding machine, please give it back right away.

5. Those shoes are my favorites; I wear them only on Saturday nights.

6. Each of the students is doing well in this class.

7. When either of the division managers gets back from Tokyo, please let me know.

8. Whom did she see at the museum? I myself met nobody.

9. "These windows look out on Mount Tamalpais," he explained to anyone listening.

10. Which of the two committees do you think meets more frequently?

II. **Replace the nouns in parentheses with personal pronouns.**

1. (Jenny and Howard) _____ met in Taiwan.

2. (The family) _____ is moving in June when the children are out of school.

3. When the bird disappeared, (the bird's) _____ mate became unhappy.

4. When you are finished with the magazine, please give (the magazine) _____ to my mother.

5. When sales went up, (the corporation) _____ advertised more heavily.

Chapter Test 3-2

Underline each of the personal pronouns in the following memo. Put two lines under the interrogative pronouns, a circle around the demonstrative pronouns, and a square around indefinite pronouns.

To: All Consultants

From: Nancy Olsen

Topic: Mental Health

Date: August 12, 19xx

You have been doing a great job finishing the Keller contract. I know it has been a lot of work. Since this is the first big contract we have had, each of us had to put in extra hours. I know these have taken their toll on us.

What would be the best solution? After some thought, I've decided we can afford a little time off. I have designated the week of August 23 a "mental health week" for each of us. You can stay home and unplug your phones or take off for a few days.

Please return on August 30 with a lot of enthusiasm for our next big project— the James account.

Exercise for Experts

Write a paragraph describing your job goals or career plans. In your explanation, include at least one personal pronoun, one demonstrative pronoun, and one indefinite pronoun. When you have finished, underline the personal, demonstrative, and indefinite pronouns and mark them with *P, D,* or *I.*

CHAPTER 4

ADJECTIVES

OBJECTIVES: To recognize articles, demonstrative adjectives, common and proper adjectives, and compound adjectives in sentences; to recognize the positive, comparative, and superlative forms of adjectives.

Can you spot the adjectives in the following sentences?

Jean saw a calico cat crossing the highway.
French cheese goes well with this delicious bread.

If you recognized *a, calico, the, French, this,* and *delicious,* you already know something about adjectives.

ADJECTIVES DESCRIBE NOUNS AND PRONOUNS

Adjectives add color and interest to our sentences. While verbs, nouns, and pronouns might be thought of as the meat and potatoes of our sentences, the adjectives could be described as the garnishes. Adjectives turn a room with carpets and furniture into a *spacious* room with *plush Oriental* carpets and *antique* furniture. Adjectives can turn a speech into an *emotional* speech, a merger into a *dangerous* or *profitable* merger.

Typically, adjectives help to answer questions that your reader might have about nouns and pronouns. What color are they? What size are they? What kind are they? How many are there?

Adjectives are called **MODIFIERS** because they describe or *modify* other elements in a sentence. Modifying a car means to change the way it looks; modifying a noun or pronoun is a similar process.

purple dish	*short* novel
cheery greeting	*three-inch* hem
American holiday	*five* books

Self-Check Test 4-1

Put a check after each of the following words that may be used to describe a noun or pronoun. (Check answers at end of text.)

handsome   _____
apply   _____
terrible   _____

when   ———
believe   ———
unhappy   ———
brown   ———
ticklish   ———
argue   ———
random   ———

LOCATING ADJECTIVES

Usually adjectives will appear in front of the nouns they describe. However, they may also appear after linking verbs such as *be, feel, seem,* and *appear.*

> This road is rough. [*Rough* is adjective describing *road.*]
> My hands are icy. [*Icy* is adjective describing *hands.*]
> This assignment seems difficult. [*Difficult* is adjective describing *assignment.*]
> Herman appears tired. [*Tired* is adjective describing *Herman.*]

Note: Adjectives, adverbs, and nouns following linking verbs are called *complements.* Complements *complete* the meaning of the verb. We discuss them in greater detail in Chapter 10 (pp. 116–117).

Occasionally, adjectives appear directly after the nouns they describe:

> The road, *hot* and *dusty,* stretched before us.
> The employee, *intelligent* but *lazy,* was not promoted.

Because this format is unusual, you may want to use it when you particularly want to emphasize a point.

When looking for adjectives, try these locations in your sentences:
1. Before a noun: _____ ← NOUN
2. After a linking verb: LINKING VERB → _____
3. After a noun: NOUN → _____

Self-Check Test 4-2

Fill in the blanks with appropriate adjectives. (See suggested answers at end of text.)

1. The _____ supervisor has bought two _____ file cabinets.

2. Our old copier is _____ and _____.

3. My secretary loaned me his _____ dictionary and his _____ _____ pen.

4. I hope you will let me drive your _____ car.

5. The accountant seems _____ but _____.

ARTICLES

Articles are some of the most common adjectives. They are simply the words *a*, *an*, and *the*. *The* refers to a specific noun; *an* and *a* refer to less definite nouns.

> Here is *the* book I wanted. [refers to one specific book]
> Here is *a* book I wanted. [refers to one of several]
> *The* salesman stopped by. [one specific salesman]
> *A* salesman stopped by. [any salesman]

Note: *A* is used before words that begin with consonant sounds; *an* is used before words that begin with vowel sounds.

> I bought a computer terminal; I bought an address book.
> We visited a hospital; they visited an elementary school.

DEMONSTRATIVE ADJECTIVES

Demonstrative adjectives are the same words we discussed as demonstrative pronouns in Chapter 3: *this*, *these*, *that*, and *those*. As adjectives, these words appear before nouns.

> This typewriter is broken.
> These cookies taste stale.
> That Buick needs a new tire.
> Those memos should be saved.

Note that *them* may never be used as an adjective.

> Them clothes are mine. [incorrect]
> Those clothes are mine. [correct]
> These clothes are mine. [correct]

Self-Check Test 4-3

Underline the articles and demonstrative adjectives in the following sentences. Put an *A* over the articles, a *D* over the demonstrative adjectives. (See answers at end of text.)

Example: These tests show the results we wanted.

1. Where are the photographs we need for the presentation?

2. I have often seen a resemblance between Dr. Perrini and Mr. Lambert.

3. We knew this was the last chance for keeping the project afloat: we simply

    had to find a few more supporters.

4. When that file is complete, please give a copy to me.

5. Those were his last words before he took that brochure and left the room.

ADJECTIVE ENDINGS

Many adjectives are formed from nouns and have characteristic endings that help us recognize them: *-able, -al, -ous, -ful, -ish, -ing, -ive, -y, -tic.*

> The boat is *colorful* and *comfortable.*
> A *stylish* scarf may be worn with this *silky* dress.
> This *exciting* occasion calls for a *festive* dessert.
> This book has a *funny, surprising* conclusion.

Self-Check Test 4-4

On the left is a list of nouns, on the right a list of adjective endings. Form adjectives by linking each noun with an appropriate ending. You may have to make some spelling changes as well. (See end of text for answers.)

NOUNS	ENDINGS	
enthusiasm	-able	_____
beauty	-ary	_____
refreshment	-al	_____
expense	-ful	_____
taste	-ish	_____
self	-ive	_____
belief	-ing	_____
practice	-y	_____
necessity	-ous	_____
peril	-tic	_____

Since adjectives come in many forms, the ending is not always a key to identifying an adjective. You will often have to identify an adjective simply by its position and function in the sentence. In fact, many words are both nouns and adjectives. Their function changes with their use in a sentence.

> The *cotton* is grown in these fields. [noun]
> The *cotton* dress is on sale. [adjective describing *dress*]
> This department is devoted to *research*. [noun]
> The *research* committee will meet in 30 minutes. [adjective describing *committee*]

To locate adjectives, you must be able to find the noun or pronoun being described in the sentence.

Self-Check Test 4-5

Put one line under the adjectives in the following sentences; put two lines under the nouns or pronouns being described. (See answers at end of text.)

1. This attractive house sits at the end of a long street.

2. Although the proposition seems interesting, we need to think about it.

3. Have you wondered whether the heavy paperwork could be handled by a temporary clerical worker?

4. When the new proposal was ready, we presented it to the executive directors.

5. He seems temperamental and erratic.

6. Carmen examined the flooded basement before she called an experienced plumber.

7. These projections seem correct; however, you should check them against the older figures.

8. This simple command enables you to copy information onto a second file.

9. The well-defined boundaries were established by surveyors in the last century.

10. As a recent graduate, you may have to wait for the accounting position you want.

PROPER ADJECTIVES

So far we have looked at common adjectives, articles, and demonstrative adjectives. Proper adjectives are formed from proper nouns. Like proper nouns, proper adjectives are usually capitalized.

PROPER NOUN	PROPER ADJECTIVE
America	American
China	Chinese
Darwin	Darwinian
Asia	Asian
Washington	Washingtonian

Once again, many proper nouns may also function as adjectives:

> The young *German* was interested in our personnel policy. [noun—a person]
> The *German* cameras have arrived. [adjective describing *cameras*]

> Martin has visited *New York*. [noun—a place]
> The *New York* office is opening soon. [adjective describing *office*]

Self-Check Test 4-6

Put an *A* after these sentences if the italicized words are adjectives; put an *N* after the sentences if the italicized words are nouns. (See answers at end of text.)

Example: He is a true *Connecticut* Yankee.   A

1. The *Cornish* game hens have been basted with orange sauce.   _____

2. The *Japanese* have increased their production by 50 percent.   _____

3. The singers will perform *Spanish* songs after dinner.   _____

4. This *Bordeaux* wine is very dry and pleasant.   _____

5. The new crop of *Idaho* potatoes is the best in years.   _____

ADJECTIVE FORMS

Most adjectives have three forms: positive, comparative, and superlative. The positive form is used to describe one noun; the comparative form is used to compare two nouns; the superlative form is used to compare three or more nouns.

> She is a *pretty* child. [positive form]
> Tara is a *prettier* child than Sheila. [comparative form]
> Olga is the *prettiest* child in the classroom. [superlative form]

Adjectives often follow the format we see in the previous examples: the comparative form ends in *-er* and the superlative in *-est*.

POSITIVE	COMPARATIVE	SUPERLATIVE
fair	fairer	fairest
mean	meaner	meanest
dirty	dirtier	dirtiest

Other adjectives require *more* or *less* in the comparative forms, *most* or *least* in the superlative forms. (Adjectives with three or more syllables always require these forms.)

POSITIVE	COMPARATIVE	SUPERLATIVE
intelligent	more intelligent less intelligent	most intelligent least intelligent
industrious	more industrious less industrious	most industrious least industrious
extravagant	more extravagant less extravagant	most extravagant least extravagant

False Friends: Irregular Adjectives

Caution: Some adjectives change completely in the comparative and superlative forms.

Positive	Comparative	Superlative
bad	worse	worst
good	better	best

If you are unsure about the forms of an adjective, check your dictionary: it will list any irregular forms.

Self-Check Test 4-7

I. Put the adjective in parentheses in a comparative form.

Example: Sheila took the (short) <u>shorter</u> route home.

1. Nelly is more creative than Tom simply because she is (imaginative) _____.

2. Mr. and Mrs. Hill feel (good) _____ today than they did yesterday.

3. Now that we have installed this computer, typing letters will be (tiring) _____ than before.

4. As a child, Charlie was (cute) _____ than Polly.

5. Now that the exits are clearly marked, this freeway is (dangerous) _____ than it was.

II. Put the adjective in parentheses in a superlative form.

1. Stanley, who is over five feet tall, is the (good) _____ basketball player in his fourth grade class.

2. Because she worked at it so hard, Marla wrote the (informative) _____ report in her department.

3. Since this is the hottest time of year, we should take our (light) _____ clothing.

4. Our family spent a week on the Amazon, one of the (long) _____ rivers in the world.

5. Our local airport, miles from a major road, could be the (lonely)
    _____ airport in Kansas.

Caution: Use with Care

Although adjectives are wonderful additions to your writing, be careful not to overuse them. Most writing related to your work should be concise and efficient: too many adjectives can detract from rather than add to the effectiveness of a memo or letter. When editing, you may have to cut some of those adjectives.

Wordy: Only four people can fit in the *small* lunchroom.
Better: Only four people can fit in the lunchroom. [You *know* it must be small if only four people fit in it.]
Wordy: The *expensive* sports car cost $30,000.
Better: The sports car cost $30,000. [The car *must* be expensive if it cost $30,000.]

Checklist for Chapter 4

1. Adjectives describe nouns or pronouns.

2. Adjectives usually appear immediately before or after nouns or after linking verbs.

3. *The, an,* and *a* are adjectives called *articles.*

4. *This, these, that,* and *those* are demonstrative adjectives when they appear before nouns.

5. Adjectives are defined by their use in the sentence; many words can be either nouns or adjectives.

6. Proper adjectives are derived from proper nouns and capitalized.

7. Most adjectives have positive, comparative, and superlative forms.

Adjective Review

Underline all the adjectives in the following paragraph.

This report addresses the problems with our new sim-

plified contracts. Analysts have thoroughly surveyed our

customers and have found both positive and negative reac-

tions. I have summarized these in the opening section of

the report, listed further findings of the analysts in the

second section, and outlined my recommendations in the

conclusion.

List the articles you found.

List the demonstrative adjectives.

List the common adjectives.

List the proper adjectives.

Check your answers at end of text.

Chapter Test 4-1

I. Underline the articles and demonstrative adjectives in the following sentences. Put an *A* over the articles, a *D* over the demonstrative adjectives.

1. These buildings will be finished by the end of May.

2. Can you tell me which of the answers is correct?

3. Please illustrate a problem like the one in this article.

4. I hope these will satisfy the client until the final versions are proofread.

5. When you want me to address the seminar, put a note in my mailbox.

II. Underline the common adjectives in the following sentences. Circle the nouns or pronouns they are describing.

1. Let me finish this exciting chapter before dinner.

2. When we begin filming this short segment, we will review the opening scenes.

3. Felicia is considered the hardest worker in the Boston office.

4. I feel tired, but a good sleep should restore my natural energy.

5. Although Mr. Tyrone is excited about the new job, the relocation problems disturb him.

Chapter Test 4-2

I. Write sentences using a superlative form of the following adjectives.

Example: rare *This stone is one of the rarest we have found.*

1. [dull]

2. [sensitive]

3. [confusing]

4. [elaborate]

5. [random]

II. **Underline all the adjectives in the following paragraphs from a business letter. Put an *A* over the articles, a *D* over the demonstrative adjectives, a *C* over the common adjectives, a *P* over the proper adjectives. Count comparative and superlative forms as one adjective.**

                                 C   A

Example: The <u>least</u> <u>talkative</u> child ate <u>a</u> sandwich.

I was happy to hear from you last week regarding our most recent plans. This opportunity should enable us to open a retail outlet in Baltimore. The Baltimore planning committee is eager for a fine furniture store in that area, and the city residents appear interested.

I will talk with you next week. Maybe we can set up a productive meeting in May.

Exercise for Experts

I. **Use the following words as adjectives in sentences. Look up any unfamiliar words.**

1. [prevalent]

2. [exaggerated]

3. [conspicuous]

4. [plausible]

5. [controversial]

II. **Use each of the following words in two sentences. First use it as a noun; then use it as an adjective. Do not change the form of the word.**

1. [parallel]

2. [leisure]

3. [deductible]

4. [safety]

5. [representative]

CHAPTER 5

ADVERBS

OBJECTIVES: To recognize adverbs in sentences; to distinguish adverbs from adjectives; to recognize the positive, comparative, and superlative forms of adverbs.

Can you locate the adverbs in the following sentences?

> Have you thoroughly investigated the wiring system?
> Since the class meets exactly at noon, many of us never eat lunch on Wednesdays.
> I hope Jack will arrive soon.

If you chose *thoroughly, exactly, never,* and *soon,* you were correct.

Adverbs are modifying words that can describe verbs, adjectives, other adverbs, **PHRASES,** and even whole **SENTENCES.** In fact, if a word in a sentence is describing something other than a noun or pronoun, you can be sure it is an adverb.

Like adjectives, adverbs add color and intensity to your sentences. They change *We swam* to *We swam energetically.* They change *I read* to *I read slowly and painfully.*

You can often recognize adverbs because they answer questions such as HOW? WHEN? TO WHAT DEGREE? WHERE?

> I ran *quickly.* [HOW did I run?]
> The car will arrive *soon.* [WHEN will it arrive?]
> Bob was *extremely* impressed. [TO WHAT DEGREE was he impressed?]
> He will sit *here.* [WHERE will he sit?]

Self-Check Test 5-1

Put a check next to each of the words that could describe verbs or adjectives. (Check answers at end of text.)

immediately _____   mutual _____

corridor _____   favor _____

attractively _____   faster _____

never _____   often _____

month _____   quickly _____

ADVERBS MODIFY VERBS

Once you have located the verb in your sentence, determine whether an adverb is describing the action:

> He ran *slowly*. [adverb modifying *ran*]
> Janet will *not* sing at the party tomorrow. [adverb modifying *will sing*]
> Barry speaks *loudly*. [adverb modifying *speaks*]

Self-Check Test 5-2

Put one line under the adverbs in the following sentences; put two lines under the verbs they modify. Remember to underline helping verbs as well as main verbs. (See answers at end of text.)

1. Fran is running quickly toward the finish line.

2. Mr. Cooper has never seen these beautiful photos.

3. I was heading faithfully toward the Idaho border when the storm struck viciously.

4. The news reports are arriving steadily from India.

5. Our dog is definitely trying to tell us something.

ADVERBS MODIFY ADJECTIVES

You can usually recognize an adverb describing an adjective by asking HOW + ADJECTIVE?

> The extremely fragile bowl is broken. [*Fragile* is an adjective modifying *bowl*.]
> How fragile? *Extremely* fragile. [*Extremely* is an adverb modifying *fragile*.]

> Mr. Johnson made a very effective speech last night. [*Effective* is an adjective modifying *speech*.]
> How effective? *Very* effective. [*Very* is an adverb modifying *effective*.]

> The California condor is practically extinct. [*Extinct* is an adjective complement for *condor*.]
> How extinct? *Practically* extinct. [*Practically* is an adverb modifying *extinct*.]

Self-Check Test 5-3

Underline the adverbs in the following sentences. Put two lines under the words they modify. (See answers at end of text.)

1. The summer attendance is generally low.

2. Charles seems very uncertain about the consequences.

3. This is a highly secret project sponsored by IBM.

4. We seem altogether unprepared for this decision.

5. I gave him some really good advice.

ADVERBS MODIFY OTHER ADVERBS

Some adverbs can modify either an adjective or an adverb. *Very* and *really* are among the most common of these adverbs. (In fact, they are *such* common adverbs that you may have to cut them when you are revising your writing. Ask yourself if they add anything to your sentence.)

> He speaks really clearly. [*Clearly* is an adverb modifying *speaks. Really* is an adverb modifying *clearly*.]
> The policemen wandered very purposefully through the crowd. [*Purposefully* is an adverb describing *wandered. Very* is an adverb modifying *purposefully*.]

Self-Check Test 5-4

Underline the adverbs in the following sentences.

1. Are you definitely interested in this project, Suzanne?

2. Our new car is idling somewhat fast.

3. Did you think the new system was working efficiently?

4. The young man is highly intelligent but poorly motivated.

5. Henry was gesturing animatedly to the unfriendly crowd.

ADVERBS CAN ACT AS CONNECTORS

Some adverbs connect parts of a sentence or connect one sentence to another sentence. Because of their connective function, these adverbs are called *conjunctive adverbs.*

> **Common Conjunctive Adverbs**
>
> besides, consequently, however, indeed, nevertheless, otherwise, similarly, then, therefore, thus

I have a cold; *consequently*, I am going home.
Marianne was surprised; *indeed*, she was astounded.

CONFUSING ADJECTIVES WITH ADVERBS

One major pitfall for writers is using adjectives instead of adverbs to modify verbs or other adjectives. Many adverbs are formed by adding *-ly* to an adjective.

He is an *efficient* worker. [Correct: Adjective modifies noun.]

He works *efficient*. [Incorrect: Adjective modifies verb *works*.]

He works *efficiently*. [Correct: Adverb modifies verb.]

She is a *quick* reader. [Correct: Adjective modifies noun.]

She reads the material *quick*. [Incorrect: Adjective modifies verb *reads*.]

She reads the material *quickly*. [Correct: Adverb modifies verb.]

> **Caution: Real vs. Really**
>
> Use *real* only when describing nouns or pronouns: He is a *real* athlete.
> Use *really* when describing adjectives: He is *really* athletic.

Some of our most common adverbs have no adjectival form, while others may also function as adjectives:

ADJECTIVE	ADVERB
—	again
—	ahead
better	better
fast	fast
good	well*
more	more
only	only
—	therefore

*Note: *Well* is an adjective when referring to health: *I feel well*. (Usually it will appear after a linking verb.) However, *well* is an adverb with nonlinking verbs: *He swims well*.

WRITING HINT: DELETE UNNECESSARY ADJECTIVES AND ADVERBS

Alice's First Draft   *Alice's Second Draft*

Source: Ford Button

LINKING VERBS

Adverbs describe action verbs: I run *swiftly*. A linking verb, however, cannot be modified by an adverb. Because a linking verb links a noun or pronoun to the word or words that follow the verb, an adjective, not an adverb, will usually follow the linking verb.

> I feel *fine*. [not *finely*]
> Bob is *angry*. [not *angrily*]
> The staff seems *unhappy*. [not *unhappily*]

> **Caution: Linking Verbs**
> subject + action verb → adverb
> subject + linking verb → adjective

Verbs like *taste, smell,* and *sound* may be linking verbs if they show a state of being rather than an action. Then these linking verbs, too, will be followed by adjectives, not adverbs.

> The bread tastes *strange*. [not *strangely*]
> The milk smells *bad*. [not *badly*]

Self-Check Test 5-5

Correct any adverb errors in the following sentences. (Check end of text for answers.)

1. Maurie Golden's welcoming speech to the student body concludes different every year.

2. He speaks good but cannot express himself effectively on the written page.

3. I have not felt well since I ran that race so quick.

4. This item will be mailed direct to you if you enclose a self-addressed stamped envelope.

5. Mrs. Jergins is not real enthusiastic about the change in administration.

6. My supervisor felt badly when she heard we had performed poorly.

7. This record sounds terribly; I will return it immediately.

8. She speaks persuasive, but she doesn't always know the facts.

9. We are all feeling awfully today, so we will leave the office at noon.

10. I know the lesson pretty good, but I must review it real quick.

Caution: Wandering Adverbs

Adverbs are sometimes migratory workers in sentences. You may find them almost anywhere. If they get too far from the word they are describing, however, they lose their effectiveness. Do your adverbs a service: send them back to the word they are describing.

> We talked about the proposed changes in the agenda *eventually*. [wandering adverb]
> We talked *eventually* about the proposed changes in the agenda.
> The company will become a subsidiary of TUP Industries *soon*. [wandering adverb]
> The company will *soon* become a subsidiary of TUP Industries.

POSITIVE, COMPARATIVE, AND SUPERLATIVE FORMS

Most forms of comparison for adverbs are the same as for adjectives: You will add *-er*, *more*, or *less* for the comparative, *-est*, *most*, or *least* for the superlative forms.

POSITIVE	COMPARATIVE	SUPERLATIVE
cruelly	more cruelly	most cruelly
	less cruelly	least cruelly
casually	more casually	most casually
	less casually	least casually
fast	faster	fastest

He hits the ball *hard*.
He hits the ball *harder* than Jason does.
Of all these players, he hits the ball *hardest*.

False Friends: Irregular Adverbs

Positive	Comparative	Superlative
bad	worse	worst
good	better	best

Many adverbs have no comparative or superlative forms. Some of these adverbs are *never*, *then*, *almost*, *not*, *hardly*, *only*, *very*, *really*, and *surely*. Conjunctive adverbs, also, have only one form.

Self-Check Test 5-6

I. Indicate whether the italicized words are adjectives (*ADJ*) or adverbs (*ADV*). (See answers at end of text.)

1. Kerry is healing more *rapidly* than we had expected.   _____

2. At this point, the international talks are practically *worthless*.   _____

3. Jeanine was the *only* woman in the class.   _____

4. Oil prices will *definitely* affect inflation rates.   _____

5. Have you *ever* considered renting a hot-air balloon?   _____

II. Put the adverb form of the following adjectives in the spaces provided. (In some cases, the adverb and adjective forms may be identical.) If there is no adverb form, leave the space blank.

	ADJECTIVE	ADVERB
1.	clear	
2.	good	
3.	effective	
4.	worse	
5.	random	

Checklist for Chapter 5

1. Adverbs usually modify verbs, adjectives, and other adverbs; they may modify almost any sentence element except a noun.

2. Conjunctive adverbs connect parts of a sentence or connect two sentences.

3. Many adverbs are formed from adjectives; some adverbs are identical to adjectives.

4. An adjective, not an adverb, will usually follow a linking verb.

5. Most adjectives have a positive, comparative, and superlative form.

Adverb and Adjective Review

Read the following paragraph. Put one line under the adverbs, two lines under the adjectives. (Consider comparative and superlative forms as a unit.)

You will usually find that a simple sentence conveys

thoughts more effectively than a complicated one. A com-

plex sentence may sound more imposing or impressive;

however, it is not very valuable if your audience cannot

easily understand it. Go carefully through your letters,

memos, and reports to delete the unnecessarily complicated

phrases and difficult words.

Check your answers at end of text.

Chapter Test 5-1

I. **Write the adjective form of the following adverbs. If there is no adjective form, write 0 in the space.**

ADVERB   ADJECTIVE

1. properly

2. delightfully

3. therefore

4. badly

5. better

II. Fill in the blanks with an appropriate adverb.

1. The young horse galloped _____ over the hills.

2. Gerry will lead the meeting today; _____, he has made some handouts for us.

3. My dentist is _____ knowledgeable about gum disease.

4. Do you think Laura has _____ decided on a color scheme?

5. I am _____ unhappy about the upcoming election.

III. Correct any adverb errors in the following sentences.

1. I really regret not having finished my coursework in management.

2. Bill is a good worker, but he types poor.

3. The problem is that the car runs worser than it did before.

4. Mr. Kalinowski is real disturbed about the production errors.

5. My mother always speaks kind to small children and dogs.

Chapter Test 5-2

I. **Underline the adverbs in the following memo.**

To: All Staff

From: Myrna Peck

Subject: Annual Report

Date: December 3, 19xx

You are probably aware that our annual report must be at the printer by February 1. Some departments have already begun systematically compiling necessary statistics and other data; however, we all must begin consciously organizing our information so that department representatives can review it easily and efficiently.

If you have not read last year's report, review it very carefully: it is an excellent model for us.

I will be extremely happy to assist any of you who want more information on what we need.

II. Write sentences following the directions given. Underline all the adverbs in your sentences.

Example: [a sentence with two adverbs] George's new program runs <u>smoothly</u> and <u>quickly</u>.

1. [a sentence with an adverb modifying an adjective]

2. [a sentence with a linking verb followed by an adjective]

3. [a sentence with an adverb modifying another adverb]

4. [a sentence with an adverb connecting two parts of a sentence]

5. [a sentence with an adverb in the comparative form]

**Exercise for
Experts**

Write the adverb form of each of the following adjectives. Then use each adverb in a sentence. Look up any unfamiliar words.

1. [irritable]

2. [disproportionate]

3. [retroactive]

4. [antagonistic]

5. [negligent]

6. [inexhaustible]

7. [irreparable]

8. [unscrupulous]

9. [exorbitant]

10. [zealous]

CHAPTER 6

PREPOSITIONS

OBJECTIVE: To recognize prepositions, prepositional phrases, and objects of prepositions in sentences.

Can you recognize the prepositions in the following sentences?

1. Has Mr. Larimer gone to the doctor for his shots?

2. From my experience, his analysis of the problem is practical and efficient.

3. The staff, confused about several issues, has decided to meet in the conference room.

4. Will you go with me to the symposium?

5. All the students except Joe will join us after the game.

If you picked out *to* and *for* in #1, *from* and *of* in #2, *about* and *in* in #3, *with* and *to* in #4, and *except* and *after* in #5, you were correct.

PREPOSITIONS ARE CONNECTING WORDS

Prepositions are hard to define because they perform a wide number of roles. Usually you can recognize them as words that connect nouns or pronouns with other words in a sentence. Many prepositions, for example, indicate a geographical or *place* relationship:

> William is going *toward* the bank.
> The train is headed *into* the tunnel.
> The balloon sailed *over* the crowd.
> Our office building sits *beside* a grocery store.

Some prepositions indicate a *time* relationship:

> We will meet *before* noon.
> Jane Healy will speak *during* the meeting.
> The director called an emergency session *after* lunch.
> The case will be closed *by* three o'clock.

Since English has hundreds of prepositions, we cannot list them all here. The following is a sampling of the most common. As you can see, some prepositions are formed from more than one word.

> **Some Common Prepositions**
>
> | about | during | through |
> |---|---|---|
> | above | except | to |
> | according to | from | toward |
> | after | in | under |
> | among | in front of | until |
> | at | in regard to | upon |
> | before | like | with |
> | below | on | within |
> | beside | onto | without |
> | between | on account of | with respect to |
> | by | over | |
> | by means of | since | |

Note: As we have seen before, many words have double and triple identities as different parts of speech. Prepositions are no exception. You will have to examine its function in a sentence to make sure a word is a preposition.

Self-Check Test 6-1

Fill in the blanks with an appropriate preposition. (See suggested answers at end of text.)

Example: He voted in favor of a salary increase.

1. The head ___of___ production is waiting ___for___ a new shipment.

2. His secretary sent the file ___to___ the district attorney ___by___ express mail.

3. ___From___ the crowd came a cry ___of___ protest.

4. Linda walked ___from___ Sixth Avenue ___to___ the beach.

5. The book is either ___on___ my desk or ___in___ the file cabinet.

6. We attended the conference ___for___ three hours and then decided to eat lunch ___at___ the Hilton.

7. Thomas spoke ___with___ enthusiasm ___during___ dinner.

8. ___Until___ now, this commission has done very little ___for___ the community.

9. My typewriter is ___in front of___ a window so I can sit ___in___ the sun as I type.

10. ___From___ 1984 ___until___ 1986, this plan was discussed ___with___ the management team.

PREPOSITIONAL PHRASES

A preposition introduces a word or series of words that we term a *phrase*. You can usually sense that these words belong together:

> We voted *for a new chairman.*
> Jack waited *until midnight.*
> I heard the news *on the radio.*
> The reasons *for his decision* are unclear.
> *At the meeting,* Lowell introduced several issues *to the committee.*

Often several prepositional phrases will follow one another. A new preposition is the beginning of a new prepositional phrase:

> We went *to the job interview / with high hopes / about the job.*
> The site is *on a hill / near a small shopping center / within a mile / of the freeway.*

Self-Check Test 6-2

Underline the prepositional phrases in the following sentences. Draw a vertical line between phrases if they directly follow one another. (Check answers at end of text.)

Example: Henry went <u>with Sally</u> / <u>to the award ceremony.</u>

1. Have you ever driven across that intersection to the used car lot?

2. Phyllis examined the issues with the help of her two assistants.

3. According to real estate analysts, many home buyers are entering the

   market at a later age.

4. Please meet with us before April 1.

5. Lawrence gave the notes to Harry without Pat's consent.

OBJECTS OF PREPOSITIONS

A prepositional phrase contains a noun or pronoun that the preposition is connecting to the rest of the sentence. This noun or pronoun is called the *object of the preposition*.

To recognize the object of the preposition in a phrase, ask yourself WHOM? or WHAT? after the preposition. Your answer will be the object of the preposition.

He is looking for the paper. [for WHAT? for *paper*]
I am going with Frances. [with WHOM? with *Frances*]

The object of a preposition will be a noun or pronoun. Do not consider adjectives, for example, when looking for the object of the preposition.

The plans *for the new track* are almost completed. [*The* and *new* are adjectives; the object of the preposition is *track*.]
We met *by the old drugstore on the deserted street*. [*The* and *old* are adjectives; *drugstore* is the object of the preposition *by*; *the* and *deserted* are adjectives, so *street* is the object of the preposition *on*.]
Someone told that same story *to me at Tim's party*. [*Me* is the object of the preposition *to*; *Tim's* is modifying *party*; *party* is the object of the preposition *at*.]

Sometimes you will have two or more objects in a prepositional phrase. Once again, ask yourself WHOM? or WHAT? after the preposition.

We fought for *God* and *country*.
Thomas waved to *Henry* and *me*.

Note: Noun **CLAUSES** may also be objects of prepositions. We will discuss noun clauses in Part Two.

Caution: Infinitives are not Prepositional Phrases

Do not confuse *to* as a preposition with *to* as it appears in the infinitive form of verbs: *To run, to subtract, to revise, to swim,* and so on are not prepositional phrases.

An infinitive is composed of *to* + a verb; a prepositional phrase containing *to* will be composed of *to* + a noun or pronoun. Note the difference between the following:

I have begun *to learn* accounting methods. [*To learn* is an infinitive.]
I have run *to the store*. [*To the store* is a prepositional phrase.]

Self-Check Test 6-3

Look again at the sentences you examined at the beginning of this chapter. Underline the prepositional phrases in each sentence and circle the object of the preposition. (See end of text for answers.)

1. Has Mr. Larimer gone to the doctor for his shots?

2. From my experience, his analysis of the problem is practical and efficient.

3. The staff, confused about several issues, has decided to meet in the

conference room.

4. Will you go with me to the symposium?

5. All the students except Joe will join us after the game.

THE CHANGING PREPOSITION

Many words must be followed by a particular preposition. In some cases, the preposition actually determines the meaning of the word it accompanies. Watch for these word pairs and make sure you choose the correct form for your sentences.

> AGREE TO [a proposal]: I *agree to* your modification of the report.
> AGREE WITH [a person]: I always *agree with* George.
> COMPLY WITH [not *to*]: I will not *comply with* those rules.
> CONVENIENT FOR [handy for]: This device is *convenient for* slicing small vegetables.
> CONVENIENT TO [close by]: The house is *convenient to* the shopping center.
> DIFFERENT FROM [not *than* or *to*]: This version is quite *different from* the original.
> INDEPENDENT OF [not *from*]: His company is *independent of* ours.
> SPEAK TO [tell someone something]: Mrs. Kahn will *speak to* the crowd.
> SPEAK WITH [have a conversation]: Mandy and Janie will *speak with* the manager.
> WAIT FOR [a person, event, and so on]: Myron is *waiting for* a train.
> WAIT ON [a customer or guest]: Jerry *waited on* six customers.

Self-Check Test 6-4

Fill in the blanks with an appropriate preposition. (See end of text for answers.)

1. While corresponding _____ Mike Matthews, I learned he had some data that would be beneficial _____ us.

2. To comply _____ the law, we are enclosing all the forms necessary _____ the project.

3. This new employee will be independent _____ this office, but he will confer _____ me every day.

4. These blueprints are different _____ the earlier ones.

5. We are waiting _____ the final decision; you can be certain that we will abide _____ it.

A FINAL WORD

You may have learned the rule "Never end a sentence with a preposition." This is a handy reference, since many final prepositions are unnecessary or even redundant.

> Poor: Where is the report at?
> Better: Where is the report?
> Poor: Where is Barbara going to?
> Better: Where is Barbara going?

Sometimes, however, sentences that are both grammatical and effective may end with a preposition. By moving the preposition, you may create a far worse sentence. Supposedly it was Winston Churchill who illustrated this point by commenting, "This is the sort of English up with which I will not put."

Checklist for Chapter 6

1. Prepositions usually connect nouns or pronouns with other words in a sentence.

2. The noun or pronoun that the preposition connects with the rest of the sentence is called the *object of the preposition*.

3. The related words following a preposition are called a prepositional phrase.

Preposition Review

Underline the prepositional phrases in the following paragraph; then circle the prepositions and put a square around the objects of the prepositions. (Check your answers at end of text.)

At noon, Jordan Glover will give a speech on the problems of small businesses in today's economy. Representatives of 20 small businesses will be at the meeting. Kathryn Horne, founder of GHA Corporation, and her assistant, Marilyn McNamara, will speak to us after Mr. Glover's speech; they will also conclude the proceedings. Please let us know if you can attend.

Chapter Test 6-1

I.   **Choose appropriate prepositions for the following sentences.**

1.   I doubt that Mr. Peters will agree _____to_____ these conditions.

2.   Please furnish us ____with____ your salary history and references.

3.   We have found that Mr. Lyons is never in his office ____during____ lunchtime.

4.   ____For____ your information, I have attached the relevant invoices.

5.   If you walk ____by____ the river, you will see the warehouse.

II. **Underline the prepositional phrases in the following sentences. Circle the prepositions and put a square around the object of the prepositions.**

1.   Please accompany Mr. and Mrs. Forester to the baseball stadium.

2.   When you finish the Newton project, please send a copy of the report to Max Bell.

3.   I have outlined the problem, but George will have to develop a solution for it.

4.   Above my desk on a shelf is a copy of Roget's *Thesaurus*.

5.   Since the beginning of June, we have been trying to finish the new employee handbook.

6.   If you get to the restaurant before me, order me a dozen oysters.

7.   My answer depends on your analysis.

8.   As Steve had canceled the order, we were unable to deliver the light fixtures to the customer.

9.   When he retired from the army, Pete returned to school.

10. I reimbursed the clerks from my own pocket.

Chapter Test 6-2

I. **Underline the prepositional phrases in the following paragraphs. Place a vertical line between any connected phrases.**

We hope you will introduce your customers to our exciting new product. This lightweight fabric is attractive and inexpensive, and it will never wrinkle or fade. Our research and development team has been working on the Fabulon fabric since 1982; satisfied only with perfection, we are now sure that Fabulon is the best sportswear fabric in the world.

Please read the enclosed catalog. We know you will be amazed at the prices, at the colors, at the variety of our products. If you want us to send you some samples, please return the attached card by the end of March.

II. **Write a sentence using each of the following sets of prepositions.**

Example: [since, except] Since April, everyone except Hugh has been promoted.

1. [to, from]

2. [before, by]

3. [over, below]

4. [near, toward]

5. [during, within]

Exercise for Experts

Write a sentence using each of the following words followed by an appropriate preposition. Underline the prepositions. Look up any unfamiliar words.

   Example: [admit] The man will not admit <u>to</u> the crime.

   1. [detract]

   2. [characterized]

   3. [emigrate]

   4. [impervious]

   5. [oblivious]

   6. [incompatible]

   7. [regardless]

   8. [attest]

   9. [dependent]

   10. [dissimilar]

CHAPTER 7

CONJUNCTIONS

OBJECTIVE: To recognize coordinate, correlative, and subordinate conjunctions in sentences.

Which words in the following sentences are conjunctions?

1. George and Sandra will revise the proposal until Mr. Williams approves of it.

2. Although we are uncertain of the results, we are trying the experiment.

3. The clerks are not only dissatisfied but also angry.

If you selected *and* and *until* in #1, *although* in #2, and *not only . . . but also* in #3, you are already familiar with conjunctions.

As their name implies, conjunctions are linking words. They may join individual words or groups of words. Conjunctions help you convey a precise meaning to your readers. In following chapters, you will find that recognizing conjunctions will help you to punctuate sentences and to avoid a wide variety of grammatical errors.

There are three types of conjunctions: coordinate, correlative, and subordinate.

COORDINATE CONJUNCTIONS

Coordinate conjunctions are probably the most familiar to you.

Coordinate Conjunctions
and   nor   yet   but   or   for   so

AND indicates *addition*: Herb *and* Belle are impatient.

BUT indicates a *qualification or contrast*: He is talented *but* lazy.

FOR indicates a *cause*: The arena was empty, *for* the game had ended an hour earlier.

NOR indicates an *additional negative*: I have not contacted Sam, *nor* has he contacted me.

OR indicates a *choice*: Randy will drive *or* walk.

SO indicates a *result*: No one was in the office, *so* Paul came home.

YET indicates a *qualification* or *contrast* similar to *but*: He is exhausted, *yet* he is still working.

Self-Check Test 7-1

Fill in the blanks with appropriate coordinate conjunctions. (Check answers at end of text.)

1. Bradley _____ Williams have been named co-chairmen of the project.

2. The team has been developing ideas for over a month, _____ it has not begun the tests or the report.

3. When you get to Atlanta, give me a call _____ I can relay your message to Henry.

4. I have not seen Inez, _____ have I seen her typescript.

5. If you have any stamps, please give them to Greg _____ let him do the mailing.

Coordinate conjunctions link items of the same type. For example, they may connect two or more nouns: I will choose the desk *or* the chair.

They may connect verbs: Mr. Milligan jogs, sails, *and* skis.

They may connect adjectives: This attractive *but* useful gadget costs $34.99.

They may connect adverbs: I will complete the project honestly *and* successfully.

They may connect two prepositional phrases: Marjorie is going to the conference *and* to the dinner.

You will not use a coordinate conjunction to link an adverb to a noun, for example, or to link a verb to a prepositional phrase.

Coordinate conjunctions may link groups of words (or *phrases*) beginning with participles, gerunds, and infinitives.

The man wearing a blue suit and carrying a briefcase is our attorney. [two participial phrases]

Flying airplanes or driving sports cars were his career choices. [two gerund phrases]

Charles Sullivan plans to analyze and to solve the problem. [two infinitive phrases]

We will discuss these phrases further in Chapter 11; for now you should see that the groups of words linked by the coordinate conjunction perform the same grammatical function in the sentence.

Self-Check Test 7-2

Underline the coordinate conjunctions in the following sentences. Then, in the space to the right, indicate the type of words being connected by the conjunctions: verbs, nouns, adjectives, adverbs, or phrases.

1. My supervisor and friend, Jill Holroyd, has been promoted. _____

2. The coffee tastes strong but sweet. _____

3. Jack is always debugging or creating new programs. _____

4. The sales manager spoke quietly yet emphatically. _____

5. Today Mr. Sumner will accept or reject the proposal. _____

COORDINATE CONJUNCTIONS AND CLAUSES

Coordinate conjunctions may also connect clauses.

A clause is a group of words that has a subject (the doer of an action) and a verb (an action).

An independent (or main) clause may stand alone as a sentence: *Jack runs.* A dependent (or subordinate) clause cannot stand by itself: *since Jack runs.*

A coordinate conjunction may combine two independent clauses or two dependent clauses; it may *not* connect a dependent to an independent clause.

independent clause + coordinate conjunction + independent clause

dependent clause + coordinate conjunction + dependent clause

> *Hilary has described the procedures,* so *she can now leave you on your own.* [So links two independent clauses.]
> I believe *that we will survive* but *that we will not prosper.*
> [But links two dependent clauses.]

Note: *That we will survive* and *that we will not prosper* cannot stand by themselves as sentences; they are *dependent* on the rest of the sentence.

Self-Check Test 7-3

Put an appropriate coordinate conjunction in each blank. In the space to the right, indicate whether the words being linked are nouns, verbs, adjectives, adverbs, phrases, or clauses. (See end of text for answers.)

1. I will hire one of the candidates: Norman _____ Keith. _____

2. Gary helped us out _____ we could finish the work on time. _____

3. The thunder scared them, _____ the team kept on playing. _____

4. I am trying to work quickly _____ conscientiously. _____

5. We will not be done by 5:00 p.m., _____ we will be done by 7:00 p.m. _____

CORRELATIVE CONJUNCTIONS

The name of correlative conjunctions may be confusing. *Correlative* simply means that two words or groups of words are related. (Some people call them *comparative* conjunctions.)

The six correlative conjunctions come in pairs. Like coordinating conjunctions, they link words, phrases, or clauses that have similar functions in a sentence.

Correlative Conjunctions

both . . . and	either . . . or
neither . . . nor	not only . . . but also
not . . . but	whether . . . or

In Chapter 20 (pp. 228–230), we will examine correlative conjunctions in depth; right now, you should simply be able to recognize them and see that they compare two items in a sentence.

> *Not only* Jack *but also* Bob will meet us at the airport.
> *Both* Jack *and* Bob will meet us at the airport.
> *Neither* Jack *nor* Bob will meet us at the airport.

Self-Check Test 7-4

Fill in the blanks with appropriate correlative conjunctions. Then, in the space to the right, indicate whether the words being linked are verbs, nouns, adjectives, adverbs, phrases, or clauses. (See sample answers at end of text.)

1. Marianne will _____ promote _____

   fire Wilfrid.   _____

2. The Samuelsons are _____ wealthy

   _____ generous.   _____

3. I have not decided _____ to major in engineering

   _____ to major in chemistry.   _____

4. _____ Harry _____ Susannah will give

   in to the strikers' demands.   _____

5. This company will go bankrupt _____ because it

   was poorly managed _____ because it was

   inadequately financed.   _____

SUBORDINATE CONJUNCTIONS

Subordinate conjunctions link independent clauses to dependent clauses. (For more on independent and dependent clauses, see Chapter 12.) There are too many subordinate conjunctions to list them all here, but the following box includes some of the most common.

Some Common Subordinate Conjunctions			
after	although	as	as if
as long as	as though	because	before
how	if	in case	in order that
since	that	though	unless
until	when	where	while

Subordinate conjunctions indicate a logical connection between two thoughts; they show cause, qualification, contrast, simultaneous action, and many other relationships between two clauses. At the same time, a subordinate conjunction indicates that the following clause is less important than (or *subordinate* to) the independent clause.

A clause beginning with a subordinate conjunction may not stand alone as a sentence.

<u>Although the issue is important,</u> we have not discussed it.
    dependent clause   + independent clause

We will go to the cafeteria <u>unless you prefer to eat here.</u>
    independent clause   + dependent clause

In the previous examples, the underlined clauses cannot stand by themselves as sentences. The independent clauses, however, could be detached from the dependent clauses to stand alone as sentences.

Dependent clauses may come before or after main clauses; in fact, dependent clauses may even appear in the middle of independent clauses.

We decided *while you were gone* to finish the project.

Many of the words that serve as subordinate conjunctions may also serve as prepositions, pronouns, or other parts of speech. Once again, you must look at the function of a word in a sentence to determine which part of speech it is.

That is my goal. [*that* is a demonstrative pronoun.]
I hope *that* you will win. [*That* is a subordinate conjunction.]

Self-Check Test 7-5

I. Fill in the blanks with appropriate subordinate conjunctions. (Check suggested answers at end of text.)

1. _____ we have considered your application, we will contact your references.

WRITING HINT: AVOID SLANG
Henry's First Draft   *Henry's Second Draft*

Source: Ford Button

2. Capitol Movers is holding our furniture _____ we send the company a check.

3. _____ the summer is just starting, morale in the office has been high.

4. Please call me this afternoon _____ you would like to use the modem.

5. _____ we were meeting with Dickerson, Eugene was meeting with Patricia.

II. Underline the conjunctions in the following sentences. Put *CRD* over the coordinate conjunctions, *SUB* over the subordinate conjunctions, and *COR* over the correlative conjunctions. (Check answers at end of text.)

1. Chemical waste has been a problem for these companies, but they are

    rapidly arriving at some solutions.

2. The job interviews were both lengthy and inefficient.

3. The company has built an expensive and impressive complex in downtown Cleveland.

4. Although the cliffs are over a thousand feet high, geologists have been going carefully through the area.

5. This is an excellent reference tool for people who want to do more detailed research, but it is neither easy to read nor easy to understand.

6. Since the trip takes over six hours by train, we brought sandwiches, a thermos, and a pile of magazines.

7. Try to get a memo to Herman before noon so he can begin work on the statistical data.

8. The Regis oil field is an expensive experiment that may make us millionaires or paupers.

9. Either Jones will win this election or he will lose embarrassingly.

10. Experience has shown us that our investments should be cautious as long as our profits are so slim.

Checklist for Chapter 7

1. Coordinate conjunctions connect words, phrases, or clauses that have similar functions in a sentence.

2. Correlative conjunctions come in pairs to link words, phrases, and clauses that have similar functions in a sentence.

3. Subordinate conjunctions connect independent clauses to dependent clauses.

4. A clause is a group of words that has a subject (the doer of an action) and a verb (an action). Independent clauses may stand alone as sentences; dependent clauses may not stand alone.

Conjunction Review

Underline the conjunctions in the following paragraphs. Then mark them *CRD*, *COR*, or *SUB* to indicate whether they are coordinate, correlative, or subordinate conjunctions.

A good interview can be a very strenuous and tiring experience, but it is always productive for both the prospective employer and the prospective candidate. If interviewers do their job correctly, they will not only learn about the candidate's background and experience, but they will convey vital information to the candidate.

Although inexperienced candidates are often too timid to ask many questions, they should remember that the interview is a two-way process; a job candidate should be finding out about the job and the company while the interviewer is finding out about the candidate.

Check your answers at end of text.

Chapter Test 7-1

I. **Indicate whether each underlined conjunction is coordinate, subordinate, or correlative by writing** *CRD, SUB,* **or** *COR* **in the space provided.**

1. We will have the wedding outside <u>whether</u> it is rainy <u>or</u> it is sunny. _____

2. Interest rates <u>and</u> unemployment rates are both rising. _____

3. <u>If</u> you would like to see our brochure, call Max. _____

4. Lerner Company will have its annual sale <u>unless</u> the clerks go on strike. _____

5. Randy <u>or</u> Austin can explain the construction problems. _____

II. **Fill in the blanks with appropriate subordinate conjunctions.**

1. _____ he was on his way to Los Angeles, Mike Herden lost his wallet.

2. The inventory will be overpriced _____ we make some changes now.

3. _____ we got our holiday bonuses, some staff members still resent the Christmas overtime.

4. Lawrence said, "Let me go to Chicago _____ Hilda returns."

5. _____ the new manager can overcome some personnel problems, she should be a success.

Chapter Test 7-2

I. **Write sentences according to the following directions; then underline the conjunctions.**

Example: [a sentence with correlative conjunctions linking two nouns] He is <u>either</u> a doctor <u>or</u> a lawyer.

1. [a sentence with a coordinate conjunction linking two nouns]

2. [a sentence beginning with a subordinate conjunction]

3. [a sentence with correlative conjunctions linking two prepositional phrases]

4. [a sentence with a coordinate conjunction between two adjectives]

5. [a sentence with a subordinate conjunction and a coordinate conjunction]

II. **Underline the conjunctions in the following sentences. Write *CRD, SUB,* or *COR* over each conjunction to indicate whether it is coordinate, subordinate, or correlative.**

Proofreading your letters and memos is a vital part of good writing. If you go carefully through your final draft, you will usually find misspellings, punctuation errors, and even logical problems. When you have just completed a draft, however, you often cannot see any errors. Since spotting your own typos can be a time-consuming and painful business, you may want to either give your draft to someone else for a final proofreading or wait a few hours before checking your draft.

One rule for good writing is to leave yourself enough time for writing and revising. Hasty writing can be the downfall of both inexperienced and seasoned writers.

Exercises for Experts

I. **Write sentences using each of the following words as subordinate conjunctions.**

1. [until]

2. [whenever]

3. [even though]

4. [while]

5. [because]

6. [so that]

7. [before]

8. [wherever]

9. [since]

10. [unless]

II. **After rereading the following paragraphs, identify the underlined words as nouns, pronouns, verbs, adjectives, adverbs, prepositions, or conjunctions.**

Proofreading your letters and memos is a vital part of good writing. If you go carefully through your final draft, you will usually find misspellings, punctuation errors, and even logical problems. When you have just completed a draft, however, you often cannot see any errors. Since spotting your own typos can be a time-consuming and painful business, you may want to either give your draft to someone else for a final proofreading or wait a few hours before checking your draft.

One rule for good writing is to leave yourself enough time for both writing and revising. Hasty writing can be the downfall of both inexperienced and seasoned writers.

1.	6.	11.
2.	7.	12.
3.	8.	13.
4.	9.	14.
5.	10.	15.

CHAPTER 8

INTERJECTIONS

OBJECTIVE: To recognize interjections in sentences.

Do you recognize the interjections in these sentences?

"Ouch!" said the child suddenly.
"Darn, I've forgotten my briefcase," muttered Paul.

If you said *Ouch* and *Darn*, you were right. *To interject* means *to throw*: an interjection is an expression or exclamation thrown into a sentence. Interjections are simply words that indicate an emotion or strong reaction of some type; they usually remain separate from the rest of the sentence.

Some interjections, as you might guess, are not appropriate for a textbook—or for your business writing. A few common (and tame) interjections include:

darn	gosh	golly	hey
hurray	ow	sssh	wow

Words such as *yes*, *no*, and *indeed* are interjections if they stand apart from the rest of the sentence.

Yes, the check has been cashed.
"Indeed, the money is in the bank," said Freddie.

Interjections are most common in dialogue. Since they are used infrequently in business writing, we will not discuss them in detail. Simply recognize them as one of the eight parts of speech; when we discuss exclamation points in Chapter 21 and commas in Chapter 22 we will mention interjections again.

Self-Check Test 8-1

Underline the interjections in the following dialogue. (See end of text for answers.)

"Well," said Phil, "I am not sure that I agree with your

analysis."

Marsha frowned. "Gee, that's too bad. Your support is

essential."

"It is," agreed Terry. "Hey, have you considered talk-

ing with Mildred about it?"

"No!" announced Phil. "I refuse to discuss the matter

with her."

"Drat!" exclaimed Marsha. "Then I guess the matter is

settled."

_____

Checklist for Chapter 8   Interjections are words set apart from the rest of the sentence that show strong emotions or reactions.

PART ONE REVIEW TESTS

Review Test 1-1

Here is the paragraph you worked on at the beginning of Part One. Read it again and answer the questions that follow.

> George began his job at ARMCO after he had worked as a technician for ten years. His new job requires more hours, but the increased pay and exciting work keep his morale high.
>
> "Oh, I cannot spend enough time with my family," he says, "but they completely understand the situation. In two years I will cut my hours at the plant and stay at home on Saturdays."

1. Go back through the paragraphs and look for every noun. Now list all the nouns you found. (Hint: There are more than 15.)

2. Now list all the helping verbs in the previous paragraph.

3. List all the *main* verbs.

4. List all the adjectives.

5. List all the adverbs.

6. List all the prepositions.

7. List all the conjunctions.

8. List all the pronouns.

9. List all the interjections.

Review Test 1-2

The following are paragraphs you worked on at the end of Chapter 3. Read them again and answer the questions that follow.

You have all been doing a great job finishing the Keller contract. I know it has been a lot of work. Since this is the first big contract we have had, each of us had to put in extra hours. I know these have taken their toll on us.

What would be the best solution? After some thought, I've decided we can afford a little time off. I have designated the week of August 23 a "mental health week" for all of us. You can stay home and unplug your phones or take off for a few days.

Please return on August 30 with a lot of enthusiasm for our next big project—the James account.

1. Underline each prepositional phrase. Put a vertical line between adjoining prepositional phrases. Now list each preposition.

2. Circle each helping verb. Now list each helping verb.

3. Put a square around each main verb; then list each one below.

Review Test 1-3

Underline the pronouns in the following sentences and circle the nouns.

1. When each of us is done with lunch, Jack will meet us in the new clubhouse.

2. Have you decided when you will finish those articles?

3. What is your opinion on the small increases in salaries?

4. Although the decision was made on Monday, the staff is not yet aware of it.

5. If these are your papers, please take them immediately to your office.

List the personal pronouns you found:

List the indefinite pronouns you found:

List the demonstrative pronouns you found:

List the nouns you found:

Now go through these sentences again. Underline the adjectives; circle the adverbs; put two lines under the conjunctions.

1. When each of us is done with lunch, Jack will meet us in the new club-
    house.

2. Have you decided when you will finish those articles?

3. What is your opinion on the small increases in salaries?

4. Although the decision was made on Monday, the staff is not yet aware of
    it.

5. If these are your papers, please take them immediately to your office.

List the adjectives you found:

List the adverbs you found:

List the coordinate conjunctions you found:

List the subordinate conjunctions you found:

**Review Test
1-4**

Write sentences using the parts of speech designated. Underline the part of speech you were requested to include in the sentence.

1. [an adverb]

2. [a coordinate conjunction]

3. [an interrogative pronoun]

4. [two main verbs]

5. [a prepositional phrase]

6. [a proper noun]

7. [two demonstrative adjectives]

8. [an indefinite pronoun]

9. [an interjection]

10. [a subordinate conjunction]

11. [two articles]

12. [a helping verb]

13. [a proper adjective]

14. [an adjective in superlative form]

15. [a demonstrative pronoun]

Review Test 1-5

After reading the following memo, identify each of the underlined words as one of the eight parts of speech according to its function in the sentence. Indicate whether an underlined verb is a main verb or helping verb; indicate whether a conjunction is coordinate, correlative, or subordinate.

Example: The manager has called us. [has: helping verb]

To: Rhonda Cooper

From: David Brill

Subject: Updated Personnel Manual

Date: February 9, 19xx

Now that we have hired 200 additional clerical employees, we find that the present personnel manual does not supply sufficient information in two key areas: medical benefits and overtime pay.

The Personnel Department staff will meet next Monday to discuss further areas that could be improved. This week, however, please outline these areas so we can discuss them on Monday before the meeting.

With your help, I am sure the revision process will be thorough and efficient.

---

1. we:

2. additional:

3. find:

4. present:

5. supply:

6. in:

7. benefits:

8. staff:

9. will:

10. Monday:

11. this:

12. however:

13. so:

14. before:

15. thorough:

CONSTRUCTING SENTENCES

FAMOUS FIRST DRAFTS: GENESIS
Writing Hint: Be Concrete

AND AT THE CONCLUSION OF THE WORK WEEK, THE LORD TOOK ADVANTAGE OF SOME COMPENSATION TIME...

And on the seventh day, God rested.

Source: Ford Button

Reading for Resourceful Writers

Sample Memos: The Carnivorous Cat Food Company

Memo

To: Robin Run-On

From: Philip Fragment

Subject: Sales Manual

Date: June 12, 19xx

New sales manual needed. Urgent. Since salespeople not following orders. Don't know product. Trying to sell cat food to cocker spaniels.

Memo

To: Corey Comma-Splice

From: Robin Run-On

Subject: Carnivorous Cat Cakes

Date: June 13, 19xx

Philip wants a sales manual written immediately but I don't have enough information on Carnivorous Cat Cakes please send product samples and ingredient list right away I appreciate your help.

Memo

To: Robin Run-On

From: Corey Comma-Splice

Subject: Creamed Goldfish

Date: June 13, 19xx

I am sending you some Carnivorous Cat Cakes, however, I don't have a complete ingredient list, I believe the cakes contain creamed goldfish, but maybe it's Mandarin spiced tuna, I will get back to you as soon as possible with the full list, I hope the wait isn't too inconvenient.

Memo

To: All Staff

From: Philip Fragment

Subject: Delectable Dog Food Deli

Date: June 14, 19xx

Change of plans. Carnivorous Cat Food defunct. Sales to cocker spaniels okay. Company name now Delectable Dog Food Deli. Key ingredient in Carnivorous Cakes: creamed goldfish. Also good on croissants, bagels, and English muffins.

PART TWO OBJECTIVES: To learn how sentences are put together and to construct complete sentences rather than fragments, run-ons, or comma splices.

Recognizing parts of speech is important to good writing, but it is not the final goal: you should be able to see how words function in each sentence you write. If you can recognize the relationships between different parts of a sentence, you can heighten your ability to use those parts effectively. When you know the essentials of constructing sentences, you will be well on your way to creating effective pieces of business writing.

The Reading for Resourceful Writers that you have just read provides humorous examples of what happens when people do not write in sentences. When the reader is forced to supply missing components of a sentence, the business writer has not carried out his or her primary function: to communicate clearly and accurately.

Sentences, as the basic building blocks of your thoughts, must be constructed carefully if you want to get results.

Before you begin Chapter 9, take the Part Two Pre-Test to check your proficiency in recognizing the components of sentences.

PART TWO PRE-TEST

I. **Put a check after each of the following if it is a complete sentence.**

1. Barbara, racing for the bus.   _____

2. Jack will head the project.   _____

3. Our goal is to succeed.   _____

4. Because the seminar has begun.   _____

5. Make three copies for Pete.   _____

II. **Read the following paragraphs and answer the questions given.**

> If you want your speech to be effective, you should organize your material very carefully.(1) Determine your major point, make sure that you support the point in every section of the speech.(2)
>
> A good speech, while it may be serious, is never dull.(3) Remember to keep your audience alert and interested.(4) Your speech should give your audience one major idea.(5) Something to remember and to think about.(6)

1. Which sentences have dependent as well as independent clauses? (List the numbers.)   _____

2. What is the subject of the independent clause in number 1? _____

3. What is the subject of the independent clause in number 3? _____
    Number 4?   _____

4. Are there any sentence fragments in these paragraphs? If yes, give the number(s).   _____

5. Are there any comma splices in these paragraphs? If yes, give the number(s).   _____

6. What is the direct object in number 5?   _____

7. What is the indirect object in number 5?   _____

8. Do any of these sentences have prepositional phrases? If so, give the number(s).   _____

After you have answered these questions to the best of your ability, check your answers at end of text. If you had trouble with the Pre-Test, come back to it after you have studied Chapters 9 through 14.

CHAPTER 9

SUBJECTS

OBJECTIVE: Locating the subjects of sentences.

Can you identify the subjects of the following sentences?

This spring, Lynn and Bob will go to Canada.
We will begin painting the house in July.
There will be a pause in the proceedings.
Has Mick already met Daniel?

If you selected *Lynn, Bob, we, pause,* and *Mick,* you are already experienced in locating subjects.

SENTENCES HAVE SUBJECTS

A simple sentence can be divided into two sections: the **SUBJECT** (the person, place, thing, or idea named) and the **PREDICATE** (what is said about the thing named).

A sentence is a group of words that contains a subject and a predicate and expresses a complete thought.

Most sentences will follow a pattern like this:

Complete Subject	+	Complete Predicate
Sandra		jogs.
The *house*		was sold on Saturday.
The *union* and *management*		disagree about wages.
A serious *problem*		is developing.

The complete subject of a sentence contains adjectives and other words that help to describe the simple subject. In the previous sentences, the simple subjects are in italics; the predicate provides more information about the simple subject. The predicate must contain a verb or verb phrase.

In Chapter 1, you worked on recognizing verbs. In this chapter, you will put your knowledge of verbs to work again. Now you will use verbs to find the subjects of your sentences.

Finding the subject is a two-part process:

1. Locate the helping and main verbs.

2. Ask yourself WHO or WHAT + VERB?

Sarah runs a bakery in Georgetown.

1. The verb is *runs.*

2. *Who* runs? *Sarah.*

Has Mick already met Daniel?

1. The verb is *has met*.

2. *Who* has met? *Mick*.

Self-Check Test 9-1

Underline the complete subjects of the following sentences; circle the simple subjects. (See answers at end of text.)

1. My work was inaccurate.

2. A new building has been planned.

3. George and Greg have made a decision.

4. Our chocolate desserts tasted peculiar.

5. Have you ordered the new copier?

6. The incoming administration has altered its tax proposals.

7. We will move to Honolulu next April.

8. Upon graduation, Gregory began working for IBM.

9. The azaleas are blooming outside our office windows.

10. Has anyone seen the telephone book?

POSITION OF SUBJECTS

Usually a subject will appear directly before the verb.

subject   verb
Claudia bought the small business.

subject   verb
The personnel *manager* has promoted Tim.

subject   verb
We are hoping for a green Christmas.

Questions, as we have seen, often alter the order of the sentence: usually the subject is between the helping verb and the main verb.

helping verb   subject   main verb
Will *Mr. Doolittle* make the presentations?

helping verb subject main verb
Does *Marta* have the necessary information?

helping verb subject   main verb
Can Florence deliver the office supplies?

Verbs occasionally precede their subjects. This reversal occurs most frequently when sentences begin with *there*.

verb   subject
There were problems with the transmission.

verb   subject
There was a mistake in the printing.

verb   subject
Was there a change in the agenda?

Sometimes writers reverse the normal subject-verb order to bring variety to their sentences:

In the last chapter occurred some dramatic moments.

1. The verb is *occurred*.

2. *What* occurred? *moments*.

Especially fascinating were his points on the economy.

1. The verb is *were*.

2. *What* were? *points*.

On the agenda appeared several financial issues.

1. The verb is *appeared*.

2. *What* appeared? *issues*.

To check the subjects of such sentences, you can usually rewrite the sentence in your mind:

subject
Some dramatic moments occurred in the last chapter.

subject
His points on the economy were especially fascinating.

subject
Several financial issues appeared on the agenda.

In fact, when you are editing your writing, you *should* rewrite most of the sentences beginning with *there*: your sentences will usually be more concise and effective if they begin with the subject. (See Chapter 33 for more on editing sentences beginning with *there*.)

Self-Check Test 9-2

Underline the subjects in the following sentences. (Check your answers at end of text.)

1. Joan will travel to Chicago before September.

2. Has my checkbook appeared in this office?

3. Often a delay will irritate the audience.

4. There has been a question regarding business ethics.

5. Will you change these dollars into francs?

MULTIPLE SUBJECTS

Just as a sentence may have more than one verb, a verb may have more than one subject. These subjects will be connected by *and, or,* or correlative conjunctions.

subjects
The *suppliers* and *retailers* are discussing the problem.

subjects
Mr. Black or *Mrs. Jamison* will join the marketing effort.

subjects
Neither the *manager* nor the *salesperson* has returned my call.

Sometimes a list of items will be the subjects of a sentence:

subjects
Rice, beans, detergent, and *eggs* were featured in today's sale.

subjects
Quality, reliability, and *service* are their goals.

Watch for sentences in which the compound subjects are separated by other material:

subject
Karen, who is president of the accounting club, and
subject
Tim, who is head of the Student Body Association, are

being photographed for a campus publication.

subject
The *vice-president*, who is an attorney, and

subject
Perry Lamont will coauthor the manual.

Self-Check Test 9-3

Underline the subjects in the following sentences. (Check your answers at end of text.)

1. William Beane, Larry Smith, and the young doctor are going on a ski trip

   this winter.

2. Can the United States or the Soviet Union arrive at a decision on this

   matter?

3. There are positive points and negative points about each option.

4. At the end of April, Max, the shop steward, and Lew, the sales manager, will meet with the staff.

5. On Memorial Day, not only our neighbors but also our close friends from Illinois get together for a barbecue.

FORMS OF SUBJECTS

Most of the time, the subject of a sentence will be a noun or pronoun:

> *Teddy* saw the movie.
> The *leader* is thinking about the situation.
> *He* brought in a good manager.

Commands or instructions may not have a defined subject: the subject is understood to be *you*.

> Please file these papers. [Subject is *you*.]
> Follow the signs to the garage sale. [Subject is *you*.]

Note: Make sure you do not identify a verb, adjective, or adverb as a subject.

Sometimes a gerund or infinitive will function as a subject. Remember, infinitives begin with *to* and gerunds end in *-ing*. Once again, you can locate these words as subjects by asking WHO or WHAT + VERB?

> Reading can be entertaining as well as educational.

1. Verb is *can be*.
2. *What* can be? *Reading*.

> To see is to believe.

1. Verb is *is*.
2. What *is*? *To see*.

Do not, however, confuse these verbals with a verb phrase.

> Cooking is my release. [Subject is *cooking*.]
> Fred was cooking some beans. [Verb is *was cooking*.]

Self-Check Test 9-4

Underline the subjects in the following sentences. (Check your answers at end of text.)

1. Losing was a traumatic experience.

2. At dawn in this field, bird-watching is great fun.

3. Try revising the memo before this afternoon.

4. To succeed is his aim.

5. Has Clyde been writing the comedy material?

NOUN PHRASES AS SUBJECTS

Sometimes a phrase will function as a noun and, thus, may be a subject. Gerund and infinitive phrases are the most common types of noun phrases.

Gerund Phrases as Subjects	+	Predicate
Selling these offices		was a drastic move.
Writing a book		takes time.
Running a marathon		is usually exhausting.

Infinitive Phrases as Subjects	+	Predicate
To win at poker		is his goal.
To fly to Atlanta		proved impossible.
To arrange a meeting		was a poor idea.

Note in the prior examples that the entire phrase must function as the subject. In the first example, *selling* is not the subject since *selling* does not tell us *what* was a drastic move; the word *offices*, also, does not tell us what was drastic. We need the entire phrase as subject.

Self-Check Test 9-5

Fill in the blanks with an appropriate noun phrase. (See end of text for sample answers.)

Example: *To see her* is to love her.

1. _____ was the answer to our problem.

2. _____ could be unavoidable.

3. _____ ended our conversation.

4. _____ is to admit defeat.

5. _____ cost him a fortune.

DEPENDENT CLAUSES AS SUBJECTS

A dependent clause contains a subject and a verb, but it cannot stand alone as a sentence. Sometimes, like a phrase, a dependent clause may function as a noun and can be the subject of a sentence. Many noun clauses begin with *why, what, whichever, whatever, who, whoever, whomever, that,* and *where.*

Dependent Clause as Subject	+	Predicate
What I have decided		is irrelevant.
Whatever you want		will be considered.
Where Paul is going		is a company secret.

You cannot choose one word in the clause to act as subject; you need the entire clause.

Self-Check Test 9-6

Underline the subjects of the following sentences. Then indicate whether each subject is a noun, pronoun, gerund, infinitive, noun phrase, or noun clause. (See answers at end of text.)

1. Whoever runs for governor must know the issues. _____

2. Winning makes no difference to Greg. _____

3. Where are you planning to build the garage? _____

4. What the report recommends is diversification. _____

5. Ordering a hundred cases was the action of an ambitious man. _____

6. Swimming Lake Tober took two hours. _____

7. Whichever set you want can be yours. _____

8. Memorizing this text requires intense concentration. _____

9. Whomever you designate will wear the badge. _____

10. Why this door is stuck remains a mystery. _____

CHECKLIST FOR CHAPTER 9

1. The subject may be located by finding the verb and asking WHO or WHAT + VERB?

2. Usually the subject precedes the verb. In some sentences, especially those starting with *there*, the subject follows the verb.

3. In questions, subjects often come between the helping verb and main verb.

4. Some sentences contain more than one subject. Compound subjects are connected by *and, or,* or correlative conjunctions.

5. Subjects may be nouns, pronouns, gerunds, or infinitives. Subjects may also be noun phrases or noun clauses.

6. Commands often have *you* as an implied subject.

SUBJECT REVIEW

Underline the simple subjects in the following sentences. (Check your answers at end of text.)

At noon, Jordan Glover will speak on the problems fac-

ing small businesses in today's economy.(1) Representa-

tives of 20 businesses will be in attendance.(2) Kathryn

Horne, founder of GHA Corporation, and her assistant will

offer us some refreshments after Mr. Glover's speech.(3)

Kathryn will also conclude the proceedings.(4) Please let us

know if you can attend.(5)

Are there any implied subjects in these sentences? If so, which sentences? (Give the numbers.) _____
Check your answers at end of text.

CHAPTER TEST 9-1

I. Put one line under the helping and main verbs in these sentences. Put two lines under the subjects.

1. Can you telephone Janet before Thursday?

2. There have been some snags in the building construction.

3. Smith, Kemble, and Franks are representatives for the union.

4. Tell me how to get in touch with Wilbur Greene.

5. Playing can be as important as working.

6. Competing and winning are two very different things.

7. Before the opening, we encountered some financial difficulties.

8. Naturally, both employees will be thoroughly tested.

9. The coach or the manager will speak to the team.

10. In the long pause between the acts, someone began coughing.

II. Fill in the blanks with appropriate subjects.

1. _____ has promised to work until eight o'clock.

2. Between noon and five, _____ broke into my office.

3. There has been a (n) _____ in the basement.

4. _____ for two weeks straight is exhausting.

5. Are _____ and _____ able to play tennis?

III. Fill in the blanks with appropriate pronoun subjects. Use personal or indefinite pronouns.

1. _____ and Mary Ruth are collecting the evidence.

2. _____ of the doctors checked for intestinal infections.

3. Will _____ arrive before midnight?

4. What are _____ looking for?

5. Hugh or _____ will be appointed chairperson.

CHAPTER TEST 9-2

Underline the subjects in the following paragraphs.

Today's meeting has been extremely important for our company. For the first time, the representatives of PULL Industries and our own executives have agreed on the strategic points of a merger. With some effort, we will come up with an agreement beneficial to all parties concerned.

There must be a waiting period between now and Thursday. By then the basic points should be in writing; we will meet with our respective department heads at that time and work out the matter in more detail. Samuel Surtees and Leila Matthews will be happy to discuss the merger with you next week. Until then, you may call me for information.

CHAPTER TEST 9-3

Write sentences according to the instructions provided. Then underline the subjects in each sentence.

Example: [a sentence with a common noun as subject] The chair is missing one of its legs.

1. [a sentence with two noun subjects connected by *and*]

2. [a sentence beginning with *there*]

3. [a command with an implied subject]

4. [a sentence in which the subject follows the verb]

5. [a question with the subject between the helping verb and main verb]

6. [a sentence with a proper noun as subject]

7. [a question with a personal pronoun as subject]

8. [a sentence with an indefinite pronoun as subject]

9. [a sentence with a noun clause as subject]

10. [a sentence with a noun phrase as subject]

EXERCISE FOR EXPERTS   Write sentences using each of the following words or groups of words as subjects. Look up any unfamiliar words.

1. [liquidation]

2. [criticizing his supervisor]

3. [cylinder]

4. [to appoint a successor]

5. [facsimile]

6. [neither physicians nor patients]

7. [proving incompetence]

8. [whatever is decided]

9. [to repave the highway]

10. [proportion]

CHAPTER 10

DIRECT OBJECTS, INDIRECT OBJECTS, AND COMPLEMENTS

OBJECTIVE: Locating direct objects, indirect objects, and complements in sentences.

Can you identify the objects in these sentences? Can you identify the indirect objects? Are there any complements?

> I mailed Joan the report.
> Please buy George a new receiver.
> These people will sell you a small size.
> The man is a detective.

If you chose *report, receiver,* and *size* as direct objects, you were correct. *Joan, George,* and *you* are the indirect objects. *Detective* is the only complement.

DIRECT OBJECTS

The object of a sentence is a noun or noun substitute (pronoun, verbal, noun phrase, noun clause) that receives the action of the verb. Usually you can find the direct object by locating the verb and asking VERB + WHOM or WHAT?

> I mailed a letter. [mailed *what*? letter]
> Gayle saw Peter. [saw *whom*? Peter]
> The secretary ignored the comment. [ignored *what*? comment]

Self-Check Test 10-1

Underline the direct objects in the following sentences. (Check answers at end of text.)

1. I am not purchasing those shoddy supplies.

2. Korea has cut its rice imports.

3. Philips sent the photographs to Mrs. Maple.

4.   In December, ARBO will publish the results of the tests.

5.   We will repair the terminals as soon as possible.

S + V + DO SENTENCES

Direct objects, like subjects, may be phrases or dependent clauses. Whatever the form of the object, most of your sentences will fall into a pattern we can call Subject + Verb + Direct Object: S + V + DO.

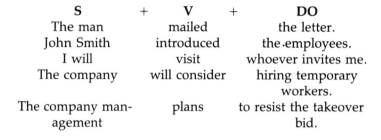

S	+	V	+	DO
The man		mailed		the letter.
John Smith		introduced		the employees.
I will		visit		whoever invites me.
The company		will consider		hiring temporary workers.
The company management		plans		to resist the takeover bid.

Self-Check Test 10-2

I.   Underline the direct objects in the following sentences. (See end of text for answers.)

1.   We cannot cancel the meeting.

2.   Mr. Miller is meeting Bob and Randy.

3.   We are planning to fly west.

4.   I do not know why you are leaving.

5.   That company hires whoever applies.

II.   Fill in the blanks with appropriate objects.

1.   Mr. Jackson fired _____. [noun object]

2.   Harold and Milly have decided _____. [infinitive phrase object]

3.   Conway Company has opened a(n) _____. [noun object]

4.   I cannot hear _____. [noun clause object]

5.   His message irritated _____. [pronoun object]

WRITING HINT: AVOID UNEXPLAINED ACRONYMS AND ABBREVIATIONS

Translation: Immediately send a statement of work on the Satellite Low Orbit Bombardment to the Commander, Service Force, South Pacific Subordinate Command.

Source: Ford Button

INDIRECT OBJECTS

Sentences with verbs such as *lend, mail, send, give, buy, offer*, and *sell* may have indirect as well as direct objects. Since an indirect object comes between a verb and a direct object, these sentences will usually take the form subject + verb + indirect object + direct object: S + V + IO + DO. (The indirect object will come between the verb and the direct object.)

To locate an indirect object:

1. Locate the verb, subject, and direct object.

2. Ask VERB + DIRECT OBJECT + TO WHOM or TO WHAT?

> Ed lent me a book.
> Lent + book + to whom? *Me.*

>   S   V   DO
> I mailed Joan the report.
> mailed the report *to whom*? Joan.

>   S   V   DO
> Sam bought George a new receiver.
> bought a new receiver *for whom*? George.

>   S   V   DO
> I offered Mr. Chung the taxi.
> offered the taxi *to whom*? Mr. Chung.

>   S   V   DO
> The company lent Henry the computer.
> lent the computer *to whom*? Henry.

Self-Check Test 10-3

Put *DO* over the direct objects in the following sentences; put *IO* over the indirect objects. (Check answers at end of text.)

1. The United States sent Poland a clear message.

2. Phil has offered the employees a raise.

3. The new methods will give us new opportunities.

4. His height gives him some authority.

5. Please ship Phyllis the washing machine.

6. Patterson sent Jackson our condolences.

7. Despite his promise, Jake did not lend Hal the typewriter.

8. Please forward the data by September 3.

9. Have you offered Harriet the new job?

10. Did the salesman sell you the sedan or the truck?

Note: Some sentences, of course, have no direct or indirect objects. A sentence with an indirect object, however, will also have a direct object.

You may have two or more direct and indirect objects in a sentence: they will be connected by *and, or,* or correlative conjunctions.

> Give *Harold* and *Kathy* the chart. [compound indirect objects]
>
> Have you sent Paul a birthday *card* or a *present*? [compound direct object]
>
> Give Marie either the *book* or the *paper*. [compound direct object]

Self-Check Test 10-4

I. Write sentences using the S + V + DO form. Use the following words as direct objects. (See sample answers at end of text.)

1. [congratulations]

2. [organization and efficiency]

3. [my desk]

4. [whoever draws the lucky card]

5. [neither clerks nor supervisors]

II. Write sentences using the S + V + IO + DO form. Use the following words as indirect objects.

1. [Irene and Bill]

2. [him]

3. [waiters]

4. [company]

5. [both Steve and his sisters]

COMPLEMENTS

As we noted in Chapter 1, some verbs indicate a state of being rather than an action. These *linking verbs* will be followed by a subject complement rather than an object. Your sentences will take the form subject + verb + complement: S + V + C.

Linking verbs include the following:

be (am, is, are, was, were, etc.)
seem   appear
feel   taste
sound   look
become   smell

I feel *ridiculous*. [adjective complement]
He is a *judge*. [noun complement]
It might be *she* who is knocking at the door. [pronoun complement]
Marilyn seems *to be uneasy*. [phrase complement]

Note: Linking verbs do not usually take a direct object. Since linking verbs do not show action, nothing in the sentence can receive the action.

Self-Check Test 10-5

I. Indicate whether the italicized words are direct objects (DO), indirect objects (IO), or complements (C). (See answers at end of text.)

1. I know his offer seems very *low*.   _____

2. Have you seen the latest rating *system*?   _____

3. When will Ernie be *ready* to graduate?   _____

4. Frances will offer *Nancy* the contract.   _____

5. The corporation management sounded *serious* about the proposal.   _____

II. Write sentences using each of the following words as subject complements.

1. [insecure]

2. [attorney]

3. [either careless or unlucky]

4. [accurate]

5. [student]

CHECKLIST FOR CHAPTER 10

1. Direct and indirect objects are nouns or noun substitutes.
2. A direct object may be located by asking VERB + WHOM or WHAT?
3. An indirect object may be located by asking VERB + DIRECT OBJECT + TO WHOM or TO WHAT?
4. A complement usually follows a linking verb.

OBJECT AND COMPLEMENT REVIEW

Read this paragraph again. Now put *DO* over the direct objects, *IO* over the indirect objects, and *C* over the complements. (Check your answers at end of text.)

At noon, Jordan Glover will give a speech on the problems of small businesses in today's economy. Representatives of 20 businesses will be in attendance. Kathryn Horne, founder of GHA Corporation, and her assistant will offer us some refreshments after Mr. Glover's speech. Kathryn will also conclude the proceedings. Please let us know if you can attend.

List the direct objects:

List the indirect objects:

List the complements:

**CHAPTER TEST
10-1**

I. Write sentences using the following words as complements. Use a variety of linking verbs.

1. purple

2. medical student

3. farsighted

4. accountant

5. motivated, energetic, and enthusiastic

II. Put one line under the direct objects, two lines under the indirect objects, and three lines under the complements in the following sentences.

1. Does Hubert sound unhappy or enthusiastic about the project?

2. Evelyn should give the neighbors some credit for the discovery.

3. William has offered his brother an enormous raise.

4. Is he really a millionaire?

5. The committee seems ambivalent about the problem.

6. Kent and Robin will send their son a graduation check.

7. I am unsure about the outcome of the debate.

8. Henry jumped the final hurdle without a pause.

9. The flood has destroyed over a hundred homes and businesses.

10. "Eugenics," declared Professor Garrison, "was an unscientific

    movement."

**CHAPTER TEST
10-2**

I. Write sentences using the following words as the verb, direct object, and indirect object. (Do not change the form of the verb.)

VERB	INDIRECT OBJECT	DIRECT OBJECT
1. send	Connie	software
2. offered	officer	position
3. lend	trainee	manual
4. bought	wife	raincoat
5. mails	supervisor	report

II. Rewrite each of the following sentences by turning a prepositional phrase into an indirect object.

1. We have decided to offer a promotion to Leslie Parkhurst.

2. The company has given a benefit for the Heart Association.

3. Who mailed the original of the letter to Mr. Keene?

4. I sent a bottle of perfume to my cousin Louise.

5. Will you please buy a carton of milk for James?

**CHAPTER TEST
10-3**

I. Indicate whether the following sentences have the S + V,
S + V + DO, S + V + IO + DO, or S + V + C forms.

1. Harry arrived before midnight.   _____

2. Management questioned the decision.   _____

3. Clara is an artist and a musician.   _____

4. Ted handed Mr. Oneida the newspaper.   _____

5. We are planning a debate for June.   _____

II. Write five different sentences using the following forms.

1. [S + V + IO + DO]

2. [S + V + C]

3. [S + V]

4. [S + V + DO]

5. [S + V + C]

**EXERCISE FOR
EXPERTS**

Read the following memo. Then answer the questions that follow.

To: Matthew Gruber

From: Tara Willson

Subject: Presidential Tour

Date: June 3, 19xx

Mr. Bland, our president, will tour our offices on Monday, June 12.(1) He is interested in our office efficiency, organizational methods, and general appearance.(2) Joan will give him the tour.(3) You should offer him lunch.(4) Also, the office must be impeccably clean.(5) Check carpets, desk tops, and tables.(6)

1. Which sentences follow an S + V + IO + DO pattern? _____

2. Which sentences have subject complements? _____

3. List the direct objects in each sentence. Put 0 if there is none.

    1.

    2.

    3.

    4.

    5.

    6.

CHAPTER 11

PHRASES

OBJECTIVE: To recognize each type of phrase in a sentence.

Which of the following are phrases?

> To win an award
> Toward a goal
> In the long run
> Delighting the audience
> Covered with ice

If you said all of them were phrases, you were correct. A phrase may be described as a group of words that works as a unit in a sentence but does not have a subject and verb. Phrases come in many shapes and sizes; they also serve many functions in a sentence.

TYPES OF PHRASES

We have already examined some types of phrases. The following chart summarizes the common types.

A prepositional phrase begins with a preposition.
> P.J. looked *under the desk*.

A participial phrase contains a participle, which is formed from either the present participle of a verb (ending in *-ing*) or the past participle of a verb (usually ending in *-d* or *-ed*)
> *Looking for more data*, we discovered a major error.
> The shirt *covered with ink* is mine.

A gerund phrase contains a gerund, which is formed from the form of a verb ending in *-ing*. Gerunds act as nouns.
> *Cooking dinner* is a chore.
> *Running backward* will not become a popular sport.

An infinitive phrase contains an infinitive, which is formed from *to* + the present or past form of a verb.
> *To solve the problem* requires patience.
> Sheila hopes *to have written the report* by Wednesday.

Note: We discussed verb phrases in Chapter 1. A verb phrase is simply a main verb with its helping verb(s): I *have decided*.

Self-Check Test 11-1

Underline the phrases in the following sentences. Put vertical lines between adjoining phrases. (Check answers at end of text.)

1. Losing a game can be painful.

2. We hope to win the award by July.

3. Baking cookies is a fun project for children.

4. To conquer the world was the aim of Alexander the Great.

5. That suit stained with mud sold for $45.99.

6. Employees without a sense of responsibility will not succeed at Patton Industries.

7. Having finished all the items on the agenda, Phil Jackson asked us for our thoughts on the investment question.

8. To finish this project on time means we must ignore all other projects.

9. If you have a moment, you might write a memo to the staff.

10. Working with the biochemist, Dr. Gresham produced some important data.

PHRASES AS NOUNS

We have already seen that phrases may function as nouns; thus, they may be subjects, objects of prepositions, objects, or complements in a sentence.

> *Breaking the habit* was difficult for Harry. [phrase as subject]
> Harry talked about *breaking the habit*. [phrase as object of preposition]
> He longed *to read the report*. [phrase as object]
> Our goal is *to capture the prize*. [phrase as complement]

Self-Check Test 11-2

Write sentences following the directions given. (See end of text for suggested answers.)

1. [Use *to remember names* as a direct object.]

2. [Use *developing guidelines* as a subject.]

3. [Use *standing in line* as a subject.]

4. [Use *to consider each person's opinion* as an object.]

5. [Use *breaking the copier* as a subject.]

PHRASES AS ADJECTIVES

Prepositional phrases, infinitive phrases, and participial phrases often function as adjectives.

> The man *from Washington* is here. [prepositional phrase describing *man*]
> Claude, *followed by his dog*, appeared in the store. [participial phrase describing *Claude*]
> *Coming to an agreement*, the opponents ended the battle. [participial phrase describing *opponents*]
> This is an outfit *to wear tonight*. [infinitive phrase describing *outfit*]

PHRASES AS ADVERBS

Prepositional phrases and infinitive phrases may function as adverbs.

> He writes *with ease*. [prepositional phrase describing *writes*]
> The manager smiled *to show his appreciation*. [infinitive phrase describing *smiled*]

NOUN PHRASES	ADJECTIVE PHRASES	ADVERB PHRASES
prepositional phrase	prepositional phrase	prepositional phrase
infinitive phrase	infinitive phrase	infinitive phrase
gerund phrase	participial phrase	

Self-Check Test 11-3

Underline the phrases in the following sentences. Then indicate the function of each phrase by writing *N*, *ADJ*, or *ADV* above it. (See end of text for answers.)

1. He rode the bicycle with uncertainty.

2. We are planning to win the election.

3. Bill, surprised by the rain, ran indoors.

4. I hope you will stand near the podium.

5. The company sold its furniture to avoid bankruptcy.

6. I am speaking from a pay telephone.

7. Just graduated from college, my sister is looking for a job.

8. The corporate offices will move to the suburbs.

9. He lost his job due to the new regulations.

10. Having stopped, the pedestrian eyed the heavy traffic.

CHECKLIST FOR CHAPTER 11

1. A phrase is a group of words that acts as a unit in a sentence but does not have a subject and verb.

2. Prepositional, gerund, and infinitive phrases may function as nouns.

3. Prepositional phrases, infinitive phrases, and participial phrases may function as adjectives.

4. Prepositional and infinitive phrases may function as adverbs.

PHRASE REVIEW

Underline any prepositional, infinitive, gerund, or participial phrases in the following paragraph. (Check your answers at end of text.)

This study has been proposed because our company

has recently suffered a drop in sales within two major

lines: our nutty fruit bars and our diet grape juice. To find

reasons for these losses, we have hired a team of research-

ers. Working in the South and Northeast, the team will

conduct thorough consumer surveys, analyze our competi-

tion, and speak with selected retailers.

**CHAPTER TEST
11-1**

Fill in the blanks with appropriate phrases.

1. [infinitive phrase] _____ is a difficult task.

2. We searched [prepositional phrase] _____
   for Harry's book.

3. The executive [participial phrase] _____ is
   from South Dakota.

4. [gerund phrase] _____ requires attention to
   detail.

5. I swim every day [infinitive phrase] _____.

6. [prepositional phrase] _____ lies the
   answer to the question.

7. [*past* participial phrase] _____, we went
   home.

8. [gerund phrase] _____ has become an
   obsession with him.

9. The company planned [infinitive phrase]

   _____.

10. The new secretary [participial phrase]

    _____ is terrified of Mrs. Cooper.

**CHAPTER TEST
11-2**

Write sentences following the directions given.

1. [Use an infinitive phrase as subject.]

2. [Use a gerund phrase as subject.]

3. [Use a prepositional phrase as an adverb.]

4. [Use an infinitive phrase as an adverb.]

5. [Use a prepositional phrase as an adjective.]

6. [Use a participial phrase as an adjective.]

7. [Use an infinitive phrase as an object.]

8. [Use a gerund phrase as an object.]

9. [Use a past participial phrase as an adjective.]

10. [Use an infinitive phrase as a subject and a prepositional phrase as an adjective.]

EXERCISE FOR EXPERTS

Indicate whether each of the underlined phrases is a prepositional, infinitive, gerund, or participial phrase. Then indicate whether it is a noun, adjectival, or adverbial phrase.

Example: He likes to work. [infinitive phrase/noun]

I read quickly through the reports(1) and discovered a discrepancy in the budget.(2) To fix the error(3) requires revising the transportation expenses.(4)

I am afraid you are the one person who can do the job with speed and accuracy.(5) The page covered with my notes(6) is the one you should examine most carefully. Please let me know if you have trouble with the figures.(7) Maybe I can find someone working in the Accounting Department(8) who can help you.

1.
2.
3.
4.
5.
6.
7.
8.

CHAPTER 12

CLAUSES

OBJECTIVES: To distinguish phrases from clauses; to distinguish dependent from independent clauses; to distinguish noun, adjective, and adverb clauses.

Which of the following are phrases (P) and which are clauses (C)?

1. When we got back from Amsterdam   _____

2. Under the Pacific Ocean   _____

3. She gave Jim a raise   _____

4. To continue the discussion   _____

5. Requesting application materials   _____

Numbers 2, 4, and 5 are phrases; numbers 1 and 3 are clauses.

As we have seen in previous chapters, a clause is a group of words that acts as a unit and contains a subject and verb. A clause will be either independent or dependent.

INDEPENDENT CLAUSES

An independent clause, as the name implies, can stand alone as a sentence.

$$\begin{array}{cc} \text{S} & \text{V} \\ \text{Johnson writes.} \\ \text{S} & \text{V} \\ \text{Marilyn dictates.} \\ \text{S} \quad \text{S} & \text{V} \\ \text{Carol and Bob are leaving.} \end{array}$$

Of course, most independent clauses are more complicated than the previous examples: they may also contain direct and indirect objects, phrases, and the various parts of speech we studied in Part One.

Johnson has written Smith a letter. [independent clause with indirect and direct objects]

Marilyn dictates her correspondence to Hilary. [independent clause with direct object and prepositional phrase]

Having stayed over two hours, Carol and Bob are leaving. [independent clause with participial phrase]

Despite all the material that appears in most sentences, you should still be able to pick out the two vital components: subject and verb. If you can spot those two elements, you know you are looking at a clause.

Self-Check Test 12-1

Put one line under the subjects, two lines under the helping and main verbs in the following clauses. Circle any phrases. Put vertical lines between adjoining phrases. (See end of text for answers.)

1. Have Randy and Bill seen the new TV studio?

2. To make his point, Jim pounded on the table.

3. At dusk, we were still sitting around the conference table.

4. You are the first candidate to bring a portfolio.

5. The new manager is studying the flowcharts.

6. Despite our planning, the project went badly.

7. With this technology came a change in the work force.

8. They were stopped by the highway patrol before getting to Texas.

9. Our lettuce has been attacked by several types of insects.

10. Will you meet us in Tijuana?

DEPENDENT CLAUSES

Dependent clauses (also called *subordinate clauses*) have a subject and verb, but, unlike independent clauses, they cannot stand alone as sentences. Usually you will sense that a dependent clause is not a complete thought; however, most dependent clauses begin with a word to warn you that what follows is dependent or subordinate material.

> *while* he was reading the report
> *until* the committee has met
> *if* we stay the night
> *after* the salaries had dropped
> *whoever* comes to the meeting
> *that* we have described
> *which* I had rejected yesterday
> *who* had been nominated

You may confuse a dependent clause with a sentence because the clause has a subject and verb. But a dependent clause cannot stand as a sentence. To make a complete sentence, you must join a dependent clause to an independent clause. Many dependent clauses begin with the subordinate conjunctions we studied in Chapter 7 (pp. 79–80).

DEPENDENT CLAUSE	INDEPENDENT CLAUSE
Before the meeting started	we had some coffee.
Since the war ended	General Hendricks has been working for the IRS.
Because the pound was down	many tourists visited Britain.

You will find dependent clauses preceding, following, and even coming in the middle of independent clauses. (A phrase will be part of either a dependent or an independent clause.)

> We will meet the train / *even if it is late.* [independent clause followed by dependent clause]
>
> *Although the negotiations had ended favorably,* / Mrs. Peters was still worried about a strike. [dependent clause followed by independent clause]
>
> We are inviting you, *since you enjoy opera,* to see the opening performance. [dependent clause inside an independent clause]
>
> *After the mail has arrived,* bring it to me *while I am speaking with Mindy.* [one dependent clause precedes and one follows the independent clause]

Self-Check Test 12-2

I.   Underline all dependent clauses in the following sentences. Put vertical lines between any adjoining dependent clauses. (See answers at end of text.)

1. If you would like the manual, you should write to Leroy.

2. After Anna Baines received the message, she made a copy of it for Mrs. Harter.

3. I will be happy to stay late unless you want us to come on Saturday.

4. I realized that she knew the truth because she called me after the meeting.

5. Being impatient has always been a drawback for Bill.

6. The governor hopes that the tax increases will help the state's school system.

7. If we are going to succeed, we must acquire capital.

8. At dawn we met in the lobby while George ordered breakfast.

9. If you give me a week to get a team together, the project will be a great success.

10. This article must have been revised before we began the Herley campaign.

II. Now go through these sentences again and put *S* over the subjects in each clause and *V* over the helping and main verbs in each clause.

1. If you would like the manual, you should write to Leroy.

2. After Anna Baines received the message, she made a copy of it for Mrs. Harter.

3. I will be happy to stay late unless you want us to come on Saturday.

4. I realized that she knew the truth because she called me after the meeting.

5. Being impatient has always been a drawback for Bill.

6. The governor hopes that the tax increases will help the state's school system.

7. If we are going to succeed, we must acquire capital.

8. At dawn we met in the lobby while George ordered breakfast.

9. If you give me a week to get a team together, the project will be a great success.

10. This article must have been revised before we began the Herley campaign.

If you had trouble with the preceding exercise, do not feel discouraged: you are learning some fairly complicated concepts. Practice will help you see what goes into a sentence; you may want to review some preceding chapters (particularly Chapters 1, 7, and 9) to get a stronger grasp on these principles.

Self-Check Test 12-3

Indicate whether the following are independent clauses (I), dependent clauses (D), or phrases (P). (See answers at end of text.)

1. Sailing swiftly across the bay   _____

2. This is the final decision   _____

3. When the assets are liquidated   _____

4. Before we settle the dispute   _____

5. Except for the new employees   _____

RELATIVE PRONOUNS

Many times, as we have said, a dependent clause will be introduced by a sub-ordinate conjunction. Some dependent clauses, however, may be introduced by relative pronouns.

Relative Pronouns

that, what, whatever, which, whichever, who, whoever, whom, whomever, whose

---

These pronouns often introduce dependent clauses that function as nouns or adjectives. The pronouns then act as subjects or objects in the dependent clause.

> The condominum *that is for sale* is overpriced. [Dependent clause introduced by *that* is adjective describing *condominium. That* is subject of dependent clause.]
>
> My brother, *who is a musician,* will be staying with us. [Dependent clause introduced by *who* acts as adjective describing *brother. Who* is subject of dependent clause.]
>
> The statistics, *which were developed in 1975,* are hopelessly out-of-date. [Dependent clause introduced by *which* is adjective describing *statistics. Which* is subject of dependent clause.]
>
> They will elect *whoever supports tax reform.* [Dependent clause introduced by *whoever* is noun acting as object of the sentence; *whoever* is subject of dependent clause.]
>
> Sarah will invite *whomever she wants.* [Dependent clause introduced by *whomever* functions as object of sentence. *Whomever* is the object in the dependent clause.]

Occasionally a dependent clause will have no warning word. Almost always, however, the word *that* has simply been omitted from the sentence. You may add *that* to the clause to check if it is dependent.

> I am sure Mr. Greene is correct. [*That* has been omitted.]
>
> I am sure [*that*] *Mr. Greene is correct.*
>
> The staff hopes the promotions are in effect. [*That* has been omitted.]
>
> The staff hopes [*that*] *the promotions are in effect.*

Self-Check Test 12-4

I. Underline the dependent clauses in the following sentences. Put vertical lines between any adjoining dependent clauses. (See answers at end of text.)

1. When you are sure that you know the answers, send me a letter.

2. If Carole sees the package I am waiting for, she should open it.

3. We have been debating the issue ever since the incident in Munich.

4. The managers who are visiting the New York office are amazed at the working environment.

5. The new museum, which has already cost a million dollars, will not be completed for three years.

II. Indicate with an *S, DO, IO, OP,* or *C* whether the underlined dependent clauses function as subjects, direct objects, indirect objects, objects of prepositions, or complements.

1. Theresa will support whomever you want. _____
2. Whom I vote for is none of your business. _____
3. Mr. Ricardo has already forgotten who I am. _____
4. The chairperson will lend her notes to whoever asks for them. _____
5. My client has agreed not to question whoever returns the money. _____

CHECKLIST FOR CHAPTER 12

1. A clause is a group of words that works as a unit and has a subject and verb.

2. An independent clause may stand alone as a sentence; a dependent clause cannot stand alone as a sentence.

3. A dependent clause is usually preceded by a "warning word." Most warning words are either subordinate conjunctions or relative pronouns.

4. A sentence may be composed of any number of phrases and dependent clauses, but it must also contain at least one independent clause.

5. A dependent clause may act as a subject, direct object, object of a preposition, indirect object, or complement.

6. A dependent clause may act as an adjective or adverb.

**CLAUSE
REVIEW**

Underline the independent clauses in the following paragraph. Put two lines under the dependent clauses. (See answers at end of text.)

Although our great advertising campaign has doubled demand for our Humanoid Dolls, we need to continue and expand our marketing efforts. The television commercials that have been so successful for us are being copied by all our competitors. The print ads in local newspapers have lost their appeal since TarnyToys came out with its Rubberman ads. We need to expand our present market and make Humanoid a household word all over America.

CHAPTER TEST 12-1 Mark each of the following clauses with a *D* if it is a dependent clause or with an *I* if it is independent.

1. The decision was made _____

2. Because I am trying a new diet program _____

3. When the payroll has been automated _____

4. Where the breezes are balmy _____

5. John Keller is here _____

6. What the new manager claims _____

7. Are you ready? _____

8. Although the office manager is absent _____

9. Since Mrs. Floris has agreed _____

10. Which has been postponed _____

CHAPTER TEST 12-2

I. Underline the dependent clauses in the following sentences.

1. Though crime statistics are down, people's fears are still increasing.

2. Please call me when you get to Tulsa.

3. If there is a problem, Howard can solve it after he gets home.

4. I cannot tell whether the streets are darker tonight.

5. Mason's new account, which he worked on for six months, has brought in exactly $18.92.

II. Put one line under the subjects, two lines under the helping and main verbs in the following independent *and* dependent clauses.

1. Maurie has decided to retire when interest rates hit 18 percent.

2. Plomber Corporation, which is being taken over by RTA, will close its Oakland offices.

3. If the incoming president wants some information on the rate increases, she should speak with Jeremy.

4. Unless the Coyotes win this game, they have no chance for the pennant.

5. Neither of them is interested in watching television while election results are coming in.

CHAPTER TEST 12-3

I. **Underline the independent clauses in the following sentences; put two lines under the dependent clauses.**

1. A phrase is a group of related words that does not contain a subject or a verb.

2. A dependent clause, like a phrase, cannot stand alone.

3. Marion Harris runs marathons because she enjoys the thrill of competition.

4. A progress report that has been prepared by the division manager will be delivered at noon.

5. The origin of our species is still being studied by eminent scientists.

II. **In the following sentences, put a line under the subjects of the independent clauses; put two lines under the helping and main verbs of the independent clauses.**

1. Due to the strain of working and going to school, Ferris has decided to take only 12 units this semester.

2. George announced today that he is joining the Peace Corps.

3. Have you ever wondered if prices will go down?

4. While he was in London, Haydn created some of his most famous symphonies.

5. Although I have not yet seen the new building, I have heard it is one of the most impressive in New York.

EXERCISE FOR EXPERTS

Write a memo to employees informing them that the company has just elected Phyllis Rogers to the board of directors. Tell your readers something about her previous work experience and interests. Limit the memo to 7–8 sentences.

Your memo should include (1) an adjective clause beginning with *who*; (2) an adverb clause beginning with *since*; and (3) at least one sentence in the S + V + IO + DO form.

CHAPTER 13

FRAGMENTS, RUN-ONS, AND COMMA SPLICES

OBJECTIVES: To recognize and write complete sentences rather than fragments, run-ons, or comma splices.

Which of the following are complete, grammatical sentences?

1. Give me the telephone number.

2. Developing a good idea.

3. Which is not operative.

4. To fulfill the agreement.

5. We hope to return tonight, however, we may be late.

Only number 1 is a complete, grammatical sentence; numbers 2, 3, and 4 are fragments, while number 5 is a comma splice.

A sentence contains a subject and predicate. In a piece of writing, a sentence is a complete unit; it conveys a complete thought. If you make part of a sentence *look* like it is a complete sentence, you will communicate only a partial idea to your reader. On the other hand, if you string together two or more independent clauses so they *look* like a single sentence, you will confuse your reader.

Remember that the basic precept of effective business writing is to convey your ideas as clearly as possible; creating complete sentences is vital to clear communication.

FRAGMENT

A fragment is a part of a sentence punctuated to look like a sentence. A fragment may be a phrase or a dependent clause—or any group of words that does not contain a subject and predicate. Check every sentence you write for completeness. Every phrase and dependent clause must be attached to an independent clause.

Self-Check Test 13-1

I. Indicate whether the following are fragments (F) or sentences (S). (Check answers at end of text.)

1. Because manual typewriters have virtually disappeared.   _____
2. Give my regards to the Dan Ryan Expressway.   _____
3. Water dripping through the office ceilings.   _____
4. Until we can determine who is responsible.   _____
5. There are over a hundred possibilities.   _____
6. Where is the new stapler?   _____
7. Emerging from the meeting.   _____
8. To assess the situation.   _____
9. Having taken the easiest route.   _____
10. Hand George the folder.   _____

II. Now, in the space below, add appropriate material to turn any fragments in the previous exercise into sentences.

RUN-ON SENTENCES

You will create a run-on (or *fused*) sentence if you put together two independent clauses without any punctuation. How many independent clauses have been run together in this paragraph?

> Peter Jacobson will interview all the clerical employees he will ask them about their work environment and supervisors each interview should take about fifteen minutes he will then put the information he gathers into his report.

You should have spotted four independent clauses:

> Peter Jacobson will interview all the clerical employees. He will ask them about their work environment and supervisors. Each interview should take about fifteen minutes. He will then put the information he gathers into his report.

To separate two independent clauses, you have a number of choices.

Run-On: I draft the schedule John approves it.

1. Put a period between the clauses.

   I draft the schedule. John approves it.

2. Put a semicolon between the clauses.

   I draft the schedule; John approves it.

3. Put a comma *and* a coordinate conjunction between the clauses.

   I draft the schedule, but John approves it.

4. Turn one independent clause into a dependent clause.

   When I draft the schedule, John approves it.
   I draft the schedule if John approves it.

Separating clauses with different techniques will add interest and variety to your writing.

Self-Check Test 13-2

Revise each of the following run-on sentences according to the directions. [See end of text for suggested answers.]

1. [Use a semicolon.] Police questioned Katie she was terrified.

2. [Use a comma and coordinating conjunction.] The building is almost finished the furniture has not been ordered.

3. [Use a dependent clause.] Thomas is annoyed with the staff members they have been wasting company supplies.

4. [Use a dependent clause.] Give me my typewriter it is on your shelf.

5. [Use a period.] The project was a disaster we lost $5,000.

COMMA SPLICES

If you put a comma between two independent clauses and do not use a coordinate conjunction, you create a comma splice. Once again, you may revise in several ways.

Comma Splice: The battle was won after two hours, the enemy retreated across the river.

Revisions: The battle was won after two hours. The enemy retreated across the river.

The battle was won after two hours; the enemy retreated across the river.

The battle was won after two hours, and the enemy retreated across the river.

The battle was won after two hours when the enemy retreated across the river.

Caution: Coordinate Conjunctions

The only coordinate conjunctions are *and, but, for, nor, or, so,* and *yet.* Do not confuse coordinate conjunctions with subordinate conjunctions (see pp. 75–80) or with conjunctive adverbs. Words such as *consequently, however, hence, furthermore,* and *therefore* may not be used with commas to connect independent clauses.

Comma Splice: Perry is engaged, however, he will not be married until August.

Revision: Perry is engaged; however, he will not be married until August.

Comma Splice: The merger was successful, therefore, the corporate executives are congratulating themselves.

Revision: The merger was successful; therefore, the corporate executives are congratulating themselves.

You may, however, use a conjunctive adverb with commas within a single independent clause. (See preceding sentence for an example.)

Self-Check Test 13-3

Revise the following to eliminate run-ons and comma splices. (See sample answers at end of text.)

1. The mountain lion was wounded, however, he managed to kill the bobcat.

2. The shirt does not fit Paul has given it to his brother.

3. July is our slowest month we are, therefore, going to close for two weeks.

4. My supervisor was not amused by his birthday present from the staff, he has returned it to Max's Magic Store.

5. Tell the receptionist your name, then ask for Mr. Withers.

WRITING HINT: AVOID TRENDY WORDS
Marsha Philips' Memo   *Mike Hanley's Translation*

Source: Ford Button

CHECKLIST FOR CHAPTER 13

1. A fragment is part of a sentence punctuated to look like a sentence.

2. A run-on is two or more independent clauses linked without punctuation or appropriate conjunctions.

3. A comma splice is two independent clauses joined only by a comma.

4. Conjunctive adverbs and subordinate conjunctions may not be used with commas to link two independent clauses.

SENTENCE REVIEW

Revise any fragments, run-ons, or comma splices in the following paragraph. Make sure new sentences start with capital letters. (Check answers at end of text.)

Modern technology has led to a large number of specialized areas many companies assign highly specialized teams to work on small segments of a project deciding how to advertise a product, for example, might necessitate specialists in production, marketing, and finance to coordinate activities, however, one person is usually assigned to supervise the project. And coordinate the activities of each specialist.

CHAPTER TEST 13-1

If any of the following are fragments, add appropriate material to make them into sentences. Do not alter already existing sentences.

1. Unless the rain stops.

2. To the railroad station in Newark.

3. Fill out the purchase orders immediately.

4. Probably the best-known bank president in America.

5. John is going to vote for Plummley tomorrow.

6. Talking his way out of the situation.

7. Your credit rating has not been affected.

8. With more detail than we needed.

9. Will you be here tomorrow?

10. Since the airport was very crowded.

CHAPTER TEST 13-2

I. Use *subordinate* conjunctions to revise the following:

1. Ten years ago this cabin would have cost a fortune, now it might sell for $15,000.

2. Petey Markeson, a well-known consultant, has been hired to help the company, we are giving him a guided tour.

3. Many immigrants to this country are learning technical skills, several technical schools in this area now have bilingual instructors.

4. The storm is getting worse, the windows are rattling.

5. Marion has joined the army she has finally found a job she likes.

II. Revise each of the following run-on sentences in TWO ways.

1. The party was over everyone went home.

    a.

    b.

2. Fletcher bought the company he risked a fortune.

    a.

    b.

3. The applicant ruined the job interview she admitted she wanted the job only
    for six weeks.

    a.

    b.

4. At the age of 11, Dave discovered he loved computers now he is designing his
    own software.

    a.

    b.

5. Oklahoma is my home state I always go back there for holidays.

a.

b.

EXERCISE FOR EXPERTS

Revise the following paragraph to eliminate fragments, run-on sentences, and comma splices. You may have to alter capital letters as well. Do not change a correct sentence.

Ted Bradley opened his mail-order business in 1905, just after he had spent two months searching for a comfortable suit. Since he was over 6 feet tall. Ted could rarely find a ready-made suit that he could afford. And that fit him perfectly. He asked his sister Imogene to design some suits for tall men and write a sample sales letter, she told the readers that any man over 6 feet tall or over 200 pounds should order one of these suits from Bradley's Big Men's Outfitter. Ted sent the letter to every household in Wilson, Nebraska. Two orders came in, she started sewing. On the $50 profit from those orders, Ted hired a second tailor, the rest is history.

CHAPTER 14

SENTENCE VARIATIONS

OBJECTIVES: To recognize and construct (1) simple, compound, complex, and compound-complex sentences; and (2) active and passive sentences.

Do you know which of the following are compound sentences? Do you know which are active and which are passive?

1. Tom and Larry were seen at the meeting.

2. I enjoyed the film, but Joe despised it.

3. Although the convention runs until Sunday, we left on Saturday morning.

If you said number 2 was compound, you were correct. The first is a simple sentence; the third is a complex sentence. The first sentence is passive; the second and third are active.

Good business writers do not put together their letters, memos, and reports at random; they design their sentences to create certain effects and to convey information as effectively as possible. To get the results they want from their writing, they have to understand how their sentences operate.

By now you should have a good understanding of the components of a sentence. This chapter shows you how these components can be formed into a variety of patterns. As you practice dissecting sentences, you will begin to recognize these recurring patterns and to see how writers use different types of sentences to achieve different results. If you understand how sentences operate, you will be able to create and control them more effectively.

SIMPLE SENTENCES

Simple sentences, which should play a major part in your writing, are formed from one independent clause. A simple sentence may be composed of a subject and a verb: S + V.

$$\overset{\text{S}}{\text{The man}} \overset{\text{V}}{\text{talked.}}$$

$$\overset{\text{S}}{\text{The meeting}} \overset{\text{V}}{\text{was convened.}}$$

Simple sentences may contain direct and indirect objects: S + V + DO and S + V + IO + DO.

$$\overset{\text{S}}{\text{Tom}} \overset{\text{V}}{\text{struck}} \overset{\text{DO}}{\text{the nail.}}$$

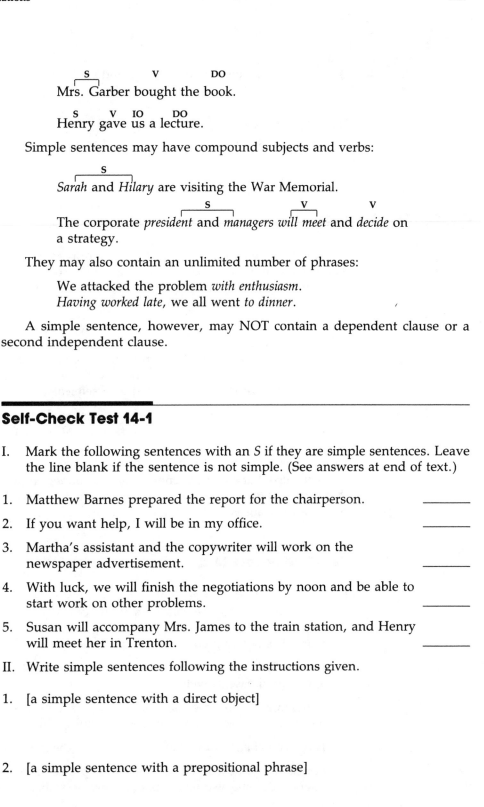

S   V   DO
Mrs. Garber bought the book.

S   V   IO   DO
Henry gave us a lecture.

Simple sentences may have compound subjects and verbs:

S
Sarah and *Hilary* are visiting the War Memorial.

S   V   V
The corporate *president* and *managers will meet* and *decide* on
a strategy.

They may also contain an unlimited number of phrases:

We attacked the problem *with enthusiasm.*
Having worked late, we all went *to dinner.*

A simple sentence, however, may NOT contain a dependent clause or a
second independent clause.

Self-Check Test 14-1

I.   Mark the following sentences with an *S* if they are simple sentences. Leave
     the line blank if the sentence is not simple. (See answers at end of text.)

1.   Matthew Barnes prepared the report for the chairperson.   _____

2.   If you want help, I will be in my office.   _____

3.   Martha's assistant and the copywriter will work on the
     newspaper advertisement.   _____

4.   With luck, we will finish the negotiations by noon and be able to
     start work on other problems.   _____

5.   Susan will accompany Mrs. James to the train station, and Henry
     will meet her in Trenton.   _____

II. Write simple sentences following the instructions given.

1.   [a simple sentence with a direct object]

2.   [a simple sentence with a prepositional phrase]

3.   [a simple sentence with an indirect and a direct object]

4. [a simple sentence with a compound subject]

5. [a simple sentence with a compound verb]

COMPOUND SENTENCES

A compound sentence is formed from two or more independent clauses. As we saw in Chapter 13, independent clauses may be connected in a variety of ways. A compound sentence cannot have a dependent clause, but it may have any number of independent clauses and phrases.

> Jonah wrote the report, and Susan edited it. [two independent clauses connected by a coordinate conjunction]
> Representatives from France will attend the conference; representatives from Germany will not be there. [two independent clauses connected by a semicolon]

Note that, in the previous examples, you could break the clauses into two short sentences: *Jonah wrote the report. Susan edited it.* Because you can create separate sentences from the two clauses, you know they are both *independent clauses*: they can stand on their own as sentences.

Note also that two independent clauses connected by a coordinate conjunction usually require a *comma* before the conjunction. (See Part Four for more on punctuating clauses.)

Self-Check Test 14-2

Put *S* after the following sentences if they are simple; put *CD* after them if they are compound. (See answers at end of text.)

1. Marty has determined the cause of the morale problems.   _____

2. Lombardy is the industrial heart of Italy; it has a strong agricultural base as well.   _____

3. Zebulon Pike, an American soldier and explorer, discovered a mountain in Colorado and was killed during the War of 1812.   _____

4. Have you changed the date or the time of the meeting?   _____

5. Louise has been working on a research project in computer science, but she also has time to lecture on statistics.   _____

COMPLEX SENTENCES

A complex sentence is formed from one independent clause and one or more dependent clauses. As we noted in Chapter 12 (pp. 129–133), a dependent clause will usually be introduced by a subordinate conjunction or relative pronoun.

Dependent clauses may come before or after the independent clause, or they may be inside the independent clause.

> While the meeting was going on, James Tenney took notes. [dependent clause + independent clause]
> James Tenney took notes while the meeting was going on. [independent clause + dependent clause]
> James Tenney, who attends every meeting, was in charge of taking notes. [dependent clause inside independent clause]

A complex sentence may have any number of dependent clauses.

> While the meeting was going on [dependent clause], James Tenney took notes [independent clause] because the secretary was ill [dependent clause].
> When I got married [dependent clause] after I graduated from college [dependent clause], I soon realized [independent clause] that I was unfit for domestic life [dependent clause].
> Although Marion Miles is a new employee [dependent clause], she has agreed to act as our supervisor [independent clause] until we find a full-time replacement [dependent clause].

The key to a complex sentence is one independent clause and any number of dependent clauses. To avoid writing fragments, practice watching for the warning words that introduce dependent clauses. Watch, too, for subjects and verbs: as long as you have a subject and verb, you know you have a clause.

Self-Check Test 14-3

I. Put *S* after simple sentences, *CD* after compound sentences, and *CX* after complex sentences. Underline the independent clauses. (See end of text for answers.)

1. Although the debate is still going on, Good Foods Inc. is

    manufacturing Sno-White Cookies in the gold package.   _____

2. With the rise in interest rates, housing starts have decreased,

    and banks are advertising more heavily.   _____

3. Unless there is a change in plans, we will meet at noon in

    the Madison Hotel.   _____

4. Calvin Smith will fly to New York on June 30 in order to set

    up the meeting with Frozen Foods International.   _____

5. Have you considered whether we should cut back employee

    hours for this month?   _____

II. Write sentences following the instructions given.

1. [a compound sentence using the conjunction *so*]

2. [a complex sentence beginning with a dependent clause]

3. [a simple sentence with two phrases]

4. [a compound sentence beginning with a phrase]

5. [a complex sentence with two dependent clauses]

COMPOUND-COMPLEX SENTENCES

As you might guess, a compound-complex sentence contains at least two independent clauses as well as at least one dependent clause.

Since these sentences tend to be long and complicated, you should not use them very often in your writing. Compound-complex sentences may be effective in some circumstances, but they can also create problems. Use them with care.

> While this company is undergoing management changes, GRY Company is increasing its market share, and Curtis Inc. is developing new products. [dependent clause followed by two independent clauses]
> Emilio Pucci, who began his career as a designer in 1947, is famed for elegant sportswear; the designer Madeleine Vionnet is known for sensuous evening wear. [dependent clause inside one independent clause; second independent clause following the semicolon.]

Self-Check Test 14-4

Underline the independent clauses in the following sentences. Put *S* after simple sentences, *CD* after compound sentences, *CX* after complex sentences, and *CC* after compound-complex sentences. (See end of text for answers.)

1. Although we are suffering some cash-flow problems, the company will be able to increase salaries and benefits in May. _____

2. In the following diagram, data flow is indicated by broken lines, and control signals are indicated by solid lines. _____

3. Zion National Park, which is renowned for its colored rock formations, is being studied by an international team of geologists. _____

4. When we work through lunch, Mr. Rowley brings us slices of pizza, and Mr. Kipps brings us potato salad. _____

5. Neither the technicians nor the research staff completely understands the problem. _____

ACTIVE AND PASSIVE SENTENCES

The vast majority of your sentences should be active: one of your editing tasks (see Chapter 33) will be to eliminate unnecessary passive sentences. Some passive sentences are effective and even necessary. However, before using them effectively, you must be able to recognize them.

An active sentence combines a subject, the *doer*, with a verb, the *action*. The subject actually *performs* an action.

> John [subject] reads [verb].
> Jerry [subject] saw [verb] the headline.
> The committee [subject] has adjourned [verb].

In a passive sentence, however, the logical direct object or indirect object (the person or thing acted upon) becomes the grammatical subject. The doer of the action either is omitted from the sentence or appears in a prepositional phrase.

>   s   v
> PASSIVE: The report was delivered by the chairperson.
> [*Report* is the subject, but the chairman actually performs the action.]
>   s   v
> PASSIVE: The evaluation had been completed by the market research staff. [The staff performs the action.]

Occasionally a passive sentence is necessary. We may not know who performed an action: *Our house was robbed.* Or the doer of the action may be obvious: *Harry Truman was elected president.* (We know the voters elected him.) Sometimes, too, a passive sentence can help to convey unpleasant information without making anyone responsible for the situation. For example, *In the past week, two minor mistakes have been made* might be more tactful than *In the past week, you made two minor mistakes.*

Business writers, however, tend to overuse the passive. Learn to recognize passive sentences and to change them to active ones whenever possible.

Two clues will help you recognize passive constructions: (1) the subject will not be performing any action; and (2) the verb *be* will appear in some form: *are, is, were, was, will be, has been, have been,* and so on.

> I have mailed the letter. [active]
> The letter *was mailed* by me. [passive]
> The letter *was mailed.* [passive]
> Peter recommends a change. [active]
> A change *is recommended* by Peter. [passive]
> A change *is recommended.* [passive]

Self-Check Test 14-5

I. Put a *P* after the passive sentences; put an *A* after active sentences. (Check answers at end of text.)

1. A decision has been reached by the committee.   _____

2. Were the guidelines followed?   _____

3. I hope you were satisfied with the job.   _____

4. When you are revising the proposal, consider Harry's recommendations.   _____

5. If the evaluations have been completed, they should be collected. _____

II. Revise any passive sentences in the previous exercise by making them active. You may have to add a doer of the action.

> Example: The windows were washed.
> I washed the windows.

CHECKLIST FOR CHAPTER 14

1. A simple sentence is formed from one independent clause.

2. A compound sentence is formed from two or more independent clauses.

3. A complex sentence is formed from one or more dependent clauses joined to an independent clause.

4. A compound-complex sentence is formed from two or more independent clauses joined to at least one dependent clause.

5. An active sentence is one in which the subject is the doer of the action.

6. A passive sentence is one in which the logical direct or indirect object becomes the grammatical subject.

7. Passive sentences should be kept to a minimum in business writing.

SENTENCE REVIEW

Read the following paragraph and answer the questions given. (Check answers at end of text.)

Although our great advertising campaign has doubled demand for our Humanoid Dolls, we need to continue and expand our marketing efforts.(1) The television commercials that have been so successful for us are being copied by our competitors.(2) The print ads in local newspapers have lost appeal since TarnyToys came out with its Rubberman ads.(3) We need to expand our present market and make Humanoid a household word all over America.(4)

1. Which of the preceding are simple sentences? (Give numbers.) _____

2. Which are compound? _____

3. Which are complex? _____

4. Which are compound-complex? _____

5. Which are active? _____

6. Which are passive? _____

CHAPTER TEST 14-1

I. Create compound sentences from the following simple sentences.

1. We arranged a meeting date. Ferris Miles will not be able to attend.

2. Somerset Maugham wrote the famous novel *Of Human Bondage*. He is also well known for his short stories.

3. Mr. Speirs is welcoming newcomers to the convention. He has forgotten to give them their name tags.

4. I have not seen Mrs. Marshall since last Wednesday. I have not spoken with her on the phone.

5. Tomorrow is Christmas. We are closing today at noon.

II. Create complex sentences from the following simple sentences.

1. We will not be able to meet the demand. We have increased production.

2. No one is working in the Records Department this afternoon. A flu epidemic has swept through the company.

3. The new accounting software is inexpensive. It is inefficient.

4. You are done with the photocopying. Please help Maureen with the telephones.

5. Ms. Peery is a recent graduate. She has some excellent experience.

CHAPTER TEST 14-2

I. Write sentences according to the instructions given.

1. [a compound sentence opening with a prepositional phrase]

2. [a complex sentence ending with a dependent clause]

3. [a compound-complex sentence opening with a dependent clause]

4. [a simple sentence with a compound subject]

5. [a complex sentence with a dependent clause inside an independent clause]

II. Change the following passive sentences to active.

1. The regulations have been rewritten by the secretary.

2. Have the holiday itineraries been outlined by the division managers?

3. A new tariff on imports is being considered by Congress.

4. Has the course curriculum been altered by the instructors?

5. Seven hundred applicants were screened by the personnel officers.

EXERCISE FOR EXPERTS

I. Change passive sentences to active ones in the following memo. Do not alter any active sentences.

To: All Employees

From: Frank Geer

Subject: Time Clocks

Date: October 3, 19xx

Since the Production Department has doubled in size, the installation of a time clock has been agreed upon by management. It is hoped by management that your productivity will be increased and the work of the Payroll Department decreased by the clock.

On Monday, October 15, you will be given a time card by your supervisor. The card should be inserted in the clock upon your arrival in the morning and your departure at 5:00 p.m. Overtime, absences, and late arrivals will be noted by the Payroll Department.

Any questions about this new procedure will be answered by your supervisor.

II. Now that you have improved the memo with active sentences, does it seem more effective and "human"? Can you suggest any changes that would improve the memo even more? Try rewriting the memo so it will convey information but not annoy the readers.

PART TWO REVIEW TESTS

Review Test 2-1   Review this test that you took at the beginning of Part Two.

I.   Put a check after each of the following if it is a complete sentence.

1.   Barbara, racing for the bus.   _____

2.   Jack will head the project.   _____

3.   Our goal is to succeed.   _____

4.   Because the seminar has begun.   _____

5.   Make three copies for Pete.   _____

II. Read the following paragraphs and answer the questions given.

> If you want your speech to be effective, you should organize your material very carefully.(1) Determine your major point, make sure that you support the point in every section of the speech.(2)
>
> A good speech, while it may be serious, is never dull.(3) Remember to keep your audience alert and interested.(4) Your speech should give your audience one major idea.(5) Something to remember and to think about.(6)

1.   Which sentences have dependent as well as independent clauses? (List the numbers.)   _____

2.   What is the subject of the independent clause in number 1?   _____

3.   What is the subject of the independent clause in number 3?   _____

     Number 4?   _____

4.   Are there any sentence fragments in these paragraphs? If yes, give the number(s).   _____

5.   Are there any comma splices in these paragraphs? If yes, give the number(s).   _____

6.   What is the direct object in number 5?   _____

7.   What is the indirect object in number 5?   _____

8.   Do any of these sentences have prepositional phrases? If so, give the number(s).   _____

     Check your answers at end of text.

Review Test 2-2

I. Put one line under the subjects of the following sentences; put two lines under the helping verbs and main verbs.

1. In the crisis, Louise has acted very responsibly.

2. Will Jones or Jackson ever consider a job change?

3. Earnings are up 3 percent this quarter.

4. Portugal lies on the western edge of the Iberian Peninsula.

5. Having kept his promise to the committee, Gerald wrote a farewell letter and retired.

II. Put one line under the direct objects in the following sentences; put two lines under the indirect objects.

1. Please lend Hank five dollars until payday.

2. I have never seen a more efficient system.

3. Unfortunately, the Records Department has given us the wrong file and the wrong financial data.

4. Typing at top speed, Cheryl still could not finish the letters in time.

5. Phyllis Cambray has sent PhotoCorp a hundred pictures.

Review Test 2-3

I. Put one line under the subjects and two lines under the verbs in the *independent* clauses of the following sentences.

1. When Mr. Winn has completed his speech, he will take a cab to the airport.

2. Since noon, seven unhappy students have been waiting outside your office.

3. I hope that I will get a hotel reservation before I leave for New York.

4. Both Felicia and Fred have decided to move to Tampa until the end of the year.

5. Despite Mr. Conway's illness, we will not cancel or delay the proceedings.

II. Put one line under the independent clauses and two lines under the dependent clauses in the following sentences.

1. While we have been arguing about wage increases, Joe Ready has quietly been instituting some new regulations.

2. I know that I will convince Paul of his error, since he usually listens to reason.

3. Even if you are not finished with the report, Alice Hall would like to see it.

4. I assume that we will be promoted, but Tom Tarrington believes that we will also be relocated.

5. Have you ever evaluated this company's hiring policies?

6. I know about the spending cuts because I have already seen a copy of the budget.

7. Although spring is in the air, TLC must begin planning for Christmas.

8. Mr. Lerner has bought the building, but Mrs. Lerner has bought the parking lot.

9. I want to stress that these months could be vital for our product.

10. Will you object to my asking about the insurance before we leave?

Review Test 2-4

I. Underline any fragments in the following exercise. Then, in the space below each item, combine the elements to make one sentence. You may rearrange the order of the elements and add or subtract words as necessary.

> Example: I am going to work on Friday. If I feel any better.
>
> I am going to work on Friday if I feel any better.

1. With the help of my assistant, I will finish the report. By Wednesday at the latest.

2. Smoking regulations are being enforced in these offices. According to the latest departmental newsletter.

3. Please attend the monthly meeting in September. Check with me for any changes in the agenda.

4. The number of employable applicants is declining rapidly in engineering fields. Although some figures conflict with these findings.

5. The Farradays' letter from Hawaii arrived today. It is filled with anecdotes about hotels and restaurants. Which do not interest me very much.

II. Underline the independent clauses in the following sentences. Put an *S* over the subjects and a *V* over the verbs of independent AND dependent clauses.

$$\quad\quad\quad\quad\quad\quad S \quad\ V \quad\quad\quad S \quad\ V \quad\ V$$
Example: If we have trouble, <u>we will call you</u>.

1. The new season of situation comedies is even more depressing than it

   was last year.

2. The Aspen Music Festival, which was started in 1949, has become a

   popular summer event for thousands of people.

3. Many athletes and coaches have wondered if the Olympics could be held

   in Greece every four years.

4. Iwo Jima, an island in the West Pacific that was captured by U.S. Marines

   in 1945, is the most famous of the Volcano Islands.

5. Management has agreed that the largest offices in the western wing

   should be made into an employee lounge.

III. Combine the following sentences so that each contains both an independent and a dependent clause. You may add, subtract, or rearrange words as necessary.

> Example: The agenda of this meeting has been altered. Mr. Baird wants to discuss the possibility of a merger with ATY Industries.
> The agenda of this meeting has been altered because Mr. Baird wants to discuss the possibility of a merger with ATY Industries.

1. The local newspaper is becoming increasingly conservative. The editors recently fired all the staff members under 35 years old.

2. The new fall marketing campaign needs to be more imaginative and less expensive. Michael Radley is in charge of making strategic changes.

3. Newport, Rhode Island, was settled in 1639. The city contains many beautiful mansions built in the 19th century.

4. Heavy fog settled over Denver Monday night. Unable to make his plane to Toledo, Mark Flores spent the night in a Denver motel near the airport.

5. Marion Barnes has chosen the six most promising candidates for the position. We must now choose the best of the six.

Review Test 2-5

Write sentences according to the directions given. (Sentences should be active unless specified otherwise.)

1. [a simple passive sentence with a compound subject]

2. [a compound sentence using the coordinate conjunction *but*]

3. [a compound-complex sentence opening with an independent clause]

4. [a complex sentence opening with a subordinate conjunction]

5. [a passive compound sentence]

6. [a simple sentence with two phrases]

7. [a compound sentence with an indirect and direct object]

8. [a compound-complex sentence with a dependent clause beginning with *who*]

9. [a complex sentence beginning with *because*]

10. [a simple sentence with two direct objects]

**Review Test
2-6**

Revise the following letter so every sentence is complete. Fix fragments, run-on sentences, and comma splices.

Payne's Department Store
13 Crestline Avenue
New York, NY 12342

December 12, 19xx

Ms. Germaine Teller
1538 Newbury Street
Westfield, CT 03562

Dear Ms. Teller:

Make plans to shop on December 23!

We are pleased to invite you to our annual pre-Christmas sale. This sale is limited to our credit customers, in fact, the store will be open only to shoppers who show us a copy of this letter. Or who have a Payne's credit card.

On December 23, everything in this store will be HALF PRICE: rugs, furniture, housewares. Everything you want to give for Christmas. And buy for yourself.

So come to Payne's on December 23, our entire staff will be there to help you find just what you want. And to help you save.

Remember: bring your charge card or a copy of this letter.

Sincerely,

Margot Atkins
Manager
Payne's Department Store

WRITING GRAMMATICALLY

FAMOUS FIRST DRAFTS: ABRAHAM LINCOLN
Writing Hint: Use Parallel Structure for Parallel Ideas

" ... GOVERNMENT OF THE PEOPLE, BY THE GENERAL POPULACE, AND FOR THE BENEFIT OF THE INHABITANTS MENTIONED ABOVE, SHALL NOT PERISH ... "

"... government of the people, by the people, and for the people, shall not perish from the earth."

Source: Ford Button

Madeline Brimble
42 Sunshine Court
Belleville, IN 48903

February 21, 19xx

Mr. David Douglas
Douglas Detective Agency
1538 A Street
Chestertown, IN 48904

Dear Mr. Douglas:

Thinking carefully about a recent situation in my neighborhood, it seemed best to write you. Maybe you've saw in the *Belleville Bulletin* last Monday poor Mr. George Potter died of a heart attack. (Well, that's what the doctor *says*.)

There seems to be several *odd* things going on in the Potter household, and I don't think poor George's death were natural at all!

First, what about that shameless wife of his, Harriet, whom has wore curlers to the Safeway every day this week?

And his son-in-law, Alfie, what will inherit George's portable table saw and hedge clippers?

I won't even tell you about George and Harriet's daughter Vera, who would of run off with Bill Banham the mailman last week if Ted Cotler's dachshund hadn't bit him in the ankle while delivering 15 valentines to Patsy Lee Trevor.

To put it bluntly, Mr. Douglas, someone in this neighborhood has got away with *murder*. Please call me so we can discuss the other clues I have acquired as soon as possible.

Waiting anxiously,

Madeline Brimble

PART THREE OBJECTIVE: To write grammatically correct sentences.

Every day in business, poor writing leads to loss of time and money. Confusing memos are followed by explanatory memos; company policy manuals are misunderstood; shipments are filled incorrectly—simply because the writers did not express themselves coherently or correctly. We all know the difficulties of IRS forms; many of us know how confusing computer manuals can be. Often the complexities arise from poor grammar and word choice, not from highly complex subject matter.

Many people who haven't been thinking about their writing in a long time are shocked to learn their sentences contain errors. "I write the way I talk," they argue, "and everyone understands me when I talk." Of course, writing and speaking have a great deal in common, but they are far from identical. When you are present before your listener, your face, body, and voice are communicating as much as your words. On the phone, your voice is conveying a tremendous amount of information. Have you ever watched a foreign film without subtitles? You can learn a lot about the characters and situation without understanding a word.

Writing, however, consists only of marks on a page. (Looking at a *book* in a foreign language will probably convey very little to you.) When your words are confusing, the readers cannot ask you to repeat your sentence, nor can they learn anything from your tone or body language.

In the Reading for Resourceful Writers at the beginning of this section, you read a letter written the way the writer *speaks*. You may not have trouble understanding the letter, but the errors (as well as the subject matter) keep it from being an ideal piece of business correspondence. (Try spotting the errors in that letter; then go back to it after you have studied Chapters 15 through 20.)

Because the conventions of grammar are vital to effective business writing, the following chapters review the basic principles and most common pitfalls. Before you start this section, try testing yourself on the following Pre-Test.

PART THREE PRE-TEST

Correct the grammatical errors in the following memo.

To: All Employees
From: Horace Wheeler
Subject: Photocopying Policy
Date: December 4, 19xx

Each of you realize, I am sure, the problems we have been experiencing with our photocopying machines. One of the two machines are always broken; the other always has a line of people in front of it. To ease the photocopying problems, two more machines have been ordered. Until they arrive, however, we should follow these guidelines:

1. Before copying, make sure you really *need* extra copies. We do not need copies of every letter and memo we write.

2. More than five copies of any document should be made on the mimeograph machine, saving time and money.

3. After photocopying, sign the sheet next to the machine. Put both your name and also put the number of copies you made.

4. Whomever uses the machine at the end of the day should give the sheet to Mel Rose or I.

5. There appears to be coffee stains inside the machine that is now being repaired. Do not put coffee cups on the copier!

Thank you for your attention to these guidelines.

After correcting the memo to the best of your ability, check your answers at end of text.

CHAPTER 15

VERB FORMS

OBJECTIVE: To choose the correct form of common regular and irregular verbs.

Can you spot any verb errors in the following sentences?

1. The news had only recently came to our office.
2. The reports have lain here for over a week.
3. Terry has swore she knew nothing about the accounting problems.
4. The airplane had flown past before we could see it clearly.

If you said #1 and #3 are incorrect, you were right: the verb in #1 should be *had come*; the verb in #3 should be *has sworn*.

Most English speakers use verbs correctly much of the time without realizing what they are doing: their "ears" inform them of the correct usage. In certain situations, however, many people make errors. In order to avoid these mistakes, we need to have a better grasp of how English verbs are put together.

PERSON AND NUMBER

Verbs change according to the person and number of their subjects. As we discussed in Chapter 3, the first person is the writer; the second person is someone being addressed; the third person is anybody or anything being written about. These persons may come singly or in groups (singular or plural).

The following chart illustrates the change in a regular verb:

EXPLAIN

	FIRST PERSON	SECOND PERSON	THIRD PERSON
singular	I explain	you explain	he, she, it explains
plural	we explain	you explain	they explain

English verbs are actually fairly simple compared with the verbs in many other languages. As you can see, a regular verb changes only in the third-person singular. An *s* will appear: *he runs*. Irregular verbs, like *be* and *have*, are slightly different, but an *s* still remains part of the third-person singular form: *he is* and *he has*.

PRESENT TENSE

As we discussed in Chapter 1, verbs also come in different forms according to the time they are indicating. The time of the verb is called the *tense*: thus, verbs indicating present action are in the present tense.

WALK	DIRECT
I walk	I direct
you walk	you direct
he, she, it walks	he, she, it directs
we walk	we direct
you walk	you direct
they walk	they direct

Self-Check Test 15-1

Fill in the blank with the correct *present tense* form of the verb in parentheses. (See answers at end of text.)

1. Jill (*settle*) _____ her accounts every evening.

2. We (*sell*) _____ a wide variety of hardware.

3. They (*know*) _____ the answers to these calculus problems.

4. I (*intend*) _____ to paint my boat in the fall.

5. She (*manage*) _____ the direct mail business.

Some verbs are irregular in the present tense. The most common of these are the ones we use frequently as helping verbs: *be, do,* and *have.*

BE	DO	HAVE
I am	I do	I have
you are	you do	you have
he, she, it is	he, she, it does	he, she, it has
we are	we do	we have
you are	you do	you have
they are	they do	they have

Self-Check Test 15-2

Write the correct present tense form of the verb in parentheses. (See answers at end of text.)

1. George (*have*) _____ the contract on his desk.

WRITING HINT: USE WORDS THAT YOUR READER UNDERSTANDS

What Suzanne Wrote   *What Kathleen Thought*

Revision: I am sure the local inhabitants will appreciate the company's charitable work.

Source: Ford Button

2. It (*do*) _____ seem to be the moment to start.

3. We (*be*) _____ delighted to be invited.

4. He (*have*) _____ a proposal we (*to be*) _____ considering.

5. (*be*) _____ I invited to the concert after the dinner?

SIMPLE PAST TENSE

The simple past tense indicates action in the past. Often the past tense of a verb is formed by adding *-ed* to the present tense form:

PRESENT	PAST
add	added
consider	considered
demand	demanded
paint	painted

To make the past tense of a verb ending in *y*, change the *y* to *i* and add *-ed*.

PRESENT	PAST
carry	carried
hurry	hurried
worry	worried

Verbs ending in *e* usually have only *-d* added in the past:

PRESENT	PAST
agree	agreed
debate	debated
orchestrate	orchestrated

Some verbs, however, are irregular in the past. (Your dictionary will tell you if a verb has an irregular past tense.) Among the common irregular verbs, again, are the helping verbs *be, do,* and *have*.

BE (past tense)	HAVE (past tense)	DO (past tense)
I was	I had	I did
you were	you had	you did
he, she, it was	he, she, it had	he, she, it did
we were	we had	we did
you were	you had	you did
they were	they had	they did

The past tense of *be* is unique in that it changes in the first-person singular and the third-person singular; other verbs, like *have* and *do*, have only one form in the simple past.

The following are some common verbs that are irregular in the simple past. (For a more complete list, see page 176.)

PRESENT	PAST
buy	bought
do	did
go	went
run	ran
sit	sat
spin	spun
tear	tore
think	thought

Self-Check Test 15-3

Fill in the blank with the correct *past tense* form of the verb in parentheses. (Check your dictionary or end of text for answers.)

1. James (*ride*) _____ the Metroliner to Philadelphia.

2. I (*be*) _____ not aware of the change in plans.

3. They (*have*) _____ the answer right here.

4. He (*give*) _____ the receipt to the clerk.

5. I (*drink*) _____ the diet cola.

FUTURE TENSE

The future tense, which indicates future action, is formed by combining *will* or *shall* and the root (or *stem*) of the verb. In most business writing, you should use *will* rather than *shall*.

PRESENT: I run.   I see.
FUTURE: I will run.   I will see.

Self-Check Test 15-4

I. Fill in the blanks with a correct verb form. (See end of text for suggested answers.)

To: All Employees

From: Maryanne Lewes

Subject: Fire Drill

Date: October 13, 19xx

Tomorrow, October 14, we (1)_____ a fire drill here in Building C.

As soon as you (2)_____ the fire alarm, please (3)_____

your desks and (4)_____ to the parking lot in an orderly fashion.

Your supervisor (5)_____ you when to resume work.

I hope you (6)_____ this drill seriously. Last time, people

(7)_____ out for hamburgers during the drill, and several employ-

ees (8)_____ late. I (9)_____ this drill (10)_____

more successful.

II. When you have filled in the blanks, list the verbs you used and the *tense* you chose for each.

1.

2.

3.

4.

5.

6.

7.

8.

9.

10.

PERFECT TENSES

Perfect tenses are formed by combining the helping verbs *has, have, had,* or *will have* with the past participle of a verb.

Present Perfect Tense

The present perfect tense indicates an action begun in the past but continuing up to the present. Form the present perfect tense by combining *has* or *have* + the past participle of a verb.

> I *have seen* the effects of the strike.
> Cheryl *has finished* the letter.

Past Perfect Tense

The past perfect tense is used to indicate an action completed at a specific time in the past. Form the past perfect tense by combining *had* + the past participle of a verb.

> The secretaries *had finished* their work by 6:00 p.m.
> Mrs. McWilliams *had added* the figures while I was eating lunch.

Future Perfect Tense

The future perfect tense is formed by combining *will have* + the past participle of a verb. The future perfect tense is used to indicate action that will be completed at a specific time in the future.

> In 2004, the company *will have been* in business for fifty years.
> By dinner time, we *will have finished* the letters.

Self-Check Test 15-5

I. Fix any errors in the underlined verbs. (See answers at end of text.)

Dear Fred:

While you were away last week, Mr. Wilson <u>asks</u>_____(1) us if we
<u>see</u> _____(2) his dog, Fritzie. Apparently the dog <u>escapes</u> _____
_____(3) every day this week, since there is a hole in Mr. Wilson's fence.

To Mr. Wilson's surprise, I said I actually <u>notice</u> _____(4) Fritzie at
8:00 a.m. while I was on my way to work. The dog <u>burrows</u> _____(5)
under Tom Gregor's fence and was playing with Tom's collie. Mr. Wilson assures
me that he <u>fix</u> _____(6) his fence by five o'clock this afternoon.

II. Now name the tenses that you used when you corrected the verbs.

1.

2.

3.

4.

5.

6.

PAST PARTICIPLES

Forming the perfect tenses, as you have seen, requires the past participle. This
form causes trouble for many writers. The past participles of regular verbs have
the same form as the simple past tense.

> I *recall* the question. [present tense]
> I *recalled* the question. [past tense]
> I have *recalled* the question. [past participle]
> I had *recalled* the question. [past participle]

Many verbs, however, have irregular participles. Make sure you do not use
the simple past form instead of an irregular participle. Check your dictionary
whenever you are in doubt. (If no past participle form is listed in the dictionary,
the verb takes the usual *-ed* form.)

The following chart outlines some of the most commonly misused verb
forms.

PRESENT	PAST	PAST PARTI- CIPLE	PRESENT	PAST	PAST PARTI- CIPLE
begin	began	begun	hang	hung	hung
blow	blew	blown	know	knew	known
break	broke	broken	lay*	laid	laid
bring	brought	brought	lie*	lay	lain
buy	bought	bought	ride	rode	ridden
catch	caught	caught	rise*	rose	risen
choose	chose	chosen	see	saw	seen
come	came	come	set*	set	set
do	did	done	shake	shook	shaken
draw	drew	drawn	sit*	sat	sat
drink	drank	drunk	slide	slid	slid
drive	drove	driven	speak	spoke	spoken
fly	flew	flown	spring	sprang	sprung
forbid	forbade	forbidden	swear	swore	sworn
forgive	forgave	forgiven	swim	swam	swum
freeze	froze	frozen	throw	threw	thrown
get	got	gotten	wear	wore	worn
go	went	gone	write	wrote	written

*See also Chapter 30.

Self-Check Test 15-6

In the following sentences, change the verb in the *independent clause* from the present tense to the present perfect tense. (See end of text for answers.)

> Example: The students buy their books at this store.
> The students *have bought* their books at this store.

1. Since she won her medal, Sheila swims the Maine River every day.

2. Henry rides his bicycle to work even in heavy snowstorms.

3. Mr. Tuttle lies in the sun until he is the color of a cooked lobster.

4. This company flies promising job applicants from New York to Miami

   Beach.

5. Mary Livermore goes to Malibu every summer.

PROGRESSIVE TENSES

The six tenses we have just discussed also appear in what are called *progressive* forms: that is, the verbs indicate an action *in progress*. The six progressive tenses are formed by combining a form of *be* + the present participle.

The present participle is formed by adding *-ing* to the stem of the verb. You may have to make other spelling changes as well.

PRESENT PROGRESSIVE:	I am eating.
PAST PROGRESSIVE:	I was eating.
FUTURE PROGRESSIVE:	I will be eating.
PRESENT PERFECT PROGRESSIVE:	I have been eating.
PAST PERFECT PROGRESSIVE:	I had been eating.
FUTURE PERFECT PROGRESSIVE:	I will have been eating.

EMPHATIC FORMS

As their name implies, emphatic forms are used for emphasis. They are made by combining *do, does,* or *did* + the stem of a verb.

Paul *does work* quickly.
We *do have* a problem.
I *did finish* the project.

Self-Check Test 15-7

Fill in the blanks with the correct verb form. (See answers at end of text.)

1. Usually I [be] _____ careful to check the office lights after everyone [leave] _____ for the night. Tonight, however, I [hurry] _____ to catch my bus, so I [forget] _____ the lights.

2. Last year, after Theresa [see] _____ BGR Company's Christmas decorations, she [decide] _____ to stage a similar display for our company. While she [speak] _____ with one of the managers about the idea, however, she [learn] _____ that the display would be too expensive.

3. In 1929, while the company [increase] _____ its market share, the employees [begin] _____ to suspect the wisdom of the corporate investments.

4. As the paper [burst] _____ into flames, Mark [spring]

    _____ into action. He [throw] _____ blankets over

    the flames right before the fire trucks [appear] _____.

5. We [lie] _____ in the sun for six hours by the time Polly

    [arrive] _____ with the suntan lotion.

Caution: Verb Errors

Watch for verb forms that may *sound* correct to you but are actually common errors.

Poor	Correct
use to	*used* to
would of	would *have*
might of	might *have*

Incorrect: I use to play tennis.
Correct: I used to play tennis.
Incorrect: Paul would of won if he had played by the rules.
Correct: Paul would have won if he had played by the rules.
Incorrect: We might of finished first.
Correct: We might have finished first.

CHECKLIST FOR CHAPTER 15

1. Verbs change according to the person and number of their subjects.

2. Verbs also change according to the time they are indicating.

3. The simple past is usually formed by adding -d or -ed to the stem of a verb.

4. Perfect tenses are formed by combining *has, have, had,* or *will have* and the past participle of a verb.

5. Watch for irregular past tense and past participle forms.

6. Progressive tenses are formed by combining a form of the verb *be* and the present participle of a verb. Progressive tenses indicate ongoing action.

7. Present participles are formed by adding -*ing* to the stem of a verb.

8. Emphatic tenses are formed by combining *do, does,* or *did* with the stem of a verb.

VERB FORM REVIEW

Fill in the blanks with the correct forms of the verbs in parentheses. (Check answers at end of text.)

We have (*speak*) _____ to the three managers who (*bring*) _____ us information on the morale problems. These managers, who (*begin*) _____ interviewing clerical employees last June, have (*take*) _____ extensive notes and also (*go*) _____ into our files of similar problems. Having reviewed their work, we (*come*) _____ to some important decisions.

CHAPTER TEST I. **Rewrite the following sentences, changing the verbs in the independent**
15-1   **clauses to the simple past.**

1. I think that you should consider these job options.

2. Are you in your office?

3. Paul will continue the report for you.

4. The manager whom we interviewed is interested in a new organizational plan.

5. The supervisor buys all the office supplies that we need.

II. **Rewrite the following sentences, changing the verbs to the past perfect tense.**

1. The stock market fluctuation influences our investment decisions.

2. Finally the battle for the corporate takeover begins.

3. Sandra lay the model airplanes under the Plexiglas.

4. We are very concerned about the hostage situation.

5. Mr. Clegg wears his college tie on special occasions.

CHAPTER TEST 15-2   Underline the correct form of the verb in the following sentences.

1. Accounting (has been / was) my major before I (took / had taken) a computer science course.

2. When George (is studying / was studying), we were playing music.

3. I had not (begun / began) the forecasting project by the end of last week.

4. Have you (got / gotten) an answer from Forbes?

5. We (have relied / relied) on Millicent since 1956.

6. The figures in the snow were (froze / frozen) solid.

7. Thomas (has been lying / has been laying) on that couch ever since he (had broken / broke) his ankle.

8. Had Coldwell (spoke / spoken) with the attorneys by the time Mr. Sims (had arrived / arrived)?

9. Please let me know when Phyllis (had / has) recovered.

10. Our competitors (have been suing / are suing) us for six years now.

CHAPTER TEST 15-3   Fill in the blanks with appropriate forms of the verbs.

Until recently our office [operate] _____ on a very simple seniority system: the person who [work] _____ here the longest [receive] _____ the first choice of vacation dates. When that person [choose] _____ his or her dates, the next person on the seniority list [make] _____ a choice. In this way, we [ensure] _____ that no vacation dates [overlap] _____.

Last year, however, a problem [arise] _____. Phil Jergins, the employee who [work] _____ here the longest, [decide] _____ to change his dates after three other employees [make] _____ their choices. The arguments that [ensue] _____ [remember] _____ for years to come.

Finally Phil [agree] _____ to his original dates, but everyone

[feel] _____ terrible about the whole situation for several weeks. Our office manager [be] _____ now in the process of devising a new system for choosing vacation dates.

EXERCISE FOR EXPERTS

Write sentences following the directions given.

1. [a sentence with the past perfect tense of *swim*]

2. [a sentence with the simple past form of *do*]

3. [a sentence with the present perfect tense of *ride*]

4. [a sentence with the future tense of *be*]

5. [a sentence with the subject *he* and the present tense of the verb *finish*]

6. [a sentence with the subject *they* and the simple past tense of *shake*]

7. [a sentence with the subject *reports* and the past progressive form of *examine*]

8. [a sentence with the subject *Mr. Brown* and the future perfect tense of *fly*]

9. [a sentence with the subjects *Hal* and *Tom* and the past progressive tense of *go*]

10. [a sentence with the subject *I* and an emphatic form of *ring*]

CHAPTER 16

SUBJECT-VERB AGREEMENT

OBJECTIVE: To avoid the common pitfalls of subject-verb agreement.

Do you see any verb errors in the following sentences?

1. There has been some problems with the new terminal.

2. Neither Joe nor Tom know the difference between the two systems.

3. Procter & Gamble are experimenting with several new products.

If you said all these sentences have verb errors, you were correct. The verbs should be *have* in #1, *knows* in #2, and *is* in #3.

We have already seen that we cannot always rely on our *ears* to tell us when a word or sentence is correct. We can afford to make a few errors when we speak, but in writing—particularly business writing—we must be precise and correct.

One of the problem areas in writing is subject-verb agreement. Your verbs must agree with their subjects in *person* and *number*. Because the action and the noun performing the action are central to every sentence, you must make sure they convey consistent, not contradictory, information to the reader.

Most of the time you will find your subjects and verbs agree naturally; your ear will help you make the correct choice. This chapter will focus on the problem areas, the pitfalls that await the unwary writer.

First, review your knowledge of subject-verb agreement in the following exercise.

Self-Check Test 16-1

I. In the following sentences, change the plural subjects of the *independent clauses* to singular and make the necessary verb changes. Make sure you do NOT change the *tense* of the verb. (Check end of text for the answers.)

> Example: The students are registering this week.
> The *student is* registering this week.

1. Having been in the new offices for a week, the division managers have

   finally discovered how to operate the elevators.

2. They are the most aggressive of all the salespeople.

3. The tuna sandwiches on my plate become less appealing when I spot cockroaches on the table.

4. Usually the easiest routes for getting to the company picnic have been laid out by Margie Simpson.

5. Upon passing the CPA exam, the young accountants are going to open an office in Riverside.

II. In the following sentences, change the singular subjects of the independent clauses to plural and make the necessary verb changes.

1. He is in charge of checking the shipments each day, and he does all the necessary paperwork.

2. The attorney has received all the material and will be in our office by noon on Thursday.

3. After Mr. and Mrs. Doolittle arrive, the department head plans to make a presentation.

4. Is the new secretary going to attend the meeting?

5. The yellow daisy flourishes throughout most of North America.

If you had trouble recognizing the subjects in the previous exercise, you should review Chapter 9.

SEPARATION OF SUBJECT AND VERB

Sometimes the subject and verb are so far apart in a sentence that we tend to agree the verb with the wrong word. Modifiers coming between the subject and verb can trick us into choosing the wrong verb. Remember to look for the *subject* of the clause.

> The constant pressure on these employees cause morale problems. [incorrect: subject is *pressure*]
> The constant pressure on these employees causes morale problems. [correct]

Simple logic should tell you that the *pressure* has caused the morale problems, not the employees themselves.

An evaluation of the reports have been presented to the committee. [incorrect: subject is *evaluation*]
An evaluation of the reports has been presented to the committee. [correct]
The manager who wrote these letters are now working upstairs. [incorrect: subject is *manager*]
The manager who wrote these letters is now working upstairs. [correct]

Self-Check Test 16-2

Fix any verb errors in the following sentences. Put a C after a sentence if it is correct. Do not change the verb *tense*. (Check answers at end of text.)

1. The advertising campaign developed by our marketing interns look very promising.

2. Henry and his brother, who arrived last month from Colorado, is establishing the procedures for the contract settlement.

3. The status of the new departments have not been affected by the budget cuts.

4. The efficiency of the computerized inventory systems is remarkable.

5. John Lang, who has acted as chief executive and as secretary, was the only man nominated.

SENTENCES WITH SUBJECT COMPLEMENTS

When a sentence has a subject complement, make the verb agree with the *subject*, not the complement.

The door prize *is* two trips to Hawaii. [Verb agrees with *prize*, not *trips*.]
Two Cadillacs *are* his gift to Nancy this year. [Verb agrees with *Cadillacs*, not *gift*.]

PHRASE AND CLAUSE SUBJECTS

As we saw in Chapter 9, a phrase or clause may be the subject of a sentence. A gerund or infinitive phrase will take a singular verb:

Translating computer instructions *is* a difficult task.
To increase efficiency *seems* to be his goal.

Two subject phrases joined by *and* will take a plural verb:

Running marathons and playing basketball *are* his hobbies.
To try and to succeed *are* very different things.

A noun clause as subject will also take a singular verb:

What management strives for *is* profit.
Whom Fred will vote for *has* become a controversial topic.

Two noun clause subjects connected by *and* take a plural verb:

Why Ian is not in school and why he is not looking for
a job *are* questions I cannot answer.

Self-Check Test 16-3

Fix any verb errors in the following sentences. Put a C after correct sentences. (See answers at end of text.)

1. Whatever they have on their minds appear to be delaying this entire dis-

   cussion.

2. Training white mice have long been one of Howard's favorite activities.

3. Whom I speak with concerning the merger does not concern Mr. Milpass.

4. Betting on horses and participating in football pools is not encouraged in

   this organization.

5. The award this year is two bronze statuettes.

REVERSAL OF SUBJECT AND VERB

We are used to our subjects preceding our verbs, so we sometimes become confused when the usual order is reversed. If you can confidently identify the subjects of your sentences, you will not make mistakes. Just remember: find the verb, and then ask WHO or WHAT + VERB?

From these reports have emerged a final solution. [Incorrect: subject is *solution*, not *reports*.]
From these reports has emerged a final solution. [Correct: A final solution has emerged from these reports.]
On the desk was some important papers. [Incorrect: Subject is *papers*, not *desk*.]
On the desk were some important papers. [Correct: Some important papers were on the desk.]

As we mentioned in Chapter 9, pay particular attention to sentences beginning with *there*: the verb will always precede the subject:

> There are seven bluejays in the tree. [*Bluejays* is plural, so verb is plural.]
> There is a bluejay in the tree. [*Bluejay* is singular, so verb is singular.]

COMPOUND SUBJECTS

Two or more subjects that are connected by *and* and that refer to different people or things require a plural verb.

> Max Johnson and Marie McVeigh *are* making a presentation.
> The chairs and the tables *have been replaced*.

If the compound subject refers to the *same* person or thing, however, the verb should be singular.

> His attorney and best friend, Marsha Mason, *has* the material. [Marsha is both the attorney and the best friend.]
> The president and chairman of the board, G. K. Wheatland, *is* announcing a change. [G. K. is both president and chairman.]

Note that prepositional phrases such as *together with, as well as*, and *in addition to* do not introduce a compound subject.

> Mr. Glassman, together with his sons, plan to attend the book fair. [incorrect]
> Mr. Glassman, together with his sons, *plans* to attend the book fair. [correct]

Remember that compound subjects may *follow* a verb:

> Here *come* Bob and Suzie.

Self-Check Test 16-4

Correct any verb errors in the following sentences. Do not change the *tense* of the verb. Put a *C* after any correct sentences. (Check answers at end of text.)

1. The founder and president of this company are Matthew Kelp.

2. Both Mr. Hayes and Mrs. Landers has arrived from Tucson to teach the summer classes.

3. I feel certain that the rise in unemployment, together with the fluctuation in interest rates, have had some severe effects on housing starts.

4. There is an unusual sense of expectancy in the air today.

5. In the first few minutes of these meetings come the bad news.

OR SENTENCES

When a sentence has two subjects connected by *or, either/or,* or *neither/nor,* the verb form will depend on the subject closest to the verb: if the closest subject is singular, the verb will be singular; if the closest subject is plural, the verb will be plural.

> Either Jay or Monique is going to the film. [Verb agrees with *Monique,* the closest subject.]
> Jay or his parents are going to the film. [Verb agrees with *parents.*]
> Neither his parents nor Jay is going to the film. [Verb agrees with *Jay.*]
> Either Max Carlson or the division managers are giving the awards. [Verb agrees with *managers.*]

In general, you should put the plural subject closer to the verb; your sentence will *sound* better, and you will be less apt to make an error.

TITLES

The name of a book, movie, company, and so on is always singular:

> *Jaws* was a very successful book and movie.
> Johnson & Johnson has been recruiting at this university.
> Reilly, Karpin, and Frogg is merging with AMP Corporation.

COLLECTIVE NOUNS

As we mentioned in Chapter 2, some nouns indicate a group of people, places, or things: *university, class, management, corporation, team,* and so on. If you are using these nouns to indicate a unit, use a singular verb.

> The class is meeting at my house tonight.
> Management has decided on a new investment plan.
> The corporation does not have holdings in South Africa.
> The government has not agreed to a change.

If you want to emphasize the individual members of the group, use a plural verb.

> The class have quickly opened their books.

To make your sentences sound more natural, you may want to use a plural subject:

The class *members* have quickly opened their books.

False Friends: The Number vs. A Number

Watch for the difference between *a number* and *the number*. As a subject, *the number* is usually singular:
The number of clerks *is* growing smaller.
As a subject, *a number* (meaning *several*) is usually plural:
A number of students *have* dropped the statistics class.

Self-Check Test 16-5

Fix any verb errors in the following sentences. Put a *C* after the sentence if it is correct. Do not change the tense of the verbs. (See answers at end of text.)

1. *Wuthering Heights* have been made into several movies.

2. Neither Jonas nor his two cousins are able to track down the bug in this software.

3. The university, together with the city government, are working toward a unified plan for the area.

4. Either his wife or his daughters has demanded a change in his work schedule.

5. The company of Lamonte, Draper, & Woods are buying this property.

SINGULAR PRONOUNS

Many of the indefinite pronouns that we studied in Chapter 3 are always singular: *anybody, anyone, each, either, everybody, everyone, neither, someone, somebody*. If one of these is the subject of a clause, the verb will be singular. (Review the chart on page 38 to see which indefinite pronouns are singular and which are plural.)

Do not be confused by plural constructions following singular indefinite pronouns.

Neither of the men *is* coming. [subject: *Neither*]
Everyone here *has* a pen and notebook. [subject: *Everyone*]
Each of us *knows* the routine. [subject: *Each*]
Someone here *has* the right answer. [subject: *Someone*]

Self-Check Test 16-6

Change any errors in subject-verb agreement in the following sentences by fixing the verbs. Do not alter the subjects or the tense of the verb. (Check your answers at end of text.)

1. Each of the executives have ordered two hamburgers.

2. Everyone in these two offices affect the profits of this company.

3. Neither George nor his cousin are going to the recruitment meeting.

4. *Star Wars* provide an interesting update to many old science fiction

   themes.

5. There has been several changes in the agenda since we last spoke.

6. The number of investment firms are growing rapidly.

7. Both Henryson and Peters have attended the convention in Los Angeles.

8. A statistical analysis of facts gathered by the researchers have proven

   nothing new about the situation.

9. From the first chapters come a sense of doom that stays with you

   throughout the book.

10. Please let me know if neither of the doctors have arrived by noon.

11. The fear of failure and need for reinforcement has created a critical situa-

    tion for some of our patients.

12. The firm of Kurtz and Calhoun have decided to open an office in

    Toronto.

13. Have both of the personnel managers reviewed these surveys?

14. Neither of the managers bring any new information to this conference.

15. There seem to be several leaks in our security system.

CHECKLIST FOR CHAPTER 16

1. Verbs must agree with their subjects in both *person* (first, second, or third) and *number* (singular or plural).

2. When a sentence has both a helping verb and a main verb, the helping verb agrees with the subject of the clause.

3. When a sentence has a subject complement, the verb should agree with the subject of the clause, not the complement.

4. If a single noun clause or noun phrase is a subject, the verb agreeing with it should be singular.

5. Two or more subjects connected by *and* that refer to different people, places, or things require a plural verb.

6. If subjects are connected by *or*, *either/or*, or *neither/nor*, the verb agrees with the subject closest to the verb.

7. The titles of books, movies, companies, and so on are always singular.

8. Collective nouns such as *university* and *management* are singular when being used as a unit.

9. Indefinite pronouns such as *any*, *each*, *everyone*, and *no one* are singular.

SUBJECT-VERB AGREEMENT REVIEW

Cross out any incorrect verb forms in the following paragraph and write in the correct form. (See answers at end of text.)

Mike Jones, together with Karen DeLora, have studied

our expenses over the past six months and have seen

problems in a number of areas. This company, despite its

excellent employees and products, face financial disaster

unless there is a few changes. Each of us have to make

some sacrifices. The following list of problem areas are in-

tended to show you how you can help.

Every one of us know that cutting costs are unpleasant,

but at this point, we have very little choice.

CHAPTER TEST 16-1   Fix any errors in verb form or agreement in the dependent and independent clauses of the following sentences by changing the verbs. Do not alter the tense of the verb. (Some sentences may be correct.)

1. The final result of the test scores have been submitted to Mrs. Peabody.

2. The class of 1983, as well as friends and spouses, have been invited to the Hilton for a gala dinner.

3. There appears to be many reasons for the sudden rise and decline of interest rates.

4. Although both Mr. Yarnell and Ms. Housman are being interviewed, neither of them are actually eligible for the position.

5. The new corporation, established in Oregon in late March, has already set up subsidiaries in California and Washington.

6. Mr. Thomson has finally laid down the law for the whole division.

7. Everyone elected to this position in the last decade are being audited.

8. Neither the government officials nor Mr. Petrovich have decided what to do about the impending financial crisis.

9. We stayed at the hotel until we had drank toasts to everyone present— including the waiters.

10. From these investigations, an appalling attempt at fraud and conspiracy have been discovered.

11. At this institute, there has always been a few specialists studying the development of ancient languages.

12. Have any of these employees tried the new accounting software?

13. Charles has wore the same tie every day for over eight months.

14. The opening of promotional letters have to appeal to a reader's emotions or pocketbook.

15. Laura will speak with each of the managers who have requested a transfer.

16. The shortage of good electrical engineers have altered the hiring strategies of this company.

17. One of the new personal computers come with over five hundred pages of documentation.

18. Theodore and Frederick have finally began the reinstatement procedures.

19. Neither the accountant nor the programmer agree to the solution.

20. The winds of change has blown over this corporation for a year.

CHAPTER TEST 16-2   **Fix any verb errors in the following memo.**

To: William McCord
From: Agnes Dewey
Subject: Marketing Diet AppleSider
Date: November 1, 19xx

As you may know, there has been a number of problems with the marketing strategy for our new Diet AppleSider mix. Despite some excellent newspaper advertisements and television commercials, sales of the product has dropped 30 percent since July. At next week's meeting, targeting appropriate consumer groups have to be thoroughly discussed.

Margaret Hathaway, along with Sam Tweedy, are developing some questions that we should consider at the meeting. Each of the people involved in the original marketing plan have agreed to attend the meeting and participate in the discussion.

The whole marketing team are going to work together to solve this problem. Please attend the meeting on November 7 at 2:00 p.m. in the conference room.

EXERCISE FOR EXPERTS   Write sentences according to the directions given.

1. [a sentence with *each* as the subject and a form of *have* as the verb]

2. [a sentence beginning with *there* that has the present tense of *be* as the verb]

3. [a sentence with a collective noun as the subject and the present tense of *share* as the verb]

4. [a sentence with *either* and *or* before the subjects]

5. [a sentence with the verb in the past perfect tense and with *marketing* as the subject]

6. [a sentence in the present tense with *everyone* as the subject]

7. [a sentence in which the verb precedes the subject]

8. [a sentence in which a prepositional phrase separates the subject and verb]

9. [a sentence with compound subjects and a verb in the present tense]

10. [a sentence with the subjects connected by *or* and the verb in the past progressive tense]

CHAPTER 17

PRONOUN AGREEMENT AND REFERENCE

OBJECTIVES: To make sure you establish clear antecedents for pronouns; to make pronouns agree with their antecedents.

Do you recognize any pronoun errors in these sentences?

1. Tim reminded Sam that his secretary was absent.

2. Each employee may take an hour for their lunch.

3. The university is raising their tuition fees.

If you recognized an error in each of the preceding sentences, you were correct. In #1 *his* is unclear; in #2 *their* should be *his/her*; in #3, *their* should be *its*.

CLEAR ANTECEDENTS

As you know, personal, demonstrative, and relative pronouns are used to replace words we do not want to keep repeating. The noun that the pronoun replaces is called the *antecedent*. (An *antecedent* is something that precedes or *goes before* something else; usually a noun will precede the pronoun that replaces it.) You must make sure that the antecedent is always clear to your reader and that the pronoun *agrees* with the antecedent.

Because pronouns take the place of nouns, make sure your reader always knows exactly what noun the pronoun is replacing. You can't refer to *her, it,* or *him* without first telling your reader what or whom you are writing about.

> Mary gave Sue *her* notebook. [confusing]
> Mary returned Sue's notebook to her. [clear]
> The managers had lunch with the clerks after *they* returned from Bermuda. [confusing]
> After the managers returned from Bermuda, they had lunch with the clerks. [clear]

Which, that, this, these, and *those* may also replace nouns. We often make these words work harder than they should. These words, like other pronouns, take the place of nouns that closely precede them.

> Winnie grew three inches last year, which her mother did not expect. [Poor: *Which* does not replace a noun.]

In the preceding example, the immediate noun is *year*, but clearly Winnie's mother was not surprised by the year; she was surprised by the three inches of growth. The sentence should be rewritten clearly:

> Winnie's mother did not expect her to grow three inches last year. [clear]

Your reader should not have to read between the lines of your writing!

> I do not understand this accounting problem. That is frustrating. [Confusing: *What* is frustrating? The problem or not understanding it?]
>
> I am frustrated by not understanding the accounting problem. [clear]
>
> I do not understand the frustrating accounting problem. [clear]

> The international conferences have been postponed because of a terrorist threat. This is creating a real problem for our company. [Confusing: Is the threat or the postponement creating a problem?
>
> The postponement of the international conferences due to a terrorist threat has created a real problem for our company. [Clear: Subject is *postponement*, so the reader knows the postponement has created the problem.]
>
> The terrorist threat that caused the postponement of international conferences has created a real problem for our company. [Clear: Subject is *threat*, so reader knows that the threat created the problem.]

> The candidates will be interviewed by four division managers. This will help us ascertain their strengths and weaknesses. [Two pronoun errors: *This* has no antecedent; *their* could refer to either the managers or the candidates.]
>
> The candidates will be interviewed by four division managers. These interviews will help us ascertain the candidates' strengths and weaknesses. [clear]
>
> When the four division managers have interviewed the candidates, we will be able to ascertain the candidates' strengths and weaknesses. [clear]

Self-Check Test 17-1

Fix any pronoun errors in the following sentences. If necessary, rewrite the sentences. (Check end of text for suggested revisions.)

1. The bank would not cover our payroll checks, which shocked the employees.

2. After the clerks have met with the accountants, tell them to speak with me.

3. I have finished writing reports on taxes and price increases. Please let me know what you think of them.

4. Maurice Constance will be speaking on the upcoming woodwind concert. This will be very interesting.

5. The ancient god Moloch was offered sacrifices of children by the Canaanites. They were condemned by Hebrew law.

6. Sam has been studying management methods in Japanese companies. It has been very beneficial for our corporation.

7. Lorraine is majoring in both economics and marketing. This has delayed her graduation by two years.

8. When Phil saw his brother yesterday, he was wearing a hat.

9. Ever since William Snell and Bonnie Grey began working with the new employees, they have been meeting every deadline.

10. When James Harding spoke to us about Philip Todd's accomplishments, many of us felt proud of him.

When you have established to whom or what the pronoun is referring, you must then make sure the pronoun agrees with its antecedent. As we mentioned in Chapter 3, the pronoun must be the same (1) gender, (2) number, and (3) person as its antecedent.

PRONOUN GENDER

In English, only people are masculine and feminine. All animals, places, things, and so on are neuter. You probably speak of your dog or cat as *he* or *she*, but in business writing you should refer to a pet as *it*. (In formal writing even ships are neuter.) The plural pronouns are the same for all genders, so you have to consider the gender of singular nouns only.

You may use *he/she, him/her*, or *his/her* when a singular antecedent refers to both sexes:

> When a student reads this catalog, he/she might be impressed by the number of management classes.
> A new employee must wear a name tag during his/her first month with the company.

When referring to an individual person, though, you will have to decide which gender is correct:

> When that incoming student reads our catalog, *he* will be impressed by the number of management classes.
> When I spoke with the instructor, *she* adjusted my grade.

PRONOUN NUMBER

Nouns are either singular or plural, and the pronoun must agree in number with the noun it replaces.

> I saw Mr. Paul this afternoon. He invited me to lunch. [singular noun/singular pronoun]
> I saw the Paul brothers this afternoon. They invited me to lunch. [plural noun/plural pronoun]

False Friends: They/Them/Their/Theirs

In speaking, we have gotten into the habit of referring to a singular person as *they*. We must be very careful not to make this mistake in writing.

When I called the operator, they gave me the number. [incorrect]

When I called the operator, he gave me the number. [correct]

When I ran into my best friend today, they took me out to lunch. [incorrect]

When I ran into my best friend today, she took me out to lunch. [correct]

Again, remember that *he/she* would be inappropriate in the prior examples: you should know the person's gender!

WRITING HINT: MAKE CLEAR PRONOUN REFERENCES

What Ms. Hooper Wrote   *What Mr. Klein Thought*

Revision: Department managers will interview the following applicants after they graduate from college.

Source: Ford Button

INDEFINITE PRONOUNS

Remember the singular pronouns we discussed in Chapter 3 and Chapter 16. Unlike personal pronouns, indefinite pronouns, as you might guess from their name, do not have specific antecedents.

> *Someone* is outside my door.
> Has *anyone* seen my watch?

You can see in the preceding sentences that the pronouns do not refer to anyone in particular. Most of the indefinite pronouns, however, are singular. If a singular indefinite pronoun is the subject of a clause, the pronouns (as well as the verbs) pertaining to that subject must be singular.

> Everyone here brought his hat. [not *their* hat]
> Each of the women has been assigned to her own
> office. [not *their* office]

In some situations, the *he/she* or *his/her* approach may be appropriate.

Neither of the assistants has purchased his/her own typewriter.

Each of the marketing majors has requested a change in his/her curriculum.

Note: To avoid the awkwardness of *she/he, her/him, and her/his*, you may want to make your subject plural:

The marketing majors have requested a change in *their* curriculum.

If a plural indefinite pronoun is the subject of a clause, the pronouns and verbs related to the subject must be plural. (See page 000 for list of plural indefinite pronouns.)

Several of the students brought their books.
Both of the managers have arrived.

PRONOUN PERSON

Your third consideration, when agreeing pronouns with their antecedents, is the person of the noun. The categories are the same as those we discussed in Chapter 3 (page 34): first, second, and third person.

When referring to yourself in writing, you should use *I* or *me*. If you start out speaking to your audience as *you*, make sure you do not switch to *they*. Be consistent!

The *You* Error   The most common error in the person of pronouns occurs with *you*. We often use *you*, the second-person pronoun, when we are referring to a third-person noun.

When a senior is about to graduate, you often become very interested in your future. [incorrect]
When a senior is about to graduate, he or she often becomes very interested in his/her future. [correct]
When seniors are about to graduate, they often become very interested in their futures. [correct]
When a person sleeps for a long time, you often wake up disoriented. [incorrect]
When a person sleeps for a long time, he or she often wakes up disoriented. [correct]

You, which is meant for addressing one or more people, should not be used as a substitute for *they, he, she,* or *one*.

Self-Check Test 17-2

Fix any pronoun errors in the following sentences. You may have to fix some verbs as well. (See end of text for answers.)

1. Every one of the doctors here has spoken on television about their specialty.

2. When you are not feeling well, an employee may see the company nurse for a checkup.

3. Have any of these students considered trying to match their wits with the chess-playing computer?

4. Now that each retiring clerk can make their own choice, many are choosing to take a check instead of a plaque and farewell dinner.

5. Management has decided to turn their offices over to the Easter Seals gala.

6. Neither the players nor the coach have decided whether they want to move the club to Dry Tongue, Nevada.

7. The university has changed their rules concerning transferring students.

8. Somebody in this group is going to regret they ever decided to attend the Christmas party at GRW Corporation.

9. If any of you can speak Cantonese, we would appreciate it if he would let us know.

10. Even though I gave the waitress my order in a very clear voice, they still brought me tuna on a bagel.

[Note: if you made subject-verb agreement errors in this test, review the rules in Chapter 16.]

CHECKLIST FOR CHAPTER 17

1. Make sure your reader can always tell what noun is being replaced by the personal, relative, and demonstrative pronouns you use.

2. Use *that, which, these* and *those* to replace a single noun in a sentence. Do not use them to refer to an entire idea.

3. Make sure that pronouns agree with their noun antecedents in gender, number, and person.

4. Do not use *they* or *them* when referring to a singular noun; do not use *you* when referring to a third-person noun.

PRONOUN AGREEMENT AND REFERENCE REVIEW

Correct the pronoun errors in the following paragraph. (Check answers at end of text.)

Snell & Company is offering you a chance to see their products in an exciting new manner. Now you can view a *videotape* of each of our exquisite dining room and bedroom sets in their elegantly decorated settings. For only $12.95 (refundable with your first purchase), our best customers can save themselves a trip to our retail outlet and can shop in the privacy of your own homes.

**CHAPTER TEST
17-1**

If the underlined pronouns in the following sentences are used correctly, write *C* in the blank. If a pronoun is used incorrectly, write a correct word or words in the blank.

1. A person should hand in their time sheet every Friday.   _____

2. Charles Miller insisted that the new managers lunch with the accounting staff after they have completed their training.   _____

3. Sometimes when an employee moves ahead too quickly, they will suddenly become upset and depressed.   _____

4. Neither of the rival advertising firms has established their rights to the account   _____

5. When you get up in the morning, a person should touch his toes a hundred times.   _____

6. After management reconsiders the terms of this proposal, they will review the budget.   _____

7. When we see a new student lost on campus, my friends and I try to help them out in whatever ways we can.   _____

8. Dow and Summerfield Corporation will move its offices to Tulsa in June.   _____

9. When I saw my supervisor today, he/she assured me that we would not be laid off before Christmas.   _____

10. Neither of the clerks has been able to work at his/her own desk.   _____

**CHAPTER TEST
17-2**

Fix any pronoun errors in the following sentences. You may have to change some verbs as well, but do not alter the tense of the verbs.

1. Laura Ferris will be studying Arabic in Morocco this autumn, which she is very excited about.

2. The university has decided to invest some of their resources in a new gymnasium.

3. When Philip is through meeting with the supervisor, he will speak to us for a few minutes.

4. Since each of the men is interested in accounting, they should attend the seminar on Tuesday.

5. Now that the company moved their headquarters from Atlanta to Baltimore, more people have been applying for management positions.

6. Each of the attorneys began the trial with their opening statement.

7. Now that you have read these magazine articles on auto imports, please give me your impressions of them.

8. In my conversation with the personnel manager, she/he recommended that I apply for the job in person.

9. Neither of the secretaries has ever before purchased their own office materials.

10. We managers had a meeting today at Ryan's Restaurant to decide who would correct the programming error. It was quite productive.

11. When Frannie hired Sharon, she was very unsure about company goals.

12. I know management has been considering other plans for the long term, but for now each of the women has been assigned to an office of their own.

13. When a person first starts working here at Tryon Corporation, they often find it hard to take the hard work and long hours.

14. I hope the company picnic will be scheduled for early June. That is always a lot of fun.

15. When Bill and George are finished speaking, please give him the necessary paperwork.

**EXERCISE FOR
EXPERTS**   Fix any verb or pronoun errors in the following letter.

ARGON CORPORATION

2121 Hilltop Terrace

Wellesley, MA 04671

September 23, 19xx

Ms. Eliza Escher

19 Seacliff Street

Ames, CT 01345

Dear Ms. Escher:

Thank you for sending me your resume and application letter. When I have reviewed it carefully, I will send it on to Bill Fine in the Personnel Department. Your application will then be evaluated by a hiring committee that have been drawn from three company departments. This should take about three weeks.

The committee will then request that each of the six most qualified candidates send in detailed descriptions of the software they have developed. The top three candidates will be interviewed by committee members. They should know the status of their candidacy by October 15.

If you have any questions about the review process, please call me.

Sincerely,

Bill Hagen

Vice-President

CHAPTER 18

PRONOUN CASE

OBJECTIVES: To use the subjective, objective, and possessive cases correctly; to use intensive and reflexive pronouns correctly.

Do you see any pronoun errors in the following sentences?

1. Give the information to Katie and myself.
2. Who is this memo for?
3. Prepare the hotel suite for Henry and I.
4. Us managers are meeting in Bay River.

If you said that all these sentences contain errors, you already know something about pronoun case. In #1, *myself* should be *me*; in #2, *Who* should be *Whom*; in #3, *I* should be *me*; in #4 *Us* should be *We*.

English speakers have been simplifying the language through the centuries. Nouns and verbs no longer have many of the forms they had a thousand years ago. Every English noun used to have a multitude of forms that changed according to the function of the noun in a sentence. Now a noun changes from its standard form only when we want to make it plural or possessive. (See Chapter 25 for more on possessive nouns.)

Pronouns, however, still retain some of the characteristics that nouns lost through the centuries. Most of our personal pronouns have three forms or cases: subjective, objective, and possessive. (These cases are called *nominative*, *accusative*, and *genitive* in older grammar books.)

> SUBJECTIVE: I, you, he, she, it, we, they, who
> OBJECTIVE: me, you, him, her, it, them, whom
> POSSESSIVE: my (mine), your (yours), his, her (hers),
> its, our (ours), their (theirs), whose
> (*You* and *it* change only in the possessive.)

When we use nouns, the placement of the words tells us who is doing action and who is receiving it: *Harry loves Jill*. If we reverse the order, the sentence means something else: *Jill loves Harry*.

The form of personal pronouns, however, depends upon the function of the pronoun in its clause. If the pronoun is the subject of a clause, it will be in the subjective form; if it is the direct object, indirect object, or object of a preposition, it will be in the objective form. (We will discuss the possessive form later in this chapter.)

> *I* love *him*. [*I* is the subject; *him* is the object.]
> *He* loves *me*. (*He* is the subject; *me* is the object.]

As we found with verb forms, most people use pronouns correctly without knowing what they are doing. If you rely totally on your "ear," however, you are apt to make mistakes. You should watch particularly for common pitfalls.

COMPOUND SUBJECTS AND OBJECTS

If you are substituting a pronoun for a subject noun in a sentence, you will use a subject pronoun regardless of other subjects in the sentence. The same rule applies for objects. If you are uncertain, try mentally deleting the other subjects and objects to see how the sentence looks and sounds without them.

> Holly and them are going to the movies. [incorrect: You wouldn't say "Them are going."]
> Holly and they are going to the movies. [correct]
> Greg loves Tammy and I. [incorrect: You wouldn't say "Greg loves I."]
> Greg loves Tammy and me. [correct]

If a pronoun is the object of a preposition, the pronoun should be in the objective form.

> Give the book to me. [*Me* is object of preposition *to*.]

Again, do not be confused if the phrase has more than one object: the pronoun should remain objective.

> Give the book to Karen and I. [incorrect]
> Give the book to Karen and me. [correct]
> Sheila is going to the meeting with Tom and he. [incorrect]
> Sheila is going to the meeting with Tom and him. [correct]

PRONOUNS FOLLOWED BY NOUNS

Sometimes pronouns are followed by nouns that make us forget whether the pronoun is a subject or an object.

> Us students are signing a petition. [incorrect: The pronoun is the subject.]
> We students are signing a petition. [correct]
> When you are through with the proposal, please give it to we managers. [incorrect: The pronoun is object of the preposition.]
> When you are through with the proposal, please give it to us managers. [correct]

Self-Check Test 18-1

Correct any pronoun errors in the following sentences. Put a C after a sentence if it is correct. (See end of text for answers.)

1. Flannery and he are going to attend the Valentine's Ball with Johanna
    and I.

2. Thomas Morel and her are going to write the annual report.

3. I gave the tickets to Mike and he before the game started.

4. Please listen to we council members tonight.

5. Carole and them are planning a surprise for us retirees.

COMPARISONS WITH *THAN* OR *AS*

In sentences that make a comparison, *than* and *as* actually introduce dependent clauses even though we do not always say or write the verb of the clause. If the pronoun is the subject of the clause, it must be in the subjective form.

> Winnie is taller than he is. [correct: *He* is the subject of the dependent clause.]

The pronoun remains subjective even if you delete the final verb:

> Winnie is taller than him. [incorrect]
> Winnie is taller than he. [correct]
> Frank is as intelligent as them. [incorrect]
> Frank is as intelligent as they. [correct]
> The new employee works less than me. [incorrect]
> The new employee works less than I. [correct]

SENTENCES WITH *BE*

As we saw in Chapter 10 (pages 116–117), forms of the verb *be* are usually followed by a *complement*; they will not usually be followed by a direct object. After the verb *be*, you should use a subject pronoun.

> It is he at the door. [not *him*]
> It was they who made the decision. [not *them*]

Self-Check Test 18-2

Correct any pronoun errors in the following sentences. Put a C after any correct sentences. (Check your answers at end of text.)

1. This candidate has more experience than Renee, but he

    is not as efficient as her.   _____

2. I am waiting for a call from Wesley; please see if that is

    him.   _____

3. If I were her, I'd give the award to either you or him.   _____

4. We typists are requesting that work requests be

    forwarded through Frannie and you.   _____

5. Gwen works more quickly than Tom; I hope she is as

    careful as him.   _____

WHO AND WHOM

The two pronouns *who* and *whom* function in the same way as other pronouns, but, since they confuse many people, they deserve a few words to themselves.

Who is simply a subject pronoun like *I, he, they,* and so on. *Whom* is an object pronoun like *me, him,* and *them.* To determine which one to use, you must decide whether the pronoun is a subject or an object in its own clause.

> Who broke the vase? [*Who* is doing the action, so the pronoun is subjective.]
> Whom did you see? [*You* is the subject; *whom* is receiving the action of being seen, so it is in the objective form.]
> Who lent him the book? [*Who* is doing the action; *him* is receiving the action.]
> To whom did you lend the book? [*Whom* is object of the preposition *to.*]

Sometimes we put the object of prepositional phrases at the beginning of the sentence and leave the preposition at the end. The form of the pronoun remains the same.

> *Whom* did you lend the book *to?*
> *Whom* did you go to the meeting *with?*

To check the case, you may find it helpful to substitute another subject or object pronoun in your sentence. For example, if you are wondering about a sentence like *Who(m) gave you the details?* try substituting *he* or *him.*

> Him gave you the details. [incorrect]
> He gave you the details. [correct]

Since the subject form *he* is correct, the subject form *who* will also be correct.

Another pitfall occurs in sentences where expressions such as *do you think, do you believe,* and *do you recommend* come in the middle of the clause with *who* or *whom.* Do not let these expressions throw you off. Look for the verb that goes with *who* or *whom.*

> Who *do you think* will be the winner?
> Who *did I tell you* would give the awards?

If you mentally delete the interrupting expression, you will see which pronoun is correct.

>   Who will be the winner? [correct]
>   Who would give the awards? [correct]

The major rule to remember is that A PRONOUN TAKES ITS FORM FROM ITS OWN CLAUSE. In Chapter 12, we discussed dependent clauses that may function as subjects, objects, or complements in a sentence. The function of the whole clause in a sentence, however, does not affect the pronouns inside the dependent clause.

In the following sentence, for example, a dependent clause acts as subject of the sentence.

>   *Whomever we elect* will be very pleased.

The case of the pronouns in the dependent clause is determined solely by their own clause. [*We* is the subject of the verb *elect*, and *whomever* is the direct object of the dependent clause.]

>   I saluted whoever was wearing a uniform. [*Whoever was
>   wearing a uniform* is a dependent clause acting as a direct
>   object: *whoever* is the subject; *was wearing* is the verb in the
>   dependent clause.]
>   I will give the booby prize to whomever I choose.
>   [*Whomever I choose* is a dependent clause acting as object of
>   the preposition: *I* is the subject; *whomever* is the object in
>   the dependent clause.]

As you can see in the preceding example, the object of a preposition can be a clause. If the group of words following the preposition has a subject and a verb, you know it is a clause. Note the difference between the following:

>   Give the book to him. [*To him* is a prepositional phrase;
>   *him* is the object of the preposition.]
>   Give the book to whoever wants it. [*Whoever wants it* is
>   a clause acting as the object of the preposition: *whoever* is
>   the subject; *it* is the object.]
>   Give the book to whomever you like. [*Whomever you like*
>   is a clause acting as object of the preposition: *you* is the
>   subject; *whomever* is the object of the dependent clause.]

Self-Check Test 18-3

Correct any pronoun errors in the following sentences. Put a *C* after any correct sentences. (Check your answers at end of text.)

1. Who will be leading the curriculum committee this spring?

2. Who do you think will second the motion for amending the report?

3. When I decided to retire, I wondered who would be the best person to

    nominate as my successor.

4. Now that I have graduated, I will be glad to speak with whomever wants information about the campus.

5. When Fenton McDonnell was in the army, he never knew whom was giving orders.

6. Bobby Jones was an American golfer who also worked as an attorney.

7. Do you remember who you voted for in the last election or who voted for you?

8. Whom do you suppose will Thompson decide to hire for the personnel position?

9. The student who the instructor trusted with the test scores has disappeared from campus.

10. Carla is very even tempered except when she is being pressured to tell whom she is going to nominate.

POSSESSIVE CASE

Possessive pronouns, as their name implies, indicate ownership. Do not confuse them with subjective or objective pronouns.

Possessive Personal Pronouns						
my	our	your	his, her	its	their	whose
mine	ours	yours	hers		theirs	

Mainly you should remember that, unlike nouns that indicate possession, possessive personal pronouns do not take an apostrophe. *Her's, our's,* or *their's* are NOT acceptable words. Of course, *it's* is a word, but it is a contraction for *it is* or *it has.* The possessive of *it* is simply *its.*

> The bird flew back to its nest. [possessive pronoun]
> It's been a great experience. [contraction for *it is.*]

. To form the possessive of indefinite pronouns such as *anyone* and *everybody,* add an apostrophe + s.

> Is this *anyone's* tennis ball?
> I thought *everybody's* spirits were low.

INTENSIVE/REFLEXIVE PRONOUNS

As we saw on page 37, intensive/reflexive pronouns end in *-self* or *-selves*. They have only two functions: (1) to emphasize a noun or pronoun and (2) to reflect on or refer to the subject.

Do not use these pronouns as subjects or objects.

> George went to the meeting with Philip and myself.
> [incorrect]
> George went to the meeting with Philip and me.
> [correct]

Note: Some writers mistakenly use *theirselves* and *themself*: remember that *themselves* is the only acceptable third-person plural reflexive or intensive form.

Self-Check Test 18-4

Correct any pronoun errors in the following sentences. Put a *C* after any correct sentences. (See end of text for answers.)

1. Both Barbara and myself were very impressed with everyones efforts.

2. James returned the book to it's shelf before he left for the office.

3. Even though the tenants claim the carpeting is their's, the landlord carried it off to the dump yesterday.

4. Having seen himself on the video screen, Jerry sadly put the cassette in its box.

5. "I have always maintained that its vital to vote," Anne insisted, "even though I myself have never tried it."

CHECKLIST FOR CHAPTER 18

1. Pronouns may be in the subjective, objective, or possessive case.

2. Pronoun case is determined by the function of the pronoun in its own clause.

3. Possessive personal pronouns do not have possessive apostrophes.

4. Possessive indefinite pronouns are formed by adding apostrophe + *s* to the indefinite pronoun.

5. Intensive and reflexive pronouns may not be used in place of subject or object pronouns.

PRONOUN CASE REVIEW   Fix any pronoun errors in the following sentences. (Check answers at end of text.)

Since its important for each department to have sufficient office supplies, Jorge and Fred have developed a new ordering method. Please review their revised procedures.

1. Every Monday, please give we supervisors a list of the supplies you need.

2. Fred will ask either Jorge or myself to check each department's list and log the items requested in the supplies book.

3. Supplies will be purchased by whomever Fred assigns each month.

4. Please assess you're needs carefully. We do not want you to run out of supplies during the week.

CHAPTER TEST 18-1   Cross out the wrong words in the parentheses.

1. (We/Us) bus drivers are considering a strike beginning in April.

2. When you and (he/him) are through with the copier, please let Anne and (I/me) know.

3. (Whomever/Whoever) wins the race will also win a thousand dollars.

4. Jimmy is more proficient in Spanish than (me/I/myself) because he lived in Madrid for six years.

5. The new employees—Bill and (he/him)—are working on the UNIX system.

6. Since (you're/your) vacation, you have been very relaxed.

7. I hope this is (him/he), since we can't leave without him.

8. (Who/Whom) do you suspect has been robbing the employee refrigerator?

9. As soon as the students saw (themselves/theirselves) on the television screen, they demanded an explanation from Charlie and (myself/me/I).

10. It seems Hal and (him/he) are the only clerks interested in the decision.

CHAPTER TEST 18-2   I. Fill in the blanks with *who, whom, whoever,* or *whomever.*

On the plane to Marseilles, I met an eccentric old man

_____ insisted on giving me four hints for touring

Europe. First, he said, make sure that _____ you

hire as a guide has lived in the area for at least ten years;

otherwise the information will be worthless. Second, you

should tip _____ carries your bags according to

his height: add a franc for every inch over five feet. Third,

before you tell someone _____ you are, ask to see

his driver's license and one credit card. And, finally, make

sure that _____ you go out to dinner with will

not order calves' brains or tripe.

II. Fix any pronoun errors in the following sentences. You may have to fix some verbs as well, but do not alter the tense of the verbs.

1. Will you be attending the conference with Mildred and myself?

2. At the end of the seminar, Mrs. Ogilvie presented three awards to we accountants.

3. I am sure that neither Terry nor them have come to a decision.

4. This keyboard presents some difficulties for whomever uses it.

5. This is the first year its been so clear to me that everybodys tax forms need to be simplified.

6. Fred works harder than Linda, but she is more efficient than him.

7. Please give us candidates a second chance.

8. Both Marianne and myself were startled to hear about the merger.

9. I consider Tom and she to be my two closest associates.

10. That must be her knocking at the door right now.

EXERCISE FOR EXPERTS   Fix any verb or pronoun errors in the following memo.

To: Mike Blythe, Orion Thomas, Wilson Waters
From: Myron Bloom
Topic: Customer Crises
Date: April 5, 19xx

Since each of you have to deal occasionally with unhappy customers, Pat Lewis and myself have compiled some guidelines for dealing with customer crises.

1. If the client is having trouble with a product, make sure they have spoken with a service representative. Also, make sure that *you* speak with whomever has been working with the client before you write to them.

2. If a product is broken and the product warranty has expired, provide the client with full details on our service contracts and repair facilities. They should know who to call about repairs.

3. If the client has written to say they are unhappy with our service, summarize the whole problem in you're letter before offering a solution. The client should be sure you and him are dealing with the same facts.

4. If the client is *very* unhappy with our service (especially if he mentions an attorney), talk with Phil Barker or I before writing an answering letter. Our client files might be useful to you.

CHAPTER 19

MODIFIERS

OBJECTIVES: To recognize modifiers; to avoid misplaced, squinting, and dangling modifiers.

Do you see any errors in the following sentences?

1. The newsletter is being published by an independent contractor with color photographs.

2. I knew by 1985 she would graduate.

3. Working quickly, the house was built in thirty days.

The first sentence has a misplaced modifier; the second has a squinting modifier; the third has a dangling modifier. The sentences could be written in a number of ways. Three possibilities are as follows:

1. The newsletter with color photographs is being published by an independent contractor.

2. I knew she would graduate by 1985.

3. Working quickly, we built the house in thirty days.

RECOGNIZING MODIFIERS

Modifiers come in many forms. They may be adjectives, adverbs, phrases, or clauses.

A. Adjectives are single words that describe nouns.

Tanya is designing a *new* project.

B. Adverbs are single words that modify a verb, an adjective, or another adverb.

I ran *quickly* and *awkwardly*. [adverbs modify verb]
Mr. Hobshead was an *irritatingly* nervous driver. [adverb modifies adjective]
George speaks *extremely quickly*. [adverb *extremely* modifies adverb *quickly*]

C. Modifying phrases (pp. 124–125) may be adjectival or adverbial.

The manager wore a tie *covered with gravy stains*. [adjectival participial phrase modifying *tie*]
Kathleen works *with both care and precision*. [adverbial prepositional phrase modifying *works*]

D. Modifying dependent clauses (page 129ff.) may also be adverbial or adjectival.

> *Because she lacks funds*, Marcia has taken a second job.
> [Clause is adverbial, as it modifies *has taken*.]
> The consulate, *which is now located on the waterfront*, will be moved to a residential area. [Dependent clause modifies *consulate*, so it is adjectival.]

Self-Check Test 19-1

Underline the modifying words, phrases, and clauses in the following sentences. Do not underline single articles. (Check end of text for answers.)

> Example: I know with certainty that the elderly accountant has recently retired.

1. The attorney in the pinstripe suit was speaking quickly.

2. With deliberation, Marjorie announced the lucky winner.

3. Phil saw only two students.

4. To win the debate, I used my quick wit; Jackie used her solid knowledge of the extensive material.

5. The student wearing a yellow shirt is writing an autobiography that begins two years before his birth.

MISPLACED MODIFIERS

The basic principle for using modifiers is simply to put them as close as possible to the word or words they are modifying. Naturally, if you wanted to discuss a *red dress*, you would want *red* to appear right before *dress*; you wouldn't put the modifier in some distant part of the sentence.

> I ran to the store for some stamps and envelopes *quickly*. [poor: Adverb is too far from verb *ran*.]
> I ran *quickly* to the store for some stamps and envelopes. [correct]
> Mr. Farnham has ordered doughnuts for employees with vanilla glaze. [poor: *With vanilla glaze* modifies *doughnuts*, not *employees*.]
> Mr. Farnham has ordered doughnuts with vanilla glaze for employees. [correct]

Some modifiers are easily misplaced. We are often careless about common words like *only, just, almost, even,* and *merely*. The principle for them, however, is

WRITING HINT: AVOID MISPLACED MODIFIERS

What Mrs. Wilson Wrote   *What Mrs. Baker Thought*

Revision: We have ordered a hundred cupcakes dipped in chocolate for the children.

Source: Ford Button

the same as for all modifiers: put them as close as you can to the word they are modifying. Compare the following sentences:

1.   Only I nibbled the sandwiches.

2.   I only nibbled the sandwiches.

3.   I nibbled only the sandwiches.

In #1, *only* modifies the subject and indicates that only the speaker nibbled the sandwiches; in #2, the writer indicates that the sandwiches were only nibbled, not eaten entirely; and in #3, we understand that only the sandwiches were eaten—the other food was untouched.

We tend to put these modifiers in front of the verb, regardless of our meaning, but this error can seriously affect our reader's understanding of the sentence.

> I just glanced through the information once. [correct if you mean that you *only glanced*—that you didn't read carefully]

> I glanced through the information just once. [correct if you are emphasizing that you glanced only one time]

PHRASE MODIFIERS

Watch for participial and infinitive phrases at the beginning and end of your sentences: make sure they are connected to the word or words they modify. Careless errors can create very odd images for your reader.

Lightly fried in butter, I ate the flounder. [poor]
I ate the flounder that was lightly fried in butter. [correct]
The trainer worked with the horse wearing running shorts. [poor]
Wearing running shorts, the trainer worked with the horse. [correct]

SQUINTING MODIFIERS

One form of the misplaced modifier is the so-called squinting modifier. This problem occurs when a modifier could be describing either of two things:

The day we were defeated *thoroughly* disgusted us.
[Squinting: Was the speaker thoroughly defeated or thoroughly disgusted?]
The day we were thoroughly defeated disgusted us.
[correct]
The day we were defeated disgusted us thoroughly.
[correct]

Self-Check Test 19-2

Fix any modifier errors in the following sentences. (Check end of text for answers.)

1. The new accountant addressed the IRS auditor with a shaking voice.

2. I just studied the most essential chapters for the test.

3. Covered with pepperoni and sausage, my friends devoured the pizza.

4. Jorge established within a week he would be victorious.

5. Management has only decided to cover the first three items on the agenda.

DANGLING MODIFIERS

Dangling modifiers are phrases that are not attached to a word in the sentence. Note that an introductory modifying phrase cannot modify an adjective or a possessive form: the phrase must modify the subject of the clause:

Swimming to shore, Mark's contact lens came out. [dangling: *swimming* cannot modify *lens*.]

While Mark was swimming to shore, his contact lens came out. [correct]

While swimming to shore, Mark lost his contact lens. [correct]

If you write a sentence with a modifier dangling at the beginning, you have two choices: (1) rewrite the sentence so the subject being modified *directly* follows the modifier; or (2) change the modifying phrase to a clause.

Climbing Mount Hood, snow began to fall. [poor: Who was climbing? Modifier appears to describe *snow*.]

1. Climbing Mount Hood, we ran into some snow. [correct: *We* were doing the climbing.]

2. While we were climbing Mount Hood, snow began to fall. [correct: Opening clause clarifies the sentence.]

Having agreed to a solution, the meeting ended. [poor: Who agreed to the solution? Meetings can't agree to things.]

1. Having agreed to a solution, the division managers ended the meeting. [clear]

2. When the division managers had agreed to a solution, the meeting ended. [clear]

Note that moving a dangling modifier from the beginning to the end of the sentence does not solve the problem:

Upon graduation, my career began. [poor: *whose* graduation?]

My career began upon graduation. [still unclear]

When I graduated, my career began. [clear]

As a modifier, *Upon graduation* requires a word adjacent to it indicating who graduated:

Upon graduation, John began his career. [clear]

Self-Check Test 19-3

Fix the modifier errors in the following sentences. (See end of text for suggested revisions.)

1. Traveling to Arkansas, our tire fell off.

2. To increase attendance, absentee members will be fined.

3. While still haggling over the issues, unfair tax laws are not being challenged by the politicians.

4. Unable to finish her education, Ariadne's desire for success never faltered.

5. As the youngest person in the room, my opinion was rarely taken seriously.

CHECKLIST FOR CHAPTER 19

1. Modifiers are words, phrases, or clauses that describe or qualify a noun, verb, adjective, or adverb.

2. Make sure your modifiers are placed as close as possible to the words they are modifying; your reader should know exactly what the modifier is describing. A *misplaced* modifier is placed close to a word it is not meant to describe. A *squinting* modifier could be describing either of two items in a sentence.

3. Make sure a modifying word or group of words is attached to a word in the sentence. A *dangling* modifier is not attached to a word in the sentence.

MODIFIER REVIEW

Rewrite the following paragraph so it is free from modifier errors. (See end of text for suggested revisions.)

Having studied the financial and statistical data thoroughly, this report has been written by the evaluation committee. We have only considered the most recent information; however, a secondary committee has been established by the division managers that will research the historical background of the problem carefully. When complete, both committees will make the reports available to all employees.

CHAPTER TEST 19-1   Fix any modifier errors in the following sentences. In some cases, you may have to add missing information.

1. Please acknowledge by October 15 the invitation to the farewell dinner.

2. The notice to all personnel hanging in the lobby was destroyed by a vandal.

3. As a student, research materials filled my desk drawers.

4. Tim only decided to visit Pleasanton this week.

5. After working on the plans for six months, the new building was abandoned by the committee.

6. Upon being promoted, my job will be a real challenge.

7. Eager to make his way through the ranks, Edgar only took two days of sick leave in over five years.

8. Traveling through the South Pacific islands, our enjoyment of warm weather and blue skies increased.

9. Having rudely interrupted, the question from Rufus was ignored by the panelists.

10. Women's soccer is a sport at this university that is gaining interest.

11. Unable to finish the program, Flo's depression increased.

12. Having been carefully evaluated, the team finally accepted the proposal.

13. I just have enough time to finish the projections.

14. Joe has graduated from Greenwich College in Maine with honors.

15. Lorraine decided by Monday to declare bankruptcy.

CHAPTER TEST 19-2   Revise each of the following sentences in two ways.

1. Having studied thoroughly, the exam did not scare me.

   a.

   b.

2. Perry had decided in a week to get married.

   a.

   b.

3. I reluctantly approached the flat tire wearing my new suit.

   a.

   b.

4. Having decided to go into business, it is essential that you study management techniques.

   a.

   b.

5. Having seen the film five times, it was time for us to go home.

   a.

   b.

6. As a graduate student, my interest in archaeology disappeared.

   a.

   b.

7. While revising these letters, an error was spotted.

    a.

    b.

8. To attract college graduates, ads about the job were placed in local newspapers.

    a.

    b.

9. Flying to Tokyo, the storm became intense.

    a.

    b.

10. While walking quickly to work, Jim's ankle became injured.

    a.

    b.

EXERCISE FOR EXPERTS   Revise the following memo. Pay particular attention to problems with modifiers, verbs, and pronouns.

To: All Sales Representatives
From: Allison Hall
Subject: Sales Presentations
Date: June 11, 19xx

Knowing that each of you are planning to make sales presentations in the next month, some guidelines for good presentations seems advisable.

1. Prepare carefully. To be effective, solid preparation is vital. Before arriving for the presentation, your products and guidelines should be carefully reviewed.

2. Know your client. Each client is different and has their own interests. Appealing to those interests are a key to your success.

3. Consider your setting. To be fully effective, the setting for your presentation should be considered. Ask the client to provide a room with enough space and proper lighting whenever possible.

4. Organize your thoughts. Make sure your presentation is well organized, with a strong beginning, middle, and conclusion. This will help your client remember your product.

5. Know your product. Maintaining a personal contact with the client, the presentation should still be professional and accurate. Do not make mistakes about the product.

6. Leave when you're done. While giving each client sufficient time to understand your product, the presentation should not be too long. Overstaying your welcome can harm your good impression at a company. They will remember you as being pushy or irritating.

7. Make follow-up calls. Remember to follow up with each client soon after the presentation in a friendly manner.

CHAPTER 20

PARALLELISM

OBJECTIVES: To recognize parallel structures and use them correctly; to avoid parallelism errors with correlative conjunctions.

Can you spot the errors in the following sentences?

1. Milly is either a marketing major or is a management major.
2. Neither does he head this division nor this office.
3. This company is both interested in energy problems and in their solutions.

Each of these sentences has a parallelism error. The sentences may be revised like this:

1. Milly is either a marketing major or a management major.
2. He heads neither this division nor this office.
3. This company is interested both in energy problems and in their solutions.

Parallelism is a very powerful tool for communicating effectively. It may be used throughout a piece of writing or limited to a single sentence.

As the name implies, a parallel structure sets up and balances similar ideas. These similar ideas, which may be expressed in words, phrases, or clauses, must be written in parallel grammatical forms. Hamlet uses parallel structure in his famous soliloquy:

> To die, to sleep;
> To sleep; perchance to dream: ay, there's the rub.

President John F. Kennedy also used parallelism effectively in many of his speeches:

> All this will not be finished in the first one hundred days.
> Nor will it be finished in the first one thousand days, nor
> in the life of this Administration, nor even perhaps in our
> lifetime on this planet. But let us begin.

If you set up a reader's expectations with a list or a sentence that indicates a balance of ideas, then the grammatical form of your sentence should also be symmetrical.

> I bought a pen, an eraser, and a typewriter ribbon.
> [parallel list of nouns]

> Francis traveled over the hill, through the town, and into the valley. [parallel list of prepositional phrases]
>
> This contract guarantees that we will be paid, that we will work at least thirty hours a week, and that we will receive health benefits. [parallel list of dependent clauses]

LISTS

Parallelism is particularly important in the list format common to memos, reports, outlines, and resumes. Once you decide on a format for your list, stick to it.

> Gerald likes skiing, playing tennis, and to fish. [not parallel]
>
> Gerald likes skiing, playing tennis, and fishing. [parallel: Each item is a gerund used as a direct object.]
>
> Gerald likes to ski, to play tennis, and to fish. [parallel: Each item is an infinitive used as a direct object.]

> My job duties consisted of serving clients, answering the phone, and correspondence. [not parallel]
>
> My job duties consisted of serving clients, answering the phone, and handling correspondence. [parallel: Each item is a gerund phrase.]

> This report was designed (1) to inform employees of the financial situation, (2) to outline possible solutions, (3) and three recommendations. [not parallel]
>
> This report was designed (1) to inform employees of the financial situation, (2) to outline three possible solutions, and (3) to offer three recommendations. [parallel: Each item is an infinitive phrase.]

To cut excess words, you might write the previous sentence like this:

> This report was designed to (1) inform employees of the financial situation, (2) outline three possible solutions, and (3) offer three recommendations.

Self-Check Test 20-1

Fix any parallelism errors in the following sentences. (See end of text for suggested revisions.)

1. We are determined to increase profits, reduce cost overruns, and to raise employee morale.

2. AMC Corporation is in favor of diversification, developing new products, and increasing its market share.

3. Market researchers asked us questions about financial security, personal

    relationships, and whether we owned a home.

4. The interviewers questioned job candidates about their experience and

    what their goals were.

5. We recommend (1) higher wages, (2) better conditions, and (3) having

    fewer hourly employees.

CORRELATIVE CONJUNCTIONS

Correlative conjunctions, which you studied in Chapter 7 (page 78), naturally set
up balanced ideas:

> not only . . . but also
> not . . . but
> both . . . and
> either . . . or
> neither . . . nor
> whether . . . or

Correlative conjunctions demand that you create a grammatical balance in
your sentences.

We not only	went to the seminar
but also	attended the luncheon.
We both	ate the sturgeon
and	drank the martinis.
George either	saw the film
or	read the book.
Kay neither	obeyed the law
nor	obeyed her conscience.

In each of the preceding examples, the words after each correlative conjunction consist of a verb + noun used as a direct object. You can vary this format as
long as both parts of the sentence are balanced:

We ate both	the sturgeon
and	the cream cheese.
We obeyed not	law
but	conscience.
We considered whether	to run
or	to sleep.

SAMPLE PARALLEL STRUCTURES

1. She is neither	an accountant	(noun complement)
nor	an attorney.	(noun complement)
2. Fran not only	writes	(verb)
but also	sings.	(verb)
3. We not only	discussed loans	(verb + direct object)
but also	mentioned insurance.	(verb + direct object)
4. I am traveling both	to Arizona	(prepositional phrase)
and	to Iowa.	(prepositional phrase)
5. Bill is deciding		
whether	to change jobs	(infinitive phrase)
or	to retire early.	(infinitive phrase)
6. Jan has both	taken algebra	(main verb + direct object)
and	studied geometry	(main verb + direct object)
7. We will consider		
either	buying the house	(gerund phrase)
or	renting it.	(gerund phrase)
8. He is not only	competent	(adjective complement)
but also	industrious	(adjective complement)
9. Either	the company will diversify	(independent clause)
or	it will go bankrupt	(independent clause)
10. Henry's suit was		
both	covered with confetti	(participial phrase)
and	stained with wine	(participial phrase)

If you are uncertain whether a sentence is parallel, outline it so you can see the parts more clearly.

> We neither considered the consequences nor the embarrassment. [not parallel]
>
> | We neither | *considered the consequences* |
> |---|---|
> | nor | *considered the embarrassment.* [correct] |
> | We considered neither | *the consequences* |
> | nor | *the embarrassment.* [parallel] |

Naturally, if you *begin* your sentence with the first part of these correlative conjunctions, an entire clause will follow it; therefore, an entire clause must follow the second part.

> | Not only | am I exhausted | |
> |---|---|---|
> | but also | I am disappointed | [Note reversal of subject and verb with *not only*.] |
> | Either | Johnson will retire | |
> | or | he will resign. | |

Self-Check Test 20-2

I. Fix any parallelism errors in the following sentences. (See end of text for suggested revisions.)

1. John Townsend will either major in accounting or in economics.

2. Not only is the new manager a dynamic speaker, but also a good writer.

3. Patty McGonigle can neither type accurately nor can she program computers, but she got an excellent job.

4. The president not only asked us difficult questions, but he also made several personal comments.

5. Determined to start his own business, Lyle has invested both in office furniture and computers.

II. Write sentences of your own using the following components.

1. [*neither . . . nor* followed by nouns]

2. [a parallel sentence with two infinitive phrases]

3. [*not only . . . but also* followed by prepositional phrases]

4. [*either . . . or* followed by clauses]

5. [a parallel sentence with two gerund phrases]

CHECKLIST FOR CHAPTER 20

1. Parallel concepts in a sentence should be presented in parallel grammatical forms.

2. Parallel forms may be single words, phrases, or clauses.

3. Correlative conjunctions divide sentences in two parts, each of which should be grammatically parallel.

PARALLELISM REVIEW

Rewrite the following sentences so they are parallel. Do not *delete* any correlative conjunctions. (See suggested answers at end of text.)

Management is very happy both with the staff's enthusiasm and productivity. To reward you for excellent work, division heads are considering either a memorable company party or offering bonuses. Not only does the company want to encourage such excellent work, but also to let you know that your work is being recognized.

**CHAPTER TEST
20-1**

Fix any parallelism errors in the following sentences.

1. Morris Summers is either very creative or he is very lucky.

2. THF Corporation has been debating whether to declare bankruptcy or sell shares to J & R Inc.

3. The year-end report was designed for stockholders, employees, and for the IRS.

4. Still uncertain about our finances, we have decided neither to take a vacation nor buy new porch furniture.

5. While working for Pacific Investments, I handled customer complaints, accounts receivable, and maintaining the copy machine.

6. My mother told me neither to be a borrower nor a lender, but my bank tells me otherwise.

7. Having traced my memo through the clerical office, the accounting office, and up to Mr. Hammersmith's office, I finally found it in the wastebasket.

8. This plant requires sunlight, plant food, warmth, and that we water it every week.

9. Neither is he going to Spain nor to Portugal; he will be visiting only Baltimore, Maryland.

10. The new manager has decided to invite us over to his house for appetizers, beer, and for all the hot dogs we can eat.

**CHAPTER TEST
20-2**

Fix any parallelism errors in the following sentences.

1. As a marketing major, Connie tried developing and to refine essential business skills.

2. Sam McFarland plays tennis like a pro: he is graceful, accurate, and he is always confident.

3. Michelle will be elected as either chairwoman or as co-chairwoman.

4. I have come here neither to praise nor criticize.

5. Mr. Jansen is very annoyed by honking drivers, screaming baseball fans, and by chattering moviegoers.

6. Neither do I enjoy pizza restaurants nor patronize them.

7. Writing resumes, letters, and dictating memos were her favorite occupations.

8. Not only am I an excellent decision maker, but also an excellent judge of character.

9. The best life, Morris knew, was composed of eating heartily, sleeping soundly, and of making new friends.

10. The manager was not an interesting speaker and neither were his letters.

EXERCISE FOR EXPERTS

Revise the following memo. Watch particularly for parallelism, modifier, and pronoun errors.

To: All Customer Service Employees

From: Bill Gold

Subject: Review of Mail-Order Policies

Date: August 7, 19xx

While reviewing recent customer complaints, there seemed to be some confusion regarding mail-order policies. The following is a summary of problem areas.

1. If a product is either damaged in transit or does not work upon arrival, the customer should return the product C.O.D. immediately. We will both send him a new product and a letter of apology.

2. If the customer says they did not receive the item they ordered, you should both (a) check the order form and (b) the shipping documents.

If the customer ordered incorrectly, he or she must return the item at their own expense either for a refund or an exchange.

If we shipped the wrong order, we will not only send the correct product but also a letter of apology. The customer should return the wrong order at our expense.

3. If the customer says the order has not arrived, check the shipping documents. If the order should have arrived, we will send a replacement order. However, while writing to the client, the statement should be made that they *must* return the original shipment if it does eventually arrive.

PART THREE REVIEW TESTS

**Review Test
3-1**

Now that you have finished Part Three, go back over the test you took at the beginning of the section.

Correct the grammatical errors in the following memo.

To: All Employees

From: Horace Wheeler

Subject: Photocopying Policy

Date: December 4, 19xx

Each of you realize, I am sure, the problems we have been experiencing with our photocopying machines. One of the two machines are always broken; the other always has a line of people in front of it. To ease the photocopying problems, two more machines have been ordered. Until they arrive, however, we should follow these guidelines:

1. Before copying, make sure you really *need* extra copies. We do not need copies of every letter and memo we write.

2. More than five copies of any document should be made on the mimeograph machine, saving time and money.

3. After photocopying, sign the sheet next to the machine. Put both your name and also put the number of copies you made.

4. Whomever uses the machine at the end of the day should give the sheet to Mel Rose or I.

5. There appears to be coffee stains inside the machine that is now being repaired. Do not put coffee cups on the copier!

Thank you for your attention to these guidelines.

**Review Test
3-2**

Cross out the wrong word or words in parentheses.

1. If a person wants to win at sports, (you / he or she / they) can't be afraid of a little pain.

2. Neither the dietitians nor the nurse (realizes / realize) how many pounds of sugar the patient consumes each month.

3. Despite the three economists' claims, the hike in oil prices and the severity of the winter (does / do) affect the new economic policies.

4. Each contestant must submit not only his name but also (his birth date / birth date).

5. There is no doubt about (who / whom) will be the most impressive pitcher for the Jays this season.

6. If you do not want the newspaper, give it to Jennifer or (I / me / myself).

7. The meeting had just (begun / began) when the fire alarm went off.

8. There (appear / appears) to be several controversies concerning the investment policy.

9. Although Barry has worked here longer than (I / me / myself), he is not paid as much.

10. Having (lain / layed) on the couch for an hour, Pete felt well enough to mow the lawn.

Review Test 3-3

The following sentences may contain errors in grammar. Each sentence either is correct or contains one error. Fix the errors, but do *not* make unnecessary changes. (Do not, for example, change the tense of a verb unless the tense is incorrect the way it is.)

1. Driving at high speeds on the desert, our engine exploded.

2. This report is neither accurate nor is it readable.

3. Although the politicians maintain otherwise, we feel sure that the import restrictions and the new legislation does have an immediate impact on our company.

4. "Henry Lowell will award the prize to whomever says the answer first," explained Janice Reilly.

5. Please give the comics to Pam and me: neither of us have read "Peanuts" in months.

6. Sarah has been betting on whom will be our best hitter this season: either James Harvey or Mason Dowell.

7. Bailey has been real diligent in the office this week, but he still makes far too many errors.

8. Although there are fewer secretaries in the accounting office than in our's, management has asked Karen Olsen from accounting to work upstairs.

9. Meg Trenton has been more successful than him, but she is far less interested in her work.

10. In February James will either climb Mount Rose or Mount Hood.

11. If I see a new employee is having trouble, I try to schedule a meeting with them as soon as I can.

12. Having reviewed the experiments, our hypotheses are clearly incorrect.

13. "Have you ever wondered," asked Tom, "how many Pomeranians could fit inside a phone booth? Us math majors claim at least 204 will fit."

14. We didn't decide to buy a house until interest rates had rose over 13 percent.

15. Not only is this contract unfair but also unclear.

Review Test 3-4

The following sentences may contain errors in grammar. Each sentence either is correct or contains one error. Fix the errors, but do *not* make unnecessary changes. (Do not, for example, change the tense of a verb unless the tense is incorrect the way it is; do not alter the subjects of the sentences.)

1. Everyone except Miles and she will meet us at the conference hall.

2. Barry is not only willing but able to join our team.

3. Jayne is the more intelligent of all the analysts at Amtech.

4. If any one of the clerical staff need some assistance, he should call Teresa.

5. Frank plans to implement a new sales strategy for the Trion software at the end of the month, which should increase sales.

6. Who was it who said Mike Lowry would promote whomever successfully designed the company brochure?

7. Does either of the new managers understand the complexities of this product?

8. I hope it's him at the door, since both Hugh and I really need his expertise.

9. Having finished the Addison contract, it is time to begin work on the Smith contract.

10. Petulia has lain the papers somewhere in this office, but no one knows where.

11. Every one of the scientists was invited to give their opinion and read a paper.

12. I know the IRS will not approve of these deductions, but I will trust their kindness.

13. Maria, together with her cousin Elijah, are planning to attend this year's Christmas party.

14. Neither of the accountants have agreed to the ledger system we have developed.

15. John Martin believes the United States' trade policy is doomed to failure. Even if some manufacturers benefit over the short term.

Review Test 3-5

Fix any grammatical errors in the following sentences.

1. The recommendation made by our committee members have not been implemented by management.

2. "Do you prefer typing, filing, or to take dictation?" Mr. Harbison asked us.

3. Neither the sales manager nor the production manager have submitted his expense account.

4. Here is both Tom and Jenny.

5. You may either send a check or a money order.

6. My sister is somewhat shorter than me, but she weighs 10 pounds more.

7. Although its already too late to attend the clearance sale today, we can get some good bargains tomorrow.

8. Who do you believe owns the business—George or Henry?

9. While arranging the beautiful roses on the desk, the vase was broken by Beryl.

10. If you submit the reports to either Mr. Kaski or I, one of us can proofread them for you.

Review Test 3-6

I. Fix any grammatical errors in the following sentences. Do not make unnecessary changes: do not alter the tense of the verb, for example, unless the tense is currently incorrect. Do not alter the SUBJECTS of the sentences. Some sentences may be correct.

1. During a conference last month with his two advisers, Edward Murphy explained, "I don't want the news broadcast yet, but, just between you and me, this firm's in deep trouble with regard to their auditing procedures."

2. Who are you expecting to work the night shift—Huey or her? I hope it's he, since she is studying for exams.

3. After Isabelle had layed in the sun for six hours, she neither felt like standing up nor felt like eating lunch.

4. Forrest Connors has finally decided that it's best for the firm to declare bankruptcy, however, he wants to delay the announcement until spring.

5. My analysis became more confused, trying to apply all the theorems Dr. Short had condensed for the class.

6. Now that Sheila has listened to everybodys complaints, she is going to consider five recommendations.

7. The number of potential voters in Sutter County were badly underestimated by the census takers; in fact, the estimate may be as much as 20 percent too low.

8. Has Mr. and Mrs. Lee really considered the potential problems with either buying a new house or subletting their present one?

9. Although each of the marketing representatives have decided to give her presentation on Monday morning, the two division managers' presentations have been postponed until Wednesday.

10. Having withstood the strain of Juneau, Alaska, for fifteen years, my car does not seem badly affected by its last six months in Burlington, Vermont.

11. Kathy Monahan has informed her boss that, while Tim is the most creative of the two accountants, Tom is the more reliable.

12. "Every one of you," said Mrs. Cooke, "is familiar with not only the personnel manual but also with the guidelines I wrote last spring."

13. When we did not receive the printers we had ordered from our suppliers, we were told the problem stemmed from they're poor interstate delivery system.

14. Who does Randy believe telephoned about the advertising contract?

15. By September, when I begin looking for a job, I will not only have a B.S. in business administration but also six years of experience in the restaurant business.

II. Fill in the blanks with the correct form of *who, whom, whoever,* or *whomever.* Do not alter the sentences.

W_____ do you think Georgia will select to head the new division? I hope _____ it is will be dynamic and aggressive. Henry Farr told me that Georgia will select someone _____ can carry out her detailed instructions and _____ everyone here both likes and respects. Personally, I will offer congratulations to _____ can work with everyone on the staff and still remain sane.

Review Test 3-7   Revise the grammatical errors in the following memo.

To: Fred Murchison
From: Myra Turner
Subject: New Collection Letters
Date: June 10, 19xx

There seems to be some problems with our present collection letters to our loan customers. They are too long, too impersonal, and they are too difficult to understand. While shortening and clarifying these letters, it would seem we should also set up a more consistent approach. I suggest we adopt a three-letter format.

1. The first letter should be a friendly reminder. Telling the customer that they have to pay in order to keep their good credit. Enclose both a copy of the bill and enclose a postage-paid envelope with the letter.

2. The second letter must be firmer. While requesting full payment, an offer to refinance the loan could be included. Make sure you tell them that you *must* hear from them by the end of the week.

3. The third letter must be *very firm*, you should mention taking legal action for the first time. After summarizing the situation, the customer should be offered a final opportunity to pay before legal action is initiated.

When you have drafted these three letters, please send copies to Bill Herman and I. Before putting them in final form, they should be reviewed by management.

PUNCTUATING SENTENCES

FAMOUS FIRST DRAFTS: GENERAL MACARTHUR
Writing Hint: Be Personal

Source: Ford Button

I shall return.

Reading for Resourceful Writers

The Young and the Freckled A Play Without a Pause

Successful attorney Esmerelda Martinez is torn between the wealthy engineer Bart Randolph and the freckled hardworking but poor bicycle repairman Elbert Smith her parents wish her to marry Bart but she has felt duty bound to marry Elbert ever since he threw himself in front of a moving bicycle to save Birdee her canary from being run over the scene takes place in Esmereldas office while several clients wait impatiently for her in the next room

BART	You know I love you Esmerelda why wont you marry me
ELBERT	She is going to marry me Bart even though I have freck les I showed my love by rescuing Birdee from the im ported 10 speed racing bike
BART	I showed my love by buying her a dual cassette dictating machine to increase her productivity and save precious time in her working days
ESMERELDA	Stop bickering and hand me that copy of Deerings California Penal Code I have to return it to the university law library
ELBERT	If you marry me I will hand you books anytime you need them as long as I am through with my gardening and household chores
BART	If you marry me you could afford a law library of your own
ESMERELDA	Could I buy a photocopy machine as well
BART	Of course dearest Essie Id let you buy only the best just say yes and the photocopy machine will be yours
ESMERELDA	That settles it then I will marry you Bart sorry Elbert but Im afraid youve just lost your chance you can take Birdee with you when you leave

PART FOUR OBJECTIVE: To punctuate sentences correctly.

Punctuation arrived relatively late in the history of writing. Much of the trouble scholars have today while deciphering old manuscripts stems from phrases and sentences running together without a recognizable pattern of marks. In the past 200 years, however, English punctuation has been systematized so that consistent rules apply to most situations.

You may find the principles of punctuation confusing when you first begin studying them. Soon, however, you will see the utility of consistent usage. Punctuation marks provide what might be termed road signs for the reader.

In the Reading for Resourceful Writers that you have just read, you find a humorous example of what happens when a writer leaves out punctuation altogether. Because they clarify written communication, punctuation marks considerably reduce ambiguity and confusion.

Moreover, you will soon find that punctuation can contribute to the effectiveness as well as the readability of your messages: at times, punctuation may be as useful as word choice and sentence structure in producing a piece of writing that gets results.

Before you start Chapter 21, test your knowledge of punctuation with the following Pre-Test.

PART FOUR PRE-TEST

Correctly punctuate the following paragraphs. Do not add, delete, or alter any words. (Check your answers at end of text.)

Tom Carpenter who works as an executive with Towne Company makes an excellent salary, and has always been satisfied with his job. His boss says, "Tom is one of this companys best managers, he is intelligent, thorough and conscientious". Management considers Tom a practical man with skills and adaptability, that give him a maturity beyond his years.

Now that Tom has been with the company for over twenty three years he is being seriously considered for the position of vice president. Tom however is not certain he wants to make the move to New York that the promotion would entail so he is evaluating his options, and discussing them with his family and with his friends' in the company.

PERIODS, QUESTION MARKS, EXCLAMATION POINTS

OBJECTIVES: To use periods, question marks, and exclamation points correctly and effectively.

Do you recognize any punctuation errors in the following sentences?

> Jonah wondered if there were any calls for him?
> George asked, "Are you coming to lunch."
> "Help," exclaimed the startled driver.

Punctuation errors occur in each of the preceding sentences. Correctly punctuated, they should read:

> Jonah wondered if there were any calls for him.
> George asked, "Are you coming to lunch?"
> "Help!" exclaimed the startled driver.

Periods, question marks, and exclamation points are used to mark the end of sentences. Periods mark the end of declarative and imperative sentences and the end of indirect questions. Question marks indicate the end of questions. Exclamation points are used after some words, phrases, clauses, or sentences that show a strong emotion.

Periods, which are also used with abbreviations, are the most commonly used of the three marks, while exclamation points appear infrequently in business writing.

PERIODS

Declarative Sentences

A period should appear at the end of every declarative sentence. The vast majority of sentences (including this one) are declarative. Declarative sentences simply make statements.

> We hired a new programmer.
> The city is declaring a holiday.

Imperative Sentences

Imperative sentences are commands or requests. (Often the subject is understood to be *you*.) If the command is phrased mildly, end it with a period.

> Deliver the books by Friday.
> Tell me your story.

Indirect Questions

Indirect questions are paraphrases of questions: they restate questions. End indirect questions with periods.

> I wondered if Katie had finished her letter.
> Fred asked me whether there had been a change in
plans.

Fragments

As we studied in Chapter 13, a sentence must contain an independent clause. Do not put a period after a fragment.

> Mr. Bernard having won the election. [fragment]
> Having won the election, Mr. Bernard gave a speech.
[correct]

Comma Splices

A comma can only interrupt a sentence; it cannot end a sentence. If you combine two sentences with a comma, you create a comma splice. Remember, if your clause is not prefaced by a subordinate conjunction or relative pronoun, it is almost always an independent clause. Most independent clauses should end with a period.

> Mrs. Hansen has arranged the meeting, it will certainly
> be a success. [comma splice]
> Mrs. Hansen has arranged the meeting. It will certainly
> be a success. [correct]
> I have prepared the food, however, the drinks are not
> made. [comma splice]
> I have prepared the food. However, the drinks are not
> made. [correct]

Note: Remember that *however* is not a coordinate conjunction; do not use *however* plus a comma to link two independent clauses.

(For other ways to separate independent clauses, see page 269.)

Periods and Quotation Marks

Periods should always appear inside quotation marks.

> Geraldine said, "The stocks are doing well."
> "I am certain," said the engineer, "that my plans have
> been stolen."

Do not put a period in the middle of a quotation unless the quotation contains more than one sentence. A period in the middle of a sentence creates fragments.

> "I often wonder." said Jean, "Where the world is head-
> ing." [Both punctuation and capitalization are incorrect.]
> "I often wonder," said Jean. "Where the world is head-
> ing." [Punctuation and capitalization are incorrect.]
> "I often wonder," said Jean, "where the world is head-
> ing." [Correct: Jean has said only one sentence.]
> "Life is a gamble," argued Fritz. "The house always
> wins." [Correct: Fritz has said two sentences.]

(For more on punctuating quotations, see pp. 280–281.)

Abbreviations

Put a period after most abbreviations: *Dr., Mrs., dept., Jan., govt.*

Periods have disappeared from some abbreviations (*NASA*) and are optional with others (*U.S.A., USA*). Your dictionary will help you if you are in doubt, but in most cases the periods will be correct.

If the abbreviation comes at the end of the sentence, use only one period.

> I am leaving at 2:00 p.m.. [incorrect]
> I am leaving at 2:00 p.m. [correct]

Abbreviations of States

The United States Postal Service has developed two-letter abbreviations for the names of states. These abbreviations are not followed by periods: AL (Alabama), AK (Alaska), AZ (Arizona), and so on. Use these abbreviations on envelopes and the inside address of letters. (See Appendix A for business letter formats.)

Self-Check Test 21-1

Correctly punctuate the following sentences. (Check answers at end of text.)

1. This is the first day of the new project, we are very nervous about it.

2. Please let me know when it is 3:00 p.m..

3. Lend Tom a hand with the typing. If you have some free time.

4. I am looking forward to meeting Mr Howard, he is a well-known

   economist.

5. I wonder if the meeting is over?

QUESTION MARKS

Direct Questions

While a period should come after an indirect question, a question mark should appear after a direct question.

> Is there any hope for the future? [direct question]
> I wonder if there is any hope for the future. [indirect question]
> Sharon asked, "Is there any bread?" [direct question]
> Sharon asked if there was any bread. [indirect question]
> "Have you spoken to James?" asked the manager. [direct question]
> The manager kept demanding whether we had spoken to James. [indirect question]
> Janice wondered if she would get a promotion. [indirect question]
> Did Janice get the promotion? [direct question]

Make sure your question mark appears after the actual question.

Will she be promoted, I wondered? [incorrect]
Will she be promoted? I wondered. [correct]

Questions and Quotations

A question mark goes inside the quotation marks if it is part of the quoted material.

Marilyn asked, "Are you well enough to work?"

If the question is not part of the quotation, the question mark goes outside the quotation marks. Do not use both a period and a question mark at the end of a sentence.

Have you ever heard Mr. Tynan say, "Go home early, boys"?

If you are writing a question that ends with a quoted question, omit the question mark outside the quotation marks.

Have you ever seen the comedy routine titled "Who's on First?"

Self-Check Test 21-2

Fix any punctuation errors in the following sentences. (See end of text for answers.)

1. Cheryl asked me if I was well?

2. "Have you ever traveled," Herman asked. "to Brazil?"

3. "The sunset is overwhelming," said Frank, "therefore, I have ordered

   dinner on the terrace."

4. The new business has potential. If Carstairs has the capital to keep it

   going for six months.

5. May I expect a call from you next week. I look forward to hearing from

   you.

EXCLAMATION POINTS

Interjections

An interjection, as we saw in Chapter 8, is often followed by an exclamation point. You will not be using exclamations very frequently in business writing, but you may use them occasionally in dialogue.

"Hey!" exclaimed George.
"Viva!" yelled the crowd.

Emotion   You may also use exclamation points simply to make your statements more
                   emotional or emphatic, but do not use them too often.

                          Sales are up!
                          Call me!

**Exclamations   When you use exclamation points in quotations, follow the same rules as you do
in Quotations**   with question marks: put the exclamation point inside the quotation marks if the
                   exclamation is made by the speaker.

                          "Hello!" cried Laura's echo. [Exclamation is the
                          speaker's.]
                          Laura's echo cried, "Hello!" [Exclamation is the
                          speaker's.]
                          After five years, Laura finally said, "Hello"! [Exclama-
                          tion is the writer's.]

Self-Check Test 21-3

Correctly punctuate the following sentences.

1. Will we ever recover from this lawsuit.

2. "No," shouted the crowd. "We won't take it anymore"!

3. Cheryl asked us if we would consider a merger?

4. The school is putting on a production of "Oklahoma"!

5. The economy is improving, sales are sure to rise.

**Checklist for   1. Put a period after declarative and imperative sentences, after indirect
Chapter 21**   questions, and after most abbreviations.

                   2. Put a question mark after direct questions.

                   3. Put question marks inside quotation marks if the speaker is asking the
                       question.

                   4. Put exclamation points after words, phrases, clauses, and sentences that
                       indicate a strong emotion.

Punctuation Review

Punctuate the following paragraphs. Do not change any words. Some sentences may be correct; some sentences may have more than one error. (Check answers at end of text.)

There is a story about a college freshman looking for the cafeteria on the first day of school. Approaching a professor on campus. The student asked, "Excuse me, where's the cafeteria at"?

The professor looked sourly at the student, "Young man, never end a sentence with a preposition".

"Yes, sir," the student replied. "So where's the cafeteria at, fathead?"

Chapter Test 21-1   Correctly punctuate the following sentences. Do not add or delete words. Some sentences may be correct.

1. The manager was uncertain about the budget, he asked his assistant to review the figures.

2. Charlie called excitedly to his friend, "Hey! I finally graduated"!

3. Will this inflation ever stop, Jessica wondered?

4. Hank said calmly, "Randy Philips is apt to be long-winded!"

5. Will you help me with the statistics next week?

6. We are altering our benefits policy. Because employees have been leaving the company.

7. Please let me know if Mr Peterson calls the office.

8. "In advertising," someone once wrote, "there is a direct, inverse proportion between the number of adjectives and the number of facts".

9. Despite the personnel problems, this company is planning to expand

10. Thelma hopes we will be on our way to Dulles Airport by 4:00 p.m..

**Exercise for
Experts**   Correctly punctuate the following letter.

FTG Stores

5689 B Street

Loomis, IA. 49021

February 9, 19xx

Mrs Michael Lancy

456 Rich Avenue

Loomis, IA. 49022

Dear Mrs Lancy:

Thank you for ordering a Dish-King dishwasher from us, we have found that model to be particularly popular with our customers.

Because so many of our customers have ordered Dish-Kings from us this month, we have had to order more from our factory in Des Moines. The new order will arrive on February 20. Will this delay be an extreme inconvenience for you.

If you urgently need a dishwasher for the next ten days or so, we can arrange to rent you one of our Wash-All machines for a very minimal cost, just call 455-6789 to let us know.

We will be delivering your Dish-King on Friday, February 21 sometime after 1:00 p.m.. If you cannot be home that afternoon, we can also deliver on Saturday.

Thank you for your patience, Mrs Lancy. We hope you enjoy your new Dish-King. As we always say, "Our Dish-Kings are real kings"!

Sincerely,

Ed Feeney, Manager

Service Dept

CHAPTER 22

COMMAS

OBJECTIVES: To use commas correctly and effectively; to avoid using unnecessary commas.

Commas help to make your writing more understandable. They act as guides to tell your reader what is essential in your sentence and what is less important; they also tell the reader when you have come to a small break or a change in your thoughts.

Probably because commas are used more often than any other punctuation mark, they present more problems for writers than do other punctuation marks. Some people, apparently, learned to insert a comma "whenever they took a breath," while others learned that commas are elusive marks to be used more or less at the writer's discretion.

In actuality, commas are governed almost entirely by basic principles. Once you have mastered these principles, you will see that commas are an aid, not a hindrance, to your writing.

BETWEEN CLAUSES

Main Clauses

Use a comma before a coordinating conjunction (*and, but, so, or, nor, for, yet*) if it links two independent clauses.

> We have gotten their support, so we will be victorious.
> McMahon won the election, but he did not win our hearts.

You may omit the comma if the two clauses are very short and the reader cannot possibly be confused.

> Either Mason is confused or he is lying.
> Marsha appeared and the meeting began.

INTRODUCTORY ELEMENTS

Introductory Modifying Clauses

A modifying dependent clause at the beginning of a sentence must be followed by a comma.

> When I arrived, the steaks were ready.
> If I have time, I will take on the project.
> Since I turned 30, my hair has turned blonde.

These clauses begin with "warning words" such as *after, although, as, because, before, since, until, when, whether,* and *while.*

If the dependent clause acts as the subject of the sentence, it will not be set off with a comma.

> *Whoever wins this race* wins the trophy.

Self-Check Test 22-1

Correctly punctuate the following sentences. (See end of text for answers.)

1. As soon as you finish the negotiations, call Phillip Carstairs.

2. The new regulations have not affected our morale, and they have not affected sales.

3. This old product contains artificial sweeteners, but the new one is sweetened naturally.

4. Our agenda is overcrowded, we should delete the final item.

5. Whether we have time for lunch, is not an important issue.

Introductory Prepositional Phrases

If an introductory phrase runs longer than four or five words, it should be followed by a comma.

> At the turn of the last century horses were prized possessions. [incorrect]
> At the turn of the last century, horses were prized possessions. [correct]

Other Introductory Phrases

If a modifying verbal phrase appears at the beginning of a sentence, a comma should separate it from the rest of the clause.

> Singing softly, Jack removed the last candy bar.
> Having won the argument, Petrini became silent.
> To get the best perspective, we stepped backward.

Self-Check Test 22-2

Correctly punctuate the following sentences. (Check answers at end of text.)

1. Having hit the ball out of the park, Tim headed around the diamond.

2. As long as we are still increasing sales, we should not change our

approach.

3. At the beginning of the report, Klein makes several good points.

4. After their performance today, Fred Rivera and Don Field will be handling

the new account.

5. Relying heavily on his notes, the speaker droned on all morning.

SERIES

Lists

Commas are normally used between items in a list. A list consists of three or more items: do not use a comma between *two* items. A list may consist of individual words, phrases, or clauses.

> I have read every book, magazine, and journal in the house.
> The report focuses on tax deductions, on insurance, and on investments.
> We invited everyone who had won, who had lost, and who had attended.

Coordinate Adjectives

Coordinate adjectives modify the same word or group of words. These adjectives must be separated by commas OR conjunctions. If you cannot put *and* between two adjectives, you should not put commas between them.

> That *tall, handsome* man is an accountant.
> That *tall and handsome* man is an accountant.
> An *impressive, exciting* movie is playing at the Strand.
> An *impressive and exciting* movie is playing at the Strand.
> I bought a small and Irish setter. [incorrect: *Small* actually modifies both *Irish* and *setter*.]
> I bought a small, Irish setter. [incorrect]
> I bought a small Irish setter. [correct]
> Harris works on a large and remote and cattle ranch. [Correct for the first and second adjectives, not for the second and third.]
> Harris works on a large, remote cattle ranch. [correct]
> IBM has created a small and powerful and compact and personal computer. [Correct for all but the last two adjectives.]
> IBM has created a small, powerful, compact personal computer. [correct]

PUNCTUATION HINT: DO NOT PUT COMMAS AROUND MATERIAL
ESSENTIAL TO THE MAIN CLAUSE

What Phil Wrote   *What Rhoda Thought*

Revision: All our clients who have declared bankruptcy are meeting here at noon on Wednesday.
(*Improved* Revision: All our bankrupt clients are meeting here at noon on Wednesday.)

Source: Ford Button

PARENTHETICAL WORDS, PHRASES, AND CLAUSES

A parenthetical element supplements a part of the sentence but is not essential material. Because parenthetical elements may be omitted from a sentence without altering its meaning, commas are used to separate them from the rest of the sentence.

Interjections

Interjections and other nonessential additions to your sentence should be set off with commas unless the sentence calls for an exclamation point, parentheses, or dashes.

> Ah, I had hoped to see Venice this year.

or

> Ah! I had hoped to see Venice this year.
> When do you plan, then, to tour the Capitol?
> I have decided, for example, to stop in Madrid.
> Yes, Claude is very informative about microeconomics.

Appositives

An **APPOSITIVE** is a noun, noun substitute, or phrase set beside a noun to describe it.

My best friend, *Ted Ames*, lives in Kokomo.
Running backwards, *a recent fad*, is surprisingly difficult.

Sometimes appositives are essential to the meaning of a sentence. If they are essential, they should not be set off with commas.

It was my friend *Joe* who lent me the money. [The name *Joe* is essential to identify which friend is being discussed.]

If an appositive is nonessential, however, it should be set off with commas.

Baton Rouge, *the state capital*, is north of here.
Grey, *his favorite color*, does not flatter him.
Herb, *my cousin from Detroit*, works for MGM.

Self-Check Test 22-3

Correctly punctuate the following sentences. (See answers at end of text.)

1. Kentucky, the bluegrass state is famed for its horses and its whiskey.

2. This project in our opinion should be scheduled for next year.

3. "Well if you cannot attend the gallery opening," said Fred, "come to the party afterward."

4. No this production is definitely not acceptable.

5. Katrina the Austrian violinist is also a stock market expert.

Negatives and Contrasts

If you introduce a contrast or negative into your sentence, set it off with a comma.

I voted for Kannis, not Innis.
Pepper, not salt, is the obvious ingredient.

Although you should not separate two items with a comma, you should set off contrasting items. Note the difference between the following:

We have hired secretaries and programmers. [two direct objects: no comma]
We have hired secretaries, but not programmers. [contrasted items: comma]

Direct Address

Anytime you speak directly to someone in your writing, the name must be separated from the rest of the sentence with a comma or commas.

I see, Larry, that our staff has doubled.
Kathryn, Mr. Masters claims we have all done a good job.

Self-Check Test 22-4

Correctly punctuate the following sentences. Some sentences may be correct. (Check end of text for answers.)

1. This small‚elegant Swiss watch has cost us a large amount but not a

    fortune.

2. Please call me‚Mr. Barkeley‚if you are interested in the position.

3. In June I‚will begin work for a small, electronics company in Norman,

    Oklahoma.

4. As you can see‚our portable efficient home computer has two disk drives.

5. When you have seen the Tec-Tan display, write up a short, incisive

    report.

Restrictive and Nonrestrictive Clauses

Restrictive and nonrestrictive clauses are dependent clauses beginning with *that*, *which*, or *who*. Nonrestrictive clauses may be considered nonessential or parenthetical: they may be lifted out of the sentence without seriously altering its meaning.

Clauses beginning with *that* are always restrictive. Never set off a *that* clause with commas.

> I am cleaning the gun, that was hanging on the wall.
> [incorrect]
> I am cleaning the gun that was hanging on the wall.
> [correct]

Clauses beginning with *who* or *which* may be either restrictive or nonrestrictive. To check whether a clause requires commas, you must ask yourself whether it contributes substantially to the reader's understanding.

> Are you writing to the Harris who is a librarian or to the Harris who is company clerk? [Clauses are restrictive since the sentence makes no sense without them.]
> I am going to Sonoma, which is in the wine country. [Comma is needed since *which* clause is adding peripheral information.]
> I am buying the only Mazda on the lot which has been repainted. [No comma: *Which* clause is essential.]
> I have invited my cousin Jamie, who is a talented violinist. [Comma needed: *Who* clause is just adding extra information.]

Dates and Addresses

When writing a date, separate the day of the week from the date; separate the month and day from the year; separate the year from the rest of the sentence.

My mother was born on Sunday, July 4, 1935, in Dallas, Texas.

If you omit the day of the month, omit the comma.

March 1976 was an important month for this company.

If you reverse the day and month, omit the comma.

She graduated on 5 June 1935.

Use commas also between city and state, between city and country. A comma sets off the name of a state or country if it follows the name of a city.

I have often visited Cincinnati, Ohio, in the autumn.
London, England, was filled with tourists.

Self-Check Test 22-5

I. Correctly punctuate the following sentences. (See answers at end of text.)

1. Albany, which is the capital of New York, is a chilly place to spend the winter.

2. This young man is from Paris, France, but he has always wanted to live in Bar Harbor, Maine.

3. This champion collie that has won prizes all over the country, will be our mascot.

4. We arrived in Seattle on January 12, 1984, and did not leave for nearly eight months.

5. Let me know if this accountant is the man, who was recommended by Molly Peters.

II. In the following sentences, commas are used correctly. In the space below each sentence, write the comma rule or rules that apply.

Example: Harry, the best is yet to come. [Use a comma with direct address.]

1. I have moved to Tulsa, my favorite city. (appositive)

2. Marilyn put butter, not margarine, on the shopping list. *{negatives and contrast}*

3. We have seen the picture, and it is exquisite. *main clauses*

4. While Joe was swimming, he hit his head, but he isn't badly hurt. *{intro modifying clause}*

5. In view of the peculiar circumstances, you should see your dentist. *prepositional phrases*

6. Yes, when you are done, see me in my office. *(interjection)*

7. When I inherited the house on July 9, 1975, I also inherited a cockatoo. *(introd modifying clause)*

8. Vera and Willie, admirers of Truman, are writing a book about his child-hood. *(appositive)*

9. Leaping up from the table, Ursula upset the decanter. *modifying clause adverbial phrase*

10. We have won legally, so we are going to enjoy the prize. *(main clause 2)*

Business Letters

Commas are used in specific parts of business letters. (See Appendix A for business letter formats.)

Date: between day and year.

January 12, 19xx

Inside address: between name and title if they are on one line.

Mr. Alan Smith, Director

Inside address: between city and state.

>Barry, ND

After complimentary close.

>Sincerely,

Writer's identification: between name and title if they are on one line.

>Brenda Carter, Manager

EXTRANEOUS COMMAS

Most of the situations in which you must use commas are outlined in the preceding section. Before using a comma, ask yourself if it fits into one of the categories we have just discussed. If you cannot find an appropriate reason for using a comma, you probably should not use it.

Between Two Items

As we have seen, two items are not a list and should not be divided by a comma.

>I belong to both the YMCA, and the Heart Association.
>[incorrect]
>I belong to both the YMCA and the Heart Association.
>[correct]

This rule applies to phrases and even dependent clauses.

>Frank has run in marathons, and in half-marathons.
>[incorrect]
>Frank has run in marathons and in half-marathons.
>[correct]
>Hubert believes that man is potentially perfect, and that
>he is perpetually flawed. [incorrect]
>Hubert believes that man is potentially perfect and that
>he is perpetually flawed. [correct]

Between Compound Subjects and Verbs

Similarly, do not separate two subjects or verbs from each other.

>The new marketing professor, and the assistant dean
>have outlined a new program. [incorrect]
>The new marketing professor and the assistant dean
>have outlined a new program. [correct]
>Cordelia has taken a firm stance on the curriculum, and
>will not listen to complaints. [incorrect]
>Cordelia has taken a firm stance on the curriculum and
>will not listen to complaints. [correct]

Between Subjects and Verbs

Do not put a comma between a subject and verb unless you have inserted material that requires a comma.

>Most of these recent college graduates, are in search of
>technical positions. [incorrect]

Most of these recent college graduates are in search of technical positions. [correct]

Larry Gurstman, our supervisor, has bronchitis. [correct: *Our supervisor* is an appositive that must be set off with commas.]

Short Phrases   Do not interrupt your sentence by separating short internal and ending phrases from the rest of the sentence.

I had decided, in a flash, to visit New York. [incorrect]
I had decided in a flash to visit New York. [correct]
I toured Boston, to learn American history. [incorrect]
I toured Boston to learn American history. [correct]

Self-Check Test 22-6

Fix any punctuation errors in the following sentences. (See end of text for answers.)

1. Last year, Barbara Lomax decided to open a new business, and to sell her condominium on Long Island.

2. Having entered the sweepstakes, Henry, and his sister Maude, waited anxiously for the date of the drawing.

3. Christopher Barley, head of operations, is taking a Caribbean vacation, for two weeks.

4. On Christmas Herb will drive from Green Bay, to Chicago.

5. Since my promotion, in April, I have been working directly for Thelma Forbes.

Checklist for Chapter 22

1. Put a comma before a coordinating conjunction if it links two independent clauses.
2. Use commas to set off introductory elements.
3. Use commas in series and between coordinate adjectives.
4. Use commas to set off parenthetical elements and nonrestrictive clauses.
5. Use a comma to separate the day of the week from the date and to separate the month and day from the year.
6. Use commas to separate city and state, city and country.

7. Use commas to separate the year, state, and country from the rest of the sentence.

8. Use commas in accordance with conventions for writing business letters.

9. Do not use unnecessary commas.

Comma Review

Punctuate the following paragraphs. Some sentences may be correct; some sentences may have more than one error. (Check answers at end of text.)

Working closely with Sam Brown, the manager of the restaurant was the head chef Henry Plante. Henry who often attended meetings with Sam Brown and the restaurant's owner was considered as good a manager as he was a cook. With the approval of Sam Brown, Henry allowed the restaurant employees the most freedom possible.

As one of the waitresses explained, "Everyone here knows one another and working here is really a joy."

On several occasions when well-known customers complimented him Henry relayed the compliments to the rest of the kitchen staff. This courtesy was well received, and gave the employees great pride in their work. Said one employee about Henry, "I've worked in restaurants all my life, but here it's more than just a job, it's a pleasure."

Both the customers, and the owner, believed it was Henry, who made the restaurant such a success.

Chapter Test 22-1

Punctuate the following sentences. Do not change any words. Some sentences may be correct; some sentences may have more than one error.

1. We have come to understand a little of the history but not the personalities of the ancient inhabitants of southern Italy.

2. "Students often do not enjoy what they have to read, or what they have to write," claimed the retiring teacher.

3. The huge brightly lit billboard, that loomed over 42nd Street, has been pulled down.

4. Even though carrots, peas, and spinach may not be my favorite vegetables I still enjoy cooking, and eating, them.

5. Through the years I have encountered a number of sports figures whom I will never forget, many of them, however will be unfamiliar to you.

6. Today at 3:00 pm the new marble and bronze statue will be undraped, and presented to a large noisy crowd of amateur art critics.

7. Joanne asked me if I had ever eaten a truffle? Then she produced one from under the kitchen sink.

8. Some people consider *Catch-22* written by Joseph Heller to be an extremely powerful war novel.

9. Having moved to Rome, Italy the young enterprising journalist began a career which focused primarily on interviewing pasta cooks.

10. I have never read a book, or seen a show, about sports car racing yet I know quite a lot about it.

11. Johann had come to a decision obviously sometime before September 1984.

12. We were welcomed, at the hotel, by a bellboy in an orange silk jumpsuit.

13. On a dreary day in February the Ferrars decided to redecorate the house, and to build new dining room furniture.

14. Writing quickly, and smoking cigarettes, Harry finished his first full-length article in just under twelve productive hours.

15. Because sandwiches are his favorite food, Bernie puts lamb chops, parsley, and potatoes between pieces of bread, and claims nothing tastes better.

Chapter Test 22-2   Fix any punctuation errors in the following sentences. Some sentences may be correct; some may have more than one error.

1. The finance committee has been in conference since noon; however, the meeting may go on for another hour.

2. Although the company has had some setbacks this year, the forecast for sales is still excellent.

3. Mark Langley has agreed, that increased benefits, not increased salaries, will considerably improve employee morale.

4. When you get through with that letter, Martin, please call Marion Fenniman, our consultant.

5. The trip to Bermuda, in fact, is one of the most essential business expenses, listed on my tax returns.

6. Thomas Cohen, founder of DGX Industries, will be speaking today on creative accounting, which he claims is the key to his outstanding, financial and personal success.

7. We have moved our offices from San Francisco, California, to Paris, France.

8. While most of this department was on vacation, the committee voted against building the new annex, that will cost under $250,000.

9. The Smiths have decided, therefore, to put in a swimming pool and tennis courts, before the rainy weather starts again.

10. Paula Kelley, the most efficient analyst on our staff, has requested a month off, she desperately needs some rest.

11. During the long months of negotiations, our tempers grew short, and snappish, and our consumption of coffee increased.

12. Ferdinand, and his brother Maxwell, have decided to start a company that will manufacture neon necklaces at absurdly low prices.

13. Annabelle wondered whether the transaction had already taken place? .

14. This company is considering opening a retail outlet in Korea, and expanding the market for used mainframes.

15. If you like, we will consider your proposal in June, and then we will call a meeting with all department heads.

Exercise for Experts

Correct any punctuation errors in the following memo. You may have to fix some capital letters as well.

To: Staff Writers
From: Felicia Mathers
Subject: Readability of Company Documents
Date: September 4 19xx

Since many of you are new to this company I have put together some guidelines for writing clear company documents. Unlike the management of many companies our management takes pride in clear concise writing, and does not appreciate impressive documents, that mean little or nothing.

1. Remember that our readers have varied educational, and technical backgrounds so use words, which everyone will understand. Do not use a word simply because it shows off your vocabulary and if you must use a technical term, define it.

2. Short sentences are much easier to read than long sentences, with a lot of internal punctuation. Short sentences obviously will become boring if you use them all the time, however, you should try to avoid putting several long complicated sentences in a row.

3. Paragraphing is essential to readability so break up your thoughts into logical paragraphs. Like sentences paragraphs should vary in length, in general, keep them fairly short

4. Use active not passive verbs. Many business writers think that passive sentences are more "businesslike" than active ones. In fact active sentences are usually more concise and readable. Use them whenever possible.

CHAPTER 23

SEMICOLONS AND COLONS, DASHES AND HYPHENS

OBJECTIVES: To use semicolons, colons, dashes, and hyphens correctly and effectively.

Do you see any punctuation problems in the following sentences?

> Georgia suddenly knew the answer; salt.
> Hubert is forty three years old; already he is considering retirement.
> The year 1929 altered many people's ideas concerning economic theories.

They should be punctuated like this:

> Georgia suddenly knew the answer: salt.
> Hubert is forty-three years old; already he is considering retirement.
> The year 1929 altered many people's ideas concerning economic theories.

SEMICOLONS

Semicolons are easy to work with as they are used in only two major areas. Just remember not to confuse them with colons.

Independent Clauses

In Chapter 13 (p. 140), we discussed ways of separating two independent clauses. One option was to put a semicolon between the clauses.

> The corporation is merging with Reynolds. Now our head office will be in Atlanta. [correct]
> The corporation is merging with Reynolds, so now our head office will be in Atlanta. [correct]
> The corporation is merging with Reynolds; now our head office will be in Atlanta. [correct]

A semicolon usually operates like a period by combining independent clauses. Do not use a semicolon between an independent and dependent clause or between phrases.

> The Chilean government has chosen to meet privately with Peruvian representatives; not with the Brazilian leaders. [incorrect]
> The Chilean government has chosen to meet privately with Peruvian representatives; Chileans will not meet with the Brazilian leaders. [correct]
> The Chilean government has chosen to meet privately with Peruvian representatives, not with the Brazilian leaders. [correct]

As we have mentioned before, conjunctive adverbs like *therefore* and *however* may not be used with commas to separate independent clauses. On the other hand, you may want to use a semicolon with conjunctive adverbs.

> The time has come, however, we are not prepared. [incorrect]
> The time has come; however, we are not prepared. [correct]

Note that the word following the semicolon is not capitalized—unless, of course, it is a proper noun.

Lists

In most lists, as we discussed in Chapter 22 (p. 256), the items will be separated by commas. If items in the list already have commas, however, separate the items with semicolons.

> The Threepenny Circus is visiting Birmingham, England, Marseilles, France, and Zurich, Switzerland. [incorrect]
> The Threepenny Circus is visiting Birmingham, England; Marseilles, France; and Zurich, Switzerland. [correct]

COLONS

You already know to use colons when giving the time of day, such as 4:20 p.m. You will also find them after salutations in letters (see Appendix A) and before a list, quotation, or explanation.

Salutations

In a business letter, a colon, not a comma, should follow the salutation.

> Dear Mr. Leary:
> Dear Dr. Chan:

Explanations, Summaries, Series, Quotations

Colons are also used to set off or highlight the material to follow. This material might be an explanation, a summary, a series, a quotation.

> We can find only one reason for the error: carelessness.
> This report examines three problem areas: budget, personnel, organization.
> We have ordered the following items: five boxes of disks, three typewriter ribbons, eight bottles of correction fluid, and nine reams of paper.

In *True Patriotism*, Charles Eliot Norton wrote: "The voice of protest, of warning, of appeal is never more needed than when the clamor of fife and drum, echoed by the press and too often by the pulpit, is bidding all men fall in and keep step and obey in silence the tyrannous word of command. Then, more than ever, it is the duty of the good citizen not to be silent." [correct since quotation is lengthy]

Clauses

Colons may also separate two independent clauses if the second explains or enlarges upon the first.

After the first hour of the seminar, everyone was exhausted: we had already covered 15 types of word processing programs.

Note: Avoid using a colon after a form of the verb *be* when highlighting material that follows.

My favorite books are: *Bambi* and *Stuart Little*. [incorrect]
My favorite books are *Bambi* and *Stuart Little*. [correct]

Self-Check Test 23-1

Fix any punctuation errors in the following sentences. (See end of text for answers.)

1. The ice has formed crystals on every twig; a beautiful sight.

2. In the spring Jerry is traveling to Miami, Florida, New York, New York, and Boston, Massachusetts.

3. Prices are right and interest rates are falling: investors are interested in the project.

4. Over his desk, Sergeant Ames has pinned these words of Sherlock Holmes; "When you have eliminated the impossible, whatever remains, *however improbable*, must be the truth."

5. ERC has developed a new personal computer: however, production has been limited to a few hundred machines.

DASHES

Dashes mark a sudden change in thought or an interruption in your sentence. Dashes may be used at times in place of colons to precede an explanation or illustration. They can be very effective, but do not overuse them.

Dashes may replace commas, semicolons, colons, and other punctuation marks. Dashes are almost always optional; another punctuation mark may usually be used instead. But a dash may be very effective in highlighting part of your sentence.

If your keyboard does not have a dash, use two hyphens with no spaces before, after, or between them. When writing by hand, you should make a dash about twice as long as a hyphen.

Abrupt Change

Use a dash when you want to indicate a sudden change in your thought or tone.

> Jason is extremely irritated—no, *angered* is a better word—by these interruptions.

Emphasis

Dashes may set off or emphasize an explanation or example.

> Fred has learned two things that win him satisfied customers: good service and a smile. [correct]
>
> Fred has learned two things that win him satisfied customers—good service and a smile. [correct]
>
> The office has been organizing Margaret Lee's birthday party, one she'll always remember. [correct]
>
> The office has been organizing Margaret Lee's birthday party—one she'll always remember. [correct]

Parenthetical Words or Phrases

A dash may be used like a comma to set off nonessential elements in your sentence. If the parenthetical phrase already contains commas, the dash makes the sentence clearer. If you set off a parenthetical word or phrase with a dash in the middle of your sentence, make sure you set it off at the beginning and end of the interruption.

> This corporation—founded, financed, and managed by Fred Murphy is now moving its home office to Salt Lake City. [incorrect]
>
> This corporation—founded, financed, and managed by Fred Murphy—is now moving its home office to Salt Lake City. [correct]

Introductory Series

If your sentence is introduced by a series, use a dash to set off the series from the subject of the sentence.

> Clarity, conciseness, accuracy, and logic—these are essential elements of a good report.

HYPHENS

Hyphens are used when a word must be continued on the following line; they also appear in some compound words, in compound numbers, and in some phrases.

The End of Lines

If you run out of room on a line, you may hyphenate a word and put part of it on the next line. Do not hyphenate frequently; with wide enough margins, you should fit most words on a single line. If you do hyphenate words at the end of lines, consider these principles.

1. Hyphenate a word only between syllables:

    sand- wich   col- lege   com- pu- ter

    > The new and inexperienced management of this corp-
    > oration is hiring a consulting firm. [incorrect: break only
    > at syllable]
    > The new and inexperienced management of this cor-
    > poration is hiring a consulting firm. [correct]

    Check your dictionary if you are unsure where a syllable break occurs. Do not hyphenate words of one syllable such as *filled*, *through*, and *caught*.

2. Do not hyphenate a word if one or two letters must be left at the beginning of a line or a single letter at the end of a line. Avoid hyphenating the following:

    a- round   e- ven   bo- a   happi- ly   dust- ed
    > Our supervisor has assured us in a loud voice that e-
    > nough is enough. [incorrect]
    > Our supervisor has assured us in a loud voice that
    > enough is enough. [correct]

3. Do not hyphenate proper names.

    > The voters have decided to elect a governor of Mary-
    > land who is bipartisan on many key issues. [incorrect]
    > The voters have decided to elect a governor of
    > Maryland who is bipartisan on many key issues. [correct]

    Also, avoid putting a title or initials on one line and the last name on the next.

    > Please give this invitation to L. B.
    > Biggs. [poor form]
    > Please give this invitation to L. B. Biggs. [correct]

4. Do not hyphenate abbreviations such as *Ph.D., a.m., YMCA, NASA.*

    Remember, you may always choose *not* to break a word into two lines: a lot of broken words will slow down your reader.

Compound Words

Through the centuries, English speakers have added new words to the language by compounding them. Many words have gone through three phases: from two separate words, to hyphenated words, to one word. *Rail road*, for example, became *rail-road*, then *railroad. Ever green* became *ever-green*, then *evergreen.*

Many words are currently undergoing this transition, so check your dictionary when in doubt; even dictionaries, however, may differ with each other on some terms.

You are most apt to have questions about words with prefixes such as *inter-, non-, pre-,* and *co-.*

In general, the modern tendency is to eliminate the hyphen between prefix and root unless the resulting word is ambiguous or confusing. Thus, you will have *intercollegiate, nonviolent, prenatal,* and *coauthor.* If you want to indicate that someone is *creating again,* however, you will write *re-create* so your reader will not be confused by the verb *recreate.*

A number of rules pertain to the hyphenation of two or more words. If you are preparing a manuscript for printing, you should consult a handbook or reference work used by the publisher with whom you are working. Similarly, the company you work for may have a "company style" that you should follow. The most common rules for everyday business usage, however, are as follows:

1. Hyphenate numbers between twenty-one and ninety-nine.

    We have thirty-six contestants.

    Usually you will write higher numbers as numerals, but, if you do write them out, use a hyphen if they contain numbers between twenty-one and ninety-nine.

    Over six hundred forty-two people arrived.

2. Hyphenate a compound modifier composed of an adjective and a noun.

    The bank is negotiating a long-term loan.
    The cold-call salesman relies heavily on his own personality and quick wit.

3. Hyphenate a compound modifier when one word is a cardinal number and the other a noun or adjective.

    I bought the three-pound bag of potatoes.
    Carrie gave away her four-hundred-dollar dress.

4. Hyphenate a compound adverb and adjective modifier if the punctuation will clarify the sentence.

    Karen Gant has been termed the best known engineer in the country. [Confusing: Is she the best or the best-*known*?]
    Karen Gant has been termed the best-known engineer in the country. [clear]

    If the adverb ends in *-ly,* do not hyphenate the compound.

    This is a poorly designed machine.
    She wore a brightly colored scarf.

5. Watch for some nouns that are hyphenated or written as one word; they often become two unhyphenated words when used as verbs. Note: *Stand by* and *standby; hand out* and *handout; follow up* and *follow-up.*

    This young man is not looking for handouts.
    We will hand out the brochures after the lecture.

6. Be alert for phrases that commonly require hyphens: *mother-in-law, jack-o'-lantern,* and so on. If you want to combine words in a phrase to make one modifier, you should hyphenate them; but do not use this type of construction too often.

> He is one of my always-too-busy acquaintances.
> Editing this report is one of those to-be-left-till-tomorrow projects.

Self-Check Test 23-2

Correctly punctuate the following sentences. Check your dictionary if necessary. (Check end of text for answers.)

1. When our company opened an office in down-town Baltimore, we insisted on a staggered work schedule to ease employees' commutes.

2. This twenty two person division has been stream-lined by four personal computers and new operating-procedures.

3. Many extra-curricular activities have been planned by the employees-many of whom are former athletes.

4. The police have been examining the eighty pound bags of cement that appeared in our back-yard yesterday.

5. Due to a confusion about the witnesses, Harry had to resign the petition.

Checklist for Chapter 23

1. A semicolon may separate two independent clauses or complex items in a list.

2. A colon follows a salutation in business correspondence and precedes a long quotation, a summary, an explanation, or a list.

3. Dashes are usually optional. They may replace a comma or other punctuation mark to highlight part of a sentence.

4. A hyphen may carry a word over to a second line. Hyphenate only at the syllable break.

5. Hyphenate some compound words and all numbers between twenty-one and ninety-nine.

6. Hyphenate certain adjective + noun and adverb + adjective modifiers as well as phrase modifiers.

Semicolon, Colon, Dash, and Hyphen Review

Correctly punctuate the following sentences. (Check your answers at end of text.)

Since we hired twenty five new salespeople last fall, we have encountered some problems and some advantages. The problems include, more paper-work, increased ordering delays, more customer complaints, and nagging morale problems.

The advantages are obvious, we have made more sales and increased our territory by six hundred-percent.

Now we need to combine our understanding of the situation with some creative solutions. In order to get some feedback from all of you; we will be meeting at 4;30 p.-m. on Monday, August 5. Please let Lorna know if you cannot attend.

Chapter Test 23-1

Correctly punctuate the following sentences.

1. Although Barbara Jenkins is both my supervisor and my mother in law, we managed to work together very successfully to organize twenty five daycare centers nationwide.

2. ITF Incorporated has brought out a powerful new product; one destined to revolutionize the collating process.

3. All the company auditors, even Frances Duffy—agreed to reexamine the short term leases and loan packages.

4. The scalpers are offering fifty dollar tickets for a hundred dollars apiece.

5. Although working at least sixty hour weeks, Marilyn is still following-up on each possible customer.

6. Lofton describes the ordeal as a life-or-death-struggle; part of a businessman's survival strategy.

7. After establishing new guidelines for the position, the personnel committee decided to; advertise for marketing executives in local newspapers, interview four or, at most, five top-notch choices, and make someone a definite offer by mid June.

8. When Jackie Tucker claimed that Henry Mackilin, her supervisor, was doing a second rate job, forty five employees supported her position.

9. With this unprecedented decision-marked only by a star in my diary-began my efforts to found the new business.

10. Ursula claims that; if we were really such a peaceloving nation, we would never have invented the freeway.

Chapter Test 23-2

Fix any punctuation errors in the following letter.

DAYGON BUSINESS MACHINES

678 34th Avenue

Boston MA 09342

April 9 19xx

Mr James Hardy Business Manager

Conway Inc

23 Rideout Rd

Boston MA 01254

Dear Mr Hardy,

Thank you for your letter ordering thirty five BCF typewriters for your newly-constructed offices. We have processed your order immediately, and will have the typewriters to you by April 20.

As you also inquired about our new BCF computers I have enclosed a brochure for your information. These compact machines may be perfect for your business as they have many excellent features; brightness and color controls, three disk-drives, a stand, which comes in three sizes, that may be easily adjusted to each user, and an optional hard disk.

Our sales representative will call you next week to see if you would like a demonstration of the BCF computer.

Thank you once again for ordering BCF typewriters from DAYGON.

Sincerely,

Fred Carruthers, Manager

Exercise for Experts

Fix any punctuation errors in the following paragraphs.

PROOFREADING

Proofreading your work, the last part of the editing process is essential to a clear effective piece of business writing. A poorly-proofread letter or memo indicates to the readers that you do not care about them. They will react the way they would if you appeared in a dirty rumpled suit—or ragged jeans for an important meeting or sales presentation.

The following are some suggestions for effective proofreading;

1. Give yourself time. When you have just finished a piece of writing you are too involved in the work to *see* errors. Take a few hours—or days, if possible, before proofreading. Waiting twenty four hours will let you see your writing in a new light.

2. Read aloud. Many times your "ears" will find an error, that your eyes did not spot. If you read your piece of writing out loud you will often find errors in word usage or grammar. You may also hear long, awkward sentences, or notice logical errors in your presentation.

3. Find an assistant. A second person will often be able to spot errors you cannot see. That person may also give you some valuable reactions to your work. After all you are writing for an audience and an assistant can give you feedback; before you send your piece of writing off to a client, colleague, or supervisor.

CHAPTER 24

QUOTATION MARKS, ITALICS, PARENTHESES

OBJECTIVES: To use quotation marks, italics, and parentheses correctly and effectively.

Do you see any punctuation errors in these sentences?

> We are going to subscribe to "Fortune" this year.
> "Have you ever visited Sardinia"? asked Michelle.
> The company president said that "he was interested in further research."

Each of the preceding sentences has an error.

> We are going to subscribe to *Fortune* this year.
> "Have you ever visited Sardinia?" asked Michelle.
> The company president said that he was interested in further research.

QUOTATION MARKS

Quotation marks are used to mark direct quotations as well as to indicate some titles and to highlight words.

Punctuating Quotations

Put quotation marks around the exact words that someone has spoken or written. Watch carefully for the punctuation accompanying the quotation.

1. Always put commas and periods inside quotation marks.

   > "He is sure to arrange an interview," said Mrs. Fairland.
   > Mrs. Fairland said, "He is sure to arrange an interview."

2. Put a comma between the quoted material and the continuation of the sentence (even if the material from which you are quoting does not have a comma).

   Original material: "Millions for defense, but not one cent for tribute."
   (Robert Goodloe Harper)

   In quotation: "Millions for defense, but not one cent for tribute," wrote Robert Goodloe Harper.

3. Put a comma after unquoted material preceding the quotation.

> Mr. Jacobs is fond of saying, "Let's stay on for dinner."

4. Put a period at the end of a declarative sentence (even if the material from which you are quoting does not have a period).
Original material: "It snowed and snowed, the whole world over,
Snow swept the world from end to end."
(Boris Pasternak)
In quotation: A famous poem by Boris Pasternak contains the line, "It snowed and snowed, the whole world over."

5. Put colons and semicolons outside the quotation marks.

> Every morning at 9:00 a.m., Joel Farley comes in and says, "Good morning"; then he does not speak to us again until noon.

6. Put question marks and exclamation points inside the quotation marks if the questions or exclamations are part of the quoted material. (See p. 287 and pp. 248–250.)

7. Capitalize the first word of a complete quotation. If the quotation is interrupted by unquoted material, capitalize only the beginnings of sentences.

> The Mitchells kept saying, "The grass is greener in Idaho."
> "The grass," said the Mitchells, "is greener in Idaho."
> "The grass is greener in Idaho," said the Mitchells.
> "However, it is often white in the winter." [Note that a period follows *Mitchells* to mark end of first sentence.]

8. If you include an incomplete quotation within your own sentence, you should not capitalize the first letter (unless it is a proper noun) or separate it from the rest of the sentence with a comma. Also, if you quote a word or phrase in your sentence, you do not need a capital letter or commas.

> Bill Land always says that "business ethics" is a contradiction in terms.
> We believe in "keeping our noses to the grindstone."

Indirect Quotations

Make sure you do not put quotation marks around paraphrased material.

> James Detter asked about "the company's investments." [incorrect]
> James Detter asked about the company's investments. [correct: indirect quotation]
> "Tell me a little about AIM's investments," James Detter said. [correct: direct quotation]

Quotes Within Quotes

If you wish to quote material inside a quotation, put single quotation marks on either side. (Your keyboard probably does not have a single quotation mark; use the apostrophe.)

> In this report, Charles quotes an 18th-century political writer: "I have based my position on the remark of Junius, 'One precedent creates another.'"

Slang   You often see quotation marks around slang words or words used in an unusual sense. This usage is appropriate, but, in general, avoid using words that do not fit in the type of writing that you are doing. (See pp. 385–386 for more on slang.)

> If your client is getting "cold feet" about trying the new product, please ask him to call me.

You might want to revise the preceding sentence:

> If your client is hesitant about trying the new product, please ask him to call me.

Emphasis   Avoid putting quotation marks around words for emphasis. Instead, underline or italicize them.

> With this coupon, you receive a "free" barbecue grill! [incorrect]
> With this coupon, you receive a <u>free</u> barbecue grill! [correct]

Self-Check Test 24-1

Correctly punctuate the following sentences. (See end of text for answers.)

1. "In the spring" said Henrietta, "We will begin marketing in Iowa."

2. "Hooper has asked us to consider renegotiating the agreement", said Faith Terrill. "It could mean an important breakthrough for us."

3. Hanser said clearly, "I am now sure of all the facts;" then he told us his preposterous theory.

4. The new Director of Operations, Helen Wong, insisted that "she should be given copies of all her predecessors' reports."

5. When Hank mentions, "leadership," he is referring to us.

Titles   Put quotation marks around the title of a chapter, poem, short story, article, or other printed material that appears within a larger volume. (The titles of publications printed separately should be underlined or italicized.)

> An article entitled "Prices and Profits" appeared recently in *Fortune*.

Also put quotation marks around the titles of songs and episodes in a television series.

The band played an Elvis Presley song, "Jailhouse Rock."

The episode in the series that she remembers was called "In the Teeth of the Evidence."

ITALICS

Since most keyboards do not allow for italics, we must underline words to indicate they are italicized.

Titles

The title of a book, magazine, newspaper, or other publication that appears on its own should be italicized.

> *Time* is one of our most widely read newsmagazines.
> He is the author of *Accounting Made Easy*.

Do not capitalize or italicize *the* before the title of a magazine or newspaper.

> She subscribes to the *New York Times*; I subscribe to the *Washington Post*.

You should italicize or underline titles of movies, television series, and plays.

> We are going to see a performance of *Our Town* tonight.
> Have you ever seen the film *Mr. Smith Goes to Washington?*

While you use quotation marks for the name of a song, you should italicize the title of an album.

> The song "Bonnie Blue Flag" appears on the album *Civil War Songs*.

Foreign Words

Italicize words that clearly are not English. As foreign words become common in English, they are no longer italicized: *role* and *laissez-faire*, for example, now appear in regular (Roman) type. Check a dictionary if you are unsure.

Single Letters

If you wish to refer to a single letter of the alphabet, italicize it.

> Laura cannot pronounce the *r* in New York.
> I have always spelled the word without the *s*.

Emphasis

Avoid continually italicizing words simply to emphasize them. Occasionally, an italicized word can be effective, but too many italicized words will annoy your reader.

> The show is now being aired on *ABC*, not CBS.
> The bonus was awarded to *Mr. Withers*, not to the whole staff.

PARENTHESES

Parentheses, dashes, and commas are all used to set off material that is supplementary or loosely related to the main point of a sentence or paragraph.

Commas are used most commonly for separating this parenthetical material, but dashes and parentheses can be effective in certain situations. While dashes highlight material that is set off, parentheses deemphasize the words they surround.

Avoid overusing parentheses: if you have a lot of unrelated material in a paragraph, you may have organizational problems.

References

In a research paper, you may want to cite the author of a quotation by putting the name in parentheses.

> This management theory has been attacked for its inflexibility. (Addison, *The Problem of Control*, p. 234)

Almost every college department, corporation, and major publication has its own system for setting up and punctuating references: check the accepted format before putting a research paper in final form.

Sentences in Parentheses

If you are putting a full sentence in parentheses, punctuate it as you normally would—with the punctuation inside the parentheses.

> Mr. Harrington has finally agreed to these five changes. (He can be very helpful when he thinks a plan will save money.)
> The members of the legislature appear to be postponing these major issues until after Christmas. (Have you ever known them to do otherwise?)

If you are including a parenthetical sentence within another sentence, you should not capitalize or use end punctuation inside the parentheses.

> If you are planning to meet in the hotel, arrange a specific spot (there are five restaurants and four lobbies).

Non-sentences in Parentheses

If you are including a parenthetical word or phrase within your sentence, do not set off the material with commas or end it with a period.

> Ms. Thomas has contacted (by telegram) John Miller-Tynan.
> LAFF Corporation (the only textile company in Fair Oaks) is planning to hire three hundred local workers.

If the parenthetical material ends the sentence, put the period outside the parentheses.

> Please bring with you all the relevant documents and correspondence (particularly Max Duran's letters).

If the parenthetical material requires a question mark or exclamation point, the mark should be put inside the parentheses.

Lawrence Cannon (who else?) has become the district attorney.

Our new computer (which we have named Irma La Douce!) is going to straighten out our accounting procedures.

Self-Check Test 24-2

Correctly punctuate the following sentences. (See end of text for answers.)

1. Will we ever recover from this lawsuit, Mr. Harrison asked himself?

2. This company is going to build an office building across the street (in the Rose Hill Mall.)

3. We have been discussing "gigot d'agneau," the French version of leg of lamb.

4. "What," asked Manuel Marquez, "are your plans for expanding the market share"?

5. I admit that I voted against the proposal. (I have never voted for a proposal I did not understand).

6. One of my uncles is fond of saying, "Whenever I need something worthwhile in my life, I read Yeats' poem Into the Twilight."

7. My subscription to Newsweek has been renewed.

8. The letter "a" has been omitted from the last word.

9. Mike Olsen (who used to be my supervisor), is now working for MMM in Minnesota.

10. Our motto, "Give what you can give," has not worked very well this year.

WRITING HINT: AVOID DANGLING MODIFIERS

What Mr. Sullivan Wrote   *What Mr. Barry Thought*

Revision: After Max had spoken to the crowd for over an hour, the limousine took him to the airport.

Source: Ford Button

Checklist for Chapter 24

1. Quotation marks set off direct quotations. The first word of a complete quotation should be capitalized.

2. Commas and periods go inside quotation marks; question marks and exclamation points go outside the quotation marks unless they are part of the quotation.

3. Quotations within quotations should be set off with single quotation marks.

4. Quotation marks are used to set off the titles of songs, stories, television episodes, magazine and newspaper articles, poems, and other short pieces.

5. Italics, usually represented by underlining, are used for titles of books, newspapers, television series, magazines, plays, movies, and record albums.

6. Italics are used for foreign words, for single letters, and, occasionally, for words the writer wants particularly emphasized.

7. Parentheses set off and deemphasize material that is loosely related to the writer's main point.

Caution: Punctuation Pitfalls
Quotation Marks and Parentheses

Quotation marks and parentheses present special problems for writers. You should remember a few key points.

1. Periods and commas *always* go inside quotation marks.

    "Hello," she said. "You must be Jeffrey."

2. Semicolons and colons go outside quotation marks.

    I have just finished "Lobbying Wars"; it is
    an excellent article.
    Jon is a "special student": he works
    with us every day for two hours.

3. Question marks and exclamation points go *inside* the quotation marks if they are part of the material being quoted.

    "Help!" she shouted. "Is anyone there?"

4. Question marks and exclamation points go *outside* the quotation marks if they are not part of the material being quoted.

    Have you read the article entitled "Lobbying Wars"?

5. If a quotation is in parentheses, quotation marks go inside the parentheses.

    Jackie ("Bongo") Carter will arrive at noon.
    The slogan on the New Hampshire license plate
    ("Live Free or Die") was my favorite.

6. If a full sentence is in parentheses and is not inside another sentence, put the end punctuation inside the parentheses.

    Mr. Wiggins has been nominated. (He is the
    conservative candidate.)

7. If a full sentence enclosed in parentheses appears inside another sentence, do not capitalize the opening or put a period after the enclosed sentence.

    I bought two puppies (they arrived yesterday) from
    my brother.

    If the enclosed sentence is a question or exclamation, add the end punctuation inside the parentheses.

    I bought two puppies (you should see them!) from
    my brother.

8. If a sentence in parentheses appears at the end of an unenclosed sentence, put the period outside the parentheses.

    I bought two puppies from my brother (they
    arrived yesterday).

**Punctuation
Review**

Correctly punctuate the following sentences. (Check your answers at end of text.)

"Please let me know," said the customer, "when I can expect the lamps to arrive. Do you think they will be here by Friday"?

"No," said the clerk (who was growing very impatient,) "I already said the order would take at least two weeks."

"Two weeks"! The customer was outraged. "I will not be able to finish reading "Romance in Moscow" if I don't have a good lamp."

"I enjoyed that book a lot," said the clerk. "It has a very unhappy ending. You will particularly like the chapter entitled Kiss in the Snow."

Chapter Test 24-1   Correctly punctuate the following sentences. Some sentences may be correct.

1. The problems resulting from cost overruns, (according to Doyle and Rubin Contractors), cannot be solved without litigation.

2. In 1934, Sir Alan Patrick Herbert published a novel (on the problems of the English divorce system) entitled "Holy Deadlock".

3. "Bribery," Mrs. Barbery assured us, "May be common in other countries and even other companies. But it is "not" common in this corporation."

4. Even today, I find it useful to remember a certain rhyme when I write words in which "c" is followed by a combination of "e" and "i."

5. In his speech, Mike Mansard described his own position by saying, "he is the utility man for the whole division."

6. "Have you ever been curious," Luanne inquired "about the recruiting procedures used by our competitors"?

7. My parents frequently forbade us to watch the *boob tube* after dinner; they figured the family could benefit from actually speaking to one another.

8. In a line of the novel *Silas Marner*, "Nothing is so good as it seems beforehand", George Eliot captures a human experience we are all familiar with.

9. Have you ever heard Stan Murchison explain reverse taxation (as he calls it)?

10. *Follow the Leader*, an article on flaws in corporate marketing strategies, was published in a college newspaper before it appeared in the Washington Post.

Chapter Test 24-2

Correctly punctuate the following memo. This test draws on material from Chapters 21, 22, 23, and 24.

To: Sales Employees

From: Jill Monroe

Subject: Personal Service

Date: December 12, 19xx

A recent article in "The Wall Street Journal" highlights a problem we are having in this store. "The customer," writes the journalist "Is considered a commodity not a person in many large department stores. At Christmas time, the impersonal element in these stores makes shopping a nightmare for many people".

This month we expect over two-thousand customers to come through this store. Some of them (I have to admit,) will be disagreeable; all of them will be hurrying. All of us will be tired. Nonetheless, let's try to keep our reputation for "personal" service.

1. Smile at each customer. Try to make customers feel like you are interested in their questions or problems.

2. If people are waiting in line at the cash register, call for assistance, some customers can be helped at the old registers in the back of the store.

3. If a customer has a complicated problem at the cash register (for example, the person is trying to return something but has no receipt,) call me. I will handle the problem, and you can wait on other customers.

4. Wish everyone, "Happy Holidays."

Exercise for Experts
Write a short dialogue (150–250 words) between a job candidate and his or her interviewer. Describe the speakers' attitudes and tones as you quote their words. You may start at any point during the interview. Punctuate the dialogue correctly.

CHAPTER 25

APOSTROPHES

OBJECTIVES: To differentiate between possessive and plural nouns; to use apostrophes correctly with possessive nouns, proper names, dual ownership, companies, abbreviations, single letters, and contractions.

Do you see any errors in the following sentences?

1. When you see this organizations brochure, you will be amazed.
2. Deirdre has invited the Smiths' to dinner.
3. Willie's and Sandra's house is for sale.

The sentences should be punctuated like this:

1. When you see this organization's brochure, you will be amazed.
2. Deirdre has invited the Smiths to dinner.
3. Willie and Sandra's house is for sale.

POSSESSIVES AND PLURALS

Apostrophes serve a very important function, yet many people use them incorrectly. Errors have come about, most likely, because a possessive noun and a plural noun may *sound* exactly alike. People used to writing what they hear have trouble with most punctuation marks—and apostrophes become a special problem.

Once you put your mind to it, however, the difference between a plural and a possessive becomes obvious.

Most English nouns have four forms:

Singular	Singular Possessive	Plural	Plural Possessive
boy	boy's	boys	boys'
governor	governor's	governors	governors'

A few nouns are the same in the singular and plural:

Singular	Singular Possessive	Plural	Plural Possessive
sheep	sheep's	sheep	sheep's
fish	fish's	fish	fish's

A possessive noun indicates *ownership*: it will almost always be followed by another noun that in some sense belongs to the possessive noun. To check whether a noun is possessive, try rewriting the sentence using *of*.

For example, you want to check whether *companys* should be a possessive or a plural in the following sentence.

I have bought the companys computer.

Rewrite the sentence using *of*:

I have bought the computer of the company.

Since the sentence can be rewritten in this way, *companys* must be possessive—and therefore must have a possessive apostrophe.

Note that there IS no actual word *companys*: your choice will be *companies* [plural] or *company's* [possessive].

I have bought the company's computer. [correct]

If the sentence has no possessive nouns, you will not be able to rewrite it in this way. For example, you might wonder whether *secretaries* in the following sentence is possessive:

Georgia gave the bonus to the secretaries.

Can you rewrite the sentence using *of*? No—not without radically altering the meaning of the sentence. So you can be sure that *secretaries* is a simple plural; the secretaries are not yet the owners of the bonus.

FORMATION OF POSSESSIVES

To use possessives correctly, you need only four rules:

1. Before adding an apostrophe, check whether the noun is singular or plural and then check the correct spelling.

2. If your singular or plural noun does not end in *s*, add an apostrophe + *s*.

3. If the noun has more than one syllable and *does* end in *s*, add only an apostrophe.

4. If the noun has only one syllable and does end in *s*, add an apostrophe *or* an apostrophe + *s* depending on pronunciation.

> We have bought the boss's Christmas present. [Add the apostrophe + *s*, since a final *s* is pronounced.]
> The class studied Mars' orbit. [Omit the final *s*, as it is not pronounced.]

Since many singular nouns end in *s* while many plurals do not, you must check the spelling before applying rule 2 or 3. Note the kinds of spelling changes you need to watch for:

Singular	Singular Possessive	Plural	Plural Possessive
company	company's	companies	companies'
lady	lady's	ladies	ladies'
child	child's	children	children's
mouse	mouse's	mice	mice's

CAUTION: These rules for forming possessives apply only to nouns. Remember that possessive personal pronouns do not take an apostrophe. Do not confuse possessive pronouns and contractions.

Self-Check Test 25-1

I.   Write the possessive forms of the following nouns. (See answers at end of text.)

1.   authors

2.   goose

3.   patio

4.   corporation

5.   lease

II. Write the plural possessive forms of the following words. (Check your dictionary or answers at end of text if you need help.)

1.   man

2.   artery

3.   ox

4.   banner

5.   actress

III. Rewrite the following sentences using possessive nouns.

        Example: I assembled the toy of the child.
                  I assembled the child's toy.

1.   I gave the instructions of my doctor to my tennis partner.

2.   Perry has never approved of the antics of those street artists, but he has continued to fight the protests of his fellow businessmen.

3.   The book of that popular novelist is available throughout the country.

4.   I am worried that the attitudes of my colleagues may jeopardize the secrecy of our project.

5.   When the proprietor of these restaurants was in the hospital, the staff of this company helped him to maintain his business and regain his health.

PROPER NAMES

Proper names are made plural or possessive by the same rules as regular nouns; however, they cause special confusion, so they deserve special attention. Like regular nouns, most names have four forms:

Singular	Singular Possessive	Plural	Plural Possessive
Smith	Smith's	Smiths	Smiths'
McVey	McVey's	McVeys	McVeys'

Some names have -es added to the plural:

Singular	Singular Possessive	Plural	Plural Possessive
Ann Forbes	Ann Forbes'	The Forbeses	The Forbeses'
Joe Harris	Joe Harris'	The Harrises	The Harrises'

Again, form the plural possessive after you have decided how to spell the name as a regular plural. You may have to trust to your ear in some cases: do you say an extra syllable when you make the name plural? If so, write the extra syllable.

> We are going to the show with Jane and Joe Kurtz.
> We are going to the show with the Kurtzes.
> I brought Joe Kurtz's manual to the meeting.
> I brought the Kurtzes' manual to the meeting.

COMPANY NAMES

To make a company name possessive, add an apostrophe or apostrophe + s to the final word of the title.

> Jones, Klein, and Jackson's clientele has doubled in three years.
> Sears' famous early catalogs are being displayed in the library.

Some companies have apostrophes in their names: *Macy's*. The name will not change in the possessive.

> Many of Macy's employees have worked there for over twenty years.

DUAL OWNERSHIP

When two or more people own a single item, you should add a possessive apostrophe to the last name on the list:

> Kathy and Bill's lawn mower is being repaired. [They both own the lawn mower.]
> Barry and his wife's business has been successful. [They both own the business.]

If two or more people own separate items, however, you should add an apostrophe to each name.

> Both Jay's and Carl's projects are outstanding. [They have separate projects.]
> My instructor's and Mrs. Farr's automobiles have collided. [They have separate automobiles.]

ABBREVIATIONS

You may use an apostrophe to indicate the plural of an abbreviated word. You may also simply add an *s*.

> The new M.B.A.s hosted a party. [correct]
> The new MBAs hosted a party. [correct]
> The new M.B.A.'s hosted a party. [correct]
> The new MBA's hosted a party. [correct]

LETTERS AND NUMBERS

Use an apostrophe to indicate the plural of a letter of the alphabet or of a number.

> Helga was excited when five *e*'s and four 9's appeared on the screen.
> How many *k*'s are there in the word *bookkeeper?*
> Morris was in college during the 1940's.

CONTRACTIONS

Apostrophes are used in contractions to indicate that one or more letters are missing from a word: *cannot* becomes *can't, would not* becomes *wouldn't*. If you happen to be writing dialogue, you might use an apostrophe to indicate a letter missing from a speaker's dialect: you might write *gettin'* for *getting*.

Self-Check Test 25-2

Correctly punctuate the following sentences. (**See end of text for answers.**)

1. Peter James, one of the new C.P.A.s' in the firm, **has loaned us his**

   cousin Kathryn James house for the weekend.

2. These critics contend that, although Napoleons strategies' and personality

   were known all over Europe, he was actually a very insecure and private

   person.

3. I should'nt have stayed out late on Wednesday, but I enjoyed the movies'

   humor so much that I sat through the show three times.

4. Although he's belonged to the Bentleys tennis club since the 1960s', he

   has never seen they're children on the courts.

5. Lets go in either Peter's or Larry's car so we can be sure to arrive before

   the Redskins are on the field.

Checklist for Chapter 25

1. Use apostrophes with possessive nouns and contractions.
2. Use apostrophes to indicate the plural of letters and numbers.
3. If the noun ends in *s* before you make it possessive, then add only an apostrophe. (If the word has only one syllable and ends in *s*, add an *s* after the apostrophe only if you pronounce the final *s*.)
4. If the noun does not end in *s* before you make it possessive, add an apostrophe and an *s*.
5. If two or more people own the same item, make only the last name possessive; if items are owned separately, make each name possessive.
6. Remember that possessive pronouns do not have apostrophes; do not confuse possessive pronouns and contractions.

**Apostrophe
Review**

Correctly punctuate the following sentences. (Check end of text for answers.)

1. The new managers abrasive personality may seriously affect the employee's in this division.

2. Joseph Conrads books, especially *Heart of Darkness,* can be instructive for anyone studying the history of imperialism.

3. According to a recent analysis, our countries school system has been severely damaged by economic factors.

4. The mens department in this store features pink tuxedos especially for customer's with large bank accounts and little taste.

5. Since the employees morale has been hurt by the overload, everyone will be happy to see the salaries proposed for next year.

6. Both the Smiths and the Browns are taking vacations in Canada this year; we're handling they're itineraries' for them.

7. When the facultys decision is final, Karen will send a memo to all the people involved.

8. Jane's and George's car will be in the shop until Monday; until then, they will use Bill Taylors Volvo.

9. Shouldn't you examine the report before you ask the C.P.A.s to your office?

10. Both the apartments' are for rent; you might look at them before signing a lease for that doctors apartment.

Chapter Test 25-1

Correctly punctuate the following sentences. Do not alter the meaning or the words in the sentences.

1. If you are'nt going to attend the two receptions, you should leave a note in the division managers mailbox; she is developing the final guest lists.

2. Several Ph.D.s' who had been teaching in the 1970s were asked to speak on this nations' academic past and future.

3. The Goldmans house is located between Harry's Cafe and Patricia Turners' backyard.

4. Since the presidents' return from Miami, both vice-presidents have been working fifty hours a week.

5. When we have decided the Farradays' and Whitmans' departure dates, we will meet with them concerning their accommodations and ticket purchases.

6. If the United States population were as large as that of China, we might have different perspectives on hundreds of issues.

7. Filbert has'nt decided whether to do all the secretary's work while they are gone or to hire temporary clerical workers.

8. If you are interested in seeing the Braves play some home games this summer, call me at Maureen or Cathy's apartments.

9. Since its been six weeks since we last met, the consultants have summarized their work in this letter.

10. On Thursdays, Jewel Barker usually telephones her two assistant's offices to request schedules for the following week.

Exercise for Experts   Correctly punctuate the following letter.

Dear Mrs. Hollins,

I am sure you have often heard the words, "Clearance Sale"! in television and radio commercials. (Perhaps youve heard them so often that you do'nt *hear* them at all anymore). We at Bradstock's Department Store know your tired of sales. But are you still tired of saving money?

Bradstock's saves you money all day long—all "year" long. Our everyday prices on housewares, mens and womens clothing, and small appliances are lower than any other local department stores' prices. And we are not a discount house that carries only a few items or brands. Bradstocks keeps hundred's of brands, sizes, and colors in stock.

So don't come to a clearance sale. Come to Bradstocks. We "promise" to save you money.

PART FOUR REVIEW TESTS

Now that you have finished Part Four, try taking the test you worked on at the beginning of the section.

Review Test 4-1

Correctly punctuate the following paragraphs. Do not add or delete words.

Tom Carpenter who works as an executive with Towne Company makes an excellent salary, and has always been satisfied with his job. His boss says, "Tom is one of this companys best managers, he is intelligent, thorough and conscientious". Management considers Tom a practical man with skills and adaptability, that give him a maturity beyond his years.

Now that Tom has been with the company for over twenty three years he is being seriously considered for the position of vice-president. Tom however is not certain he wants to make the move to New York that the promotion would entail so he is evaluating his options, and discussing them with his family and with his friends' in the company.

Review Test 4-2

Correctly punctuate the following sentences. Some sentences may be correct; some may have more than one error. Do not alter the order of the words.

1. The two accountants theories have been tested thoroughly by both accounting firms, and graduate students.

2. Twenty three newly hired employees have been attending the videotape demonstration.

3. Frank Harper, the company's leading analyst is also a skilled writer and graphic artist.

4. Much of our European heritage is disappearing in this country with each successive generations integration into American culture.

5. "The growth of anarchy," writes one indignant historian "is assisted by the growth of liberal economics."

6. Mrs. Levin will not go to the conference, however she will send her assistant Mr. Patterson.

7. A loss of prestige is not particularly surprising; given the loss of finances that preceded it.

8. This is one of the places, in fact, where you can see thousands of seals sunbathing on the rocks.

9. "The mens department is being renovated," explained the manager, "so we will have more room for merchandise and customers".

10. Lisa maintains that three quarters of the pigeons in the world live on her roof.

11. I have often wondered if the human being is a migratory species?

12. Henry disagrees with the concept that "only in the past decade has the crime rate been used as a political tool."

13. The education specialist maintained that the major problems with childrens books are the sexual and racial biases; the stories reflect the writer's prejudices.

14. As far as you can see, the huge shiny mahogany desks are covered with useless sheets of paper.

15. Although Jo-Jo regrets nothing in his past, he sometimes dreams of being a student again, and studying astronomy and physics.

Review Test 4-3

Correctly punctuate the following sentences. Some sentences may be correct; some may have more than one error. Do not alter the order of the words.

Between the fifteenth and the eighteenth centuries, if the population went up or down everything else changed as well. When the number of people increased production and trade also increased. Manufacturing spread, villages and towns expanded. Of course, wars, disputes, and privateering also flourished, therefore armies and armed bands increased in number.

When it's population increases, a societys relationship to the space it occupies and the wealth at it's disposal, is altered. The society reaches critical thresholds and, at each one its entire structure is questioned afresh. "Demographic increases," as one historian has written "lead to a deterioration in the standard of living when they are extreme". In essence, such increases enlarge the horrors of the underfed, the poor, and the uprooted.

**Review Test
4-4**

Write sentences according to the directions given.

1. [a sentence with a semicolon]

2. [a question in a quotation]

3. [a sentence with a plural possessive]

4. [a sentence with words in parentheses]

5. [a sentence with coordinate adjectives]

6. [an indirect question]

7. [a sentence with an abbreviation]

8. [an indirect quotation]

9. [a sentence with a colon]

10. [a sentence with a dash]

Review Test 4-5   Fix any grammar or punctuation errors in the following letter.

NATIONAL CANNED GOODS FAN CLUB

394 45th Street

Oakland, CA 90872

September 21, 19xx

Mr Samuel Dwyer

President

National Canned Goods Company

97 E Lansing Drive

Platteville, CA 90596

Dear Mr Dwyer,

Its been fifteen years now since I first enjoyed your wonderful companies fine canned products. Upon entering college, they formed the major part of my lunches and dinners. Now as a married man they are even more vital to my healthy diet. I have savored the green beans in onion sauce particularly and I will always be a special fan of the imported franks and sauerkraut.

I want to mention, however an important element missing from you're selection of canned foods. You do'nt carry any chili peppers! Each of the fans of National Canned Goods who I correspond with is disappointed by this omission. Would it be possible for you to include it. I suggest that you start a line of Mexican canned goods with you're own special touch.

You will have new fans, I assure you if you follow my suggestions.

Devotedly,

Arno Flatt

Chairman

National Canned Goods

Fan Club

LEARNING MECHANICS

FAMOUS FIRST DRAFTS: Harry S Truman
Writing Hint: Get to Your Point

Source: Ford Button

The buck stops here.

**Reading for
Resourceful
Writers**
Speling for
Sukcess

To: All Reeders   Date: Soon!!!

From: Rita Ritter

Subject: "B All You Can B": Spelling B for Xperts

Wood you like to:

- Spend a hole day speling hard words?

- Spend a hole day lissening to *other peeple* speling hard words?

- Maybe win YOURE OWN copy of a small but helpfull dicshunary?

Of coarse you wood! That's why your going to take part in RITA RITTER'S
SPELING B FOR XPERTS. Beleve me, it'll be a blast. You'll be on the edge of
your seet as you and your frends spel hard words such as—well, we don't
want to give enything away. Just wate and sea.

WHEN: Wensday, Febuary 3
TIME: Noon-ish
WEAR: Bayfare Hottel
COST: FREE! (ten dollers if you leave erly)

Loosers will win a copy of *Rita Ritter's Speling Guide for Xperts*. Winners will
win there own copy of the highly aklaimed *Dicshunary for Hog-Callers and
Other Speshulized Jobs*.

CAWSHUN Don't come if you've got a week hart: the ecksitement mite be
TO MUCH!!

**PART FIVE OBJECTIVES: To spell words correctly; to capitalize words cor-
rectly; to write numbers according to conventional usage.**

The word *mechanics* emphasizes the routine operations of writing, the basic
operating procedures that keep your sentences in good working order. These
procedures may not seem particularly exciting, but they are as vital to your
writing as oil changes and lube jobs are to your car.

Good sentences not only are grammatical and well punctuated but also follow
certain standard practices. Poor spelling or word choices can ruin the effectiveness of any piece of business writing.

This section cannot cover every potential problem you may encounter, but it
can make you aware of the areas on which you should focus when you revise your
writing. Always have a good dictionary beside you as you write; look up every
word that you feel unsure about. Keep lists of troublesome words.

And, most of all, remember the importance of "mechanics." Do not say, "I've always been a bad speller, but my ideas are good, and they're the most important part of my writing." Poor spelling and capitalization have destroyed many pieces of writing. The Reading for Resourceful Writers you have just read shows you a humorous example of how poor spelling can ruin a piece of writing.

Careful attention to a few rules can make your writing much more understandable and effective.

Before starting Chapter 26, take the following Pre-Test to check your skills in writing mechanics.

PART FIVE PRE-TEST

Look for problems with spelling, capitalization, and numbers in the following letter. Cross out each error and write in your correction. (Check end of text for answers.)

November 14, 19xx

Mr. Harold Glassman
Standford office supplies
3467 Hoover blvd.
Coral Bay, MI 48489

Dear mr. Glassman:

On tuesday, November 12, we recieved your order for one hundred and fifty-five boxes of stationary and your check for six hundred dollars. We appreciate your order and look forward to accomodating you.

Before filling your order, however, we need to know the styles and colors you wish to stock; Please refer to our enclosed brochure. Many of our customers have been buying the pastel shades, so you might consider them.

If you call or write us this week, we can fill your order before thanksgiving. We look forward to hearing from you.

sincerely,

Kate Stillman

CHAPTER 26

SPELLING

OBJECTIVE: To spell words correctly.

Can you correct the spelling errors in the following sentences?

1. We did not buy new calenders until Febuary.
2. The hieght of the office building is being discused by the city counsel.
3. Thompson will not posses all the facts until the ninteenth of this month.

You should have spotted seven errors: the correctly spelled words are *calendars*, *February*, *height*, *discussed*, *council*, *possess*, and *nineteenth*.

English spelling rules are not easy. Our language was formed from words of so many languages and has gone through so many changes over the centuries that exceptions exist to almost every rule. Many words spelled in similar ways are pronounced very differently; other words with similar pronunciations are spelled differently.

Consider, for example, the words *through, enough, trough, borough, hiccough, bough,* and *tough.* These words *look* like they should be pronounced in similar ways, but actually each is quite different.

You should have a good dictionary on your desk, and you should check the pronunciation of words as you look them up; many words are misspelled because people say them incorrectly. If spelling is difficult for you, you should invest in a paperback of words commonly misspelled. This sort of book has lists of words, so you can read through them quickly. When you find the word you want, you can always double-check the meaning in a dictionary.

Keeping your own word lists is an excellent way to improve your spelling. Each time you have to look up a word—or each time you discover you have misspelled a word—write it down. Review your list frequently.

You will also find that simply *being aware* of words as you read them will help you to spell them. Many of us read quickly, not stopping to *look* at the words. If you become interested in how words are spelled, you will find your own spelling gradually improving.

Learning to spell is not an overnight process, but some concentrated effort will work wonders.

The following rules can also assist you in spelling many common words.

IE AND *EI*

The rhyme "*I* before *E* except after *C*, or when sounded like *A* as in *neighbor* or *weigh*" is helpful in many cases. It works for the majority of words with this vowel combination.

A S-H-U-R Way to Spell Correctly

Try a four-pronged approach to improve your spelling: SEE it, HEAR it, USE it, REPEAT it.

1. *See* the word. When you come across an unfamiliar word or have trouble spelling a word, try really *looking* at it. Think about why it is spelled a certain way or give yourself a memory "hook" by which to remember it. (For example, people who forget the difference between *stationery* (meaning *letter paper*) and *stationary* (meaning *not moving*) might remember that the word *letter* has an *e* in it—and so does *stationery*.

2. *Hear* the word. Say the word out loud. Listen to it. If you really hear the way a word sounds, you will often remember how to spell it. For instance, if you carefully pronounce the word *prefer* while you are looking at it, you will see it is spelled the way it should be pronounced: *prefer*, not *perfer!*

3. *Use* the word. Memorizing words is a pointless task unless you use them. Using new words when you write and speak will carve them into your memory. Do not hesitate to try new words and to look them up several times in a dictionary or word list if you have to.

4. *Repeat* the word. Using a word once or twice may not make the word "yours." You have to keep using it until it flows effortlessly onto your page. If you have been avoiding the word *possess* because you cannot remember how many *s*'s it has, write it as often as you can. Look it up a dozen times if you have to— but keep writing it. After a while, you will remember all four *s*'s!

---

1. Most words with this combination and the *ee* sound are spelled with the *i* first: *chief, grief, niece, field.* Some exceptions are *weird, seizure,* and *sheik.*
2. Words with the *ai* sound are spelled with *ei: neighbor, weigh, freight, reign.*
3. After *c* the combination is *ei: receive, ceiling, receipt.* If the *c* sounds like *sh* or *ch*, the combination is *ie: conscience, deficient, species.*
4. When a syllable break occurs between this combination of vowels, the spelling is *ie: dietary, obedience, hierarchy.*

PLURALS

We briefly discussed the formation of plurals in Chapter 2 (pp. 24–25). Most noun plurals are formed by adding *s* or *es*.

1. Words ending in *s, ch, sh,* and *x* require *es* in the plural.

SINGULAR	PLURAL
kiss	kisses
branch	branches
crash	crashes
box	boxes

2. Most words ending in *y* change to *ies* in the plural.

SINGULAR	PLURAL
seventy	seventies
university	universities
faculty	faculties
city	cities

3. Some words ending in *f* or *fe* change to *ves* in the plural.

SINGULAR	PLURAL
scarf	scarves
thief	thieves
life	lives
leaf	leaves
hoof	hooves

Exceptions include:

SINGULAR	PLURAL
brief	briefs
belief	beliefs
roof	roofs

FOREIGN WORDS

English speakers tend to regularize foreign words by making them fit English patterns. Thus, many words of foreign origin now have *s* or *es* plurals.

SINGULAR	PLURAL
adieu	adieus
femur	femurs
curriculum	curriculums

Other words of foreign origin still retain their foreign plural forms:

SINGULAR	PLURAL
alumnus	alumni
crisis	crises
phenomenon	phenomena
criterion	criteria

Self-Check Test 26-1

I. Write sentences using the following words in their plural forms. Look up any unfamiliar words. (Check your spelling in a dictionary or in answer section at end of text.)

1. circus

2. elegy

3. industry

4. ranch

5. analysis

6. speech

7. rodeo

8. calf

9. loaf

10. larynx

II. Fill in the blanks with either *ei* or *ie*.

We have found that a var___ ___ty of our pat___ ___nts bel___ ___ve that they
have w___ ___rd problems relating to their w___ ___ght, d___ ___ts, or
hyg___ ___ne. We rec___ ___ve dozens of calls each month from
gr___ ___f-stricken cl___ ___nts. Without sounding too conc___ ___ted, I will
say we have ach___ ___ved considerable success with our effic___ ___nt techniques.

_____

SUFFIXES

Suffixes are additions to the ends of words: *-ly, -able, -ance, -ed*, and so on. There are exceptions to every rule, but here are some useful hints.

1. When adding a suffix, drop the silent *e* at the end of most words.

fade	fading
combine	combining
erase	erasable
argue	arguable

2. When adding a suffix, leave the silent *e* if the word ends in *ce* or *ge*.

reinforce	reinforceable
notice	noticeable
courage	courageous

3. Double a final consonant of a one-syllable word before a suffix beginning with a vowel.

wrap	wrapped
trim	trimmed
bar	barring

4. Double a final consonant of a two-syllable word if the accent is on the second syllable.

forget	forgetting
allot	allotted
occur	occurred/occurrence

5. Watch for the suffixes *-cede, -sede*, and *-ceed*. Most English words with these suffixes end in *-cede*.

    > Only one word ends in *-sede: supersede*.
    > Only three words end in *-ceed: exceed, proceed*, and *succeed*.
    > Others end in *-cede: concede, precede, recede*, and so on.

Self-Check Test 26-2

Add a suffix to each of the following words, and then use the new word in a sentence (Check your dictionary or the answer section for spelling.)

1. accept:

2. regret:

WRITING HINT: DO NOT CONFUSE WORDS THAT SOUND ALIKE
What Pauline Wrote   *What Fred Thought*

Revision: Our import quotas may be affected by the new leaders reigning over the developing countries.

Source: Ford Button

3. betray:

4. insulate:

5. debate:

6. stall:

7. prefer:

8. control:

9. acknowledge:

10. stretch:

WORDS COMMONLY MISSPELLED

absence	condemn	innocuous	privilege
absorbent	conceivable	jeopardize	questionnaire
accessible	conscience	judgment	receipt
accommodate	conspicuous	liaison	reminisce
accuracy	definite	mileage	requisition
all right	develop	minuscule	schedule
analyze	embarrass	morale	seize
ballot	exaggerate	nickel	siege
bookkeeper	fascinate	ninth	skillful
bouillon	February	noticeable	suing
bureau	foresee	occurred	supersede
business	gauge	omission	susceptible
calendar	guarantee	peculiar	thoroughly
census	guerrilla	principal	yield
chief	harass	principle	

Self-Check Test 26-3

Underline each misspelled word in the following memo, and then write it correctly in the space at the end of the memo. (When you have done the exercise, check your spelling in your dictionary or in the answer section.)

To: All Employes
From: Fred Pryor
Subject: Order Forms
Date: Febuary 4, 19xx

Several of you have been thoroghly embarassed recently by the erors you have made while taking customor orders. You have forgoten or omited some relevent peice of information or hurredly writen the wrong datta while you were speaking on the telephone. As you know, we garantee our services and are liabel for our mistakes, so you must make sure that forgetfullness or in-attention does not jepardize our busness.

I know you are all conscientious and courteus workers. From now on, please be more conscius of the information you take from clients.

SOUND-ALIKES

Many words in English are spelled differently and have different meanings even though they sound the same: *air*, *err*, and *heir*, for example are pronounced the same but spelled differently. (These words are called *homophones*.) As you work on your list of words that you are learning to spell, watch for these sound-alikes. How many of them can you think of?

Self-Check Test 26-4

I. Use each of the following sound-alike words in a sentence. If you are unsure of the meaning of a word, check your dictionary.

1. pear

   pair

2. hale

hail

3. bare

bear

4. scene

seen

5. holy

wholly

6. fair

fare

7. bail

bale

8. lien

lean

9. bowled

bold

10. loan

lone

II. Now think of five sets of sound-alike words on your own and use each word in a sentence.

1. a.

b.

2. a.

b.

3. a.

    b.

4. a.

    b.

5. a.

    b.

Checklist for Chapter 26

1. The familiar rhyme works for most words with an *i* and *e* vowel combination.

2. Most plurals are formed by adding *s* or *es*.

3. Words ending in *s*, *ch*, *sh*, and *x* require *es* in the plural.

4. Some words ending in *f* or *fe* change to *ves* in the plural.

5. Many plurals of foreign words are now regularized according to English rules.

6. The silent *e* at the end of most words is usually dropped when a suffix is added (unless the word ends in *ce* or *ge*).

7. The final consonant of a one-syllable word is usually doubled before a suffix beginning with a vowel. (The same rule applies for two-syllable words when the emphasis is on the second syllable.)

8. Homophones are words that sound alike but are spelled differently.

Spelling Review   Cross out any misspelled words and write the correct form. (Check end of text for answers.)

1. This new ink is eraseable, so do not use it when filling out these ques-
    tionaires.

2. Mr. Thornton has always been very suseptible to the flu; his inocuous
    cough can quickly devlope into a serious illness.

3. I will reimburse you after you have tallyed your milage and accomodation
    reciepts.

4. I feel privedged to recieve this information; you can feel certian I will not
    jepardize your sckedule by telling anyone else.

5. The new bookeeper is not skilful enough for our growing bussiness.

**Chapter Test
26-1**

I. **Fill in the blanks with the correct letters.**

1. I have om_____ed [left out] the total figure.

2. The porch must be built so it is acces_____ble [can be reached] from the kitchen.

3. Try not to exc_____ [go over] your budget.

4. The company tries to acco_____date to [adjust to] its employees.

5. Have you put an advertising bro_____re [pamphlet] on Henry's desk?

II. **Write the plural form of each of the following words, and then use the plural form in a sentence.**

1. [wedge]

2. [dress]

3. [annex]

4. [battery]

5. [goose]

Chapter Test 26-2   Cross out misspelled or misused words in the following memo and write in the correct forms.

To: Henry Cohn

From: Ted Frazier and Susan Petersen

Subject: Personel Problems

Date: January 12, 19xx

We have thoroghly analysed a number of problems that occured in the two months preceeding the Christmas holiday.

We still have no definit data concerning the embarassing drop in sales, but we beleive the principle problem was low moral and overwork: our salespeople wanted to work many extra hours before Christmas, but they could not forsee how tired they would be. As a result, their scheduleing was often erratic and their customer relations were poor.

We cannot promise an enormous rise in Febuary sales now that the salespeople are back to their usual hours, but we do feel you will perceive a noticable improvement.

Exercise for Experts   Each of the following words has a homophone or sound-alike. Write the word that sounds like each of these words and then use both words in sentences. Use your dictionary if you need help.

1. a. principal

   b.

2. a. baited

   b.

3. a. all together

   b.

4. a. dual

   b.

5. a. discreet

   b.

6. a. birth

   b.

7. a. or

   b.

8. a. while

   b.

9. a. beat

   b.

10. a. time

    b.

EXTRA CREDIT:

   a. idle

   b.

   c.

CHAPTER 27

CAPITALIZATION

OBJECTIVE: To capitalize words according to accepted usage.

How many errors do you recognize in the following sentences?

> Thomas Lee, the representative of the democratic party from Brownsville, michigan, was born on december 12, 1945. He once ran for Governor while teaching at a College in Illinois. He is also the author of *My life in politics*, which sold over a million copies.

There are eight errors in the sentences. Six words should be capitalized: *Democratic Party, Michigan, December, Life,* and *Politics.* Two words should not be capitalized: *governor* and *college.*

Like spelling, capitalization is a mechanical part of writing that some people find irritating or boring. But capitalization provides helpful signposts for your reader and can also make your writing more effective.

CAPITALIZE THE FIRST WORD OF A SENTENCE

> Give the package to me.
> Today is the deadline.

Note: Do not capitalize the first word after a semicolon unless it is a proper noun.

> The company is planning a merger; no one yet knows the details. [correct]
> The company is planning a merger; Wendell Smith knows the details. [correct]

CAPITALIZE THE FIRST WORD OF DIRECTLY QUOTED SPEECH

> Jack said, "This is my first vacation in ten years."
> My supervisor asked, "Is this the missing file?"

CAPITALIZE THE FIRST WORD OF A SENTENCE IN QUOTATION

"I will be leaving the office at noon," said Frannie.
"Wait for me at Syd's Restaurant."

Note: Do not capitalize the second part of an interrupted sentence in a quotation:

"I will be leaving," said Frannie, "at noon."

CAPITALIZE THE FIRST WORD OF A SENTENCE IN PARENTHESES

We voted on the issue. (A quorum was present.)

If the words in parentheses are not a sentence, do not open with a capital letter.

The 15 members (a quorum) voted on the issue.

Do *not* capitalize the first word of a sentence in parentheses if that sentence comes inside another sentence. (See also p. 287.)

If the weather changes (it has been raining since Tuesday), we can go fishing.

Self-Check Test 27-1

Correct any errors in capitalization in the following sentences. (See end of text for answers.)

1. "We are planning," said Greg, "To leave here in the morning."

2. The meeting is scheduled for 11:00 a.m. (Or noon at the latest).

3. My supervisor retired today; She is going to start her own gardening

    business.

4. "Let me know the details," Leola requested. "we need to start on the

    project right away."

5. The new building has been painted (It is a beautiful salmon pink!), and

    now it is being furnished.

CAPITALIZE PROPER NOUNS

As you saw in Chapter 2, proper nouns name particular people, places, and things. Capitalize the names of:

A. individual people.

> Mary Jones is an accomplished violinist.
> Phil Gallagher will be visiting us this week.

B. countries and continents.

> The group is touring Europe.
> Representatives from Japan stayed for a week.

C. states, counties, cities, towns, regions.

> My cousin is from Wisconsin.
> Broward County voted for Wilson.
> St. Paul, Minnesota, has an interesting history.
> Some people say Lincoln, Nebraska, is the heart of the Midwest.

D. languages.

> John speaks Russian as well as Greek.
> Marilyn Patterson majored in English.

E. historical periods.

> Our class is studying the Mesozoic Era.
> This book examines the Middle Ages and the Renaissance.

F. political parties, organizations, religions.

> Clarkson is the Socialist candidate.
> My father belongs to the Kiwanis Club.
> The speaker is a convert to Catholicism.

G. companies, colleges.

> We are on the technical support staff at General Mills.
> Sam graduated from the University of Michigan.

H. government departments.

> Our group toured the offices of the Federal Bureau of Investigation.
> The United States Postal Service is considering some operational changes.

I. product brands.

> Cathy always eats Wheaties for breakfast.
> Their children are demanding Nestle's chocolate milk.

Note that the name of the product after the brand is not capitalized: Campbell's soup, Chevrolet station wagon.

J.   months, days of the week, holidays.

> I am transferring departments in June.
> Will Saturday be soon enough?
> Jack is graduating right before Labor Day.

Self-Check Test 27-2

Capitalize the appropriate words in the following sentences. (Check end of text for answers.)

1. We visited berlin, germany, in july.

2. Have you heard that hancock corporation is opening in tokyo?

3. Marge and pete attended the lutheran ceremony.

4. Charles, campaign manager for the republican candidate, is a former

   airplane pilot.

5. He is planning to buy some pepsi at safeway.

6. Corrie attended a seminar at the united states treasury department.

7. Peter Williams arrived on mother's day.

8. Do you think you can be ready by wednesday, march 4?

9. When Joe graduates from cornell university, he plans to work for sears.

10. Check with me before you speak with the avon representative.

CAPITALIZE MAJOR WORDS OF BOOK TITLES, MOVIE TITLES, SONG TITLES, AND SO ON

Capitalize titles of books, movies, magazines, songs, record albums, newspapers, television shows, manuals, and articles. Do not capitalize an article, preposition, or conjunction with fewer than four letters unless it is the opening or closing word of the title. Do not capitalize the *to* in infinitives.

> I am finishing George Eliot's *The Mill on the Floss.*
> Her picture appeared in the *National Enquirer.*
> Allen is writing an article called "Living with
> Diabetes."
> We recently saw a performance of *Cat on a Hot Tin Roof.*
> His column is entitled "What to Listen For."

CAPITALIZE ABBREVIATIONS DERIVED FROM CAPITALIZED WORDS

I have joined the YMCA.
Bill works for IBM.

CAPITALIZE PROPER ADJECTIVES DERIVED FROM PROPER NOUNS

We are reading about Keynesian economics.
Jill is a Marxist.

CAPITALIZE ACADEMIC DEGREES

This is Martin Bayer, Ph.D.
I received a Bachelor of Science degree from Tulane University.

CAPITALIZE TITLES WHEN THEY PRECEDE NAMES

Kerry was introduced to Governor Mason.
My friend Lieutenant Daley was the first to speak.
Please introduce me to Dr. Scanlon.

Do not capitalize titles that follow or are not attached to names.

Alan Grey is running for governor.
Paula Terry, mayor of Carterville, will lunch with us.
When Bob Cheney was captain of the cruise ship, he called himself Captain Bob.

CAPITALIZE CERTAIN PARTS OF LETTERS

Capitalize the following:

1. In the inside address, the reader's name, title, department, and company as well as street, city, and state names.

Dr. Leon Hurley
Vice-President, Operations
Olsen Company
4561 Bleeker Boulevard
Chico, CA 95478

2. All important words in attention or subject lines:

> Re: Installation of Air Conditioners
> Attention: All Clerical Staff
> Subject: Company Picnic

3. The first word of the salutation and the person's title:

> Dear Professor Smith:
> Dear Mr. Larsson:

4. First word of the complimentary close.

> Sincerely yours,
> Very truly yours,

See Appendix A for more on letter formats.

Self-Check Test 27-3

Capitalize the appropriate words in the following sentences. (Check end of text for answers.)

1. While in college, harry was in rotc.

2. "Let me know," Suzie wrote, "if you need another car when you move."

3. Carol will finish her mba in september.

4. Our sixth grade class visited the montgomery county courthouse in april

   of 1965.

5. We finally approached mr. Green and dr. Smithe to see if they could take

   part in the ceremony. (they were both very difficult to locate.)

Checklist for Chapter 27

1. Capitalize proper nouns and adjectives.
2. Capitalize the first word of a sentence.
3. Capitalize academic degrees.
4. Capitalize titles when they precede names.
5. Capitalize major words of publication titles, movie titles, song titles, and so on.
6. Capitalize abbreviations derived from proper nouns.
7. Capitalize the first word of directly quoted speech and the first word of sentences in quotations.

8. Capitalize the first word of a sentence in parentheses, unless it comes inside another sentence.

9. Capitalize certain parts of letters.

Capitalization Review

Fix any capitalization errors in the following paragraphs. (Check end of text for answers.)

Notice to employees

On friday, may 4, dr. Imogene Hart accepted a position as head of our Research and development Department. Dr. Hart, who received her ph.d. at the university of Michigan, has been working at Kotell, inc. for the past five years. Her latest book, *The Industrial world*, has been translated into french and sold in seven Countries.

I know you will welcome dr. Hart to our company; She will be a great asset to our research and development Staff.

**Chapter Test
27-1**

I. **Use the following words in sentences.**

1. Governor

2. governor

3. University

4. university

5. Democratic

6. democratic

7. Thanksgiving

8. thanksgiving

9. Federal

10. federal

II. **Write sentences according to the following directions.**

1. [a sentence that mentions a particular country]

2. [a sentence that mentions a book title]

3. [a sentence that includes another sentence in quotation marks]

4. [a sentence that contains a proper adjective]

5. [a sentence that mentions a city and state]

6. [a sentence that mentions a day, month, and year]

7. [a sentence followed by a sentence in parentheses]

8. [a sentence that mentions an academic degree]

9. [a sentence that mentions a continent]

10. [a sentence that mentions a historical period]

Chapter Test 27-2

Correctly capitalize words in the following sentences.

1. Johann came to the united states in february after spending eight months in sydney, australia.

2. When Laurie got out of college in june, she applied for the masters in business administration program at the university of colorado.

3. "When do we get to jamestown?" asked Karl. "will we get there before dinner?"

4. I enjoyed the movie of *gone with the wind*, but the book was even better.

5. The caravan crossing asia in 1785 stopped for supplies in a small chinese village.

6. The package arrived monday from the department of transportation. (only mr. Parker expected it to arrive so soon.)

7. When assemblyman Holmes came to williams, new hampshire, he was met by the mayor and representatives of local businesses.

8. "This is a very unusual geological formation," explained our tour guide, "For a desert area."

9. Our market research team is compiling data on revlon products.

10. Let me know (by thursday if possible) what you think of my article entitled "conversations with a neolithic man."

Exercise for Experts   Correct the capitalization in the following letter.

GERRY'S BOOKS FOR BUSINESSES

2381 Roundtree boulevard

Norton, connecticut 02567

august 4, 19xx

Mr. Thomas Deeley, manager

Conway consulting services

892 Apple road

Washington, d.c. 20015

dear mr. Deeley:

Thank you for your letter of july 24. We do occasionally carry financial guides written in french and german, but at the moment we would have to order them for you. Most of our european orders take six to eight weeks to arrive. If you need some tax information in those languages, the irs may be able to help you more quickly than I can.

One of our best selling tax books this year has been dawson and bleeker's *guide to the u.s. tax system*; If you are interested in a french or german translation, I will be happy to see if I can get one for you.

Please write or call me if you would like me to put an order in for you.

Sincerely Yours,

Gerry Mandeville

CHAPTER 28

NUMBERS

OBJECTIVE: To learn conventional usage for writing numbers.

Do you see any errors in the following sentences? How would you fix them?

1. This is the 10th letter we have received from Mrs. Kelso.

2. Hugh lives at two thousand thirty-five B Street.

3. I have paid only a hundred twenty-five dollars of the $235 I owe.

Corrected sentences should read:

1. This is the tenth letter we have received from Mrs. Kelso.

2. Hugh lives at 2035 B Street.

3. I have paid only $125 of the $235 I owe.

In most business writing, you will use figures (220) more than you will write out numbers (two hundred twenty). You will use figures, of course, when filling out order forms or balancing accounts. In fact, in many types of reports and letters, figures are more useful and easier to comprehend.

At times you will simply have to use your good sense with regard to numbers: make the choice that will be easiest for your reader to understand.

The following guides for using numbers apply to both cardinal numbers (9, *nine*) and ordinal numbers (*ninth*).

SPELL OUT NUMBERS TEN AND UNDER

We have ordered five books.
This is our second attempt.

DO NOT SPELL OUT COMPLICATED NUMBERS

The city has three million nine hundred thousand inhabitants. [incorrect]
The city has 3.9 million inhabitants. [correct]
The city has 3,900,000 inhabitants. [correct]

SPELL OUT NUMBERS AT THE BEGINNING OF SENTENCES

Three hundred people attended the game.

If the number contains several words, rewrite the sentence. Avoid:

Four thousand five hundred fifty-two people were at the game.

Instead, write:

The audience at the game numbered 4,552 people.

BE CONSISTENT WITH LISTS OF NUMBERS

The office ordered three boxes of stationery and 15 typewriter ribbons. [incorrect]
The office ordered three boxes of stationery and fifteen typewriter ribbons. [correct]
We ordered 3 boxes of stationery and 15 typewriter ribbons. [correct]

USE NUMERALS FOR:

1. Addresses and phone numbers.

   345 19th Avenue, Apt. 6
   Plainville, TX 67893
   (892) 567-0347

2. Dates.

   I was born August 2, 1968.
   This letter is dated June 12.

   Note: Do not write *June 12th*. You may write *the 12th of June*.

3. Decimals (including money).

   Jill owes the company $54.90.
   The patient's temperature was 100.5.

4. Times that come before a.m. or p.m.

   I met her at 12:04 p.m.

5. Page numbers, volume numbers.

   George found the answer in *The American Dictionary*,
   Volume 3, page 122.

6. Percentages.

   Sales went up 3 percent in January.

7. Ages.

> The doctors interviewed were between 34 and 38 years
> old.

8. Dimensions, distances, measures.

> The room is 40 feet long and 12 feet wide.
> Tim Haley was driving at 75 miles per hour when he
> was stopped.
> The company bought 5,000 quarts of milk.

9. Statistics/scores.

> The survey established that 5 people out of every 1,500
> buy chewing gum.
> The score was 45–12 at the end of the first half.
> Only 67 out of 189 people voted for the referendum.

SPELL OUT:

1. Indefinite amounts.

> I suspect nearly a thousand people attended the con-
> cert.
> Almost thirty-five people work in this office.

2. Times using *o'clock*.

> Karen was here at exactly four o'clock.

3. Numbers ten and under and round numbers.

> We have hired two employees.
> The company has hired a hundred people since April.
> This is our second attempt to locate the broker.
> I am happy to say that you are our ninth caller.
> The company may lose a million dollars.

Self-Check Test 28-1

Correct any errors in the following sentences. (Check end of text for answers.)

1. We arrested the suspect at 3 o'clock in his apartment at two hundred thir-

   ty Nineteenth Avenue in Salisbury.

2. 346 votes have already come in from our listeners.

3. I will call you on March 4th if I want to invest the forty-five hundred dol-

   lars.

4. The pool is forty feet long, twenty feet deep, and 156 feet wide.

5. Greg ran with the ball when the score was six to zero in the 1st quarter.

Checklist for Chapter 28

1. Write numbers as figures more than as words in business materials.

2. Spell out numbers ten and under.

3. Use numerals for complicated numbers.

4. Write out numbers at the beginning of sentences; if a complicated number appears at the beginning of a sentence, rewrite the sentence.

5. Be consistent with lists of numbers: usually numerals will be more efficient and readable.

6. Use numerals for addresses, phone numbers, dates, decimals, times with a.m. and p.m., page and volume numbers, percentages, ages, measurements, statistics, and scores.

7. Spell out indefinite amounts, times using *o'clock*, and round numbers.

Number Review

Fix any errors in the following paragraph. (Check end of text for answers.)

For our twenty-fifth anniversary in the year two thousand, we are putting out an expanded version of our annual report. This report will be large, perhaps thirteen inches by eighteen inches, will have over three hundred fifty pages, and will contain 100's of photographs of company projects and employees through the years. We already have 5 employees working on this project, which will cost nearly ten thousand dollars but which should be a work of art we can all treasure.

Chapter Test 28-1

Fix any errors with numbers in the following sentences.

1. Where do you plan to invest the four hundred fifty dollars?

2. This room is 30 by 25 feet, but it is forty feet high.

3. Let me know if you hear from Patricia Garcia by June 15th.

4. 700 employees are planning to go on strike next month unless the company offers a fifty percent pay raise.

5. We will meet here at six p.m. The meeting should last about 45 minutes.

6. Our division manager is almost 50 years old, but he still runs 3 miles every morning.

7. On September sixteenth, we ordered 4 manicure sets, 12 hair dryers, and twenty makeup mirrors.

8. When we began working here, four thousand twenty-three employees worked in the three production areas.

9. Only two and three-quarters percent of the people polled wanted to see a change in the voting procedures.

10. I saw the article in the *Automobile Owner's Guide*, Volume Three, page one hundred ninety.

Exercise for Experts

Fix any errors in the following letter.

Mrs. Leonard Whiggens

Fifty-two Court Place

Lincoln, NY 19982

January 28th, 19xx

Dear Mrs. Whiggens:

We were sorry to receive your letter of January 23rd listing your troubles with the Traveler's Coffeemaker and with our service department. The 2 clerks with whom you spoke should have agreed either to fix the coffeemaker without charge or to return your twenty-five dollars and fifteen cents.

If you wish to bring the coffeemaker to our department again, we will be happy to help you. (Bring this letter with you.) Or send the machine to us C.O.D. with a copy of this letter. Let us know whether you want a new machine or your money back.

As you seem perturbed by the small size of the Travelers's Coffeemaker, you might consider our Custom-Made line: you may choose from coffeemakers that brew ten to 20 cups of coffee at a time.

Again, we apologize for the situation. Our two clerks were recently transferred from another department, and this was their 1st experience with a product complaint. We look forward to hearing from you.

Sincerely,

Leonard Ferguson

Manager

PART FIVE REVIEW TESTS

Review Test 5-1

Now that you have completed this section, retake the test from the beginning of Part Five.

Check this letter for problems with spelling, capitalization, and numbers. Cross out each error and write in your correction.

November 14, 19xx

Mr. Harold Glassman

Standford office supplies

3467 Hoover blvd.

Coral Bay, MI 48489

Dear mr. Glassman:

On tuesday, November 12, we recieved your order for one hundred and fifty-five boxes of stationary and your check for six hundred dollars. We appreciate your order and look forward to accomodating you.

Before filling your order, however, we need to know the styles and colors you wish to stock; Please refer to our enclosed brochure. Many of our customers have been buying the pastel shades, so you might consider them.

If you call or write us this week, we can fill your order before thanksgiving. We look forward to hearing from you.

sincerely,

Kate Stillman

**Review Test
5-2**

I. Fix any mechanical errors in the following paragraphs.

David Malloy was only twenty-three years old when he 1st began to think of starting a business of his own. he had recieved a b.s. degree in Marketing, but he had no practical experience in accounting or in hiring employees.

He beleived he had 2 major assets. He had six thousand dollars that he had acquired from working as a waiter for four summers, and he had an excellent idea: he would set up a company that organized people's closets.

A market research survey of 350 apartment-dwellers showed David that most people found their closets thoroghly disagreeable and the contents inaccesible. He felt sure that, with some skilfull advertising and strong recommendations from initial clients, he would be making money within 7 months.

II. Add a suffix to the following words, and then use each new word in a sentence.

1. coordinate:

2. erase:

3. allot:

4. gauge:

5. develop:

6. reminisce:

7. exaggerate:

8. jeopardize:

9. fascinate:

10. omit:

Review Test 5-3

Fix any errors in the following sentences.

1. "It has been a priviledge doing business with you," said dr. Corley.

2. 1,745 pounds of sugar were shipped to the wrong address in brooklyn on wednesday.

3. This company cannot condone Mr. Winters' behavior, but managment cannot consider sueing the man.

4. Nearly four thousand people disappeared from the computerized list after the census had been taken.

5. The irs contended that Mrs. Poll had exagerrated the number of nickels she contributed to the children's charity.

6. This new personnel manual does not supercede the earlier ones.

7. Martin Hayes has no definit idea on how to proceed with the project, but he has spent five thousand ninety-eight dollars on it.

8. The consultants will act as a liason between this company and the foriegn investors.

9. This is Gary Young's nineth offense; We are beginning to believe he is very suseptible to certain types of fraud.

10. Karen Field hired 5 new staff members after firing 9 clerks.

11. The retiring president is only sixty-two; However, he acknowledges that he is not as interested in making profits and running a business as he used to be.

12. Some scientists now believe that the universe began about 15,000,000,000 years ago and that it has been expanding and cooling ever since.

13. Excited about finding some nike running shoes her size, Crystal did not notice that they were priced at thirty-four dollars and ninety-eight cents.

14. Now that he is a resident of Baton Rouge, louisiana instead of Wheeling, west virginia, Bob Miller has found it much easier to find good boiled crawfish.

15. Tracey Blackstone named a new chief administrator before managment had interviewed each of the two hundred thirty-five applicants.

Review Test 5-4

Write a letter to the Billing Office of a department store to complain that you did not purchase some of the items that appeared on your bill. Explain the situation carefully: include the date of purchase and the costs and quantities of other items purchased. Use a complete letter format, including both your address and the store's full address.

EDITING

FAMOUS FIRST DRAFTS: PATRICK HENRY
Writing Hint: Stick to Your Topic

" I HOPE, GENTLEMEN, THAT YOU WILL FIRST ALLOW ME TO SAY A FEW WORDS ON THE TOPIC OF LIBERTY, OR, AS SOME CALL IT, FREEDOM, WHICH IS ONE OF THE MOST IMPORTANT... "

Source: Ford Button

Give me liberty or give me death.

Reading for Resourceful Writers

Corporate Notices: A Sampling

Sesquipedalian Dictionary Company

To avoid negative consequences, it is incumbent upon employees to partake of midday refection in the designated locus.

Easy Does It T-Shirt Company

Hey, meatheads, stuff
your faces in the lunchroom,
okay?

Worldwide Defense Company Unit 13469—52

WARNING:
ANY EMPLOYEE IGNORING
LUNCH REGULATION 1-435-B
WILL BE PROSECUTED.

Cuteness-Iz-Us Toy Company

Management has a little hunch
That you would like to join the bunch
Of jolly workers who eat their lunch
In the room where it's FUN to munch.
THE CAFETERIA!

Corporation for Reasonable Writing

EMPLOYEES:
Please eat lunch in the
lunchroom.

PART SIX OBJECTIVES: To organize and revise sentences and paragraphs.

Now that we have covered the mechanics of good writing, we move on to editing techniques that will make your business writing more effective. In reviewing these techniques, we will examine words, sentences, and paragraphs.

Before beginning work on writing and rewriting strategies, however, we include a chapter on *pre-writing*: techniques you can use to organize and develop your thoughts. The chart on page 355 outlines a series of steps you can follow to develop a good piece of business writing. Note that *writing* is Step 4—not Step 1.

THREE *W*'S AND ONE *H*

Before you put together sentences and paragraphs, you should have a good sense of the three *W*'s: WHY, WHAT, and WHOM. You should know *why* you are writing, *what* you are writing about, and to *whom* you are writing. You should also know HOW you are going to present your ideas: the major points you want to cover and the order you will use to cover them. Only then should you begin writing!

When you actually begin writing, we suggest that you move quickly. Do not stop to polish your sentences or rearrange the order of your paragraphs. You might make notes to yourself as you write your first draft (*check spelling* or *use another word here*), but try to let your thoughts flow freely. When you have a rough draft (and it will be *rough*!), you can go back to revise it for word choice, wordiness, tone, sentence and paragraph structure as well as for grammar, punctuation, and mechanics.

Chapters 30 through 35 provide guidelines for this *rewriting* process. Revision is the key to good writing. You must learn to be patient; accept the fact that your first draft will have to be revised—and revised again. You may hear stories of authors who wrote famous novels in two days, but in most cases those tales are just that—tales. Even the most brilliant writers often struggle over their first, second, even third and fourth drafts.

So, especially if you are writing something important, try to leave a day or two between your first and second drafts: when you see them with fresh eyes, you will be able to solve easily many of the problems that bothered you earlier.

Before starting work on Part Six, try editing the following sentences.

PART SIX PRE-TEST

Rewrite the following sentences so they are clear, concise, and effective. You may add, delete, or replace words as needed.

1. The important essentials of this report have been summarized by me.

2. Please be advised that subsequent correspondence should be addressed to Francis Deering.

3. We were both astonished and surprised by the sudden changes and alterations in plans.

4. Maureen Hammond is in receipt of your letter, and its contents have been duly noted by her.

5. As per our conversation of March 21, your new terminal has been sent to you by us.

6. If you don't bother to contact us by May 2, your membership will be canceled.

7. A general consensus of opinion has been reached by the Board.

8. Herewith enclosed is a copy of the report with statistics for the month of June.

9. The interfacing between employees and management last week did not produce a viable resolution to the problems.

10. Philip Tremaine is both uncertain and unsure about the true facts of the matter.

See sample revisions at end of text.

SEVEN STEPS TO SUCCESSFUL WRITING

1. Define Your Subject and Purpose

Focus on your topic and goal. Are you giving information? Selling something? Arguing a point? Conveying bad news? Proposing a project?

2. Brainstorm

Jot down random thoughts about your goals, your readers' needs, your needs, the information you want to get across, the action you would like readers to take, and so on.

3. Make an Outline

Decide on the best organization for your purpose and subject. Organize a beginning, middle, and end. If possible, draft topic sentences for major paragraphs or sections.

4. Write

Begin writing without editing. Keep an eye on your outline, but do not worry if your plan begins to change.

5. Revise

Reorganize if necessary. Check word choice, tone. Delete unnecessary words. Develop a strong opening and conclusion. Provide transitions between thoughts.

6. Polish

Review grammar, punctuation, spelling, word usage, and tone. Work on sentence construction and variety.

7. Proofread

Check for mechanical and typographical errors.

CHAPTER 29

ORGANIZATION/ OUTLINES

OBJECTIVE: To organize effective letters, memos, and reports.

Before beginning any letter, memo, report—in fact, any piece of writing—you should organize it. A good outline will save you many hours of extra work and bring you to a finished product much more quickly.

Even the briefest letter requires an opening, supporting material, and conclusion. An outline helps you to see what you plan to say and what order will best convey your message.

DEFINE YOUR PURPOSE

First, however, you need to define your exact reason for writing. Knowing your purpose is vital to the coherence and unity of your final version. In the following letter, for example, the writer never defines a central purpose.

Dear Ms. Thornton:

We were all very sorry to hear about your son's illness and hope he will be out of the hospital very soon. Congratulations on your promotion to district manager! I am sure we will now see the Fair Oaks branch become even more successful under your supervision.

I hope to see you at the upcoming company picnic in Gardner Park. Have you heard any news from George Derby in New York? I am looking forward to seeing him at the picnic as well.

This letter is confusing and fragmented because the writer never establishes a focus or major point. Every piece of writing should have a *concept*. If you cannot summarize that concept in your own mind ("congratulate Ms. Thornton on her promotion"; "offer sympathy on her son's illness"; "invite her to the company picnic"), you may not be able to write coherently. You should especially avoid combining two or more unsuited topics—congratulations and condolences are not very compatible. Congratulations and an invitation to the company picnic could be more easily fused.

LIMIT YOUR TOPIC

After making sure you have only *one* major topic, establish that your topic is not too large for the time and space you have available. If you intend to write a brief report, for example, you cannot handle *all* personnel problems: instead, you need to focus on a particular area such as staff training.

Note: One way to check the scope of your topic is to find a title for a memo or report before you begin the outline. If you cannot come up with a specific title ("Training New Clerical Staff"), you may not have sufficiently limited your topic.

OUTLINE MAJOR IDEAS

Now make notes on all the major points you want to touch on. A stream of consciousness technique can be helpful here. Don't try to organize anything; just note some major areas.

For instance, when Fred Rose, the head of a mid-size consulting firm based in Milwaukee, decided to open an office in New York, he wanted to write a memo to the Personnel Department concerning interviewing management trainee candidates for positions in the new office. He jotted down this list:

1. Ascertain the candidates' long-term goals.

2. Why do they want to work for us?

3. Are they willing to move to New York? (Have they ever been to New York? Do they know what to expect?)

4. Make sure candidates are strongly people-oriented. See if they are the kind of aggressive personalities we need in our New York office.

5. Get candidates to discuss their leadership activities.

6. Ask candidates what they know about our company.

7. When can they start work?

SHAPE AND ORGANIZE
YOUR OUTLINE

From this list, Fred could see three major areas he wanted the interviewers to focus on: (1) establishing which candidates have dynamic business personalities; (2) establishing which candidates will adapt well to an aggressive urban workplace; and (3) establishing which candidates will have a long-term commitment to the company.

Numbers 4 and 5 fell under the first category, while number 3 fell under the second, and numbers 1, 2, and 6 fell under the third. Number 7, he quickly saw, did not belong in any of the three categories. Moreover, it was a standard question that interviewers always asked the candidates. It was an unnecessary part of Fred's memo, so he eliminated it.

His new outline looked like this:

1. What Are the Candidates Like?
   a. Are they people-oriented and aggressive?
   b. Have they been leaders in their colleges? Communities? Jobs?

2. Will They Be Successful in New York?
   a. Have they been to New York? How did they like it?
   b. Have they lived or worked in other large urban environments?

3. Will They Be Committed to Our Company?
   a. What do they know about our company?
   b. Why are they interested in working for us? (Did they choose us at random from a list of consulting firms?)
   c. Can they describe their long-term goals?

[Note that Fred's new outline is parallel. It consists solely of questions, not a combination of questions and things to do.]

From this reorganized outline, then, Fred could begin drafting the memo knowing he wouldn't forget a major point or put it in an illogical place.

As you can see, an outline does not have to be very formal, though a longer piece of writing often demands a more detailed outline. Basically, you want to make sure that your thoughts are falling into some sort of order, that none sticks out untidily, and that your topic is small enough to be handled in the framework you have in mind.

Many formal outlines (see Figure 29.2, p. 363) use Roman numerals for the major headings, capital letters for the first set of subheadings, numbers for the second set of subheadings, and lowercase letters for the fourth set. You may find this method useful, but it is not essential. As you can see, Fred Rose used a more informal approach that successfully accomplished his purpose.

CREATE AN EFFECTIVE OPENING

Many writers do not begin tackling their opening paragraphs until they have a good grasp on their topics. You may want to write your first paragraph after everything else, when you are sure of your purpose and major points.

An opening paragraph should provide insight into the paragraphs that follow and answer *some* of the reader's questions. It should pique the reader's interest and provide an accurate sense of what the rest of the piece of writing is about. You do not have to summarize the whole piece or reveal your arguments or conclusions; but you should not confuse your reader by discussing a minor issue or describing a topic broader than the one you are actually going to cover.

After assembling his outline, for example, Fred Rose jotted some notes on his opening paragraph, although he did not actually write the paragraph until later.

—Tell interviewers that I want them to address some special areas in interviews with these candidates.

—Assure interviewers that these areas should be addressed *in conjunction* with their usual interview techniques.

—Explain that this is a special group of candidates who must be able to function more independently than our usual management trainees.

In your opening, you may want to present the background on a certain situation or problem; establish your point of view about a topic; summarize your recommendations; describe your purpose for writing; explain a problem or ask a question; or define the scope of your piece of writing.

ORGANIZE YOUR MAJOR POINTS

The most useful feature of an outline is to organize your data in some order that will make sense to your reader. You will find it much easier to write logically if you summarize your ideas before you write them out.

For example, when Norm Lambert was inviting his co-workers to the annual company dinner, he first outlined his memo like this:

Paragraph 1:

1. Announce the date and time of the dinner

2. Tell them it's also a good-bye dinner for Gary Goodman

Paragraph 2:

1. Give time, location

2. Describe the band, the four-course dinner

Paragraph 3:

1. Mention that dress is semiformal

2. Remind them that there is no charge for the event

Paragraph 4:

1. Urge them to support company event

2. Give directions to restaurant

When he looked this outline over, Norm decided that the most important details were disorganized and spread through the whole memo. It would be more effective if he combined the pertinent information—time, date, location—in one paragraph and provided information about the event itself in another paragraph. The directions, he decided, could go in a postscript. His next outline looked like this:

Paragraph 1: Purpose of memo

1. Announce that this year's company dinner is also a good-bye to Gary Goodman

Paragraph 2: Essential information

1. Give info on time, date, location, attire

Paragraph 3: Less essential information

1. Describe four-course dinner

2. Describe band

Paragraph 4: Reasons for attending

1. Urge them to support company event

2. Remind them that the event is free

3. Say it's their chance to say good-bye to Gary

Paragraph 5 (postscript)

1. Give directions to restaurant

Self-Check Test 29-1

Outline a new letter to Ms. Thornton (see page 356), congratulating her on her promotion to district manager and inviting her to the company picnic. (See answer section at end of text for sample outline.)

The following are some methods you might consider for organizing your material.

ORDER OF INCREASING IMPORTANCE

You may want to organize your material toward a crescendo, building toward a climax.

For example, you may have three reasons why your company should purchase a certain computer system: the cost is very reasonable, the system is adaptable to your company's growth, and the software available for the system is perfect for your needs. The second two items are important, but the cost is exceptionally good as you have negotiated successfully with the dealer.

Your report on the system could first develop the strong points of the system itself and then end persuasively with the excellent price.

ORDER OF DECREASING IMPORTANCE

The major drawback to the crescendo approach to organization is that, in some situations, your reader may get tired of reading the less vital data. You will have to judge whether to hold your trump card until the end or show it at the beginning.

An organizational approach that starts with the most essential information is helpful to a busy reader who wants to get to the heart of the matter without delay. Thus, sometimes you will want to summarize your recommendations, for example, or the results of your research before you go into the background and methodology.

A report might start with a recommendation based on the significant results of a customer survey. The remainder of the report might provide less important reasons for your recommendation.

The drawback to this approach is that it can become dull, since the most interesting points are covered in the first few paragraphs or pages.

COMPARISON AND CONTRAST

If you are comparing or contrasting two or more systems, ideas, items, and so on, you may want to set up an organization that allows the reader to see the strong and weak points of each item. Once again, however, you may want to start with either the most important or the least important points.

You will also have to decide whether to describe all the points of each item before moving on to the next (see Figure 29.1) or to describe one aspect of all the items (cost, for example, or size) before moving on to the next aspect (see Figure 29.2).

PROBLEM TO SOLUTION ORDER

Many business materials are written in response to a problem. In this case, your organization will be built around stating the problem, offering and weighing solutions, and arriving at a recommendation.

To organize the possible solutions, you will probably use a pattern similar to one we have just discussed: you might start with the least feasible possibility, for example, and move to the most feasible. Or you might start with the best recommendation and then explain why others are less feasible.

When Wendy Young organized a memo to management regarding the high personnel turnover in her department, she stated the cause of the problem in her opening: too much overtime is required of part-time employees. Then she presented three possible solutions and analyzed each one in terms of costs and savings. By showing the second and third options to be more expensive and less productive than the first option, she provided an argument for the first solution.

Figure 29.1

SAMPLE OUTLINE This outline organizes information for a report on selecting a site for a drugstore. The writer establishes three criteria for making a decision and then evaluates the advantages and disadvantages of each site in relation to those criteria. The writer uses the crescendo approach, moving toward the most attractive site.

TITLE: Site Report for Farr's Drugstore

INTRODUCTION: This report evaluates three possible sites for Farr's Drugstore. The criteria used for evaluation were cost, convenience of location, and available consumer markets.

I.   Methodology

    A.   Cost: Owners and real estate agents provided figures for buying, renting, or leasing each site.

    B.   Convenience: Observational studies determined parking availability, ease of access, and visibility of each site.

    C.   Consumer markets: A market research team conducted tests to determine market segmentation and buyer habits at each site.

II.   Analysis of Freeway Location (give address)

    A.   Advantages

        1.   Location is visible to freeway travelers and parking is unlimited.

        2.   Travelers are willing to pay more for convenience of store.

    B.   Disadvantages

        1.   Travelers are only 10 percent of Farr's target market.

        2.   The 1,550 square foot space costs $3,100 per month to lease.

III.   Analysis of Downtown Location (give address)

    A.   Advantages

        1.   There are 15 office buildings and 25 small businesses within walking distance.

        2.   No multipurpose drugstore exists to accommodate lunch-hour and after-work shoppers.

        3.   The building, with 3,400 square feet, is the largest of the sites.

    B.   Disadvantages

        1.   Only limited meter parking is available.

        2.   Lease cost is $3,000 per month.

        3.   Businesspeople are only 20 percent of targeted market.

IV.   Analysis of Suburban Location (give address)

    A.   Advantages

        1.   Access is easy and plenty of free parking is available.

        2.   The population is 60 percent retired people, 25 percent families: these are the majority of Farr's targeted markets.

    B.   Disadvantages

        1.   This site is the most expensive. The building has 2,500 square feet and will cost $3,300 per month to lease. Bringing building up to code will cost an additional $7,000.

V.   Recommendation. Despite operating costs, the suburban site will be the most profitable.

Figure 29.2

SAMPLE OUTLINE This outline organizes data for a report on a company health facility. Major sections compare and contrast three options. Report will present benefits and costs before arriving at a recommendation.

Title: EMPLOYEE HEALTH FACILITY

Introduction: An employee survey indicates that 77 percent of employees would like access to a health facility. Other companies report that such a facility is economically beneficial to them.

I.   Advantages to the Facility

    A.   Employees are in favor of it. (Give survey data.)

    B.   Facility will benefit employees.

        1.   Will improve fitness/health

        2.   Will allow social interaction

    C.   Facility will benefit company.

        1.   Will improve employees' health and morale

            a.   Less absenteeism

            b.   Lower health costs

            c.   Increased production

        2.   Will help recruit new employees

        3.   Will improve company image

II. Disadvantages to Health Facility

    A.   Cost

    B.   Space problems

III. Employee Preferences for Types of Facilities

    A.   Exercise equipment/aerobics classes: 85 percent (of employees in favor of a facility)

    B.   Indoor track: 40 percent

    C.   Swimming pool: 30 percent

IV. Costs

    A.   Exercise equipment/aerobics teacher (medium cost)

    B.   Track (least expensive)

    C.   Swimming pool (most expensive)

V.   Space Problems

    A.   Exercise room (least space)

    B.   Track (moderate amount of space)

    C.   Swimming pool (most space)

VI. Recommendation: Exercise Equipment/Aerobics Classes

    A.   Much more demand for this type of facility, and building has adequate space for it.

    B.   Benefits will eventually outweigh costs.

ORDER OF TIME

The order of time organizational pattern is most useful when you are explaining procedures or giving instructions.

> Step 1: Turn on the power button at the rear left corner of the terminal.
> Step 2: Push the power button located beside the disk drives.

This type of organization is not meant to be persuasive or interesting, but it is vital to certain types of writing.

The best way to choose your organizational method is to consider the nature of your material and your audience: what are the needs and concerns of your readers? What do the readers need to know? How much do they know already? How much time are they going to spend on your writing?

When you have a clear sense of your audience and your own central purpose in writing, you will find it easier to organize your data.

Self-Check Test 29-2

I. Gerri Farr is organizing a memo that will inform her supervisor about the strong and weak points of three photocopy machines she has been researching. Which organizational method should she use? Why? (See end of text for sample answer.)

II. Heriot Patterson is writing a memo to all his store employees to explain how to use a new computerized cash register he has purchased. Which organizational method should he use? Why?

III. Peggy Martin is writing a memo to the company president. She hopes to persuade the president to change from a nine to five working schedule for employees to a flextime schedule. She has five major points in favor of flextime. What method do you suggest she use to organize the memo? Why?

CREATE A STRONG CONCLUSION

In some ways, the opening and closing of your piece of writing are the most important parts. Your reader is apt to remember the first and last paragraphs more than the middle parts—just as you might particularly remember a strong opening or closing shot in a film or an effective opening or closing to someone's speech.

Before writing his memo to the Personnel Department, Fred Rose summarized his concluding paragraph:

—Repeat that these candidates will have to be dynamic self-starters.

—Tell interviewers that top five candidates should be notified of a second interview with management staff by August 5.

—Assure interviewers that they always do an excellent job and will undoubtedly choose the best candidates.

Many ending paragraphs provide a concise restatement of major points or of the introductory paragraph; others provide recommendations or look to a future situation.

Some endings are a call for action: here is where you ask for a job interview, request that the reader meet with you regarding a special issue, ask the reader to support your cause or to call you by a certain date.

Make sure the final paragraph of your piece of writing will be a smooth, definitive conclusion. You do not want your reader to turn the page looking for more information: he or she should *know* this paragraph is the end.

USE YOUR OUTLINE

Your outline should be a useful guide. It should be flexible, something you can change as your thoughts on your topic become clearer. But, once you have an outline that works, think very carefully before you deviate from it as you write: your outline is there to keep you from wandering off your topic and to help you present your information in a clear, organized fashion.

Checklist for Chapter 29

1. Define and limit your topic before you start writing.

2. List your major ideas.

3. Create an effective opening.

4. Develop a logical order for your central data.

5. Create a strong conclusion.

Exercises

1. A friend has asked you for some ideas on how to choose a college that will be right for his or her needs. Outline a letter to the friend with at least two major headings. Make sure you organize your ideas effectively.

2. Outline an invitation to a software demonstration sponsored by Communications Technology. This is a three-hour event including lunch.

Chapter Test 29-1

The following list includes some major points that a writer wants to include in a memo concerning a new petty cash system for a company. Decide on an effective organizational structure for the memo, and then organize the list into an outline with at least two major headings. You may add items to the outline, but do not delete items from this list.

- Use petty cash only for purchasing office materials under ten dollars.
- Do not use petty cash for buying birthday gifts, shower gifts, and so on, for other employees.
- At present you take the money and then put a receipt in the petty cash box after you have purchased an item.
- When Jackie Bronson is absent, ask Hank Greene for the petty cash box.
- Sign the card inside the box whenever you take money out.
- Put the date, amount, and purpose for which you are taking the money.
- Jackie Bronson will now be in charge of the petty cash box.
- Sign each receipt you put in the box.
- Present petty cash system is inaccurate and confusing.

Chapter Test 29-2

Outline a memo to fellow students regarding a new organization on campus that you would like them to join. You will want to tell them the purpose and goals of the organization, give details of an upcoming meeting, and explain why students will benefit from joining. Use a crescendo method to order the benefits of belonging to the organization.

Exercise for Experts

Outline a two- to three-page report on communication problems you have encountered in a work situation. This is a very broad area, so make sure you limit the problems to a specific context. Assume you will be addressing the report to a communications instructor. Your outline should have at least two major headings and two or three subheadings under each major one.

CHAPTER 30

WORDS COMMONLY CONFUSED

OBJECTIVE: To use words with the correct meaning for your sentences.

Can you spot any usage errors in the following sentences?

1. I hope you will except our glass of complementary wine.

2. Our sales have been affected by the change in weather.

3. The company managers plan to adopt the rules to their own needs.

Sentences #1 and #3 contain errors: *except* should be *accept; complementary* should be *complimentary; adopt* should be *adapt*. Sentence #2 is correct.

As we saw in Chapter 26 (p. 318), many English words sound alike but mean different things. To avoid confusing words, you should follow the same principles we described while discussing spelling problems. SEE how words are used, HEAR how they are pronounced, USE troublesome words, and REPEAT them: keep using troublesome words (and looking them up in the dictionary if necessary) until you are sure of them.

A dictionary is an invaluable tool for every writer. Invest in a good dictionary that shows you alternative meanings, syllabification, and pronunciation. Many dictionaries also provide examples of how words are used in sentences. Watch for usage labels such as *obsolete, slang, informal,* and *colloquial.* These words will probably not be appropriate for business writing.

Some dictionaries provide information about the origin of the word—whether it is derived from a foreign language or from an earlier form of English. You will find it worthwhile to read about the origin of a word: not only can the source be interesting but it may also help to imprint the meaning of the word on your mind.

PREFIXES

Pay particular attention to prefixes (one or more letters preceding the root of a word). Often these prefixes will give you a clue as to the meaning of the word.

PREFIX	MEANING	
ante-	before	*ante*cedent (something coming before)
anti-	against	*anti*-aircraft (against aircraft)
co-	jointly	*co*-authored (authored jointly)
inter-	between	*inter*national (between nations)
pre-	before	*pre*view (advance viewing)
post-	after	*post*date (assign a date after the present date)

Self-Check Test 30-1

Using a dictionary, look up the meanings of the following prefixes. Then use two words with that prefix in a sentence.

1. [pro-]

a.

b.

2. [hyper-]

a.

b.

3. [super-]

a.

b.

4. [dis-]

a.

b.

5. [de-]

a.

b.

SUFFIXES

Suffixes, too, can be helpful in recognizing and using words. As we saw in Part One, endings often provide information about a word: words ending in -*ly* are often adverbs; words ending in -*tion* and -*ness* are often nouns. (Of course, endings often tell you also whether a noun is singular or plural or whether a verb is in present or past tense.)

COMMON PROBLEM WORDS

TO ACCEPT means *to receive* or *to approve. Mrs. Reilley accepted the terms of the contract.*
TO EXCEPT means *to make an exception. Except is also a preposition. Jack bought all the furniture except this.*

TO ADAPT means *to alter* or *remodel: We adapted the constitution of the former organization.*
TO ADOPT means *to take as one's own: The supervisor adopted an aggressive managerial style.*

ALOT OF Colloquial. Do not use.
A LOT OF Even this form is slightly colloquial. In formal business writing, use *many* or a similar word. *We have acquired a lot of new computers* is less acceptable than *We have acquired many new computers.*

WRITING HINT: CHECK YOUR DICTIONARY FOR DEFINITIONS

What Mrs. Browne Wrote   *What Her Sentence* Means

Source: Ford Button

TO AFFECT means *to influence. The rain affected our spirits.*
TO EFFECT means *to bring about. His research effected a cure.* (It did not simply influence a cure—it brought it into existence.)
AN EFFECT means *a result.* The yard showed the *effects* of the storm.

TO ALLUDE means *to refer to. Greg alluded to Einstein's theories.*
TO ELUDE means *to escape. The convict eluded the authorities.*

ALREADY means *by a certain time: The ships were already on the bay by noon.*
ALL READY means *completely ready: Are you all ready for the performance?*

AMOUNT should be used when referring to bulk quantities: *The warehouse stores a large amount of sugar.* (Use *amount* with singular nouns.)
A NUMBER should refer to countable items: *A large number of reporters have converged on the courtroom.* (Use *number* with plural nouns. *A number* is usually followed by a plural verb.)
THE NUMBER is usually followed by a singular noun. *The number* of applicants is still small.

TO APPRAISE means *to set a value on: The jeweler appraised the gold watch.*
TO APPRISE means *to inform: We have been apprised of the current situation.*

TO COMPLEMENT means *to go with* or *accompany: The colors complement her face.*
TO COMPLIMENT means *to say something favorable: He complimented the candidate on his experience.* (A *complimentary* item is a free item.)

CONTINUAL means *recurring at intervals: The volcano has erupted continually over a thousand years.*
CONTINUOUS means *without interruption: Warren has spoken continuously for three hours.*

DISINTERESTED means *impartial: The panel chose seven disinterested judges.*
UNINTERESTED means *without interest: Doug is uninterested in politics.*

ELICIT means *to bring out: The speaker elicited a cheer from the crowd.*
ILLICIT means illegal: *The bookkeeper had developed some illicit procedures.*

EMINENT means *distinguished: Alice is an eminent psychologist.*
IMMINENT means *soon: The bankruptcy proceedings are imminent.*

EXPLICIT means *expressed directly: The reporter explicitly accuses the man by referring to him as "the arsonist."*
IMPLICIT means *expressed indirectly: The wording is vague, but the implicit message is alarming.*

FEWER should be used with countable items: *This company employs fewer programmers than that company.* (Fewer should be followed by plural nouns.)
LESS should be used with bulk items: *I have less enthusiasm for the project than you do.* (Less should be followed by singular nouns.)

TO FLOUNDER means *to move awkwardly: Without his notes, the speaker floundered.*
TO FOUNDER means *to sink* or *to fall apart: The ship foundered on the sunken rocks.*

FORMER and **LATTER** should be used when referring to two items: *Of these two ideas, the former is too expensive and the latter is too uncertain.*
FIRST and **LAST** should be used when referring to more than two items: *Of all the items on my grocery list, I forgot only the first and the last.*

IRREGARDLESS is nonstandard. Do not use. Use REGARDLESS.

PRINCIPAL is an adjective meaning *chief: Profits are their principal concern.* Principal is also a noun referring to an administrator and to a sum of money: *The school principal is retiring. The principal has grown by 10 percent.*
A PRINCIPLE is a belief: *Alex is a man of strong principles.* A *principle* is also a personal code of conduct: *Greta maintains high principles.*

TO PRECEDE means *to go before: Wild speculation preceded the stock market crash.*
TO PROCEED means *to go ahead: The company proceeded with its plans.*

STATIONARY means *not movable: The stationary bicycle was bolted to the floor.*
STATIONERY means *letter paper and envelopes.*

THAN is used in comparison: *Quincy is taller than Harry.*
THEN refers to time: *Only then will we decide on the merger.*

WOULD OF is unacceptable. Do not confuse with the helping verbs *would have: I would have helped if I had known.* (See also p. 178.)

Self-Check Test 30-2

Look for word usage problems in the following sentences. Cross out the wrong words and put in the appropriate forms. (Check end of text for answers.)

1. I would ~~of~~ *have* seen the problem earlier if I had spent more time on the calculations.

2. Mr. Simpson often ~~eludes~~ *allude* to a number of people he met in New York.

3. The ~~stationary~~ *stationery* we have ordered has ~~illicited~~ *elicited* some controversy from the staff.

4. The ~~principals~~ *principles* in the personnel handbook have already been adapted for the new company.

5. There are ~~less~~ *fewer* people in this department now that we have a computerized system.

6. John never mentioned the employees' morale problem when he ~~appraised~~ *apprised* the Board of the financial situation.

7. Please do not ~~except~~ *accept* this job offer unless you are willing to work ~~alot~~ *a lot* of hours.

8. The ~~imminent~~ *eminent* attorney Leonard Flagg has ~~all ready~~ *already* addressed the group.

9. A large ~~amount~~ *number* of secretaries are complaining of nervous tension.

10. I believe we will survive longer ~~then~~ *than* many other companies our size.

THREE TROUBLESOME VERBS

The verbs *sit* and *set*, *rise* and *raise*, and *lie* and *lay* cause particular problems for many writers. In each case, the first verb in the pair does not take a direct object, while the second verb in the pair does take an object.

Sit and Set

The verb *sit* means to take a seat; *set* means to put something down. Both verbs are irregular in the simple past.

SIT	SET
I sit (present tense)	I set (present tense)
I sat (past tense)	I set (past tense)
I have sat (present perfect tense)	I have set (present perfect tense)
I sit on the ledge. (no d.o.)	I set the book down. (d.o.)
I sat on the ledge. (no d.o.)	

Rise and Raise

Rise means to go up or stand up; *raise* means to put in a higher position. Only *raise* takes a direct object.

RISE	RAISE
I rise (present tense)	I raise (present tense)
I rose (past tense)	I raised (past tense)
I have risen (present perfect tense)	I have raised (present perfect tense)
I rise early on weekdays. (no d.o.)	I raise tomatoes. (d.o.)
I rose early today. (no d.o.)	I raised tomatoes. (d.o.)
I have risen early since childhood. (no d.o.)	I have raised tomatoes all year. (d.o.)

Lie and Lay

Lie means to be in a horizontal position; *lay* means to put something down. Only *lay* takes a direct object.

LIE	LAY
I lie (present tense)	I lay (present tense)
I lay (past tense)	I laid (past tense)
I have lain (present perfect tense)	I have laid (present perfect tense)
I am lying (present progressive tense)	I am laying (present progressive tense)
I lie in bed every day. (no d.o.)	I lay books on the table. (d.o.)
I lay in bed yesterday. (no d.o.)	I laid books on the table. (d.o.)
I have lain in bed for a week. (no d.o.)	I have laid books on the table. (d.o.)
I was lying here when she arrived. (no d.o.)	I was laying books on the table when she arrived. (d.o.)

Self-Check Test 30-3

I. Using a dictionary, write a brief definition for the following words. Then use each in a sentence. (See answer section at end of text for sample sentences.)

1. All together:

   Altogether:

2. Imaginary:

   Imaginative:

3. Incidence:

   Incidents:

4. Conscious:

   Conscience:

5. Envelop:

   Envelope:

6. Incredible:

Incredulous:

7. Condole:

Condone:

8. Detract:

Distract:

9. Elemental:

Elementary:

10. Populace:

Populous:

II. Fill in the blanks with the correct forms of the verbs. (See end of text for answers.)

1. [sit/set] Now that Jill and Gerry have _____ here for an hour, they have finally _____ their books on the table.

2. [lie/lay] I had _____ on the sofa for an hour with a newspaper _____ on the floor beside me when I noticed that my cat had _____ her ball of twine on my knee.

3. [rise/raise] Our spirits _____ while the soldier was

_____ the flag and the crowd was _____ to its feet.

4. [sit/set] As we _____ on the porch, the sun is _____ behind the hills.

5. [lie/lay] As Felipe's dog was _____ in the sun, Felipe

_____ a sandwich under the dog's nose.

Checklist for Chapter 30

1. Use your dictionary whenever you are unsure of a word.

2. Use your dictionary to check for word origin, syllabification, pronunciation, and usage.

3. To avoid confusing similar sounding words, use the same principles we discussed for avoiding spelling errors.

4. Learn common prefixes and suffixes to help you recognize and use words.

Word Usage Review

Correct any errors in the following paragraph. (Check end of text for answers.)

After we had laid in the sun continually for an hour, we realized we were late for our appointment, so we preceded to hurry indoors. A large amount of people were also coming inside, since the temperature was raising quickly and the sand was becoming unbearably hot. By the time we left to go set in the doctor's office, we saw less than ten people on the beach.

**Chapter Test
30-1**

Cross out the words used incorrectly and write in the appropriate counterpart to each. Some sentences may be correct.

1. For your convenience, we have set up a special lane for people with ten items or less.

2. Before the trial began, everyone believed that the defendant had tried to allude the authorities.

3. Because George Martin is a man of strong principles, I knew he would of been an excellent representative of our cause.

4. The menu states explicitly that the champagne is complementary irregardless of the price of one's entrée.

5. The large amount of news stories have convinced us that the issue is important to the public.

6. Of the three issues at stake, the former is most vital.

7. Many disinterested observers have informed us that a strike is eminent.

8. I hope your opinion has not been effected by this lone incident.

9. According to a large number of commuters, these trains are continuously late.

10. These marketing experts are working on implicit messages that filter into the subconscious minds of the readers.

Chapter Test 30-2

Fill in the blanks with appropriate forms of *to lie* and *to lay*.

1. When my back went out last week, I _____ on the bed for 15 hours.

2. Sam carefully _____ the vase on the table before unwrapping it.

3. Now that she has heard the evidence, she realizes that the truth _____ _____ somewhere between the two versions of the story.

4. By _____ newspapers on the kitchen floor, Marty soaked up most of the spilled stew.

5. Harry had _____ in the bathtub an hour by the time he woke up.

6. The busboy was _____ glasses on the cart when the customer called for help.

7. Patsy _____ in the sun every morning when she is on vacation.

8. I have been _____ tile this way for six years even though I realize there are simpler methods.

9. The coat had been _____ there for days before someone claimed it.

10. Jack had just _____ the watch in the store window when Marilyn spotted it.

Exercise for Experts

Mrs. Malaprop, a character in a play by Richard Sheridan, is famous for her incorrect choice of words. In fact, a *malapropism* now means an absurd misuse of a word. In the following letter, the writer has a similar tendency to confuse words. See if you can spot the misused words and replace them with the words the writer should have used.

Dear Mrs. Winthrop:

I was most shocked and grieved yesterday to learn that you are considering Martin Hoopsdale for precedent of your club. I cannot condole such a poor choice.

Perhaps you are under the allusion that Hoopsdale is an imminent member of our community. In actuality, he is a repulsive gambler who has no conscious when it comes to money. My son loaned him five dollars last week, and Hoopsdale has been most regretful about paying it back. Would you want to make that man an officious representative of your group?

Before you come to a final derangement with Hoopsdale, I suggest you consider my son Algernon Apple for the job. The imposition would be perfect for Algernon. Even in elemental school he was a child progeny; he served as a corporeal in the army and has always been a great pillow of our community.

So, before exorcising your right to elect Hoopsdale, please dismember my son.

Sincerely,

Alfred Apple

After you have replaced the incorrect words in this letter with those the writer intended to use, make a list of the *incorrect* words. Are you familiar with all of them? If not, check their meanings in a dictionary.

CHAPTER 31

WORD CHOICE

OBJECTIVE: To improve your writing by choosing the clearest, most concrete, and most correct word for your message and your audience.

Word choice, naturally, lies at the heart of written communication. On the written page, where your reader cannot see your face or your gestures—or hear the tone of your voice—word choice is vital to effective communication. One word can radically alter the meaning of a message. And, by disrupting tone and style, a wrong word can damage the relationship you want to establish with your readers.

THE THREE *C*'S

As you work on writing and revising your business writing, consider the three C's of word choice: CLEARNESS, CONCRETENESS, and CORRECTNESS.

THE CLEAR WORD

The words you choose should be ones that your readers easily understand. Consider who your readers are. Remember: your principal concern should be to communicate—not to show off a magnificent vocabulary. For example, if you are writing a science article meant for scientists, you might discuss sodium chloride; for general readers, you would want to use the word *salt*.

In business writing, a short, common word is usually a better choice than a long, difficult one. One problem with many memos, letters, and reports is that they employ "ten dollar" words when a "ten cent" word would do just as well—or better. Why use *retrocede* when you can say *move back?* If you run out of a building yelling "Conflagration!" you will probably get less of a response than if you yell "Fire!"

Naturally, if you are writing complex or technical material, you will have to choose vocabulary suited to the field. A biologist may write about zoophytes; a linguist may discuss pre-palatal spirants. But keep remembering the *audience*. If your readers are apt to know the words in your field, you need not define them. But if your writing is not aimed at an audience specialized in the area, then choose simple vocabulary and define the words not in common use.

ABBREVIATIONS

While choosing the easiest word for your audience, remember to avoid using abbreviations, initials, and acronyms that your readers may not recognize. If you assume everyone knows what the AMA or the UUAW is, you may end up writing a completely incomprehensible memo or letter.

Besides, too many acronyms and abbreviations will make your writing sound like it was spewed from a computer—or a bureaucrat's desk.

Self-Check Test 31-1

Rewrite the following letter, making it more readable. Look up any unfamiliar words. (See end of text for suggested revisions.)

Dear Ms. Lee:

In reference to your letter under date of October 12 in which you requested purchasing the new Honeywell XZ under a bimonthly installment plan, let me assure you that we have considered the parameters of your request to the fullest possible extent.

Due in large measure, however, to circumstances beyond our control, we are forced to proffer a negative reply to your request. Enclosed herewith is a summary of our monthly installment plan which we hope you will consider favorably. We are of the opinion that the Honeywell XZ is the best micro on the market today and that you will find our terms very reasonable.

We will hold a Honeywell XZ for you pending receipt of your order.

THE CONCRETE WORD

Rough drafts are as varied as the people who write them, but most do have a few common characteristics. Most are over-wordy, as we shall see in Chapter 33, and most are vague. As you review your draft for word choices, ask yourself whether you could be more specific. Check your sentences. Do the words indicate how much, how far, how big, where, who, why, and what?

Our place of business is located near a shopping mall. [vague]

Our store is on Maple Avenue, across from the North-town Mall. [concrete]

Marlene Hardy has a business degree and some business experience. [vague]

Marlene Hardy, who has a doctorate in finance, worked two years as a financial consultant for NYP Corporation. [specific]

If you pay slightly more, you will pay back the loan in just a few years. [vague]

If you pay $122 a month, you will pay back the loan in three years. [specific]

VAGUE	CONCRETE
big	forty feet high
shallow	one inch deep
far	six hundred miles
inexpensive	less than a dollar
many people	a thousand students
good clothes	tuxedos and formal gowns
bad food	spoiled beef

Concrete words make your message not only clearer but also more interesting. Compare "Herman Schmidt drove a car" with "Herman Schmidt drove a 1952 custom Mercedes." The concrete detail makes the sentence come alive and hold some interest for your reader.

Being concrete, by the way, does not necessarily mean adding a string of adjectives to your nouns and adverbs to your verbs: it does mean choosing nouns and verbs that have some substance. As you will see in Chapter 33, concrete words can also save you time and space; you can say what you mean in fewer but more efficient words.

Self-Check Test 31-2

Make the following sentences more complete. Invent more information if necessary. (See end of text for suggested revisions.)

1. I am applying for the job you advertised in the paper as I have all the qualifications you mentioned.

2. I am a good worker, have a college degree, and excellent personal qualities. I also worked for some time for a prominent accounting firm.

3. Come to Simpson's Clothing big sale where several name brands will be greatly discounted.

4. I am sure you will be interested in our new office furniture leasing program, which enables you to lease some types of furniture at a low cost and buy them some time in the future if you prefer.

5. The new restaurant is very large and serves several interesting foreign cuisines for reasonable prices.

THE CORRECT WORD

In Chapter 30, we examined words that writers commonly confuse. Naturally, using a word with the wrong meaning is disastrous to effective communication. However, you also should be attuned to more subtle differences between words. A thesaurus is a great asset for a writer, but it is dangerous to rely on a word if you are unsure of its exact usage.

In *Alice in Wonderland*, Humpty Dumpty claims he can make words mean what he wants them to mean. Unfortunately, people *cannot* really use words in the way they want to. Our words have meanings (or *denotations*) that can be found in dictionaries; words also have connotations, the whole range of associations related to them.

Beautiful, handsome, and *pretty,* for example, have similar dictionary definitions, but each has a different connotation. While each is used to indicate physical attractiveness, we usually use *beautiful* to describe an attractive woman and *handsome* to describe an attractive man. *Pretty,* on the other hand, although usually used to describe girls or women, indicates more superficial good looks. Most women would rather be called *beautiful* than *pretty!*

At the heart of effective writing is choosing the correct word for your message and audience. Pay attention to how words are used in different situations. Correct usage also requires a sense of how the language is changing, since words constantly take on new meanings and connotations.

WORDS CHANGE

Over the centuries a word's meaning may change drastically. A few hundred years ago, *lewd* meant merely *ignorant;* a *villain* was a farm laborer. The word *fast* changed from meaning *immovable* (we still say *fasten*) to meaning *rapid. Nice* used to mean *foolish; meat* referred to all food.

Less drastic changes occur over months and years. Some slang words that would have been improper in formal writing a few years ago are now acceptable (*kudos, foul play*); some words remain slang (*guy, scram*); while others are quickly disappearing (*groovy, fab*). Good writers have a sense of the appropriateness of their words as well as their meanings.

SLANG

Your choice of words should be tailored to the context: a report should be more formal than a sales letter. In general, however, professional writing should adhere to conventional word choices and a traditional style.

An interoffice memo may be friendly and personal, but it should still be free of slang, regionalisms, nonstandard usage, and, of course, bad grammar and punctuation. Some business writers make the mistake of being overly colloquial or conversational.

In general, words and phrases such as *fixing to, busted, fink, mooch, kind of, guy, anyways,* and obscenities of any kind have no place in even the most informal of professional writing.

> We have a bunch of new clients this month. [poor]
> We have plenty of new clients this month. [poor]
> We have many new clients this month. [better]
> Be sure and give me a buzz when you've read the report. [poor]
> Please call me when you've read the report. [better]

Self-Check Test 31-3

Rewrite the following sentences to improve the word choice. (See end of text for suggested revisions.)

1. Our store was ripped off last April by a guy wearing a mask.

2. The whole staff goofed off Friday afternoon until the head honcho told us to get cracking again.

3. The new manager gets his kicks from ordering everyone around a lot.

4. The project is a flop even though we sweated over it for weeks.

5. The new dude in the office is going to squeal to the boss if we take off early from work.

POMPOUS LANGUAGE

Using standard word choices and a professional style does not mean that your writing should be pompous or inflated. On the contrary: your word choices should lead to a pleasant, readable style that is flexible enough for most purposes. Some business writers think that heavy-handed writing will impress their readers; most likely, such writing will only irritate your readers and maybe confuse them as well.

Phrases such as "Per our conversation of March 5" and "Herewith please find enclosed" reveal a lack of originality and a dependence on phrases long out of date. If you want to save time and not sound like you're writing in the 1800's, delete inflated words and replace them with more conversational language.

> Pursuant to your request, we are enclosing herewith a sampling of all colors available. [pompous]
> We enclose samples of available colors, as you requested. [better]
> We desire to acknowledge receipt of your letter of July 5, 19xx, in which you made inquiries concerning the warranty pertaining to your air conditioner. [pompous]
> As you requested on July 5, we enclose the terms of your air conditioner warranty. [better]

The following is a list of some words and phrases too pompous and inflated for most business writing.

INFLATED	IMPROVED
aforementioned	stated before
according to our records	we find
at this point in time	now
due in large measure to	because
effectuate a change	change
in view of foregoing circumstances	therefore
it has come to my attention	[delete]
it is incumbent on me	I must
subsequent to	after
taking this factor into consideration	therefore
to be cognizant of	to know

Self-Check Test 31-4

Make the following sentences more readable. (Check end of text for suggested revisions.)

1. I am sending the new brochure to you under separate cover and hope you will acknowledge receipt.

2. Please give this matter your full attention so we can make an inquiry pertaining to appropriate measures to be taken.

3. It has come to my attention that this department is going to effectuate a change in policy pertaining to sales.

4. Subsequent to the meeting, we have deemed it necessary to make provisions for sick leave in the company benefit plan.

5. If doubt is entertained concerning the aforementioned situation, please remember we will make every effort to compensate you for your efforts.

JARGON

You might think that originality belongs to fiction writing rather than to memos, letters, and reports. Within limits, you would be right: we shouldn't try to emulate the originality of James Joyce's *Ulysses* when composing business correspondence.

On the other hand, there is no reason why business and technical writing should be stale, cliché-ridden, and tedious. Many writers begin every business letter with the words "Per your letter of ———" or "Please find enclosed ———." They believe this jargon gives credibility to their letter when actually it is just an excuse for not thinking.

Jargon and clichés are the bane of writers in every field. They flow naturally from our pens (or keyboards) because we hear them so often. Almost inevitably, they will appear in your first drafts. But do not despair. Simply edit carefully: remove the dull and tedious language and insert simple, clear, but interesting words.

Jargon words often stem from the vocabulary of technical or specialized groups and then become part of our standard vocabulary. *Input* was computer jargon but is now in common use—in fact, it is overused. Business, government, and the military create jargon words by the hundreds. And much of this jargon is pompous and inflated, so it fails on two counts.

> Ever since Linda McMahon came on board as personnel adviser, this organization has prioritized maximum interfacing between management personnel and clerical employees. [tedious and filled with jargon]
>
> Since Linda McMahon began working as personnel adviser, our company has stressed communication between management and clerical staff. [clear and free of jargon]

Clichés may be even more insidious than jargon since we hear and read them constantly. At one point, most clichés were probably original and interesting; the first person who said someone was "sly as a fox" was making an interesting comparison. But, after a few hundred years, that line has worn a bit thin. You can check for clichés often by saying the first part of the phrase and deciding whether the second part is inevitable: *last but not* ———, *I have a sneaking* ———, *true beyond a shadow of a* ———.

The following are some clichés that show up with regularity in business writing. Delete them from your writing whenever you can.

acid test	enclosed herewith
aired their grievances	few and far between
ample opportunity	foreseeable future
at long last	impact (as a verb)
at this point in time	implement (as a verb)
back burner	it goes without saying
ballpark figure	leave well enough alone
benefit of the doubt	marked contrast
bottom line	other things being equal
by the same token	painfully obvious
came on board	parameter
cost effective	state of the art
due consideration	viable

Self-Check Test 31-5

Make the following letter more readable and *human* by revising some of the word choices. (See end of text for a suggested revision.)

Dear Ms. Calhoun:

This is to advise you that we have given due consideration to the bank and credit card references with which you supplied us and to thank you for same. At this point in time we are herewith raising your credit limit to $2,000.

Thanking you again for your patronage, I remain,

Sincerely,

Frank Jones
Credit Manager

Checklist for Chapter 31

1. Check to make sure your words are clear, concrete, and correct for your message and your audience.

2. Define any terms your reader might not know.

3. Avoid pompous, inflated language.

4. Avoid slang, jargon, clichés.

5. Use specific, concrete words.

Word Choice Review

Revise the word choices in the following memo to make it more readable and effective. (Check end of text for suggested revision.)

To: All Employees

From: Garnet Iverson

Subject: Christmas Overtime

Date: December 19, 19xx

It is the understanding of this writer that several employees have proposed a suggestion whereby those persons working the day shift on Christmas Day receive double their hourly wages rather than the standard time and a half. We have forwarded this proposal to management, and an investigation into its financial impact has been initiated. We will convey the outcome immediately upon termination of the investigation.

Exercises

1. Write an invitation to your fellow workers to attend a special seminar on report writing. Explain the need for the seminar and include all pertinent details (location, time, instructor, and so on). Revise the letter with special attention to your choice of words.

2. As a bank manager, write a form letter that will go to customers who have overdrawn their accounts by more than $50. Explain the charges they have incurred and suggest a new type of checking account that will bill overdrawn amounts to their credit card account. Make sure that the letter is clear and concrete and that your words are appropriate to the message and the audience.

3. As credit manager for Caswell's Department Store, write a letter refusing a credit card to a customer. Explain why he is not eligible for the card and offer some suggestions on how he could improve his credit rating.

4. Bring to class a form letter that you have recently received. Underline any jargon, clichés, vague terms, and pompous phrases that you notice in it. Rewrite the letter to make it more effective.

5. Write a letter from the outline you developed in Chapter 29, Exercise 1 or 2 (p. 365). Make sure your word choices are clear, correct, and concrete.

Chapter Test 31-1

Edit the following letter, replacing jargon and clichés with more original word choices and developing a more readable style.

Dear Mr. Climpson:

As per your request of March 12, I enclose herewith a summary of the items that you have ordered from EMF Products over the past six months. At this point in time, as you can see, you have exceeded your credit limit of $350 by nearly a hundred dollars.

In view of the fact that you are a valued customer, we have given due consideration to your request for an additional $200 credit. Although we would ordinarily be happy to implement such a change in our policy, our home office has requested particularly that we curtail credit extensions for the foreseeable future. By the same token, we must request that you finalize your present outstanding balance by the end of this month pursuant to our agreement of February 15.

We look forward to your prompt reply.

Sincerely,

Foster Kent

Chapter Test 31-2   Revise the following letter for clarity and concreteness. You may add any necessary information.

Dear Mrs. Neeman:

This will acknowledge receipt of your recent letter.

One of the principles of EFR Designs has always been: "The customer comes first." We have been pleased to serve you for so many years and hope we will continue to have a successful business relationship with you.

We will not, however, be able to act in accordance with your request for an extended line of credit for office supplies unless you or your agents fill out some papers that are being sent under separate cover. These require information about financial matters. Our company policy also requires that your company maintain a minimum monthly order with us.

In the event that you have any questions pertaining to the credit line application, please do not hesitate to contact me at your convenience.

Sincerely,

Alice Mann

**Exercise for
Experts**

Underline the clichés in the following memo. Then rewrite the memo to make it more effective.

To: All Employees
From: Ralph Hicks
Subject: Grateful Acknowledgments
Date: March 4, 19xx

I wish to offer an abject apology for the straitened circumstances in which we find ourselves at this point in time. Although, after all has been said and done, we are bloody but unbowed, we know this is just the calm before the storm: it is the beginning of the end for this company. To cut a long story short, we are going to have to beat a hasty retreat and take refuge in the tender mercies of the bankruptcy courts.

I give each and every one of you my heartfelt thanks; you have been generous to a fault through the checkered career of this firm. Although the days of this company are numbered, you have been part and parcel of some red-letter days in our industry. It goes without saying that I hope you will receive your just deserts in future positions.

CHAPTER 32

TONE

OBJECTIVE: To create a tone that is most effective for your message and your audience.

You already know the importance of tone when you speak: you can say something as simple as "hello" in tones ranging from friendly to angry, from happy to despondent. Even when you deal with people over the phone, you can tell a lot about their mood from the opening moments of the conversation—their tone often reveals more than their words. If you are like most people, you tend to be friendlier to people who are friendly to you; a hostile voice over the phone can make you hostile as well.

The same concept applies to writing. You may have to write some unpleasant memos and letters during your career, but you will find that a positive, friendly tone will usually be more effective than an angry one. After all, you are writing to get results—not to inflate your ego or damage someone else's.

Naturally, you may sometimes have to write a firm, even threatening letter to collect money or complain about a poor product or service. But first give your readers the benefit of the doubt; don't alienate them from the start. If possible, ask your readers to do something; don't order them.

BE PERSONAL

In Chapter 31, we discussed the bad effects of using long and unnatural words such as *whereas, attached herewith,* and *aforementioned*. These words not only can confuse a reader but also can lend a pretentious, legalistic feeling to your writing. Complicated sentences may add to this impersonal tone. Try to incorporate a personal touch in your writing. People prefer to work for or with a real person rather than an automaton or dictator.

Sometimes you can make your message more personal by phrasing it in the positive rather than in the negative:

> You cannot take a vacation until September. (negative, dictatorial)
> You may take a vacation starting on September 5. (positive)

Other times you may be able to add a bright aspect to your message or provide a reason which will make your reader sympathetic to your message.

> From now until May 15, employees are required to park on Cedar Avenue and take a shuttle bus to the Fairview Building. (negative)

Until May 15 when the new parking lot is finished, employees may park on Cedar Avenue and use our free shuttle bus to the Fairview Building. (positive)

The following is a memo written by a manager who was generally liked and respected by his employees. When he tried to express himself on paper, however, he appeared to have a different personality than he had in person.

To: All Employees

From: Herb Gannon

Topic: Break Times

Date: May 6, 19xx

As many of you have been transgressing on company time by taking extra-long coffee breaks in the mornings and afternoons, henceforth all breaks will be strictly limited to 15 minutes. This policy is in accordance with the rules in Chapter Four of your Personnel Manual. Breaks in this division will be taken from 10:00 to 10:15 a.m. and from 2:00 until 2:15 p.m. ONLY. You will be issued a warning by Elizabeth McElroy if you are late. If you receive more than two warnings, you will be required to speak with me and face a possible dock in pay.

To facilitate the coffee breaks, everyone must remain in the allotted lounge areas for each 15-minute period.

The impersonal, legalistic tone of this memo differed sharply from Herb Gannon's firm but amiable management style. He was shocked to find that the employees resented the memo—even though, as he had pointed out, the policy was already in their personnel manuals. If he had altered the tone of the memo, he would have won the support rather than the resentment of the employees.

The following rewritten version of Herb's memo offers reasons for the rule as well as a friendlier and more persuasive style. Note the changes from passive to active verbs. This version is a little longer than the original, but a few extra words can sometimes help promote cooperation and goodwill.

To: All Employees

From: Herb Gannon

Topic: Break Times

Date: May 6, 19xx

Coffee breaks are an important part of everyone's day. We must, however, make sure not to extend our breaks past the allotted 15 minutes: we need you at your desks, and other divisions need to use the lounge areas before and after us.

Please make sure your breaks extend only from 10:00 until 10:15 a.m. and from 2:00 until 2:15 p.m.—and please remain in the lounge areas during those times.

If you do not follow these regulations, which are explained in more detail in your Personnel Manual, Elizabeth McElroy will have to issue warnings. If you receive more than two warnings, you could receive a dock in pay.

We want your coffee breaks to be a pleasure, not a burden. Please speak with me immediately if you foresee a scheduling problem.

In summary, to maintain a friendly, personal tone, you should consider these guidelines:

- use simple words
- use active, not passive, verbs
- provide reader-oriented explanations
- make positive, not negative, statements

Self-Check Test 32-1

Rewrite the following sentences to make the tone more personal and pleasant. (See end of text for suggested revisions.)

1. Several customers have complained about the poor appearance of our salespeople. As of Friday, March 3, all male employees are required to wear a coat and tie while on the sales floor. All female employees without exception must wear dresses or skirts.

2. Your check for $50, pursuant to our written agreement, must be post-marked no later than August 4, 19xx.

3. In view of the fact that the new health insurance does not cover dental bills, employees must pay their own dental bills or pay for their own individual dental coverage.

4. Your subscription to *New Ideas* will expire on June 1 unless you immediately send in the enclosed card and a check for the appropriate amount.

5. Employees are forbidden to smoke anywhere in the offices or rest rooms of this building. Smoking is restricted to the lounge areas.

STAY CALM

Undoubtedly some of your business correspondence and memos will bear unpleasant news for your readers. You may, for instance, have to write customers about unpaid bills or write a company about a service you have not received. Once again, keep a friendly tone for as long as you can. Avoid using swear words or wild threats. Even if you eventually have to take your reader to court, you should maintain a calm, rational tone. Don't be obnoxious: your major aim should be to solve the problem that has upset you. (Also, a rational letter with concrete details will be more effective in court than a vague, obnoxious one.)

> This stupid car your moron salesman sold me won't even make it to the corner without stalling. [poor: vague and obnoxious]
> The Toyota Corolla I bought from Fred Hicks stalls every time I press the brakes. [better]
> If I don't see your lousy check in this office by Thursday, I'll be seeing you in jail. [poor]
> If I do not receive your check for $340 by Thursday, March 4, I will have to notify my attorney. [better]

BE PROFESSIONAL

Another type of tone problem can occur when the writer wants something offered by the reader—a job or special consideration of some kind. In this situation, you should still maintain a professional, friendly tone. Avoid pleading too hard, promising too much, or making a sad case for yourself. The following examples are extreme—but business people everywhere have seen sentences resembling them.

> If you don't let me postpone my vacation time until July, my children's little hearts will be broken. [unprofessional]

Since my children will be in school until the end of
June, I hope you will consider postponing my vacation until July. [better]

If you have any sympathy in your heart for someone
who has relied too much on the American credit system,
please be kind enough to allow me to make my final payment on December 1 instead of November 15. [unprofes-
sional]

If you could extend my credit two more weeks, I assure
you I will be able to make my final payment on December
1. [better]

In general, you should maintain a rational, professional tone that will not
alienate your reader. If you keep thinking of the reader's reactions, rather than
letting your own emotions dominate the situation, your writing will produce the
results you want.

Checklist for Chapter 32

1. Avoid long, legalistic words and sentences.

2. Provide reasons that will make sense to your readers.

3. Phrase statements positively rather than negatively.

4. Maintain a calm, reasonable approach. Do not lose your temper.

5. Do not grovel. Do not make rash promises.

Exercises

1. Rewrite the following letter with a more professional tone.

Dear Mr. Dithers:

Ever since my father, Dagwood Bumstead, came to work for you many
years ago, my greatest goal has been to work for and with you. I know dad
has talked to you about me, so I won't give a lot of detail about my schooling
and experience. Suffice it to say, I've graduated from State College with a degree in Business, and I have had four terrific summers working for Gemco.
Now I'm ready to put my shoulder to the grindstone for your company.

I could come in for an interview any time of the day or night. Just say the
word and let me fulfill a lifelong dream!

Sincerely,

Alexander Bumstead

2.   Improve the tone in the following memo.

To: All Clerical Employees

From: Maureen Murchison

Topic: New Employees

Date: June 12, 19xx

Five new employees will start work on the clerical staff on June 24. As they will be sharing your present offices for the next six months, you will all have to accommodate yourselves to them. You will be required to clear out your extra supplies from the desks located on the east side of Room 34 and keep all your personal possessions strictly in your own work space.

You will be sharing the four computer terminals with these five employees also, so make sure you schedule your computer work in advance. I will put a weekly sign-up sheet on the bulletin board so you can arrange times for working on the terminals.

**Chapter Test
32-1**

Rewrite the following collection letter. Assume the writer has already written once and the bill is six weeks overdue.

Dear Ms. Barlowe:

In case you haven't been reading your mail recently, I'm telling you once again that the Sanyo terminal you took out of this store on July 1 wasn't free. It cost $250 American dollars, and I better see those dollars in a check before this week is over. The check better be good, too, or you'll be hearing from my attorney.

Sincerely,

Jack Dawes

**Chapter Test
32-2**

Rewrite the following letter of complaint.

Dear Sirs:

The people working in your office must be blind, since they haven't noticed that I moved to a new address. I sent in a change of address form a month ago, and still *Poodle World* is being sent to Foster City and then arriving here two weeks later. Not only is it late—but I have to pay $.25 every damn time it comes. If you people don't have the brains to change my delivery address, cancel my subscription and refund my $15. I have better uses for my money.

Sincerely,

Horace Blackstone

Exercises for Experts

I. You have ordered a clock radio from Bells Company and charged it on your Visa card. You were told the delivery would take six to ten weeks, but four months have passed. You have written once and received no answer. Now you are writing a firmer letter.

II. This year, due to a change in the production schedule for your company's product (Christmas ornaments), most employees will not be able to take a vacation during the summer. Either they must take their weeks in the spring or else they will have to wait until October. Write a memo to employees summarizing the problem and explaining how and when they must sign up for the vacation time. (Look ahead to Chapter 36 for more on memos.)

III. You have just been offered a job with AGGO Corporation and are very happy to accept the offer. As you will have to move to a city over three hundred miles from your present home, however, you foresee difficulties with the starting date. Write to your employer accepting the offer but requesting a two-week extension on the starting date.

Make sure your tone is enthusiastic but firm.

CHAPTER 33

WORDINESS

OBJECTIVES: To sharpen your writing by: (1) eliminating redundancies; (2) changing passive sentences to active; (3) using strong verbs; (4) avoiding delayed openings; and (5) deleting unnecessary words, phrases, and clauses.

In Chapter 31, we discussed the importance of choosing words that are correct for both your message and your reader. Now we turn to another vital facet of editing: eliminating unnecessary words. This task may be painful at first. Writers often become attached to their words and hesitate to cross them off the page. But unneeded words will slow down your reader and often obscure your message.

Most rough drafts are wordier than they should be because they resemble the way we think and speak. But remember that every unnecessary word wastes a little of someone's time. And wordy writing is boring. If you don't want your efforts to end up in someone's wastebasket, make sure the writing is concise.

Remember: your goal is not to impress people with the number of words you can write; your goal is simply to get your message across to a reader.

Editing for wordiness saves your reader time and makes your message more effective. It also helps you clarify your own thoughts. If you aren't sure what you want to write, you will have trouble writing a clean, lean sentence.

When Flossie Gerber received an angry letter about a billing from one of her store's customers, she wrote back before she had decided how to handle the problem: "In view of your letter of July 15 regarding your invoice, provisions will be made in accordance with our present policy." If she had figured out what to do BEFORE she answered the letter, she might have written: "The Credit Department will adjust your bill." Six clear words (instead of twenty-one confusing ones) make the message precise and understandable.

So, to avoid using further words, let's look at some ways you can cut the flab from your sentences.

ELIMINATE REDUNDANCIES

A number of common phrases in our language actually say the same thing two or more times. Because these phrases are so common—many of them are clichés—we don't even notice they are redundant. Stop to THINK about the words that roll onto your page.

REDUNDANT	CONCISE
advance planning	planning
basic fundamentals	fundamentals

brief in length . . . . brief

brown in color . . . . brown

collect together . . . . collect

desirable benefits . . . . benefits

end results . . . . results

general consensus of opinion . . . . consensus

important essentials . . . . essentials

merge together . . . . merge

one and only . . . . only

past history . . . . history

true facts . . . . facts

First and foremost, we should cease and desist using redundancies. [redundant. 10 words]

First, we should stop using redundancies. [concise. 6 words]

The end result of our mutual cooperation is that the project will be completed during the winter months. [redundant. 18 words]

Due to our cooperation, the project will be completed this winter. [concise. 11 words]

Having cooperated, we will complete the project this winter. [concise. 9 words]

Self-Check Test 33-1

Eliminate redundancies in the following sentences. (See end of text for suggested revisions.)

1. The new accounting innovation is the first priority item on our agenda.

2. The two departments have combined together to discuss the final outcome of the project.

3. After careful thought and consideration, I have listed the following necessary requisites for the marketing survey.

4. He is now in the process of completely eliminating redundancies in his application letter.

5. The stocks have been depreciating in value throughout the whole year.

CHANGE PASSIVE SENTENCES TO ACTIVE

In most sentences, the subject should be the doer of the action. However, many business writers tend to reverse this normal order and either put the doer of the action in a prepositional phrase or eliminate him, her, or it: *The dog was seen by me* or simply *The dog was seen.* As we discussed in Chapter 14 (pp. 151–152), these reversed sentences are called *passive sentences.*

Passive sentences serve certain purposes. Sometimes you may not know who did an action: *The man was murdered.* Or the doer of the action may be obvious: *The bill was passed.* Usually, however, the doer of the action should be the subject and should appear toward the beginning of your sentence. Too many inverted sentences can be annoying. Readers want to know right away who did an action. Besides, a passive sentence usually requires more words than an active one:

> The letter was mailed by me. [passive. 6 words]
> I mailed the letter. [active. 4 words]
> A hundred employees were interviewed. [passive. *Who* interviewed them?]
> I interviewed a hundred employees. [active]
> A decision has been made by the legislature to raise taxes. [passive]
> The legislature decided to raise taxes. [active]
> The following report has been issued by management. [passive]
> Management issued the following report. [active]

Scan your writing for passives and eliminate all but those that serve a real purpose.

Self-Check Test 33-2

Change the following passive sentences to active ones. (See end of text for suggested revisions.)

1. The report on training sled dogs for television commercials was written by our Alaskan correspondent.

2. The superior court judge was elected by a vast number of misinformed voters.

3. The curve in the road was not seen by the driver.

4. Fifty envelopes were stamped and addressed by me before midnight.

5. Negotiations were started by our company to end the price war.

USE STRONG VERBS

Because the verb is the action of the sentence, it should be a focal point for the reader. We tend, however, to dilute the power of our sentences by overusing handy but dull verbs and tacking a noun onto them. Verbs such as *to be, to make,* and *to do* are vital to the language, but they don't carry much punch in a sentence. (Passive sentences are weak partly because they employ the verb *to be.*)

Weak or boring verbs may also contribute to the wordiness of your sentence because, in many cases, a noun must follow them: "make a statement," "come to a decision." If you turn these weak verb + noun combinations into verbs (*state, decide*), you will have more interesting and more concise sentences.

Mr. Pederson *made an examination* of five school districts. [wordy and dull. 9 words]

Mr. Pederson examined five school districts. [concise. 6 words]

BORING VERBS . . . . **STRONG VERBS**
are in agreement . . . . agree
bring about an improvement in . . . . improve
bring to a conclusion . . . . conclude
give an indication of . . . . indicate
is suggestive of . . . . suggests
made an experiment . . . . experimented

Self-Check Test 33-3

Rewrite the following sentences with strong verbs. (See end of text for suggested revisions.)

1. Mrs. Henrickson will soon make a decision about the contract.

2. I made use of a favorite strategy to win the match.

3. Maury Closs and I had a conversation about horse racing.

4.   Gloria has an appreciation of fine wine and art.

5.   Having given serious consideration to your proposal, I have a perception of its strengths and weaknesses.

AVOID DELAYED OPENINGS

The majority of effective English sentences begin with a subject. Many writers, however, put "fillers" at the beginning of their sentences. Although you may certainly open a sentence (such as this one) with a dependent clause or a phrase, don't pad your sentence with unnecessary words.

Delayed openings include *There is/are; The fact that; It is clear that,* and similar deadly phrases. Ruthlessly delete them!

> The fact that the dogs were barking kept me awake. [wordy. 10 words]
> The barking dogs kept me awake. [concise. 6 words]
> (In the preceding example, the revision is more accurate as well as more concise since the *barking dogs,* not the *fact,* were responsible for keeping the writer awake.)
> It seems to me that the weather has been chilly. [wordy. 10 words]
> I think the weather has been chilly. [concise. 7 words]

You might even drop *I think* in the previous example; we often preface our sentences with *I think* or *I believe* when we should simply get to our point.

> I believe we have a problem with the budget. [wordy. 9 words]
> We have a problem with the budget. [concise. 7 words]
> What I plan to do is read the report. [wordy. 9 words]
> I plan to read the report. [concise. 6 words]

Self-Check Test 33-4

I.   Remove delayed openings from the following sentences. (See end of text for suggested revisions.)

1.   There were seven people waiting in the hallway.

2.   The fact that it was raining ruined the parade.

3.   It has been a pleasure for me to meet you.

4.   What the author is saying is that life is a continuum.

5.   "It is the union wage that is inflationary," claimed Herman Fenwick.

II. Rewrite the following paragraph to make it more concise and clear.

It has come to my attention that there is a problem with our cataloging system in the company library. The fact that a periodical has been in the office for over two weeks does not mean that it should be put on the bookshelves with the old periodicals. What I mean is, instead of simply checking the date the periodical arrived at our office, check whether a more recent issue has appeared. There should be at least one recent issue of the periodical in the new periodical rack before you put older issues on the bookshelves.

DELETE UNNECESSARY PHRASES AND CLAUSES

Phrases and clauses are vital components of sentences. Many times, however, we use them unnecessarily to convey a simple thought we might have condensed.

Consider whether your thought DESERVES a whole phrase or clause—a minor idea should have a minor status in your sentence. Watch particularly for phrases that may be turned into adjectives and adverbs and for clauses that may be transformed into phrases.

> He spoke with enthusiasm in a loud voice. [wordy. 8 words]
> He spoke loudly and enthusiastically. [concise. 5 words]
> The man who is wearing a red hat is my brother. [wordy. 11 words]
> The man wearing a red hat is my brother. [concise. 9 words]
> Singers who specialize in opera often spend years learning to pronounce with accuracy words that are foreign. [wordy. 17 words]
> Opera singers often spend years learning to accurately pronounce foreign words. [concise. 11 words]

In Chapter 34 we will discuss subordinating less important parts of your sentences and emphasizing the essential material; at this point, however, you can see that turning dependent clauses into phrases and phrases into adjectives or adverbs can substantially shorten your sentences and increase their readability.

Self-Check Test 33-5

Condense the following sentences. (See end of text for suggested revisions.)

1. The woman who was wearing a clown suit ordered toast covered with butter.

2. Mr. Framley will consult an expert in the field of advertising.

3. The boy with freckles delivers the packages that are most fragile to this office.

4. The evaluation of this employee, which is complete, is very favorable.

5. Even students who are liberal arts majors have enjoyed this new text on principles of management.

DELETE UNNECESSARY MODIFIERS

On page 50, we mentioned that you should delete unnecessary modifiers from your sentences. Check back through your business writing to make sure you need all the adverbs and adjectives you have used. Sometimes these will be effective; often they will be "deadwood" and contribute little. The worst offenders are *very* and *quite*. Watch also for *extremely*, *rather*, and similar adverbs.

> This event has been very successful. [wordy]
> This event has been successful. [better]
> I am quite certain. [wordy]
> I am certain. [better]

Self-Check Test 33-6

Revise the following memo to make it less wordy. (Check end of text for a sample revision.)

To: Patty Boyd

From: Ed Burney

Subject: Increased Cash Register Services

Date: April 7, 19xx

It seems that a number of our customers have had some complaints quite recently about extremely slow service at the cash registers. What I am proposing is that from now on we have six rather than four cash registers working at the same time. When the store is very crowded, moreover, we can open up the seventh register at the very back of the store.

When I spoke with some seriousness to the checkout clerks about this plan, they seemed extremely enthusiastic. I think we should take this idea into consideration and have a discussion about it at our meeting next week.

Checklist For Chapter 33

1. Remove redundancies from your sentences.
2. Change inappropriate passive sentences to active.
3. Substitute interesting verbs for boring ones.
4. Avoid weak verb + noun combinations.
5. Remove delayed openings.
6. Delete unnecessary phrases and clauses.
7. Delete unnecessary modifiers.

Exercises   I.   Make the following sentences more concise.

1.   Vinnie Sims, who is the oldest of the members of the committee, has combined together with six other BIX employees to make an assessment of the basic fundamentals of computerized accounting.

2.   It cannot be denied that the new manager's capacity to understand and ability to give explanations of the techniques used by managers are unsurpassed.

3.   It seems as though we might be able to come to an agreement on some of the terms that you are posing here.

4.   Our office building, which will be three stories in height, will be built by a local construction company and will be located close to a bank and some stores.

5.   There are a great many ERM employees who have an interest in buying some shares of the company at a rate that is favorable.

II. John McFarland used to be famous for his verbose, confusing memos. Luckily, since taking a writing class, he has learned to edit his drafts. Identify the wordy writing techniques (passive sentences and so on) in the following memo. Then compare it with his second draft (on pages 412–413).

FIRST DRAFT MEMO

To: All Clerical Employees

From: John McFarland

Subject: Communication with Clients by Telephone

Date: June 5, 19xx

It has come to my attention that in May there were 500 telephone calls from clients logged in by the secretaries of this company. The following are some thoughts that I have had regarding using the telephone inasmuch as it is such a vital tool for communication.

As secretaries for this company, you have the function of acting as a liaison between our clients (and our potential clients) and our salespeople. In view of this fact, you must use courtesy and be efficient when speaking to clients. Lengthy conversations with callers should not be carried on, and it is important to find out what their names are right away so you can tell the salespeople who is calling for them.

There is always the possibility that the person whom the client wants to speak with is not in his or her office, so you must be prepared to get the caller's name and correct phone number as well as any pertinent message he or she wants conveyed to the salesperson. Also, it is possible that another salesperson could handle the problem, so make sure you ask the customer if he or she would like to speak to someone else.

Please remember that these guidelines are vital to our company's success and profits and that you should make sure you are familiar with and adhere to them.

If there are any questions or problems concerning these guidelines, rest assured I will be happy to answer them.

WRITING HINT: DELETE REDUNDANCIES
Mrs. Drake's First Draft   *Mrs. Drake's Second Draft*

Source: Ford Button

IMPROVED MEMO

When you compare this revised memo with McFarland's first effort, you will find it much more effective and readable. But it is not perfect. How would you make it even more effective? Try revising this memo before reading McFarland's final version.

To: Clerical Staff

From: John McFarland

Subject: Communicating by Telephone

Date: June 5, 19xx

In May, company secretaries logged in 500 phone calls. I have had some thoughts regarding the telephone, since it is a vital communication tool.

As you are a liaison between clients and salespeople, you should be courteous and efficient when speaking with clients. Do not have long conversations with them, but find out their names and whom they are calling.

(continued)

If that salesperson is not in his/her office, take down the caller's phone number and message. Also ask the client if he or she can speak with an available salesperson.

If you have any questions on these guidelines, I'll be happy to answer them.

FINAL VERSION

To: Clerical Staff

From: John McFarland

Subject: Telephone Use

Date: June 5, 19xx

As good telephone use is vital to our company's success, please follow these guidelines:

1. Answer your telephone promptly and courteously.

2. Ask whom the person is calling.

3. Ask the caller's name.

4. If the person being called is unavailable, ask if the caller can speak with someone else. If not, take the caller's phone number and message.

5. Avoid long telephone conversations.

If you have any questions regarding telephone calls, call me at Ext. 534.

[Note that this memo is not only shorter than its predecessors but better organized and more precise: (1) the opening states reason for the memo; (2) central portions logically summarize major points; (3) ending tells reader how to reach the writer. See Chapter 36 for more on organizing memos.]

III. Edit the following memo.

To: Department Heads

From: Janet Lee

Subject: Update on the Communications Seminar

Date: December 1, 19xx.

This memo is to bring you up-to-date on the plans for the upcoming seminar that have been completed by our committee at the present time. As you know, the seminar will be held on Thursday, December 19. It will be in the Conference Room on the third floor beginning at 3:00 p.m. in the afternoon, and it will be over at 5:00 p.m.

The seminar will feature Mr. Hobart Flagg, an expert in the field of business communications, who will speak to us on the topic of effective memo writing.

Employees who will be attending the seminar should read and be familiar with Mr. Flagg's article on the use of excess words in business communications. There will be a chance for employees who are interested to speak with Mr. Flagg and ask questions after the seminar.

Please let me know as soon as possible how many employees from your respective departments will be attending. Thank you.

**Chapter Test
33-1**

Revise these wordy sentences from a recent college graduate's job application letter. You may add information as necessary.

1. As per our conversation on the telephone on April 3, I would like to apply for the position of management trainee.

2. During my four years at Flair College, working toward a B.S. in Business Administration, I took each and every course in management that was offered as an elective.

3. While working in the position of assistant night clerk at Royd's Drugstore, I assumed the duties of the night clerk whenever he was away on vacation.

4. A copy of my resume has been enclosed for your review and consideration.

5. If you are interested in my qualifications, please feel free to call on me personally at your convenience.

**Chapter Test
33-2**

Edit the following memo.

To: All Employees

From: Harry Burns

Subject: Arranging Summer Vacations

Date: April 1, 19xx

Now that it is almost time for summer, employees in various departments are trying to make a decision about when to go away on their summer vacations. Inasmuch as the company cannot continue operation without a sufficient number of employees at work, the following policy has been outlined by management.

(continued)

1. Employees who wish to and are eligible to take time off in the summer should make a first and second choice of vacation dates.

2. These dates should be put on a card and handed in to Mrs. Jameson's office by April 15.

3. All first requests will be considered by Mrs. Jameson, but if too many overlap on the same dates, there will have to be some changes.

4. All final decisions will be based on the respective seniority of the employees who are involved.

It is my hope that you will find this policy to be convenient and workable.

Exercise for Experts

Write a memo giving employees details of an upcoming volleyball game. Then exchange memos with another student. Can you make his or her memo more concise and readable?

CHAPTER 34

SENTENCES

OBJECTIVES: To edit your sentences for (1) variety, (2) general readability, (3) excessive length, and (4) choppiness.

To edit your drafts successfully, you will usually find yourself doing several tasks simultaneously: fixing a comma error in one sentence, adding a more vivid verb in another, deleting an unnecessary word in another. As part of this editing process, you should also examine the length, form, and general readability of your sentences. After all, your words alone can't convey thoughts; they must be ordered properly to be effective. Sentences provide structure for your ideas.

Consider the following sentences:

1. This literature has stressed not only such problems as the proper representation of affected parties, but the preclusive effect of any final judgment on future issues that might arise between them, and, most importantly, the creation of ongoing processes for the formulation, modification, and enforcement of the complex injunctive remedies required in such cases.

2. Mr. Henryson is president of VPI. He has worked there for thirty years. He will retire in five years. He is well liked.

The first sentence could use some simpler word choices. But it is also so long that you forget what the writer is talking about before you get to the end. The second group of sentences is so choppy that it sounds like something out of a child's reading primer.

A business writer should not have a highly visible "style." Your readers should not be commenting on your beautiful sentences as they read your memos; they should be concentrating on your ideas, the content of your writing. But making your style invisible is an art in itself. If you have ever noticed how effortless a good swimmer's technique appears—or how easy it looks to play tennis well—you'll understand that writing sentences that *look* effortless is a task demanding some attention.

VARIETY

We all know the cliché about the spice of life. Well, variety certainly adds spice to any piece of writing. Just because you are writing a memo or business letter, you should not let your writing become monotonous. Many writers' sentences develop an almost hypnotic, singsong rhythm that will put their readers to sleep instead of make them pay attention to the message.

Watch for similar sentence *structures*. You already know the perils of too many passive sentences. Too many compound sentences connected by *and* can be equally tedious, as can a succession of sentences that open with long dependent clauses. Even the standard subject-verb-object format can become dull.

> Felicia read the report and sent it to Robert. He will study it and recommend changes. We will meet on Friday and discuss the project. [boring: three simple sentences with compound verbs connected by *and*]
>
> When Felicia had read the report, she sent it to Robert <u>so</u> he could study it and recommend changes. We will meet on Friday <u>to</u> discuss the project. [good variety: underlined words indicate relationships between ideas]

SUBORDINATION

The key to sentence variety is *subordination.* You can inject secondary ideas into your sentences in a multitude of ways. Once you recognize the main point of your sentence, you should be able to incorporate the less important ideas into subordinate parts of your sentence—phrases or dependent clauses. Make sure you highlight any relationship between the ideas. Did one event occur *because* of something else? Did one event *follow* another one chronologically? Does one fact *explain* another one?

You will find subordinate conjunctions (pp. 79–81) to be helpful tools in this subordinating process.

To Show Cause

WITHOUT SUBORDINATION: The project was too expensive, and it was canceled.

WITH SUBORDINATION: *Because* the project was too expensive, it was canceled.

The project was canceled *since* it was too expensive.

To Show Time

WITHOUT SUBORDINATION: The meeting ended, and we went home.

WITH SUBORDINATION: *After* the meeting ended, we went home.

When the meeting had ended, we went home.

As soon as the meeting ended, we went home.

To Show Purpose

WITHOUT SUBORDINATION: Matthew visited Utah. He studied three state agencies.

WITH SUBORDINATION: Matthew visited Utah *in order to* study three state agencies.

To Show Contrast

WITHOUT SUBORDINATION: Henry dislikes working on computers. He is excited about this accounting program.

WITH SUBORDINATION: *Although* Henry dislikes working on computers, he is excited about this accounting program.

While Henry dislikes working on computers, he is excited about this accounting program.

Self-Check Test 34-1

Rewrite each of the following sentences by using subordinate conjunctions to indicate relationships between ideas. Revise any *wordiness* in the sentences as well. (See end of text for sample revisions.)

1. I will go to Des Moines for Christmas. The snow, however, may keep my plane from leaving Chicago.

2. The new highway runs along the river. The highway does not go as far south as the river does.

3. The corporate records are incomplete. There was a fire in the document library last year.

4. Theo is meeting with union delegates in Boston. Before that, he will meet with me and Ford Guthrie in Philadelphia.

5. Mrs. Leeman works all day Saturdays. She is unable to work on Tuesdays.

You do not have to use a dependent clause to subordinate material in your sentence. In fact, once again, you should use a variety of methods. Each of the following ways to subordinate material will help you add variety to your sentences and give proper emphasis to the points you are conveying.

Choppy Sentences

Max is a salesman. Max works ten hours a day. Max is the company's best salesman.

Variation 1.   Dependent clause inside an independent clause.

Max, who is the company's best salesman, works ten hours a day.

Variation 2.   Appositive in the independent clause.

Max, the company's best salesman, works ten hours a day.

Variation 3.   Dependent clause + independent clause (showing *cause*).

> Since he works ten hours a day, Max is the company's
> best salesman.

Variation 4.   Modifying phrase + independent clause.

> Working ten hours a day, Max is the company's best
> salesman.

Variation 5.   Parallel structure.

> Max not only works ten hours a day, but he is our
> company's best salesman.

Naturally, you can vary these five structures in many ways by rearranging the elements:

> Max is our company's best salesman since he works ten
> hours a day. (variant of #3)
> The company's best salesman, Max works ten hours a
> day. (variant of #2)

Just keep in mind the major point you are conveying. If your primary idea is that Max is the company's best salesman, then don't bury that idea in a dependent clause. Also try not to put your major idea in the *middle* of your sentence; it will stand out more prominently at the beginning or the end.

Self-Check Test 34-2

Using subordinating techniques, rewrite each of the following series of sentences in two versions. Do not feel obliged to use only one sentence for each item. (See end of text for some suggested revisions.)

1.   The earthquake hit. Everyone panicked. Buildings trembled. Some trees fell. Tremors continued for an hour. No one was seriously injured.

2.   The meeting was held in the library. The meeting began at noon. Nearly fifty parents attended. They were concerned about a possible teachers' strike. The principal of the high school spoke to them.

3.   Computer security is becoming more of a problem. No computer is completely protected. Even children have broken into some computers.

4. Maurice Young teaches eighth grade. He is 37 years old. He has developed patience and a strong sense of humor. He has also learned the names of 55 rock bands.

5. The office building is new. It's on the corner of Third and South Streets. It is fifteen stories tall. It contains ten stores and three restaurants. It also contains four software companies.

GENERAL READABILITY

Variety in sentence length and structure is important, as you can see. When examining the effectiveness of your sentences, however, you should also make sure you (1) avoid lengthy delays between subject and verb and between verb and object; (2) put statements in the positive rather than negative form; and (3) avoid stringing together too many subordinate elements in one sentence.

Lengthy Delays

As you know, the typical English sentence is composed of a subject + verb + object. Probably 80 percent of your sentences will be in this form.

Once again, a little variety is nice; an occasional passive sentence or one in which the subject follows the verb can help keep your reader interested. But once you have introduced the doer of the action, do not make a habit of putting in a lot of secondary material before getting to the verb. Likewise, the object should usually appear quite soon after the verb.

> The company, because of financial problems, legal problems, and personnel problems, was disbanded. [confusing]
> The company was disbanded because of financial, legal, and personnel problems. [better]
> Stuart Hall, through no fault of his own and probably just because traffic is very heavy on Saturday nights, was late. [wordy and confusing]
> Probably just because traffic is very heavy on Saturday nights, Stuart Hall was late. [better]
> The department head gave, although with very little expertise and not much enthusiasm, a long speech. [confusing]
> The department head gave a long speech with very little expertise and not much enthusiasm. [better]

Positive Form

Positive statements are more easily understood than negative ones because your reader learns what *is* rather than what *is not*. For example, if you write that you are not happy, your reader cannot assume automatically that you are *un*happy. You might be simply meditative. Or you might even be jubilant rather than happy!

Negative statements, too, are often wordier and more confusing than positive ones.

> The new employee is not unintelligent. [confusing]
> The new employee is intelligent. [clear]

Naturally, a negative sentence, like a passive sentence, may be both appropriate and effective. But do consider *why* you are using it.

Subordinate Elements

A final consideration in editing your sentences is to keep them clean as well as clear. Try not to clutter them with too many dependent clauses or prepositional phrases. If you can't fit everything you want to say into one sentence, start another sentence. Shorter sentences, remember, will often be easier on the reader than long ones.

> Alan Fogg, my good friend who is a golf pro and hosts a talk show and who also helped to found ETY Foods, will appear tonight. [confusing]
> My good friend Alan Fogg—golf pro, talk show host, and founder of ETY Foods—will appear tonight. [better]

> The Feather River, which is one of California's most beautiful rivers and which provides water to much of the Sacramento Valley and which offers recreational enjoyment to thousands in the summers, used to overflow its banks every winter. [awkward, confusing]
> One of California's most beautiful rivers, the Feather River, provides water to much of the Sacramento Valley. Although it offers recreational enjoyment to thousands in the summers, it used to overflow its banks every winter. [better]

> You are invited to the office picnic that we hold every year at 2:00 p.m. at Columbus Park in Terryfield near the intersection of Dawn Lane and Fourth Street on Saturday, August 3. [confusing]
> You are invited to the annual office picnic in Columbus Park on August 3. Join us at 2:00 p.m. near the intersection of Dawn Lane and Fourth Street in Terryfield. [better]

Self-Check Test 34-3

Make the following sentences more readable. (See end of text for suggested revisions.)

1. The gala event, which will begin at 7:00 p.m. in the Chandelier Room of the Holter Hotel and which will move on to the PomPom Room after you have dined on lobster and champagne and listened to the amusing tales of guest speaker Rob Johnson, should be a night to remember.

2. The news story was not denied by the reporters, and the whole situation was not yet clear.

3. Mr. Ganley, for reasons known only to himself, his administrative assistant, and a dozen others but perhaps because he is tired of administrative controversy, is retiring.

4. Marion, who is a good pianist and who enjoys playing jazz as much as classical music, has planned, whether her employers agree or not, a series of lunchtime concerts.

5. The university, which is in Mayfield, Massachusetts, and enjoys a certain popularity among a new breed of liberal arts graduate students who are interested in business careers with a humanistic touch, is sponsoring a daily newspaper.

EXCESSIVE LENGTH

There is no "ideal" sentence length. Some short sentences can be difficult to read, while some long ones can be clear. An occasional two-word sentence can be effective; so can an occasional fifty-word sentence. Most of your sentences should fall somewhere in between these extremes, but watch for tedious similarity and for excessive length.

If you follow the rules for eliminating wordiness (Chapter 33), you may not have to worry about too many long sentences. Deleting passive verbs, unnecessary clauses and phrases, and redundancies will solve most of your long sentence problems. If you suspect a sentence is too long for your reader to grasp easily, read it aloud: your ear will probably tell you whether you should break up the sentence into two or more sentences.

Remember a basic rule of sentence making: most sentences should have ONE major idea. You should be able to look at your sentences and isolate one leading concept in each; if you can't, you may be packing your sentences too tightly and creating problems for your readers.

Of course, compound sentences may have two or more major ideas—one in each independent clause. But if you think you are packing too much into a sentence, try to summarize its main point. If you cannot summarize the sentence in a few words, it may be too complicated.

If the writer of the monster sentence at the beginning of this chapter had tried to reduce his sentence to a main concept, he might have seen the problem he was giving his readers. He seems much more concerned with impressing his readers with his own genius than with actually transmitting ideas.

If you are worried that breaking up long sentences will create childish, short sentences, remember that in general the short sentence will at least convey the idea to your reader—and transmitting concepts is the point of communication. Also, combining short, clear sentences is much easier than breaking up long, confusing ones.

The length of your sentence should depend partly on the sophistication of your reader, partly on the formality of your message. A sales letter, for example, will probably have shorter sentences than a year-end report. A memo to fellow employees will have shorter sentences than a technical article aimed at a professional audience.

> Recession caused millions of Americans to lose their jobs, but no group is having a rougher time finding work than disabled workers since many employers are reluctant to make jobs available to disabled workers out of fear that disabled workers will end up costing more than the nondisabled. [Too long. Tries to convey too many ideas.]

In the preceding sentence, the writer has presented four ideas:

1. Recession caused Americans to lose their jobs.

2. Disabled workers are having more trouble finding work than other groups.

3. Employers are reluctant to hire disabled workers.

4. Employers fear hiring disabled workers will cost more than hiring nondisabled workers.

Which of these ideas are the most important? The second is more important than the first, since the report is focusing on disabled workers. Numbers 3 and 4 are more equally matched than the first two, but #3 could be seen as slightly more important since it is a *result*; the fourth sentence is simply a cause. More important, though, are the connections between these sentences; #1 and #2 are clearly related; #3 and #4 are clearly related. All four of them should not be in one sentence, especially as #2 and #3 are major ideas.

While recession caused millions of Americans to lose their jobs, no group is having a rougher time finding work than disabled workers. Many employers are reluctant to hire the disabled because they fear disabled workers will be more expensive than nondisabled ones. [better]

Note that the minor idea in each sentence has been put in a dependent clause; the major ideas are in independent clauses. And the two major ideas are now in separate sentences.

Self-Check Test 34-4

Make the following sentences more readable by shortening, separating, or restructuring them. Avoid linking too many thoughts with *and*. (See end of text for suggested revisions.)

1. Concordia Home Supply increased profits by 30 percent annually over the past three years and the business is still growing rapidly, so management decided to do some research on whether to open a new branch in Stockton, Modesto, or Bakersfield in order to keep pace with the growth of the business.

2. Of these three cities, Bakersfield was considered the best choice for the new store because it met the five criteria used to determine the ideal location for the new store (number of homeowners, average income level, number of home supply stores, transportation costs, and number of construction firms in the area) and because an excellent site for the store had been found in Bakersfield.

3. In order to attract customers to the new store, Concordia planned a grand opening celebration and offered customers a 20 percent discount on all items during the first two days as well as handing out discount coupons for special items if they were purchased within the next month and offering professional consulting services in gardening, plumbing, and carpentry.

4. Research showed that the potential Bakersfield customers did not like to carry large amounts of cash and preferred cards to personal checks and also preferred using a special store credit card to putting all items on their bank credit card, so Concordia Home Supply introduced Concordia credit cards for the Bakersfield customers.

5. The Concordia Home Supply Store branch in Bakersfield has prospered partly because it has won several contracts with major construction firms in the area, currently making 40 percent of its earnings from those firms, and partly because it has effectively used the local media, particularly the newspapers, to advertise its products, special sales, convenient location, and helpful personnel, and partly because management and staff have worked very hard to make every customer a steady customer.

CHOPPINESS

In doing the preceding exercise, you may have found yourself creating short, choppy sentences that seem boring and childish. The following is an extreme example of choppiness:

(1) Concordia Home Supply Company has made big profits. (2) It has been profitable for three years. (3) Profits have increased 30 percent annually. (4) Business is growing rapidly. (5) Management is considering opening a new branch. (6) The new branch would help keep pace with the company's growth. (7) Management is considering three cities. (8) The cities are Stockton, Modesto, and Bakersfield.

You can often spot choppy sentences by checking the subjects: if the subjects of two or more short, consecutive sentences are the same, the effect is often choppy. Similarly, if the opening of a sentence uses a word or phrase that appeared at the end of the previous sentence, the effect can be choppy.

In the first two sentences of the preceding example, the subjects are the same (*Concordia Home Supply Company* and *It*). Sentence 6 opens with the words that ended sentence 5; sentence 8 opens with the words that ended sentence 7.

Each of the eight sentences in that sample paragraph is also *simple*; a paragraph with no compound or complex sentences will usually seem choppy.

Actually, while fixing choppy sentences is usually easier than tackling long, complex ones, the procedure is much the same. You should again consider the major and minor points of the sentences. Put separate points in separate sentences; then add minor points to subordinate parts of the sentences.

In this example, sentences 1, 2, 3, and 4 are clearly connected, while sentences 5, 6, 7, and 8 are clearly connected. Your rewritten draft may well have two sentences that can be summarized thus: (1) For three years, Concordia Home Supply Company has increased profits by 30 percent, and (2) Management is considering three cities for a new store site.

Self-Check Test 34-5

Make these choppy sentences more readable by combining and restructuring them. (See end of text for suggested revisions.)

1. The city needs public transportation. Highways are too crowded. Gasoline prices are soaring. Many people cannot afford cars. Young people and senior citizens find it difficult to get around without cars.

2. Martina Deloreth is an economist. She is interested in interest rate fluctuations. She has worked for several banks. Currently she works for Northeast Research Institute. Her position is senior economic adviser.

3. My experience qualifies me. I have a B.S. in Business Administration. I have three years' experience with Darth Enterprises. I worked as a personnel assistant. I was in charge of reviewing files. I also handled correspondence with prospective employees.

4. Our company has reached an agreement. The agreement is with Elmer Corporation. We will be sharing production facilities. This is a trial arrangement. We will review its success in three months.

5. The report concerns morale problems. It examines five companies. All the companies are in Tulsa. All of them experience high turnover. The turnover is predominantly a problem with clerical employees.

Checklist for Chapter 34

1. Vary structure of sentences.

2. Subordinate minor ideas.

3. Put major ideas in independent clauses.

4. Put major ideas toward beginning or end of sentences.

5. Avoid lengthy delays between subject and verb, between verb and object.

6. Word most statements positively.

7. Avoid stringing together too many subordinate elements.

Exercises

Perry McDaniel, Customer Service Manager for Kern's Department Store, wrote a form letter for Kern's inactive charge account customers. Before sending it out, however, Perry asked his assistant, Mick Granger, to edit it. By reworking Perry's sentences and some of his word choices, Mick created a much more effective letter. Read Perry's letter that follows. Note any problems in the margins. Then compare the letter with Mick's version.

Dear Charge Customer:

Our records show you haven't used your Kern's charge card for over a year. We don't like to have our customers lose interest. We are making you a special offer.

We are, to encourage you to shop at Kern's, making you a special offer when you bring in the enclosed discount coupon to Kern's during our annual February White Sale and present it at our Customer Service Desk on the second floor. You will receive, upon presenting a stamped receipt from the Customer Service Desk, an additional 25 percent off our reduced White Sale prices on any purchase of $15 or more in our Housewares Department.

During this year's White Sale, which will be in all departments of the store and which will begin February 14 and run through February 19, you will receive substantial savings on our wide selection of bed linens, dishes, cookware, and electrical appliances as well as on our well-known designer clothing. We do not want you to miss coming in to take advantage of your special discount on items you need for your home.

You are a preferred customer. We value your business. Do save the enclosed coupon. You'll be glad you did. We look forward to serving you.

Sincerely,

Perry McDaniel

MICK'S VERSION

Dear Charge Customer:

Since we want to encourage you to shop at Kern's, we're making you a special offer.

When you come to our annual February White Sale (February 14–19), bring the enclosed discount coupon to the Customer Service Desk on the second floor. You will receive a stamped receipt making you eligible for an additional 25 percent off any purchase of $15 or more in our Housewares Department.

The February White Sale extends to all departments—you'll find savings in linens, dishes, cookware, and small appliances.

You're one of our special customers, so we value your business. Save the enclosed coupon. You'll be glad you did!

Sincerely,

Perry McDaniel

When Perry saw Mick's version, he was impressed with the tighter, cleaner sentences. But he felt the letter still lacked what he called "punch"—an exciting tone that would attract customers.

Assume Perry has hired you to rewrite this letter. Make some notes in the margin of Mick's version; then write a version with a faster pace and more concrete details.

Chapter Test 34-1   Rewrite the following letter with strong, varied sentences.

Dear Consultant:

I am sure you are not unfamiliar with the increasing financial burden of a business recession. This company must ease problems for its employees. New and different methods of cost control must be applied.

It has been, in the past and actually until only a few months ago, company policy to issue American Express cards to all consultants for charging their legitimate business expenses such as gasoline and motel bills and meals while traveling from one client's office to another. Recently the board of directors determined that some bills exceeded reasonable expenses. The board issued a new policy. All consultants must now use their own credit cards. Reimbursement can be obtained by submitting Form RS430 to the Finance Department.

The new policy demands you return your previously issued American Express cards. Return your card to the Finance Department by March 1.

As a consultant for the Northern Pacific Transportation Company, you are a valued employee whose expertise is greatly appreciated, and we want you to know that this policy change is in no way a reflection upon your personal contributions, and we look forward to many years of continued association.

Sincerely,

Marianne Wibberley

**Chapter Test
34-2**

Rewrite the following memo by adding variety to the sentences.

To: Mac Brown

From: Jane Hermann

Subject: Hiring Freeze

Date: February 21, 19xx

The San Francisco branch performed well in 19xx. We led the district in revenues for three-fourths of the year. We closed 75 new accounts. That was a company record. We would like to make this year even better. We're going to need your help.

In January, two technical representatives left the company. Those reps were Karen Jones and Lydia Canner. I cannot replace them. I have to comply with the hiring freeze.

Although Bart and Susan have attempted to take up the slack, it is impossible for two tech reps to support 600 accounts, and we are getting complaints from customers (Hancock Bank and Northern Pacific) about lack of support and slow response time, while the marketing representatives are hesitant to close sales until they know what kind of technical support they can promise the customer.

Mac, I'm aware of the hiring freeze. I know we need to cut costs. But I need some help. We need to spend some money to make money. Please see what you can do about hiring two new reps.

**Exercises for
Experts**

I. As manager of a hardware store, write a memo to the salespeople telling them that customers are complaining about salespeople's apparent lack of interest. Explain what you expect a salesperson to do when a customer comes in the store and what will happen if customers continue to complain. Watch the variety of your sentences.

II. As department head, write a memo to employees telling them about a new policy for late arrivals in the morning and after lunch. Make sure your sentences are clear, strong, and positive. (See Chapter 36 for hints on memos.)

CHAPTER 35

PARAGRAPHS

OBJECTIVES: To strengthen your writing by (1) creating a design for each paragraph; (2) establishing topic sentences; (3) adding supportive information; (4) making transitions between thoughts; and (5) linking each paragraph with the ones that precede and follow it.

In Chapter 34, we discussed the structure and scope of sentences. In some ways, you might think of a paragraph as simply an expanded sentence; like a sentence, it should develop only one major thought. Because a paragraph is usually longer than one sentence, you have more opportunity to add supporting or corroborating material.

But the paragraph, like the sentence, should be well constructed, thoughtfully designed. It should bear no resemblance to a garbage can where you dump every odd thought that strays across your mind.

Like a sentence, a paragraph should have no unnecessary parts; it should contribute an important thought to your piece of writing as a whole, and its structure should help your reader to comprehend the major points of your message.

PARAGRAPH FORMATION

Usually you will indent a line five spaces to mark the beginning of a new paragraph. If your document is single-spaced, you will also double-space between paragraphs. In the block format (see Appendix A) common to many business documents, the opening line of a paragraph is not indented. Instead, you simply double-space to indicate the beginning of a new paragraph.

PARAGRAPH LENGTH

Paragraphs function as visual as well as logical markers in your writing. Long paragraphs are more difficult to read than short ones; the white space formed by margins and paragraph breaks on your page contributes to the readability of your letter, memo, or report.

In business documents, paragraphs are usually short, often with fewer than eight lines. Paragraphs in letters often have only one or two sentences. You should break your paragraphs logically and make sure each logical chunk is small enough for a reader to digest easily.

Although in the rest of this chapter we discuss the components of a fully developed paragraph, you should be aware that, in business documents, even a one-sentence paragraph is perfectly acceptable. Just don't make *every* paragraph one sentence: variety in paragraph length is as important as variety in sentence length.

Many memos and reports, also, are written predominantly in a *list* format rather than in developed paragraphs. Many times a list will be easier to scan and comprehend than a paragraph. You should consider the format of your business documents in the early stages of your organization: some topics lend themselves to a list, while others require full paragraph development. (See pp. 475–478 for sample memos that use lists.)

PARAGRAPH COMPONENTS

Most paragraphs are composed of three structuring elements: a topic sentence, supporting sentences, and transitional words or sentences.

Topic Sentences

Most paragraphs contain a sentence that summarizes the main point of the paragraph or pulls together the major ideas. Often the topic sentence appears at the beginning of a paragraph, but it may appear at the end (as a summary) or in the middle.

Check your writing for topic sentences. If you cannot find controlling sentences in your paragraphs, they are probably loose and incoherent.

The following paragraphs appeared in reports written by business students. Where are the topic sentences?

> (1) Many seniors have run into severe problems because they cannot get into the prerequisite classes for Management 4678. (2) These classes include Marketing Management, Introduction to Quantitative Methods, and Financial Management. (3) Last semester, over twenty students on the waiting list for a prerequisite class sat through three sessions, checked every day with the school office, and were finally told they could not be admitted. (4) Half of these students will have to delay graduation in order to fulfill the school requirements.

> (1) During my three years in the Business School, many fellow students have complained to me that they are not being fully prepared for real-life situations in the business world. (2) To help solve this problem, I have invented a business game in which students assume roles they might actually have after graduation. (3) Functioning somewhat like the Stock Market Game, the business game demands that students address problems common to various business situations and make decisions based on real-world data such as interest rates and stock prices.

In the first paragraph, the first sentence is clearly the topic sentence. The writer is presenting the problem that students face: being admitted into certain prerequisites for a required class. The rest of the paragraph continues with the thought.

WRITING HINT: PROVIDE EXPLANATIONS WHEN CONVEYING BAD NEWS

What George Wrote   *What Bill Thought*

Revision: With my two associates on vacation, I'm flooded with work. Can we have lunch on Monday instead of this Friday?

Source: Ford Button

In the second paragraph, the topic sentence is delayed. The student is not going to write about the lack of real-world preparation in the Business School; he is going to write about a solution to the problem—the game he has devised. In this paragraph, the topic sentence is the second sentence.

Note: As we noted in Chapter 29, one excellent way to outline a piece of writing is to list your topic sentences so you can make sure every paragraph has a focus.

Supporting Material

Naturally, most paragraphs will be longer than one sentence. Not only will you introduce a major theme, but you will write other sentences giving more information, providing examples, analyzing the topic, comparing or contrasting the major idea with other ideas. We call these sentences supporting material.

In the previous paragraph on scheduling problems, for example, the second sentence tells us exactly *which* classes the writer is talking about. The third sentence provides detail on the number of students having problems and the nature of the problems. The final sentence tells us the most unfortunate aspect of the problem: the number of students who must actually postpone graduation because of scheduling difficulty. In a standard informative paragraph, every supporting sentence adds to the information in the topic sentence.

(The paragraph you have just read follows a similar pattern, except the topic sentence appears at the end. The first three sentences provide supporting material leading to the conclusion.)

Self-Check Test 35-1

Write three or four supporting sentences for the following topic sentences. (See end of text for some examples.)

1.   The big American car is not dead.

2.   Many employers like to see a liberal arts minor and a business major on a job candidate's resume.

3.   Martin Firenzi is one of the best managers in this division.

4. The vending machines in this building are a constant source of controversy.

5. Opening a satellite office in Tulsa could be a tragic mistake for our company.

Transitional Material

When you have put together your supporting material and your topic sentence, your paragraph may still be lacking one major element: a flow between ideas. You need transitions from one sentence to the next and transitions between paragraphs. When transitions are lacking, readers sense that a paragraph is choppy or disorganized.

One rule of thumb to consider while writing and organizing paragraphs is that you do not want to surprise or confuse your readers. Instead, you should be setting up road signs along the way, telling your readers that you are adding material, providing a slightly different perspective, moving on in time, or giving examples. These road signs may consist of transitional words or phrases, pronouns, or echoes.

Transitional Words

One of the easiest ways to make transitions is to add transitional words.

The following is the opening paragraph of a marketing report for a canned goods company.

> I am the product manager of the Food Services Division. I was instructed by John Garon to evaluate our Lite Fruit marketing strategy. I have analyzed the effect of the marketing campaign on the division. The campaign has run

at a loss for two years. I studied the division's recent cost-income data and consumer-trend reports. I recommend continuing the Lite Fruit campaign. I urge increasing the price of Lite Fruit and directing a larger portion of the advertising budget to male consumers.

The information in this paragraph is acceptable for the beginning of a report: the writer states her position, who authorized the report, and what its goals are. She also summarizes her methods, the problem, and her recommendations. The rest of the report will supply the necessary supporting material for her conclusions.

The problem with the paragraph is choppiness. The writer does not provide transitional words to move us from one point to another. A few helpful words will make the paragraph much more accessible and effective.

John Garon instructed me, *as product manager of the Food Services Division*, to evaluate our Lite Fruit marketing strategy. *When* I analyzed the effect of the marketing campaign on the division, I found the campaign had run at a loss for two years. *To determine the root of the problem*, I studied the division's recent cost-income data and consumer-trend reports. *Now that I have completed my research*, I recommend continuing the Lite Fruit campaign, increasing the price of Lite Fruit, and directing a larger portion of the advertising budget to male consumers.

The few words added to these sentences provide a chronological sense as well as a logical sequence to the paragraph. By combining the last two sentences, the writer clearly summarizes her recommendations and makes a smooth transition to the rest of the report.

Some Transitional Words and Phrases

To add material: *additionally, also, and, as well as, besides, moreover, furthermore, first (second, third, finally), similarly*

To show contrast: *although, but, on the other hand, however, whereas, yet*

To show examples: *such as, for example, that is*

To summarize: *in short, in other words, in summary*

To show cause and effect: *because, since, therefore, thus, so*

Before using transitional words, decide whether your next sentence (or paragraph) is adding material, establishing causes or results, providing examples, moving through a time sequence, or comparing and contrasting ideas. Then choose a transitional word appropriate to your meaning. (Note some of these techniques are similar to the ones you used in Chapter 34 to create smooth sentences.)

I am going to the beach this summer. My doctor says I need some sun. [choppy]

I am going to the beach this summer *since* my doctor says I need some sun. [better]

> I dislike eating in restaurants. Sometimes restaurant food can be delicious. [choppy]
>
> *Although* I dislike eating in restaurants, sometimes restaurant food can be delicious. [better]

Self-Check Test 35-2

Rewrite this paragraph, making sure there is a topic sentence and transitional words to make it move more smoothly. (See end of text for sample revision.)

> John Matthews has worked for GMC Inc. for 30 years. He is young at heart. He loves watching softball and coordinating events. We put him in charge of the yearly company picnic. He is particularly good at choosing the softball teams. He does not play the game anymore. He still knows who will be most effective in each position.

Pronoun Transitions

You may also make transitions between sentences and paragraphs by using a pronoun referring to a noun in the previous sentence.

> The discussion of a strike upsets a number of the drivers. *They* are worried that they will lose their pensions or even their jobs.
>
> Individual health insurance is getting more expensive every day. Soon *it* will be a luxury item.

Echoes

You may simply echo a word from a previous sentence—or use a word very similar in meaning—to make an effective transition.

> The new banking machines are convenient. But *convenience* does not always make up for impersonal, computerized service.
>
> Christmas is traditionally a time for the annual office party. At this office *festivity* people often try to make up for a lack of friendliness during the rest of the year.

Theresa Juarez was asked to draft a memo to employees telling them that, due to financial problems, the company was going to have to terminate some clerical staff, reduce hourly employees to a 30-hour week, and eliminate the upcoming Christmas party.

Her outline looked like this:

1. Introduction
    —explain how difficult it was to arrive at these decisions
    —summarize company's perilous situation
    —say cutbacks are necessary
    —say why situation is so bad (machinists' strike)

2. Nature of Cutbacks
    —30-hour week for hourly employees
    —no Xmas party
    —6–10 clerical employees will have to be fired
    —they will know who they are by December 1
    —these employees will be first hired when company recovers

3. Conclusion
    —repeat the apologies of management

The following is the rough draft of her memo:

To: All Employees

From: Theresa Juarez, Administrative Assistant to the President

Topic: Cutbacks

Date: November 16, 19xx

The management of GHS is sorry to announce certain cutbacks that will take effect in the next month. GHS has been operating at a loss since the machinists' strike last summer. We may have to declare bankruptcy.

All full-time hourly employees will be reduced to 30-hour work weeks as of December 1. You may work even fewer hours if you desire. You may work out individual schedules with your supervisors.

The upcoming Christmas party has been canceled. If the earnings rise in the next quarter, management will sponsor a July Fourth picnic and party.

Between six and ten clerical employees will have to be terminated. We will supply the best possible references and help in your job search if we can. You will know of your status by December 1. If you want to return to GHS when we are ready to rehire, you will be considered first.

GHS apologizes for bearing bad tidings. I hope 19xx will be a better year for all of us.

Although this memo held the information Theresa wanted to convey, it was too abrupt. Transitional material and some changes in sentence ordering would make the memo flow more easily and also make the message less brusque and unpleasant. Her next draft looked like this:

Because GHS has been operating at a loss since the machinist's strike last summer, management is sorry to announce certain cutbacks will have to take effect next month. *If we do not make these cutbacks immediately*, we may have to declare bankruptcy.

First, all full-time hourly employees will be reduced to 30-hour work weeks as of December 1 *although* you may work even fewer hours if you desire. Work out individual schedules with your supervisors.

Secondly, we must also cancel the upcoming Christmas party. *To atone somewhat for this cancellation*, the company will sponsor a July Fourth picnic and party if earnings increase next quarter.

Finally and most unfortunately, between six and ten clerical employees will have to be terminated. You will know of your status by December 1. We will supply the best possible references and help in your job search if we can. If you want to return to GHS when we are ready to rehire, you will be considered first.

GHS apologizes for bearing *these* bad tidings. I hope 19xx will be a better year for all of us.

Checklist for Chapter 35

1. Most paragraphs in business documents should be short.

2. Each paragraph should be linked to the major theme of your letter, memo, article, or report.

3. Each paragraph should have a topic sentence centering on the major idea.

4. Supporting sentences in the paragraph should add information, provide comparison or contrast, establish cause or results, move through time, follow a logical thought process or analysis, or provide examples.

5. Transitional words, pronouns, echoing words, and synonyms should be added to paragraphs to help the flow of ideas.

Paragraph Review

Rewrite this paragraph with a topic sentence and transitional words. (See end of text for suggested revisions.)

The clouds are dark and ominous. It rarely rains in this part of the country in July. We are probably just in for a muggy afternoon. There is always a chance of a tornado. People are listening carefully to the weather broadcasts.

**Chapter Test
35-1**

Rewrite the following memo with a variety of transitional methods. You may break the memo into more than one paragraph if you like. (Do *not* use a list method.)

To: All Staff

From: Marianne Flaherty

Topic: Fire Drills

Date: September 4, 19xx

On Friday, September 12, we will have our first fire drill in the new building. Make sure you leave the office by the emergency exits at the end of each hall. Move rapidly but calmly. Do not push or shove. Do not take the elevators. Stay with your own office group when you are outside. Office managers should check the rest rooms and lounge areas. They should have a list of the staff at work in their office that day. Check off the names on the list when everyone is outside. The drill should take less than thirty minutes.

Chapter Test 35-2

I. You are applying for a summer job as a salesperson with a shoe store. Your final letter of application will have four paragraphs: (1) applying for the position; (2) stating your school credentials; (3) summarizing relevant work experience; and (4) asking for an interview. Write four topic sentences that will provide a focus for each of these paragraphs.

II. Write two or three supporting sentences for the second and third paragraphs. Make sure each sentence amplifies the topic sentences.

Exercises for Experts

I. Write a memo to sales employees that explains the procedures for handling customer complaints in Thompson's Department Store. Make sure every paragraph has a topic sentence, supporting material, and transitional material.

II. Cut out a front-page article from *The Wall Street Journal*. Mark the topic and supporting sentences as well as the transitional devices.

EXAMPLE OF EDITING PROCESS

I.   First Draft

```
                                              345 Palm avenue
                                              Talahassee, FLO  35782
                                              June 21st, 19xx

mr. Robert Meyer,

District manager

HJI Products

9000 Bolton Boulvard

Boulder, CO  89345

dear mr. Meyer;

      We were very happy to recieve your order for five hundred thirty-three Regal

cardbord cartons.  I am sure you will find each of our cartons are both sturdy and

attractive.  Before sending your order, however it is important for us to know the

size boxes you require and need.  Enclosed is a sheet of sizes available.  Please

call or write us with the information as soon as possible.

      Thank you again for you're order.  Its been a pleasure serving you.

                                   Very Truly Yours,

                                   Michael Griffiths

                                   Michael Griffiths,

                                   Sale's Manager
```

II. Revisions

345 Palm avenue

Talahassee, FLO 35782

June 21st, 19xx

mr. Robert Meyer

District manager

HJI Products

9000 Bolton Boulvard

Boulder, CO 89345

dear mr. Meyer:

We were very happy to recieve your order for ~~five hundred thirty-three~~ 533 Regal cardbord cartons. I am sure you will find each of our cartons ~~are~~ is both sturdy and attractive. Before sending your order, however, ~~it is important for us~~ we need to know the size boxes you require ~~and need.~~ To receive your order by July 15, Enclosed is a sheet of sizes available. please call or write us with the information ~~as soon as possible.~~ by July 1

Thank you again for ~~you're~~ your order. Its been a pleasure serving you.

Very Truly Yours,

Michael Griffiths

Michael Griffiths

Sale's Manager

III. Second Draft

```
                                                    345 Palm Avenue
                                                    Tallahassee, FL   35782
                                                    June 21, 19xx


Mr. Robert Meyer
District Manager
HJI Products
9000 Bolton Boulevard
Boulder, CO  89345

Dear Mr. Meyer:

     We were very happy to receive your order for 533 Regal cardboard cartons.  I
am sure you will find each of our cartons is both sturdy and attractive.

     Before sending your order, however, we need to know the size boxes you re-
quire.  Enclosed is a sheet of sizes available.  To receive your order by July 15,
please call or write us with the information by July 1.

     Thank you again for your order.  It's been a pleasure serving you.

                                        Very truly yours,

                                        Michael Griffiths

                                        Michael Griffiths
                                        Sales Manager
```

PART SIX REVIEW TESTS

**Review Test
6-1**

Now that you have completed Part Six, review the test you took at the beginning of the section.

Rewrite the following sentences so they are clear, concise, and effective. You may add, delete, or replace words as needed.

1. The important essentials of this report have been summarized by me.

2. Please be advised that subsequent correspondence should be addressed to Francis Deering.

3. We were both astonished and surprised by the sudden changes and alterations in plans.

4. Maureen Hammond is in receipt of your letter, and its contents have been duly noted by her.

5. As per our conversation of March 21, your new terminal has been sent to you by us.

6. If you don't bother to contact us by May 2, your membership will be canceled.

7. A general consensus of opinion has been reached by the Board.

8. Herewith enclosed is a copy of the report with statistics for the month of June.

9. The interfacing between employees and management last week did not produce a viable resolution to the problems.

10. Philip Tremaine is both uncertain and unsure about the true facts of the matter.

Review Test 6-2

Rewrite the following letter to make it more precise and effective. Check word choice, wordiness, sentences, and paragraph structure.

Dear Mrs. Hodges:

Receipt is hereby acknowledged of your inquiry of September 21 which I have at hand. With regard to your request for information about Jerry's Jellies, I am happy to acquaint you with the fact that we have a complete stock at the present writing, so that we will be in a position to take care of your valued order. Pursuant to your request, we are enclosing herewith our full-color catalog. Kindly advise us which gift packages you would like to order. Please realize that we are not in a position to ship on credit, so that you must transmit a check or money order with your order.

If you would be so kind as to let us know your wishes at your earliest convenience, we will commence to work on your order so that it can be delivered before Christmas.

Sincerely,

Jerry

Review Test 6-3

Rewrite the following beginnings and endings of letters to make them more effective.

1. I was glad to receive your letter of June 15 asking whether we carry oil-filled electric heaters, and I hasten to reply to your inquiry.

2. Please be advised that your letter has been taken under advisement by our adjustment department. Should an adjustment in your water bill be made, you will be so informed in the future. We trust you will find this procedure satisfactory.

3. It is our sincere and earnest hope that every detail of your business will be handled to your complete and entire satisfaction and that this will be the commencement of a long and pleasant business relationship.

4. We desire herewith to acknowledge receipt of your letter of April 15 in which you inquired about the provisions of a life insurance policy (235-567-09182) purchased by your husband, Mr. Robert Smith, from our agent, Ms. Luisa Ferrari, on May 2, 1985.

5. In view of the foregoing facts and figures, we are going to make an intensive study of the procedures and methods which we could utilize for more efficient accounting techniques.

Review Test 6-4

Rewrite the following paragraphs, eliminating jargon, wordiness, poor word choice, clichés, and so on.

1. Because of the current trend now in progress, I urge you to give careful consideration to the proposed merger and to proceed with caution. In the data previously researched by myself and my staff, there is more than ample evidence of the risks and dangers involved.

2. It is generally agreed that by the end of the next decade, a shortage of elementary schoolteachers will again exist due to the increased number of school-age children and the general move of women away from the teaching profession. A review of studies compiling data on this problem indicates that, unless a definite reversal trend begins in the next two years, the actual magnitude of the shortage will severely inhibit the academic standards of our schools.

Review Test 6-5

Rewrite the following letter: revise organization, word choice, sentence structure, and so on.

Dear Dave and Helena:

We at the Cancer Society would like to take this opportunity to extend a personal invitation to our friends who have supported our work throughout the year. We would like to invite you to our annual Valentine's Day Ball.

The annual Valentine's Day Ball, which will take place on Saturday, February 14, provides us with an opportunity to show our appreciation for your support and assistance. The Ball also helps us continue our vital research on cancer.

The Ball will be held at the Hyatt Regency and will be a black tie affair starting at 7:00 p.m. Dinner, which will be served at 8:00 p.m., will follow no-host cocktails. Dancing will follow dinner. Music by the Illusions will be played for your listening pleasure.

A tax-deductible $100-per-person check can be enclosed in the attached envelope. Please return the envelope with your check by February 9.

We look forward to a most enjoyable evening and hope you can join us on the 14th from 7:00 p.m. until 1:00 a.m.

Sincerely yours,

Marta Marks

Review Test 6-6

Underline the problems you see in this memo and identify them in the margins as poor word choices, awkward sentences, and so on. Then rewrite the memo.

To: All Clerical Employees

From: Winnie Johannsen, Manager, Personnel Division

Subject: New Office Manager

Date: June 2, 19xx

It has come to my attention that many clerical employees are bitching about the way the new office manager, John McLeod, has been bossing them around, butting in on matters that don't concern him, and accusing a lot of you of carrying on noisy conversations in the lunchroom.

At this point in time, I would like to advise that you postpone formulating a formal complaint until such time as Mr. McLeod has completed his first month with the firm and until management has had ample opportunity to introduce him to the rules and regulations of the company. It goes without saying, however, that I hope you will continue to informally share your grievances with me, so I can, as per your suggestions, help to effect an improvement in Mr. McLeod's interpersonal skills.

Review Test 6-7

I. You have worked for AMG Corporation for two years. Now you are in line for a promotion. The president of the company has requested that you write a page (to go in your personnel folder) that summarizes your education and experience as well as what you have done in the past two years to warrant the promotion. You want to make the page persuasive as well as factual; moreover, you want to show your abilities as a writer as well as your accomplishments for the company.

Start by outlining the major ideas you have for the page: have at at least three major headings and two or three subheadings under each major heading.

II. Now write the page (250–350 words). Make sure your paragraphs are effective, your information is concrete, and your sentences are concise.

WRITING BUSINESS MATERIALS

FAMOUS FIRST DRAFTS: WINSTON CHURCHILL
Writing Hint: Be Specific

Source: Ford Button

I have nothing
to offer but blood,
toil, tears, and sweat.

Reading for Resourceful Writers

The Specialized Resume

BOB ("THE SKUNK") CALHOUN

No permanent address: You can usually find me at the
King's X Saloon, corner of Broad and South streets,
Capitan, New Mex. Or ask my friend Bill ("Billy the Kid")
Bonney since he usually knows where I am.

JOB OBJECTIVES: I'd like something in the outdoors. I don't mind working nights as well as days, but I don't get along too well with people hanging around my neck giving me orders, so I'd like a position with a lot of independence. Prefer being paid in gold.

EDUCATION: School didn't turn out for me too well, though I've been to a lot of them. Rogers Home for Troubled Teens was one of the best as I developed several skills such as manufacturing small explosives that have proved very useful.

EXPERIENCE: Devil's Ranch, near Fort Worth, Tex. Worked with Big Sam Bass, who you might've heard of, taking care of a few thousand head of cattle. Took 10,000 of the critters from Arizona back to Texas one year and arrived with 18,000. Received commendation from the boss.
Worked for two years on my own transacting cattle deals with ranchers. Learned to handle a variety of weapons.
Had to spend four years indoors under close supervision but learned some good methods for making sharp tools out of silverware.

HOBBIES: Read home-study manuals on using and modifying handguns enjoy horseback riding; am familiar with all major New Mexico cattle ranches and with the Southern Pacific Railroad schedules; took a Banking Operations course given by Mr. Frank James and his brother, Jesse.

PERSONAL: Willing to travel and relocate; am not afraid of taking risks; prefer not to work with law enforcement officers.

PART SEVEN OBJECTIVE: To write effective memos, resumes, and letters.

You already know quite a lot about business materials. Throughout this book, you have been working on letters and memos as well as on sentences and paragraphs related to business. And chances are that you had written some business materials long before you started this book.

However, now that you are more confident in your abilities to write grammatically and clearly, the following chapters will guide you toward writing even more effectively. They will help you to direct your writing specifically toward the results you want—whether you are applying for a job or informing your readers of survey data.

Moreover, since conveying information and being persuasive are basic elements of almost every social and business relationship, understanding these principles will help you to be effective in every aspect of your life.

Before starting Chapter 36, take the Part Seven Pre-Test to test some of your skills in writing business materials.

PART SEVEN PRE-TEST

Read the following job application letter and answer the questions given.

Dear Sirs:

I can't tell you how excited I was to see your ad in today's *Bulletin*. I am sure you will be excited, too, when you see how well the qualifications on my resume (enclosed for your consideration) fit with the description in the ad.

I may not have the degree you specify in the ad, but I have the drive and ambition. You can reach me by calling the number on the resume.

Sincerely,

C. Smith

---

1. Does this letter have any major faults?

2. Is anything wrong with the opening? With the closing?

3. Is any information missing?

4. Is there anything you would delete from this letter?

5. Write your own version of this letter, adding and deleting information as you wish.

(See end of text for some hints on how the letter could be improved.)

CHAPTER 36

MEMORANDUMS

OBJECTIVES: To develop strategies (1) for memos that inform, request, and persuade; (2) for pleasant and unpleasant memos; and (3) for each section of the memo.

Memorandums (memos) are the most common type of written communication in business. Most businesspeople find they spend much of their workday writing memos—even though their jobs are in marketing, financial planning, auditing, personnel, or management.

Despite the proliferation of memos on almost every office desk in the world, people are rarely trained to write them effectively. In many companies, a random sampling of these documents reveals the majority of memos to be incomplete, unclear, verbose, offensively worded, or unnecessary. (See Figures 36.1, 36.3, 36.10.)

A few simple guidelines will help make your memos more readable and worthwhile.

CONSIDER WHETHER THE MEMO IS NECESSARY

Paper flow has become a big problem in some organizations. The copy machine seems to propagate endless reams of paper across every desk. As a result, people barely glance at most memos. A busy employee is apt to throw a memo in the wastebasket and then ask his neighbor, "Anything in that memo from Personnel?"

Before writing a memo and making 70 copies, ask yourself:

> How many people need the information in this?
> Is the information simple or complicated?
> Do we need a written record of this information?

If only two or three people really need the information and the facts are simple, a phone call might be more efficient than a memo. For example, you could call up your three fellow supervisors and suggest a lunch meeting instead of writing a memo about it.

If you want the information kept on file, however, a memo is preferable. For example, if you are announcing a change in procedures or making a monthly tally of office costs, the information should be on paper—or on a disk.

A computer mail system, of course, can alleviate the paper problem in offices where employees have access to terminals. But an informational bulletin board can be just as effective in a small company, and it can cut paper and copying costs to an astonishing extent.

DETERMINE THE MAIN POINT OF YOUR MEMO

Many memos are fuzzy or difficult to read because the writer either is unclear what the message is or has more than one message to convey. In general, you should be able to condense the focus of your memo into the subject line at the top of your memo. If you cannot come up with a clear, meaningful subject, you may not have one: you may have two or more subjects—or none at all.

Fred Toomey, for example, struggled for hours trying to put together a memo that both summarized the events of a recent meeting and outlined the findings of a company survey. One problem was that he could not write a title for his memo: he was not comfortable with any of his variations on "Hiring Committee Meeting and Employee Survey Results." He finally determined that he did not have one major point at all—he was trying to condense two major ideas into one memo.

Fred then included the results of the employee survey in a recommendation report to the Personnel Department and wrote a memo to department supervisors entitled "Minutes of Hiring Committee Meeting."

CONSIDER WHO NEEDS THE INFORMATION

Some writers send most of their memos to all employees. This procedure seems simpler because the writer does not have to look up a list of names or take the time to consider who actually needs the information. As a result, everyone's desk is flooded with unnecessary information.

Your memo will be much more effective if you send it only to people affected by the information. If the production staff does not need to know about the new software available for the accounting personnel, then don't send the memo to the Production Department.

If your memo is being sent to only a small group, you can often get a better response by listing individual names. If a memo is personally addressed, the recipient is more apt to read it. Compare:

> To: All Supervisors

with

> To: Karen Jones
>   Henry Korning
>   Bill Lawson
>   Jill Pointer
>   Patricia Wong

Most people will respond more positively to a personalized memo—just as they will respond better to a letter addressed to them rather than to "Dear Occupant."

You will also find that having a small, well-defined audience will help you write a better memo. You can usually convey information more efficiently to a smaller audience because you know exactly what the readers already know and what they need to know.

OUTLINE YOUR MEMO

Disorganization is one of the biggest problems with memos. People write them so fast—and so frequently—that the end result is jumbled. If your information is worth putting in written form, it is worth expressing clearly. So, once you have determined your main purpose, arrived at a specific title, and defined your audience, outline the major ideas as we discussed in Chapter 29.

Most memos will have three main parts: (1) an introduction stating the purpose of the memo; (2) a central portion, often in list form, providing the specifics of the topic; and (3) a conclusion informing the readers what action they should take or expect.

For example, when Grace Weatherby wanted to inform the clerical staff about new coffee break times, she outlined her memo like this:

I.   Inform employees that break times have changed due to overcrowding.

II. List break times for each office.

III. Mention when change goes into effect and what employees should do if they cannot break at time specified.

An outline not only helps you organize ideas in a manner the reader can understand, but also helps you remember all vital points. If Grace had forgotten to mention when the new break schedule went into effect—or what employees should do if they cannot break at the specified time—she would have been inundated with questions. As so often happens, she would probably have had to write yet another memo filling in the gaps of her first effort.

Self-Check Test 36-1

Marcia Forbes has outlined a memo requesting that the head of the Personnel Department consider three applicants for an entry-level programmer position. To make her outline more effective, put the following headings in a more logical order. (Check end of text for suggested revision.)

I.   We need a programmer who has finished an undergraduate degree in accounting.

II. The programmer we choose should have at least one year of experience with a small company.

III. The three applications attached to this memo seem suitable.

IV. If one of the three seems to fit our needs, have him or her call me so we can set up a second interview.

V.   Interview these applicants by July 1.

VI. The programmer should have good communication skills.

CONSIDER THE TONE OF YOUR MEMO

Keep the tone of your memo in mind as you put it in final form. Remember that your main purpose is to inform, persuade, or request, not to intimidate or alienate your readers. (Go back to Chapter 32 if you want to review some pointers on effective tone.)

When Grace Weatherby first drafted her notice about coffee breaks, she came out with a dry, impersonal memo that made the new schedule sound more like a punishment than a help for the employees (Figure 36.1). Her second draft became much more human and pleasant (Figure 36.2).

Remember, too, that your memo should sound like it came from *you*, not from a robot or computer. Having studied Chapter 31, you will be sure to avoid tired phrases like "It has come to my attention," "per your request" and "upon receipt of."

As you review the drafts of your memo, you might ask yourself questions like these:

- Have I written to my readers in much the same way I would speak to them?
- Have I used a tone that will produce results, not anger or resentment?
- Have I kept a pleasant and positive tone?
- Have I used the passive voice too often?
- Have I used too much business jargon?

WORDINESS

As we discussed in Chapter 33, wordiness is a problem for most business writers. Remember to check every sentence for unnecessary words and phrases. But also consider whether you have given the right amount of information in your memo. You may not have to summarize an entire telephone call, for example, before responding to one point that was discussed during the conversation. Or you might not have to provide all the background of a problem if you are certain your reader knows the situation.

On the other hand, if you are not sure what your readers know about a situation, give them all the details.

You might ask yourself these questions as you review your draft:

- Have I provided unnecessary or irrelevant information?
- Have I delayed getting to my major points?
- Could I make my points more concisely?
- Is there any information *missing?*

Self-Check Test 36-2

Write the memo you outlined in Self-Check Test 36-1. Check for wordiness, word choice, and tone. (See end of text for sample memo.)

To: Cheryl Birch, Head of Personnel   Date:

From: Marcia Forbes, Head of Accounting

Subject: Programmer Interviews

MEMOS TO INFORM, REQUEST, PERSUADE

Before starting your first draft, you should consider the primary *aim* of your memo. Knowing what you want to achieve will affect your organizational strategies and your tone as well as your choice of data.

So, as you consider your first draft, ask yourself, "Am I trying to convey information? Am I *asking* for information—or requesting a favor? Or do I have a recommendation that I want my readers to accept?

Informative Memos

Informative memos may give instructions, delineate a problem or situation, announce a change in procedures, or summarize proceedings. Since your major concern is conveying information, you must focus on clarity and effective organization. (See Figures 36.2 and 36.4 through 36.9 for samples of informative memos.)

Typically, an informative memo follows a three-part structure:

1. Introduction explaining point of memo

2. Central section outlining information in a logical format

3. Conclusion summarizing the information or outlining action the reader should take

Request Memos

Memos that ask the reader to do something may require a little more tact than a simple informative message. If the reader is going to resist doing what you ask, you may want to *explain* before you request: prepare the reader before asking him or her for assistance. Also work on creating a pleasant, personal tone: you will get more cooperation from your reader.

You may want to organize your request like this:

1. An opening sentence that stresses something positive

2. An explanation for the request you are making

3. The request itself with all necessary details

4. An upbeat ending that will make your reader react positively to the request

Figure 36.10 illustrates a request memo that lacks positive tone and explanations. The total effect is more apt to annoy the reader than win her help. Figure 36.11 shows a better approach to the same problem.

Persuasive Memos

A persuasive memo should focus on *evidence*. You will usually need to bolster your arguments and recommendations with specific examples, costs, benefits, and concrete language. While an informative memo will often list steps or procedures, a persuasive memo will weigh advantages and disadvantages.

You could organize a persuasive memo along the same lines as a request memo; in fact, a request memo in some ways *is* a persuasive memo. In both cases, you should provide an explanation before you really begin persuading the reader. For example, you might organize a persuasive memo like this:

1. Description of a problem or situation

2. Statement of purpose

3. Description of solutions, recommendations, and so on

4. Analysis of strong and weak points of options already described

5. Conclusion summarizing your point and indicating specific action you want the reader to take

In a persuasive memo, you need to concentrate on a clear reasoning, an objective tone, and strong, valid argument. (See Figures 36.13 and 36.14.)

PLEASANT AND UNPLEASANT MEMOS

Before writing, you should also consider how your reader is going to view your memo. If you are giving good news, start with it: "I am pleased to announce that management has agreed to our request for a 10 percent pay raise."

If your news is less agreeable, you may want to start with a delaying sentence or two. You may also want to incorporate explanations before you pass on the news. In Figure 36.7, for example, Karen Weeks explains the reasons for the new parking solutions—and emphasizes their temporary nature—*before* she summarizes them. In Figure 36.9, Patricia Holbrooke links the bad news with some good news.

PARTS OF A MEMO

Memo Headings

Once you have considered the nature of your message and how your audience will react to it, you can begin filling out the top of the memo form. Many companies have printed memo forms with headings at the top that look something like this:

To:

From:

Subject:

Date:

Sometimes the headings are arranged in two columns:

To: From:

Subject: Date:

And sometimes only the date is on the right:

To: Date:

From:

Subject:

Although filling out the appropriate information seems simple, you should consider a few points.

To and From

We have already briefly discussed the first line: limit your reader to those who need the information, and use names if you are sending the memo to a small number of people.

In some cases, you may want to include the reader's title after his or her name: *To: Fred Barnes, Sales Manager*. Use this format particularly if you do not know the reader well or if the memo is going to be kept on file.

If you include the reader's title, you should also include your own: *From: Marla Finney, Sales Representative*.

Be consistent, also, with first and last names: do not put Fred's first name and then your first *and* last names. In some companies, courtesy titles such as *Mr.*, *Mrs.*, *Ms.*, and *Dr.* are used in memo headings. If you use a courtesy title for your reader, use one for yourself:

To: Mr. Fred Barnes

From: Ms. Marla Finney

Subject

A memo is meant for fast communication. A reader should grasp the gist of it within moments. Therefore, the subject line is a vital part of the memo: it should be informative and specific, and it should make the reader want to read the memo. Avoid upsetting your readers before they have even started reading!

In Grace Weatherby's first draft (Figure 36.1), for example, she wrote "New Regulations" as a subject line. Upon revising her rough draft, she found that title unpleasantly negative as well as vague and changed it to "New Coffee Break Schedules" (Figure 36.2).

Make sure, also, that your title is clear and straightforward. Avoid jargon like "Implementation of Cost-efficient Regulations" when you mean "How to Lower Our Electricity Costs."

Self-Check Test 36-3

Write an appropriate and useful subject line for the following memo. (See end of text for suggested title.)

To: Gary Dawes   Date: March 3, 19xx

From: Karen Hill

Subject:

As you suggested this morning during our meeting, I am preparing the following information for your report:

1. Salary histories for each programmer since June 19xx

2. Overtime pay for each programmer during the past 12 months

3. Number of sick hours leave granted to each programmer over the past 12 months

I will have the information for you on Wednesday morning.

Openings   In most memos, the opening sentences should expand the subject line of the heading and give a strong sense of the memo as a whole.

The opening paragraph should be appropriate to the subject matter: for example, a memo about a serious problem should not open with a joke; a memo on a pleasant topic—like the company picnic—should not have a dull, heavy-handed beginning.

The following openings are clear, readable, and appropriate:

Subject: Budget/Biennial Convention

The finance staff has finished evaluating the projected budget for the convention. Although we found most of the figures reasonable, we questioned three areas.

(See Figure 36.8 for complete memo.)

Subject: Xerxes Mini-Classes

Since management recommends that all company accountants become familiar with the new Xerxes software, Marcia Donaldson has offered to give half-hour mini-lessons to everyone on the accounting staff.

Subject: Annual Report Deadline

Because the annual report must be at the printer's by January 30, John Cohn needs all your materials by Friday, January 5.

If the memo holds unpleasant news, the opening sentences can be slightly off the main point; they should, however, still be linked to the main theme:

Subject: Vacation Schedules

Congratulations on your excellent work over the past six months. Sales are up 30 percent—and your bonuses will reflect our success. As a result of our hard work, we have won three new contracts that must be completed by September 1.

This work load, however, means most of us will have to schedule vacations for the fall or winter months.

The following checklist may prove helpful as you write your openings:

- Is my opening paragraph linked to both my subject line and the rest of the memo?

- Is my opening going to interest my readers? Does it make someone want to read on?

- Is my opening suitable for the subject matter as a whole?

If you answer yes to these questions, you probably have a good beginning.

Hint: Many people write their opening paragraphs *last*; if you already know how you have organized your material, you will often have a better sense of how to begin the memo.

Central Paragraphs

Because your central message should be logical and easy to follow, the key task here is organization. Once again, an outline can be very useful. After listing all your major points, you can order them in a way that will be most helpful to the reader—or most effective at presenting your point.

We discussed some organizational methods in Chapter 29. You may want to consider the following:

1. Chronological steps

2. Logical narration

3. Order of increasing importance

4. Order of decreasing importance

5. Comparison/contrast

Methods 1 and 2 are more common with informative memos; methods 3, 4, and 5 are more common with persuasive memos. Request memos will vary with the subject matter.

Chronological Steps

Many informative memos follow the chronological pattern. If you are telling your readers about a new procedure or illustrating how something works, for example, a step-by-step description is usually most useful.

For examples of memos organized chronologically, see Figures 36.5 and 36.6. In Figure 36.5, Carol Dunn informs readers what steps to take before applying for research funds; in Figure 36.6, Joe Robertson outlines new procedures for ordering supplies.

If you use this method, make sure your steps *are* chronological. You would not want to describe starting a car, for instance, with a list like this:

1. Insert key.

2. Turn it to the right until engine comes on.

3. Press accelerator.

4. Make sure car is in Park.

Logical Narration

In a logically developed memo, the writer organizes material in a manner useful for the reader; often the writer answers unspoken questions in the order they would naturally come to the reader's mind.

Figures 36.4, 36.7, and 36.13 illustrate a logical method of organizing material.

In Figure 36.4, Jay Mann provides the essential data about a seminar. He begins by giving basic time/date/location, moves on to the purpose and method of the seminar, and concludes with details important to readers attending and not attending.

In Figure 36.7, Karen Weeks organizes parking alternatives for employees by opening with the most obvious (the company lot) and moving toward less obvious—and possibly less pleasant—options.

In Figure 36.13, Janet Ogilvie describes the costs and benefits of starting a company aerobics program. By beginning with costs, she answers her readers' first questions; then she goes on to turn those costs into advantages for the company.

Increasing Importance/ Decreasing Importance

Organizing your memo by the importance of the elements can be particularly useful in a persuasive memo. You will have to decide, however, whether to start by playing your trump cards or by holding out until the reader has been partially persuaded by your less impressive arguments or details.

In Figure 36.8 Michael Kurtz lists questionable estimates in convention costs. He wants to catch his reader's attention right from the start, so he begins with the worst error and then moves to the next most important. In Figure 36.9, on the other hand, Patricia Holbrooke analyzes the results of the customer survey by building up to a grand finale.

Even without explicitly stating their organizational methods, both writers have heightened the effectiveness of their message by the order of their data. The reader senses a progression and, usually without realizing it, is persuaded in part by the logic behind the organization.

Comparison/ Contrast

The comparison/contrast method will be most useful in a persuasive memo in which you are describing options. You may want to establish advantages versus disadvantages, costs versus benefits, and so on.

In Figure 36.14, Vince Lonigan's comparison of two catering services leads logically to his final recommendation.

To be persuasive, you must answer your readers' questions and doubts: you cannot stress the good points of an option without delineating the costs or the weaknesses. By comparing and contrasting options, you actually end up with a more persuasive piece of writing.

Endings

Usually the final paragraph accomplishes one or more of the following:

1. Summarizes the information from the central paragraphs

2. Requests the reader to act

3. Returns the memo to an upbeat point made at the opening

4. Summarizes the writer's recommendations

The last paragraph should provide a definite ending; do not leave your reader in midair. (He or she should not have to turn the page to see if you wrote more.) Also make sure you include nothing *new* in the ending: restate points—do not introduce new information.

Sometimes a simple list at the end will catch the reader's eye and help him or her remember your most important points. In Figure 36.4, for example, the writer concludes with a list of the time, date, and location of the seminar: this ending not only reinforces the writer's point but serves as easy reference for the reader.

Charts and Graphs

Charts and graphs often accompany memos. If you can summarize sales data in a pie chart or bar graph, for example, you can save yourself and your reader a lot of time. A graphic representation of the costs and benefits of your recommendations allows the reader to glance over the data before reading the entire memo.

Remember the keys to an effective memo:

- Readability
- Accuracy
- Thoroughness
- Personal tone

Readable language, concise presentation, lists, visual aids, and an appropriate organizational method will help you create an effective and worthwhile memo.

Self-Check Test 36-4

I. Reorganize the central points in this persuasive memo so they are more effective. You may simply renumber the list. (See end of text for suggested revision.)

To: Management

From: Corey Bates

Subject: New Building Location

Date: July 5, 19xx

During the last week in June, I visited the three lots that our consultants chose as possible sites for our new building. The site next to Plumtree Mall seems the best choice for us.

1. Plumtree Mall is a landmark in the area, so our clients will easily locate our building.

2. The Plumtree Mall site costs nearly $50,000 less than the site at Gladding Village and nearly $60,000 less than the site in Addison Heights.

3. The Plumtree site has much more room for parking than the other sites.

4. We could immediately begin building at the Plumtree site; building at the other sites would have to be delayed until the local Planning Commission reviewed our plans.

5. The Plumtree lot is large enough to accommodate the building we need; the other two lots would require that we substantially revise our present plans (at considerable expense).

I will present my findings in more detail at our meeting on July 10, but I am sure you will find the Plumtree location far superior to the others.

II. What organizational method did you use to reorganize the memo? Why?

Checklist for Chapter 36

1. Write memos only when necessary.
2. Send memos only to readers who need the information.
3. Consider whether the primary function of your memo is to inform, request, or persuade.
4. Consider whether the information in the memo is pleasant or unpleasant.
5. Make sure the subject line is helpful to the reader.
6. Make sure the opening paragraph gives a strong sense of the memo as a whole.
7. Organize your central points so they are persuasive and easily understood.
8. Include a summary, request for action, or positive note at the end.
9. Use charts, graphs, and lists if they will make your memos more readable and persuasive.
10. Make sure your memos are concise, complete, and pleasant.

Exercises

Rewrite the following memo to make it more organized and readable.

To: All Staff, Finance Division   Date: May 2, 19xx

From: Len Pine

Subject: New Hires

As you know, we have welcomed on board with us three analysts who will be working with us and with Information Processing. If you have not already met George Derby, Jackie Ross, and Mo Peters, go and introduce yourself. You will be glad to know that George is a renowned first baseman—so we may finally have a chance against the Accounting Department!

To welcome these new people and to celebrate spring, we are having a company picnic for all department members and their families. There will be volleyball, Ping-Pong, and swimming. Bring food for your family and some to share. Barbecues are available. The picnic will run from noon till dusk.

If you are interested, bring your softball equipment, too. The picnic will take place at Howatt Park. Let me know by Wednesday if you can attend. See you there.

Chapter Test 36-1

After hearing some discontented comments, you have surveyed the thoughts of the clerical staff on the working environment (lights, ventilation, work space, and so on) in your company. Now you are presenting the survey results to Mr. Blake, company president, in memo form.

Chapter Test 36-2

As manager of a department, write a memo to three other managers requesting help on a project. You are putting together a list of all the software presently available in the company and the software that employees are requesting. Ask the managers to submit names of programs their employees would find useful as well as programs they are currently using.

Chapter Test 36-3

The present petty cash system is inadequate. Amounts are never tallied properly, receipts are missing, and money may have been stolen. As a supervisor, write a memo to your employees explaining a new procedure for obtaining petty cash.

Chapter Test 36-4

You are the head of a clerical staff. Write a memo to the staff informing them of a new policy: they may no longer eat lunch at their desks. Tell them where they may eat, where they may not eat, and when the policy goes into effect. Make sure the memo is clear, well organized, concise, and friendly.

Chapter Test 36-5

Write a memo to the staff informing them of new regulations regarding smoking. Tell them where and when they may smoke.

Chapter Test 36-6

As a member of a professional association or college club, write a memo to members who could not attend the last meeting. Tell them the main points covered in the meeting and include details about upcoming events or meetings.

Chapter Test 36-7   This memo suffers from poor organization and tone. Rewrite it by starting on a positive note and adding any concrete detail that could help the readers.

To: All Employees

From: Marcie Katz

Date: February 12, 19xx

Subject: Customer Complaints

Some of our customers are complaining about the way salespeople are dressed while at work. Needless to say, we are in business to make customers happy, so we need to shape up. On Friday morning at 9:00, Harriet Chou will meet with all salespeople to review proper methods of dressing— including makeup, hairstyle, and footwear.

I know this means getting to work an hour earlier, but the situation is critical, so sacrifices have to be made. Meanwhile, I suggest you use discretion in choosing outfits for work. We will meet in the upstairs lounge. Please be prompt.

Exercises for Experts   Write the memo that you outlined in Chapter Test 29-1.
Write the memo that you outlined in Chapter Test 29-2.

Figure 36.1   **POOR INFORMATIVE MEMO**

negative and vague
subject line

negative opening
passive voice

central points difficult
to read

impersonal passives

To: Clerical Staff

From: Grace Weatherby *GW*

Subject: New Regulations

Date: May 2, 19xx

Since complaints have been received regarding overcrowding during coffee breaks, breaks will now be taken at designated times only.

Division 1 will break from 10:00 a.m. to 10:15 a.m. and from 2:00 p.m. to 2:15 p.m. Division 2 will break from 10:15 a.m. to 10:30 a.m. and from 2:15 p.m. to 2:30 p.m. Division 3 will break from 10:30 a.m. to 10:45 a.m. and from 2:30 p.m. to 2:45 p.m.

If a break cannot be taken at the times specified, alternative arrangements can be made with the appropriate division supervisor.

This memo is both impersonal and difficult to read. The subject line of the memo is vague, and the second paragraph prevents a reader from glancing quickly at the schedule. Moreover, Grace does not mention when the new procedure goes into effect. Finally, because many of her sentences are in the passive voice, the tone is cold and impersonal.

See Figure 36.2 for an improved version of this memo.

Figure 36.2   **GOOD INFORMATIVE MEMO**

positive and specific
subject line

reason for new
schedules
main point of memo

key details in list form

personal, upbeat
ending

> To: All Clerical Staff
>
> From: Grace Weatherby (GW)
>
> Subject: New Coffee Break Schedules
>
> Date: May 2, 19xx
>
> Since we hired 30 new staff members in April, many of you have complained about waiting in line at the cafeteria during breaks. As a result, starting May 5, each division will break at different times:
>
> Division 1: 10:00 a.m.-10:15 a.m.
>   2:00 p.m.-2:15 p.m.
>
> Division 2: 10:15 a.m.-10:30 a.m.
>   2:15 p.m.-2:30 p.m.
>
> Division 3: 10:30 a.m.-10:45 a.m.
>   2:30 p.m.-2:45 p.m.
>
> If you can't break at the times specified, please speak with your supervisor.
>
> I hope your breaks will be more relaxed from now on. Enjoy your coffee and dough-nuts!

A specific subject line and a list format make this memo much easier to read than the first version. And, because Grace has written active sentences and included a *reader-oriented* rationale for the change, the tone is more pleasant.

Figure 36.3   **POOR INFORMATIVE MEMO**

To: All Managers

From: Jay Mann

Subject: Business Communication Seminar

Date: September 13, 19xx

The Organizational Development Department will give a seminar on business communication on Saturday, September 20, from 9:00 a.m. till 3:00 p.m. The seminar will be held in the multi-use facility. All managers and supervisors are expected to attend.

This seminar will improve your skills in several important areas. The morning session will focus on effective group communication. The afternoon session will concentrate on efficient phone usage and memo writing.

Informal attire will be encouraged, and lunch will be provided. Compensatory time will be granted for attendees. Anyone unable to attend should notify the OD Department in writing by September 17.

The beginning of this memo is well organized: the essential information appears in paragraph 1; more detail follows in paragraph 2. Paragraph 3, however, is disorganized: it opens with yet more detail, and then moves on to what action should be taken by people unable to attend.

A more serious problem lies in the tone: the writer is impersonal, even threatening. He uses the passive voice in several key sentences and offers few details about the seminar that make it appear worthwhile or interesting.

Rather than looking forward to the seminar, Jay's readers would probably have been dismayed by a Saturday wasted on a dull, 8-hour seminar. The compensatory time would not compensate for the aggravation.

For a more effective memo, see Jay's second draft (Figure 36.4).

Figure 36.4   **GOOD INFORMATIVE MEMO**

To: All Managers

From: Jay Mann

Subject: Business Communication Seminar

Date: September 13, 19xx

Brenda Lee from our Organizational Development Department will give a seminar on
business communication skills on September 20, from 9:00 a.m. to 3:00 p.m., in
the multi-use facility. All managers and supervisors should attend.

If you have ever left a meeting knowing nothing was accomplished--or hung up the
phone knowing you haven't made your major point--this seminar can help you control
these situations and make them productive.

In the morning session, focusing on group communication, Brenda will direct you
through role-playing exercises emphasizing techniques you will find useful in your
own departments. In the afternoon, you will practice ways to make your memos and
phone calls more effective. The whole day should be fun as well as educational.

Please dress informally--especially as you will be enjoying lunch provided by
Flint's Barbecue.

After attending the seminar, you may take eight hours of compensatory time at your
convenience. If you cannot attend, please notify the OD Department by September
17.

          Date: Saturday, September 20

          Time: 9:00 a.m. to 3:00 p.m.

          Place: Multi-Use Facility

Jay's second version is longer than his first, but the extra words will pay off in terms of his readers'
response. Although they may still not be delighted at spending a Saturday away from home, they will
at least see the day as profitable and even entertaining.

Figure 36.5   **GOOD INFORMATIVE MEMO**

To: Craig Almon, Bernie Ferragamo, Page Garrison, Larry Matthews

From: Carol Dunn

Topic: NRI Research Funds

Date: February 1, 19xx

As some of you are working on intercultural training projects, you may want to apply for funding from NRI.

NRI, a privately supported foundation, has notified me that funds may be available for research on aspects of employee training. George Fermin, the director, has told me that the institute is particularly interested in projects focusing on international business needs. I have attached a copy of the institute's guidelines.

Before you begin developing a proposal, I recommend the following:

    1. Speak to me about the project. I may have some additional information for you.

    2. Read the summaries of previously funded NRI projects that I have left in the company library.

    3. Prepare a preproposal as described by the guidelines. If you get a draft to me before March 1, I may be able to discuss it with George before you put it in final form.

    4. Start working right away, as the deadline for the proposal is April 18.

    This memo is well organized. Carol makes her major point in the opening sentence, and then provides a step-by-step, chronological picture of what the interested reader should do next.

    One strength of this memo is that the writer has made the point clear from the beginning. After reading the topic line and opening sentence, the readers can tell whether the memo holds any relevance for them. A good memo will not waste a reader's time.

| Figure 36.6 | **GOOD INFORMATIVE MEMO** |

To: Bob Freeman

From: Joe Robertson *JR*

Topic: Ordering Procedures

Date: June 5, 19xx

On Friday, June 2, I met with Wilson Cullen and Pam Owens about the ordering problems we have been having. We agreed to the following procedures, subject to your approval.

1. Triplicate order forms will go to Marsha at the beginning of each month.

2. Having checked the forms for completeness and accuracy, Marsha will call department heads if she sees a problem.

3. She will put pertinent information into the computer.

4. She will send pink copies of the form back to the departments for final verification and retain the yellow copies. Then she will send the white copies to suppliers.

The whole procedure should still take less than two days, and we should avoid the double ordering and confusion we have been experiencing.

Let me know your thoughts as soon as possible. I'd like to have the system set up for July.

This is one of the most common types of memo: defining a procedure. Joe tells his reader the point of the memo; then he outlines the procedure step by step. His conclusion requests the reader to act promptly. The memo is short and to the point without being impersonal or abrupt.

Figure 36.7   **GOOD MEMO CONVEYING BAD NEWS**

subject line presents *solutions*, not problems

explanation of problem

personal tone

list of options from most pleasant to least pleasant

upbeat ending

To: All Employees

From: Karen Weeks

Topic: Temporary Parking Solutions

Date: June 13, 19xx

Now that the western portion of our parking lot has been taken over for the new building, we are encountering severe parking problems. We will have a permanent solution in August when the new lot is paved, but until then we must ask you to be patient.

Department heads met this week and arrived at the following temporary solutions.

   1. As our lot now accommodates only 40 cars, we will allocate each of these spaces to an employee by giving each car a numbered sticker corresponding to a parking place. If you want us to consider you for one of these places, please give me a note with your name and any special considerations you may have, i.e., disability, distance from work, etc. We will allocate these spaces by need before seniority. You will know by Friday if you are one of the 40.

   2. If possible, the remaining 35 employees should try to car pool or take public transportation. I have started a Car Poolers' Telephone Listing on the downstairs bulletin board. The 40 bus will take you to the corner of Forbes and Market.

   3. For a small fee, Lerner Foods has agreed to let 15 cars park in the lot adjacent to the plant on Mill Street. As Lerner's is almost a mile from here, you will have to take a long walk, arrange a ride, or take a bicycle in your car. Sign the Lerner's List on the downstairs bulletin board if you want to be one of the 15.

   4. If more than eight people still have severe transportation difficulties, we can start a van pool with a hired van. I will let you know next week if this will be necessary.

I know these procedures cannot please everyone, but at least they should ease some of the early morning tensions and late arrivals we have been experiencing. And remember--the situation will be remedied by August!

Before giving her solutions, Karen provides a rationale for her somewhat unpleasant alternatives and mentions a time by which all the problems will be permanently solved.

She then lists the options from the most pleasant to the least pleasant—and from the most obvious to the least obvious. Her upbeat ending brings the reader back to the temporary nature of the problem.

Figure 36.8   **GOOD MEMO CONVEYING BAD NEWS**

From: Michael Kurtz, Finance Department

To: Thelma Townsend, Convention Committee Chairperson

Subject: Budget/Biennial Convention

Date: October 12, 19xx

The finance staff has finished evaluating the projected budget for the convention. Although we found most of the figures reasonable, we questioned three areas.

1. Travel costs: The budget seems to be based on one-way air fares. The costs of flying 30 people to and from Los Angeles will run closer to $6,000 than $3,000.

2. Programs: Printing programs will cost $300, not $225.

3. Flowers: Flowers at the head table will run $50, not $40.

I hope this $3,085 difference will not adversely affect convention plans. If you want us to discuss our findings with the convention committee, we will be happy to do so.

This concise memo begins with the largest problems and moves to the smallest. The tone is formal but polite. By opening with a sentence approving most of the budget, Michael makes the memo more positive and reader-oriented.

Figure 36.9   **GOOD MEMO CONVEYING GOOD AND BAD NEWS**

To: Jan Marnet

From: Patricia Holbrooke

Subject: Results of Customer Survey

Date: April 13, 19xx

On Thursday, April 9, we finished compiling results of the 300 surveys our customers filled out over the past 3 weeks. In general, the results indicate we are on the right track: customers like our new vegetarian entrees and want to see more diet entrees. We also have a good rate of repeat customers.

On the other hand, many customers found our food bland and the service poor. Almost 25 percent said they wouldn't return. So we have some work ahead of us!

Here is a more complete picture of the results. (I have starred the problem areas.)

	Yes	No
Do you find our atmosphere appealing?	230	70
Do you like our vegetarian entrees?	213	87
Would you like more of our diet entrees?	210	90
*Will you come back after today?	230	70

	Very Good	OK	Poor
*How do you rate our service?	175	82	43

	Tasty	Bland	Too Spicy
*Do you find our food	205	90	5

Let me know if you want to discuss how we might improve these figures.

This informative memo starts with an overview of the survey and then presents actual figures in a chart form. The memo directs the reader to problem areas but also emphasizes the good things that the survey pointed out.

Figure 36.10   **POOR REQUEST MEMO**

To: Kim Reed

From: Harry O'Gara *HO*

Subject: Absenteeism

Date: July 5, 19xx

opening is passive, impersonal—focuses on *problems*

this is a demand, not a request

Problems with our volunteers have to be solved immediately. As volunteer coordi-nator, you will have to figure out a policy that will keep us from being stranded by absent volunteers at the last minute. Last month, seven workshops had to be canceled, and three were led by poorly trained trainers called in at the last minute.

writer-oriented statement

vague, passive

The buck stops with you, Kim. I'm being driven crazy by this problem, and I don't have time to help you find volunteers two hours before a workshop starts. Since we have 15 workshops scheduled for August, a proposal from you regarding this problem would be greatly appreciated.

Harry wrote this memo in a fit of temper—and quickly regretted it. He had a real problem, but he saw that a memo like this was not going to get a positive response from his reader. He was, after all, making a request. When he realized that he was asking Kim to do something, he rewrote the memo with a pleasant tone indicating that he saw a *mutual* problem.

See Figure 36.11 for his revised version.

Figure 36.11   **GOOD REQUEST MEMO**

To: Kim Reed

From: Harry O'Gara

Subject: Absenteeism

Date: July 5, 19xx

positive opening

description of problem

Since Jobs Unlimited depends on the fine work of its volunteers, each volunteer is vital to the smooth functioning of our organization. As you know, however, we have been having increasing problems: many volunteers have been calling in sick, and several have been absent without notice. We can't go on canceling workshops or calling on poorly prepared trainers at the last minute.

reason for request

As volunteer coordinator, you may be able to help. A more complete and clear absentee policy could spare us some of this confusion. We might lose a few volunteers, but we could keep the ones that really want to work.

I would appreciate your drafting a proposal that we could discuss when we meet next week. You might consider:

specific details of request

    1. a firm policy on volunteers who are absent more than twice in three weeks;

    2. a backup system for replacing volunteers who become ill;

    3. an organizational system that will help volunteers find their own replacements.

Also, if you have some idea about what is causing the absenteeism, please discuss it with me. I am sure that, with a little effort, we can get the system working smoothly again.

upbeat ending

This memo is longer than the first version, but it is much more effective. Harry starts with a commendation; then he makes his request. When he does ask for a report, he shows his appreciation and offers concrete ideas on what he wants and when he wants it. His emphasis on cooperation will ensure that he gets it.

Figure 36.12   **GOOD REQUEST MEMO**

```
        To:      George Franks

        From:    Michi Low

        Subject: Temporary Clerical Staff

        Date:    August 21, 19xx


        Since we won the Turner account, our office has had almost double the word
        processing and filing work that we had last year.  We have, as you know, hired one
        more full-time typist, and we are interviewing for a second full-time position.
        For the past 2 weeks, however, the entire staff has been working overtime.

        Once we get caught up, our larger staff should successfully take care of the new
        work load.  But first we must get through the backlog.  I estimate that two more
        people working 40 hours for one week should put us on track.

        I would greatly appreciate your authorizing two temporary typists for a week.
        Paying them by the hour will cost less than paying regular workers overtime, and
        the temporaries will be more efficient:  we are all getting burned out from the
        long hours.

        Please let me know by Friday if I can go ahead and hire the temporaries.  I am
        sure you'll be pleased with our efficiency from now on.
```

This request memo combines informative and persuasive strategies. Michi explains that the problem is only short-term and points out several good reasons for hiring the temporaries. She does not complain about the stress incurred by the long hours, but she emphasizes considerations of cost and morale to persuade the reader to do as she requests.

Figure 36.13   **GOOD PERSUASIVE MEMO**

To: Henry Watts

From: Janet Ogilvie

Topic: Proposed Aerobics Program

Date: February 20, 19xx

Having examined over ten health and exercise programs for our employees, I have found Mark and Betty Olsen's aerobics classes to be best suited to our budget, facilities, and employees' time and interests.

The Olsens will charge us $1,000/month for ten one-hour classes every week. Five classes will meet at 7:00 a.m., five will meet at noon. We benefit from hiring the Olsens by the month, as their usual $50/hour price is double that of their monthly charge.

A thousand dollars a month, also, is a low figure since it represents almost our only cost: we will not have to remodel facilities except to add some lockers and carpet the downstairs lounge, which is presently unused. Our other options-- building racquetball courts or signing employees up with a local health club-- would be considerably more expensive.

Our employees, moreover, strongly favor the aerobics classes. The time schedule is good for almost all of them, and the convenience of classes in our own building will encourage them to participate.

If research on company health and wellness programs is accurate, we should end up saving money on absentee workers and health benefits. Dave Hamon at GDH Corporation says the Olsens' evening classes have noticeably improved the morale and fitness of his employees.

Further, hiring the Olsens is reversible: if employees lose interest, we can end the classes without having invested in expensive facilities or yearly club memberships.

Please let me know this week if I should sign a month-to-month contract with the Olsens. If we get the lounge carpeted, classes could start April 1.

This persuasive memo starts with the bad news—the cost of the aerobics classes. Then the writer proceeds to show that the price is actually a bargain—and should actually end up saving the company money.

Janet is careful to cover questions most apt to enter the reader's mind: what the classes will cost; what facilities are needed; what reputation the Olsens have; and what this company's employees want.

The memo ends with a request for action and a deadline to motivate the reader.

Figure 36.14   **GOOD PERSUASIVE MEMO**

To: Fred Fogarty, Vice-President

From: Vince Lonigan, Operations Manager

Subject: Cafeteria Suppliers

Date: July 21, 19xx

description of problem

Over the past six months, employees have been complaining about the food provided by CDS Cafeteria Services for our cafeteria. Almost every day, someone tells me about wilted salad, unappetizing meatloaf, stale bread, or cold soup.

recommendation for solving problem

As we are about to end our six-month contract with CDS, I recommend changing caterers. Six months ago, CDS was the only local company providing such services; now two others are competing: Company Caterers and Mrs. Green's Company Kitchen. Company Caterers seems the better choice, as Mrs. Green's is still too small to serve all our employees.

Consider some of Company Caterers' qualifications:

persuasive details beginning with most important

1. Company Caterers will charge our employees approximately the same as CDS for sandwiches, salads, and hot meals.

2. Company Caterers guarantees its quality: unlike CDS, this company welcomes suggestions from employees. Mike Brierly, the manager, will visit our cafeteria every week to check on food, service, and customer reactions.

3. Company Caterers offers a broader menu than CDS: the daily specials include Chinese and Mexican dishes as well as other ethnic favorites.

4. Company Caterers provides lunches for Torey Company and McPhee's, Inc. Both companies recommend the food and invite us to stop by and try it.

request for action

I have told Mike Brierly that we would decide on our caterer by August 1, since our contract with CDS runs out August 15. Please let me know your decision by July 31. (You might try the chow mein at Torey Company before you decide!)

This persuasive memo contrasts two catering services and offers several persuasive reasons for changing to Company Caterers. The opening gets the reader's attention with specific details of the problem and a recommendation. The central list format emphasizes Company Caterers' strong points. The end urges immediate action—and concludes on a personal note.

CHAPTER 37

RESUMES

OBJECTIVES: To (1) understand what makes the most successful resumes and (2) be able to create a resume suitable for your unique background and goals.

The resume may be one of the most important documents you ever write. Not only is it essential to the job-hunting process, but it may prove useful throughout your career. Many companies keep employees' resumes on file, insert them in corporate capability statements, and include them in proposals for grants or government contracts. Your resume may be examined when internal promotions are discussed or when management teams are being organized.

Because resumes are used so frequently and for so many reasons, you should constantly keep yours updated and ready for viewing.

Resume styles are as varied as the people who write them, but the best are clear, precise, and professional. Written in phrases rather than sentences, they focus on objective aspects of your experience, not on descriptions of your personal qualities. For example, most prospective employers expect to see some information on where you went to school rather than statements like, "I am well versed in all aspects of business."

A resume is not a life history. The word *resume* comes from a French word meaning *to summarize*. It is an outline meant to be glanced at: a prospective employer might look at your resume for less than 30 seconds before putting it in a *yes* or *no* pile. Make sure the best things about yourself can be spotted quickly!

RESUME STRATEGY

One of the most important things to remember about a resume is that it is *yours*. The format should be adapted to your particular goals, experience, and strengths. Nothing negative should appear on the page.

Also, remember, your resume is not meant to impress a reader with your charm or enthusiasm. It should be factual and straightforward; leave the enthusiastic tone to your cover letters and interviews.

Do look at your friends' resumes and at the examples in this book; but, ultimately, you will have to design a format that best suits you and your needs.

Before you start, bear in mind a few pointers:

- Keep it short—no more than two pages.
- Make it easy on the eye—easy to *glance* at.
- Include only positive aspects of yourself.
- Put the most important information toward the beginning—most people glance at a resume from top to bottom.

BRAINSTORMING

To get started, jot down a list of your major strengths and skills as well as the factual details about your education and experience. Also consider who your reader will be (an accountant, an advertising executive, a personnel manager) and what that reader will probably want to see. Someone hiring a salesperson will be looking for different qualities than a person searching for an entry-level accountant.

Naturally, one vital component to this brainstorming process is figuring out what you want the resume for: you should have a good sense of your goals so you can highlight the appropriate skills and experience. You may, in fact, end up having to write two or more resumes if you are applying for different kinds of positions.

If you are going to apply for two types of summer jobs, for example—as a lifeguard and as a salesperson—you may want to develop two resumes. One would highlight your swimming and sports experience, while the other would emphasize your experience and skill in sales. Both would emphasize your skills with people.

A grasp of your own strengths and weaknesses will help you determine the format and content of your resume: you will be highlighting your strengths, of course, and de-emphasizing your weaknesses.

When Carl Johnson was looking for an entry-level accounting position, part of his first brainstorming list looked like this:

Positive	Negative
summer internship at AA	took 6 years to get my B.S.
B.S. in accounting	first major in sociology
member of Accounting Assoc.	took 3 years off from school
supervised 16 people	worked odd jobs for 7 years
willing to travel	30 years old (good or bad?)
high G.P.A.	not willing to relocate
financed my education	went to three jr. colleges

Carl believed that many recruiters for the big public accounting firms he was interested in would not like his apparent lack of direction: he had taken time off from school, worked at various jobs, and attended several schools before deciding on and completing his accounting degree. Employers, he figured, might not be as interested in someone who had worked as a waiter and construction foreman as they were in 22-year olds who had devoted themselves to accounting since high school.

Carl's major strengths, on the other hand, were his successful internship at a Big Eight accounting firm, his good grades, and his B.S. from a reputable business school. He also had a maturity and range of skills acquired from his diverse experience. He developed a resume that played down dates and highlighted his education, internship, and activities in a professional organization.

He summarized his work experience in terms of skills: the supervisory experience he gained as a construction foreman and the understanding of small businesses he learned while working for a retail outlet. He included the positive line that he was willing to travel but deleted the negative note that he was unwilling to relocate. (See Figure 37.4 for his final resume.)

Self-Check Test 37-1

Rita Dawes, a college junior, is applying for a summer position as counselor in a girls' camp. She has randomly listed her experience and skills but now must decide which ones to highlight on her resume. Put a star next to the items that you suggest she emphasize. (See end of text for suggested answers.)

1. played varsity field hockey in high school

2. coached a girls' swimming team two summers ago

3. am majoring in fashion design and merchandising

4. have attended three colleges

5. sold encyclopedias for two months

6. have a lifeguard certificate

7. was sales manager for high school yearbook

8. was president of college sorority

9. can play guitar

10. plan to become a buyer for a retail store

11. have completed three semesters of accounting classes

RESUME TYPES

Traditionally, resumes have fallen into two formats: the chronological and the functional (or skills) resume. The first type takes a reader from the present to the past. (See Figures 37.2 and 37.3.) It mentions job titles, employers, and dates.

The second type, as the name implies, highlights skills. It does not state what you were doing when, but what you *can* do. Rather than saying you took an advanced programming seminar in 1986, it states that you have developed accounting software for a small business—not mentioning that the software was a special project for the seminar. (See Figure 37.5.)

Until recently, almost everyone used a chronological resume. More and more, however, as people began changing careers more frequently and older people began returning to the work force, the functional resume has gained in popularity.

Also, people are now combining the two types: you may want to have both a summary of skills and an outline of your work history. (See Figures 37.6 and 37.7 for examples of composite resumes.)

Basically, the key to a good resume is how effectively it displays your strong points and links you with the position or goal you have in mind.

RESUME HINT: DO NOT EXAGGERATE

Source: Ford Button

APPEARANCE OF RESUME

The resume must look *perfect*: no typos, faded print, misaligned margins or misspellings. Check all your information: someone seeing *Sear's* instead of *Sears* or *Arthur Anderson* instead of *Arthur Andersen* might decide not to read your resume any further.

Because the reader of a resume usually has only a piece of paper with which to judge your ability, you want that paper to be attractive as well as informative. Arrange your information with an artistic eye. You may want to have the resume typeset; at least have it typed on a good typewriter and photocopied neatly and clearly.

A computer is a great tool for writing a resume since you can easily update it. But do use a good printer and quality paper for the final copy.

If you are applying for a job, use that same quality paper for your cover letter and envelope. In essence, you are designing a marketing package for yourself. The appearance of that package can be almost as important as the contents.

RESUME FORMAT

Your resume should be typed in black or maybe brown ink on 8-½-by-11-inch paper. The paper should be white or, at its wildest, beige. Your resume should stand out because of its quality, not because it is printed on turquoise paper.

The general arrangement of entries is more or less up to you: you may want to center your titles and print them in boldface, or underline them and put them in the margin. You may choose to set off your entries with stars, bullets, or dashes.

Whatever your artistic choices, make sure you leave a sizable amount of white space on the page, so entries may be read easily. Avoid using fancy print that will slow down a reader.

BE CONSISTENT IN YOUR FORMAT

If you choose to write your graduation date as *6/87*, do not write out a month (*April 1985*) elsewhere in the resume. Do not underline one heading, then put another in boldface. Do not provide dates for one job but not for another.

USE ACTIVE VERBS

To make your resume as dynamic as possible, use verbs that highlight action. Avoid sluggish phrases such as "Helped new employees learn their job duties" when you can say, "Trained new employees."

The following are some verbs you might consider in a resume:

Achieved	Determined	Interviewed	Produced
Administered	Developed	Introduced	Programmed
Analyzed	Directed	Launched	Promoted
Assessed	Established	Maintained	Recruited
Audited	Expedited	Marketed	Revised
Centralized	Formulated	Monitored	Scheduled
Composed	Hired	Negotiated	Staffed
Conducted	Implemented	Operated	Streamlined
Created	Initiated	Organized	Supervised
Demonstrated	Instructed	Planned	Surveyed
			Tested

Self-Check Test 37-2

Turn the following sluggish descriptions into more interesting ones. Write in phrases, not complete sentences; remove personal pronouns. (See suggested revisions at end of text.)

> Example: I was responsible for seven employees
> Revision: Supervised seven employees

1. When the company needed a new manual on personnel procedures, I helped to organize and write it.

2. Was instructed to draw the illustrations for the company's newspaper advertisements.

3. Showed clerical employees how to operate new computer hardware.

4. When job applicants telephoned, I would talk to them before scheduling their interviews with appropriate department managers.

5. When the supervisor was out of town, I made sure the office ran smoothly.

ENTRIES

Heading

Some resumes are titled *RESUME*. This heading is purely optional: most people will recognize what it is without being told. If you are short of space, omit the heading. (Note: The French word *résumé* has an accent over each *e*. In English, it is perfectly acceptable to omit the accents, especially as they are often not included on English keyboards. However, do avoid using just *one* accent.)

Name, Address, Telephone

You must put your name, address, and phone number at the top of your resume. You may include both a permanent address and a school address, a home and a business telephone number, but avoid cluttering the resume with too many addresses and numbers. You want an address where you will definitely receive your mail; and you want a phone number that will be answered consistently by you or by a friend, family member, answering service, or machine.

Design the top of your resume to make it attractive and appealing to the eye.

Job Objective

Many resumes have an objective or job goal toward the top. This entry is optional. If you have a clear goal, such as computer programmer or travel agent, then include it. (If you have programmer as your objective, of course, you cannot send the resume in response to an ad for a bank teller.) If you plan to apply for several kinds of jobs, either delete this entry or design more than one resume.

Remember, a reader glancing down the page wants to know what you are applying for. If you do not have a clear objective, omit the entry. (Make sure, however, that your cover letter states clearly what position you are seeking.) Avoid vague, verbose descriptions that fill up space on the page and tell the reader nothing.

Job Objective: Seeking a position with management potential which will enable me to advance. Ideally, this would be a position in which an individual of ability and initiative would continue to grow professionally and obtain personal satisfaction. [verbose, vague]

Job Objective: Interested in a public-oriented position, preferably where business knowledge would be applied and developed. [vague]

Job Objective: Management trainee [precise, clear]

Qualified By

If you have several strong points that you want your reader to spot right away, you might summarize your qualifications toward the top of your resume. For instance, if you have several years of work experience and a master's degree, you could put this information under one heading. Do not go into a lot of detail here; simply pique your reader's interest and make him or her want to read further. (See Figures 37.2, 37.4, and 37.6.) Again, avoid long, fuzzy descriptions.

Qualified By: A Master's in Business Administration from George Washington University and four years' full-time work experience with United Airlines. [good entry]

Skills

In a functional resume, the skills section is the most important. And, as we noted earlier, you may want to include a skills section even in a chronological resume. In either case, brainstorming is probably in order. Jot down lots of skills and then organize them: organizational, computer, communication, accounting, marketing, and so on.

Starting with the skills most relevant to the job you want, list them in a way the reader will easily understand. Accountants would start with accounting skills, programmers with computer skills. You may be surprised at how many skills you have!

Remember, you do not have to explain when or where you acquired or used these skills.

Self-Check Test 37-3

Assume that Rita Dawes (Self-Check Test 37-1) is going to write a skills resume. From the items she listed, what *skills* do you think she might have? Organize your list starting with the skills that will be most relevant to the counselor job she wants. (See end of text for suggested items.)

Education

Many recent graduates will put education toward the top of their resumes. If your work experience is more impressive, however, put that first. The education entry usually includes the degree, the major, the name and location of the school, and the date of graduation. (If you are de-emphasizing dates, you do not need to include when you started the program, and you may even delete the graduation date. Remember: Include only what will speak *in your favor*.)

All items in your education and work experience entries should be arranged in *reverse* chronological order: start with the most recent items and move backward in time.

If you attended several schools, you need not mention them all. Do mention where you got your degree(s) and include any impressive or unusual programs. Include your G.P.A. if it is very good; do not include an even marginally good G.P.A.

You might also want to include awards, citations, fellowships, and so on in this section. If you have a lot of them, however, give them a separate section. (See Figures 37.2, 37.3, and 37.8.)

Coursework

Do NOT list all your classes. If you have taken some unusual or particularly impressive courses, put them down. A computer programmer might want to list all the computer language courses he has taken; an accountant need not mention that she took Principles of Accounting, but she might want to mention a tax or auditing class. (See Figures 37.7 and 37.10.)

High School

Include high school information only if you did not graduate too long ago and if the information is particularly relevant to the job you want. (For instance, Rita Dawes might mention her experience playing varsity field hockey in high school, since she is applying for a position that requires some skill in outdoor sports.)

The farther you get from high school, the less relevant it becomes. Even entries about being yearbook editor or senior class president look a little strained 15 years later. (There is no reason for Rita to mention her experience as sales manager of her high school yearbook.)

Work Experience

Education and work experience are usually the focal points of a resume. Once again, decide how your format will best highlight your strong points. (Figures 37.3, 37.4, and 37.7 present some interesting variations on the work experience entries.) You do NOT need to include:

- all your jobs
- all your duties
- the name of your supervisor
- the full address of the places you worked

And you should NEVER include:

- why you left
- your salary

Do put each entry in a consistent format: if you begin with the name of the company in capitals, then use that format throughout. Avoid listing too many duties; try to highlight the most relevant ones. For example, if you are looking for an accounting position, put any accounting-related duties first—even if you did them less frequently than, say, answering the telephone or working a cash register.

Memberships   Make sure you list any memberships in community or school organizations and any positions you have held. For some people (see Figure 37.8), memberships and activities may be more important than work experience.

Languages   Include foreign languages that you can read or speak and any computer languages with which you are familiar.

Other Entries   Include licenses, special abilities, and technical skills. (See Figures 37.2 and 37.12.)

Interests   The interests entry is optional. You may want to include some hobbies or activities if you have room on your resume. Be concrete rather than vague: *varsity swimming* is more impressive than *sports*, for instance. Put down any particularly relevant interests: someone interested in advertising might want to mention an interest in photography or graphics.

Personal Data   In years past, many resumes began with information about the writer's age, place of birth, marital status, and health. Now none of this information is mandatory; employers cannot legally ask questions about several of these areas, and most people consider applicants' eye color, weight, and height irrelevant to most jobs.
Either delete this data or put a few selected details at the *end* of the resume.

References   You may list references on the resume, add a separate sheet of references, or tell the reader that they are available on request. If your resume is crowded, you could delete the entry altogether and mention references in your cover letter. When you do list them on the resume, make sure you have more than one and no more than four. Put the full name, title, address, and phone number of each reference.

Checklist for Chapter 37

1. Make sure your resume is concise and clear.

2. Check that your resume is physically attractive and error-free.

3. Include only positive aspects of yourself.

4. Arrange chronological entries in reverse chronological order.

5. List skills in order of descending importance.

6. Do not make your resume longer than two pages.

Exercises

1. Develop a list of your strong and weak points. Make sure you consider these points from *an employer's* viewpoint.
2. Write a paragraph or two explaining what your resume strategy should be: given your particular job goals, what should you highlight? What should you de-emphasize? Should you use a chronological or functional resume—or a composite of the two?
3. Write a resume for a full-time, part-time, or summer job.
4. Design a complete skills resume for Rita Dawes (see p. 487). You may make up additional information, but use the following major headings: Job Objective, Skills, Education, Work History, and Hobbies.

Chapter Test 37-1

Rewrite the following resume so it is clearer and more effective. Develop a format that highlights the writer's best features. You may add and delete items as necessary.

THE CONFIDENTIAL RESUME OF:

James T. Parkington   Personal: 5'10", 165 lbs.

346 Green Street   single

Washington, D.C. 20014   willing to travel

(202) 235-8924

Objective: A management position that will give me an opportunity to take part in short- and long-term planning and will utilize my financial and "people" skills.

Education: B.A., mathematics
           M.B.A., operations research

Experience: I worked as a sixth-grade mathematics teacher in Baltimore, Maryland, before returning to school for my M.B.A. While in graduate school, I worked as a teaching assistant in mathematics at the University of Massachusetts.

For the past six years, I have worked for Grey Brothers Corporation as a financial clerk and then as budget accountant.

My skills include: developing a computerized warehouse system
                   using BASIC, C, and *Lotus 1-2-3* computer
                     languages
                   understanding and generating budget reports
                     and financial statements

                   working on a dynamic financial team

Employers:	Grey Brothers Corporation
	1423 G Street
19xx – present	Washington, D.C. 20012
	(202) 357-0021
	Position: Cost and Budget Accountant
19xx – 19xx	University of Massachusetts
	Department of Mathematics
	Position: Teaching Assistant
Colleges:	American College
19xx – 19xx	Baltimore, MD
19xx – 19xx	University of Massachusetts
	Amherst, MA

References available on request.

Exercises for Experts

I. Exchange resumes with a fellow classmate. Each of you should evaluate the other's resume for appearance and content. Write comments directly on the resume sheet.

II. A part-time sales job has been advertised in your local newspaper. Write or revise your resume so that it highlights skills and experience relevant to the job.

Figure 37.1   **SAMPLE RESUME FORMAT**

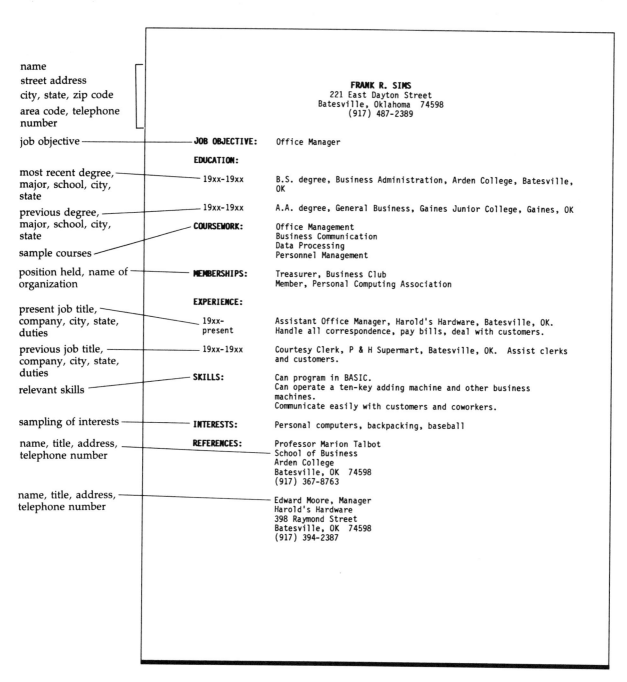

name
street address
city, state, zip code
area code, telephone
number

job objective —

most recent degree,
major, school, city,
state

previous degree,
major, school, city,
state

sample courses

position held, name of
organization

present job title,
company, city, state,
duties

previous job title,
company, city, state,
duties

relevant skills

sampling of interests

name, title, address,
telephone number

name, title, address,
telephone number

FRANK R. SIMS
221 East Dayton Street
Batesville, Oklahoma 74598
(917) 487-2389

JOB OBJECTIVE: Office Manager

EDUCATION:

19xx-19xx   B.S. degree, Business Administration, Arden College, Batesville, OK

19xx-19xx   A.A. degree, General Business, Gaines Junior College, Gaines, OK

COURSEWORK: Office Management
Business Communication
Data Processing
Personnel Management

MEMBERSHIPS: Treasurer, Business Club
Member, Personal Computing Association

EXPERIENCE:

19xx-present   Assistant Office Manager, Harold's Hardware, Batesville, OK. Handle all correspondence, pay bills, deal with customers.

19xx-19xx   Courtesy Clerk, P & H Supermart, Batesville, OK. Assist clerks and customers.

SKILLS: Can program in BASIC.
Can operate a ten-key adding machine and other business machines.
Communicate easily with customers and coworkers.

INTERESTS: Personal computers, backpacking, baseball

REFERENCES: Professor Marion Talbot
School of Business
Arden College
Batesville, OK 74598
(917) 367-8763

Edward Moore, Manager
Harold's Hardware
398 Raymond Street
Batesville, OK 74598
(917) 394-2387

Figure 37.2   **EFFECTIVE RESUME**

Georgia McVey
127 Klein Street
Oakland, CA 94765
(415) 783-2367

OBJECTIVE: Entry-level staff accountant

QUALIFIED BY: B.S. in Business Administration/Accounting and 8 years' account-
                        ing and supervisory experience

EXPERIENCE: Delta Airlines, Oakland Airport, Manager Assistant. Processed
                        pilots' payroll; posted and audited data. Trained and super-
  19xx - 19xx   vised payroll clerks; helped design program to computerize pay-
                        roll; maintained records and completed period-end reports.

                        Bank of Alex Brown, Sacramento, General Ledger Bookkeeper.
  19xx - 19xx   Maintained accurate general ledger accounts; prepared period-end
                        statements.

SPECIAL SKILLS: BASIC computer language, IFPS and SSPS computer packages; NCR
                        proof and bookkeeping machines

EDUCATION: B.S., Business Administration/Accounting, Hathaway College,
                        Sacramento, CA
                        G.P.A.: 3.8

HONORS: Achievement Award, National Association of Accountants
                        Dean's Scholar Roll, Dean's Honor Roll

REFERENCES: Career Placement Center
                        Hathaway College
                        Sacramento, CA 94556
                        (916) 564-3489

This is the classic resume format for someone whose experience is even more relevant than her degree. Because she does have an appropriate degree for the position she is looking for, however, she has mentioned both her education and her experience right beneath her objective.

See Figure 38.5 for the application letter accompanying this resume.

Figure 37.3   **EFFECTIVE RESUME**

JERROLD LAU

School Address   Permanent Address
Walters Hall, #23   1236 Garret St.
Carroll State College   Reno, NV 83456
Carroll, MN 56678   (702) 345-7895
(612) 334-6789

EDUCATION

19xx   B.S., Business Administration/Personnel Administration, Carroll State
            College

19xx   A.A. Accounting, Nevada Junior College, Reno

HONORS

Dean's Scholar Roll (every semester)
Achievement Award, Carroll State College
Lifetime member, Gamma Beta Alpha

EXPERIENCE

19xx -   Salesclerk, Gammage's Department Store, Carroll, MN.
19xx   Assisted customers in all departments, performed transactions on NCR
            terminals, trained new salesclerks, handled customer complaints. (20
            hrs/wk)

19xx -   Administrative assistant/cashier, Sears, Reno, NV.
19xx   Cleared credit purchases over $100; closed cash registers and verified
            funds; trained employees for cashier work. (full-time, summers)

19xx   Administrative assistant, Cooley's Menswear, Reno.
            Handled correspondence and telephones; input computer data to manage
            inventory. (25 hrs/wk)

INTERESTS

Tutor, Reno YMCA. Teach swimming to disabled children.

Ski team, Carroll State College

REFERENCES

Available on request

This is a basic resume for a student with no real related work experience. Because he is completing his education on schedule and has worked consistently while in school, he has placed his dates prominently in the margin. His brief job descriptions emphasize a variety of business experience: working with customers and other employees, handling cash, using computers, and so on.

Figure 37.4   **EFFECTIVE RESUME**

```
CARL JOHNSON                                      678 Rose Court
                                                  Boston, MA  04789
                                                  (617) 549-0921

                          OBJECTIVE

Entry-level Accountant

                         QUALIFIED BY

B.S. in Accounting and an internship with Arthur Andersen

                          EDUCATION

B.S., Accounting, Boston College, Boston, MA.  Advanced coursework in auditing,
small business ventures, BASIC, COBOL, and management information systems.

G.P.A.:  3.8.  Dean's List every semester.
Worked full-time while attending school full-time.

                         MEMBERSHIPS

President, Accounting Association.  Work closely with students, college adminis-
trators, faculty, and business recruiters to set up informational meetings and
seminars.

Treasurer, Boston College Ski Club.  Maintain books and collect dues from 45
student members.  Help raise funds for ski trips.

                          EXPERIENCE

As Summer Intern with public accounting firm, worked in both tax and auditing de-
partments, helped prepare financial statements for small businesses, and input
data on computer system.

As Construction Foreman, supervised 16 people; hired and trained new workers.
Solely responsible for several large construction projects.

As Assistant Store Manager, handled accounts receivable and learned inventory and
security procedures for small retail business.  Hired and trained new employees.

As Salesman, learned to deal with customers and suppliers; made cold calls and
maintained extensive list of return customers.  Twice received Salesman of the
Month Award.

                           PERSONAL

Willing to travel
```

This resume format is useful for an older applicant who wants to de-emphasize his dates and highlight his recent education and summer internship. He has both his educational data and his memberships before his work experience. His experience entries do not mention company names or dates of employment; instead, the entries focus on the skills he acquired at his jobs. (See p. 486 for more discussion of this resume.)

Figure 37.5   **EFFECTIVE RESUME**

MARILYN LEE
2347 Taylor Road
Harbour, WI 53607
(414) 347-9802

OBJECTIVE

Management Training Program

EDUCATION

<u>M.B.A.</u>, University of Wisconsin, Madison, WI
<u>B.A.</u>, American History, Clare College, Minneapolis, MN

PROFESSIONAL EXPERIENCE AND SKILLS

<u>Organization/Planning</u>

- Defined goals and established policies for two nonprofit organizations
- Chaired policy, procedures, and other organizational committees
- Designed and implemented fund-raising events
- Chaired three international drama competitions

<u>Administration</u>

- Established budgets for fund-raising events
- Organized office procedures, reduced office expenses
- Designed citywide Christmas fair

<u>Research/Analysis</u>

- Investigated budget problems for two nonprofit organizations
- Performed marketing and industrial research for management consulting firm
- Evaluated professional drama performances for fund allocations

<u>Special Skills</u>

- Program in BASIC
- Speak and read French

This is a functional resume of an older student who has worked as a volunteer while raising a family; before she was married, she worked as a secretary. Her resume, which mentions no dates or places of employment, highlights her master's degree and her skills.

Figure 37.6   **EFFECTIVE RESUME**

ROBERT ZIEGLER
23 Rose Court
Fairview, NY 10034
(518) 346-0987

EDUCATION

M.S., Environmental Science, University of Delaware (1974)
B.A., Biology, Deering University (1972)

QUALIFIED BY

• over 10 years' work experience in the environmental and consumer protection field
• managing, writing, research, and training skills

SKILLS

Managing/Coordinating

• acted as liaison with local, federal, and state officials; responsible for assuring consistency and quality of over 20 federal environmental impact statements

• worked with managers of water supply and sanitation districts as well as representatives from environmental organizations and businesses; implemented three large-scale regional reclamation studies

Writing/Research

• interpreted, reviewed, and wrote environmental and administrative legislation

• prepared investigative reports on sanitation, consumer complaints, accident/injury inquiries

• researched and wrote technical papers on ecological hazards, mass transportation, and water conservation

Training/Communication

• developed and led public participation programs on water reclamation

• trained consultants in workshops on environmental regulations

EMPLOYMENT HISTORY

Environmental Protection Scientist, U.S. Environmental Protection Agency, New York, NY (1975-present)

This is a resume of someone who has worked for the same employer over an extended period. Because he is now interested in making a career change, he has de-emphasized his place of employment and his dates while highlighting his varied skills.

Figure 37.7   **EFFECTIVE RESUME**

```
                                                    Louanne Fouchet
                                                    783 Hilltop Drive
                                                    Hillside, CA 95678
                                                    (415) 236-9870

OBJECTIVE      Technical Writer

EDUCATION      M.B.A., California State University, San Jose
                  Option:  Information Systems Management
                  G.P.A.:  3.8
                  Related coursework:  COBOL I and II, small business management,
                  mathematics, finance, statistics (June 19xx)

               B.A., Georgetown University, Washington, D.C.
                  Major:  English Literature

EXPERIENCE     Technical Writer (part-time), Ace Software Company, Sunnyvale.
  writing         Develop literature for order processing systems.

  planning     Chairperson, Christmas bazaar, Courtney Elementary School, Silver
                  Spring, MD

  accounting   Treasurer, Courtney PTA.  Responsible for $35,000 budget.

  managing     Assistant Librarian, Courtney Elementary School

  teaching     Teaching Assistant, Georgetown University

ACHIEVEMENTS   Volunteer Service Award, Maryland State PTA
               California State University Fellowship

REFERENCES     Available on request
```

This is the composite resume of a job applicant who wants to combine her liberal arts background with her more recent technical education. Like Marilyn Lee (Figure 37.5), this woman has combined volunteeer work with her paid job experience. Her resume focuses on her skills rather than on her dates.

Figure 37.8   **EFFECTIVE RESUME**

John S. Zayle
2305 Woolsey Street
Seattle, WA 98001
(206) 346-8732

OBJECTIVE	Programmer/Analyst
EDUCATION	
19xx	B.S., Information Systems Management, University of Washington, Seattle G.P.A.: 3.65
COURSEWORK	
	Management Information Systems BASIC COBOL Assembly Linear Algebra Finance Economics Organizational Behavior
ACTIVITIES	
19xx - 19xx	President, Associated Students
19xx - 19xx	Academic Senator
19xx - 19xx	Chairman, Undergraduate Business Club
19xx - 19xx	Treasurer, Delta Sigma Fraternity
19xx - 19xx	Member, Academic Fairness Council
AWARDS	
19xx	Outstanding Service to University
19xx - 19xx	Dean's List
19xx - 19xx	Fellowship, Bank of Washington State
EXPERIENCE	
19xx - 19xx	Office Clerk, Johnson and Bly Accountants, Tacoma (summers) Handle correspondence, telephones, deliveries.
19xx - 19xx	Waiter, Francesco's Restaurant, Seattle (part-time, school year)
REFERENCES	On request

This student has no related work experience, but he has a good academic record and has been very active in college. He has placed his dates prominently and has put his activities and awards before his work experience.

Figure 37.9 **POOR RESUME**

```
Lawrence Keene
23659 St. James Court
Philadelphia, PA  19784                        (215) 347-2376

CAREER OBJECTIVE   I want a position with a lot of potential that will utilize my
skills effectively.

EDUCATION   I hope to receive my B.S. degree in Business Administration in June
19xx from Temple University.  G.P.A. 3.1 in major.

EXPERIENCE   Cashier at Pay less.  I also set advertisements and helped employees
in many areas of merchandising and sales.  10/19 to current.

ACTIVITIES   JV Basketball, High School
             High School Senior Week Organizer
             Currently in Adult Choir, First Methodist Church

INTERESTS   Hiking, camping, music

REFERENCES   All references available on request
```

This reveals the problems of many student resumes. Because it is written in sentences and does not highlight anything, it is difficult to read. It is also vague, lacks details, and contains a typo (*Pay less*).

When Lawrence reevaluated his strengths and weaknesses, he found that he should have a more dynamic objective, highlight his coursework, and add a strong skills section. Then he created a visually effective composite resume. For his final version, see Figure 37.10.

Figure 37.10   **EFFECTIVE RESUME**

RESUME

LAWRENCE KEENE
23659 St. James Court
Philadelphia, PA 19784   (215) 347-2376

OBJECTIVE

Management or Sales Training Program

EDUCATION

B.S., Business Administration, Management, Temple University, Philadelphia, PA.
June 19xx.

Relevant coursework in: managerial accounting, financial management, management
information systems, business communication, BASIC programming.

EXPERIENCE

Cashier, Payless Drug Store, Bryn Mawr, PA. Work computerized cash register,
handle over 200 customers a day. Help design in-store displays and window advertisements. Assist with inventory control and train new cashiers. October 19xx -
present.

Member, Adult Choir, First Methodist Church. Work with 30 members to organize re-
hearsals and weekly performances. Developed program and raised funds for two
charity performances. 19xx - present.

Organizer, High School Senior Week, Bryn Mawr High School. Coordinated events for
700 students and guests. 19xx.

SKILLS

- Strong quantitative and communication skills
- Extensive practical experience in retail sales as well as a broad educational
  background in business
- Can program in BASIC and have operated IBM PC/XT, Apple II, and HP 2000F

INTERESTS

Singing, hiking, camping, playing basketball

References on request

In this resume, Lawrence combined his volunteer work in a church choir with his cashier experience. He deleted some of his high school activities but kept the entry about organizing Senior Week.
His entries are designed to highlight a variety of skills and experience.

Figure 37.11   POOR RESUME

RESUME OF
_____

Felicia Martin   349 Traine Ave.
(312) 821-4389   Chicago, IL 65378

PERSONAL

Born in Dallas, TX, 19xx. Height 5'6", wt. 132 lbs.
Married to Harold Martin, C.P.A.; two children ages 4 and 5
Health: excellent   Hobbies: crafts, cooking

EXPERIENCE

At 34, with 7 years' experience in C.P.A. firms and additional experience in sales
and office manager positions, I am now competent in:

Preparing financial statements and tax returns, developing procedures manual for
computerized A/R systems, training employees in administrative procedures,
handling payroll and payroll tax returns, interfacing with other departments and
with clients.

***

Last year I was hired by a local firm as a full-charge bookkeeper to help a newly
hired controller bring the books up to date. Two weeks later the controller left.
In less than two months, I organized a temporary work force, assigned and reviewed the work and presented a working trial balance to the C.P.A. auditor for
approval.

***

Earlier, I gained experience with a public accounting firm. After promotion to a
staff accountant position, I returned to school to finish my degree in accounting.
Since no one in the organization knew how to fully utilize the computer system, I
worked with the computer representative to develop a procedures manual. The
person I hired to replace me was able to use the manual immediately, indicating a
successful training document.

BACKGROUND

Lauren Murphy, C.P.A.   19xx - present
H & D Accountancy Corporation   19xx - 19xx
Capital Insurance Brokers   19xx - 19xx
American Insurance   19xx - 19xx
David Furniss, C.P.A.   19xx - 19xx

Northwestern University, expect a B.S. degree in accounting in June 19xx

I am willing to travel or relocate.

This resume is very crowded, filled with unnecessary personal detail, and lacking some necessary information. The personal style is more appropriate to a letter than to a resume, and the disorganized presentation prevents a reader from easily recognizing the applicant's strengths.

In her revised resume (see Figure 37.12), Felicia streamlined her format so a reader can quickly see that she has a wealth of experience and skills.

Figure 37.12   **EFFECTIVE RESUME**

FELICIA MARTIN
349 Traine Ave.
Chicago, IL 65378
(312) 821-4389

OBJECTIVE   Accountant

QUALIFICATIONS B.S. in Accounting and 7 years' experience in bookkeeping,
                    sales, and office manager positions

EXPERIENCE   FULL-CHARGE BOOKKEEPER, Lauren Murphy, C.P.A., Chicago, IL
                    (19xx - present)

                    STAFF ACCOUNTANT, H & D Accountancy Corporation, Chicago, IL
                    (19xx - 19xx)

                    OFFICE MANAGER, Capital Insurance Brokers, Austin, TX
                    (19xx - 19xx)

                    SALESPERSON, American Insurance, Dallas, TX (19xx - 19xx)

                    SECRETARY, David Furniss, C.P.A., Dallas, TX (19xx - 19xx)

SKILLS   Preparing financial statements and tax returns

                    Developing procedures manual for computerized A/R systems

                    Training employees in administrative procedures

                    Handling payroll and payroll tax returns

                    Working with other departments and with clients

EDUCATION   B.S., Accounting, Northwestern University (June 19xx)

PERSONAL   Willing to travel or relocate

Since many of her job duties were similar, Felicia does not list them after each job entry. Instead, she combines her skills in a separate section. Her format is clean, easy to read, and carefully geared to the kind of position she wants.

CHAPTER 38

APPLICATION AND THANK-YOU LETTERS

OBJECTIVES: To (1) learn what an employer is looking for; (2) organize and interpret your experience and skills; (3) outline effective letters; (4) arrive at an appropriate tone; and (5) organize your job search.

Now that you have a strong resume, you can begin work on your application and thank-you letters. Application letters are among the most difficult pieces of business writing you may ever attempt. So, rather than start from scratch every time you answer an advertisement, hear of an opening, or actually have an interview, you should have effective letter formats on hand so that you can reword and revise for each situation.

APPLICATION LETTERS

Why Write an Application Letter?

The application letter is a vital component to your application. Not only does the letter interpret and humanize your resume, but it also reveals your abilities as a communicator. And because they are often the most difficult type of persuasive letter to write, application letters give a prospective employer insights into your abilities that he or she cannot receive from the resume alone—or even from an interview.

The letter also allows you to demonstrate interest and excitement in the job as well as to highlight the skills and experience directly linking you with the position and the firm. And, maybe most importantly, the letter enables you to request an interview.

To get you that interview, your application letter must be flawlessly written and attractively presented. In fact, like your resume, it must be perfect.

What Is an Employer Looking For?

Naturally, every employer has different interests, different biases. But, as an applicant, you may assume a few basic principles. Employers are looking for applicants who are capable, industrious, loyal, and personable—not necessarily in that order. Your letter should reflect these qualities as well as an interest in the position.

Capable

Almost every sentence of your letter should reflect the skills that will ensure your success in the position for which you are applying.

If you are applying for the type of position you have held in the past, this aspect of your letter will be fairly easy; knowing the company is looking for someone who can program in C, you can describe your expertise and the successful work you accomplished either in school or at another company.

If the position is different from what you have held in the past, you will have a more difficult time showing your capability. In this situation, you will have to pick out areas of expertise that the job demands and then link those areas with your own skills.

For example, someone applying for a position in personnel would accentuate how his or her academic background will be useful and then perhaps highlight relevant aspects of former jobs, such as hiring, supervising, counseling, or training.

To indicate capability, also, you will want to demonstrate your success in school, at work, and even in sports or hobbies. Most employers know that exact knowledge of a job is often less important than the success applicants have demonstrated throughout their lives.

Industrious

Most employers, of course, want employees who will work hard and manage their time successfully. Without bragging, you should establish these qualities in your letter.

To show your industriousness, however, you must provide facts. Simply claiming "I work hard" does not carry much impact. By mentioning that you work part-time while going to school full-time or that you have maintained a high G.P.A. with a double major, you *show* that you can work. When you tell a prospective employer that you have been promoted—or that you were offered a full-time position after finishing a summer job—you are letting him or her know in the best possible way that you are a good worker.

Note: *Never* indicate in a letter or an interview that you have trouble managing your time or that you changed jobs or majors because you were overworked.

Loyal

Hiring and training employees take time and money. Most employers are looking for someone who will want to stay with the firm for some time. Even employers looking for part-time or summer employees want applicants with a stable work history and an interest in the job.

If you have held one or more jobs for a long time, emphasize your loyalty. Never criticize the company or the job in any way. If you have held many jobs for short durations, indicate your enthusiasm for the job you are applying for and your interest in a career with the firm.

At times you may have to use some tact. Most employers, for example, will not be happy to learn that you are hoping to start your own company someday. While your successful leadership and fascination with entrepreneurship may strike you as your most positive qualities, you will have to reveal them in some other way. If you want to continue your education, do not indicate that you will be leaving the job in order to go back to school.

Beware: A little research could help you in this area. Some firms encourage employees' education—some even fund it. Others would rather have the undivided attention of their work force. By announcing your educational plans, you might think you are showing your ambition and assertiveness, while actually you are ensuring that you do not get an interview. Before revealing your plans, try to find out the company's attitudes or policies.

One of the best ways to demonstrate your potential loyalty is to show

RESUME HINT: INCLUDE SKILLS RELEVANT TO THE JOB YOU WANT

Source: Ford Button

knowledge about the firm itself. Tailor the letter to the firm as well as to the job so the reader will sense that you really do care about the company. A little research can go a long way to assuring an employer that you will be a dedicated employee.

Personable

Probably the hardest part of writing an application letter is conveying a pleasant personality. Many times letters are pompous, assertive, groveling, or overly remote and formal. Yet an employer is often more concerned about the personality of an applicant than about his or her skills: after all, most people can be trained to perform a job, but if they do not get along with their co-workers, everyone will suffer.

The key to a good application letter is a pleasant and enthusiastic tone that will make the reader want to meet you. To accomplish this, you should avoid the major pitfalls.

- Do not copy a letter from a book. You letter should not sound like someone else wrote it.
- Do not use the clichés and common formulas of application letters such as "Thank you in advance for your time."
- Do not brag. Avoid telling the employer how much he or she needs you.
- Never mention any problems the company may be having.
- Do not go on about yourself at great length. A few concrete details will say far more than pages of autobiography.
- Do not grovel. Speak to the employer as one professional to another, not as slave to master.
- Do not include ANY negative details about yourself. Never admit that you have no full-time work experience or that your degree is not the one described in the advertisement: simply present your background in the best possible light and let the reader determine the extent of your weaknesses.
- Do not use pompous or difficult language; like the resume, the letter should be easy to read. The reader is more apt to be annoyed than impressed by ponderous words.
- Avoid the passive voice. Be personal. Compare "An interview with you at your convenience would be much appreciated" with "I look forward to meeting you." (See Figures 38.1–38.6 for good and poor application letters.)

Self-Check Test 38-1

Revise the following paragraph from an application letter to make it more effective. (See end of text for sample revision.)

> Although I have never actually held a full-time job, you will find I am by far the best candidate for the administrative assistant position. I have considerable expertise in bookkeeping. I have taken numerous courses at Grace's Business College and am presently majoring in accounting at Derby College. As administrative assistant, I am sure I can vastly improve your present bookkeeping and office procedures.

Components of Application Letters

The sections of an application letter are similar to those of a sales letter; in fact, an application letter *is* a sales letter of a very special sort. (Thinking of yourself as a product, by the way, may help you to create an effective letter.) As in a sales letter, you need to (1) get the attention of the reader; (2) create interest through concrete information; and (3) provide the reader with a plan of action.

Catch the Reader's Attention

Most application letters open with a sentence similar to: "I am responding to your advertisement in the *Sunday Post*." This is parallel with a sales letter beginning, "We found your name on a list of magazine subscribers." Such an opening would not make anyone's pulse quicken with excitement.

Remember that your application letter may well receive about the same attention as a piece of junk mail—unless you get the reader's attention from the start. How do you do this? Applicants should have their own methods—methods that suit their own needs and personality. As we mentioned earlier, lines copied from a book are as boring as television reruns. You should, however, consider some techniques that have worked in the past.

Summarize Your Qualifications

Often you can capture your reader's attention by stating your strong points in the opening sentence—particularly if they mesh with requirements listed in the job description.

> As a recent graduate with a B.S. in finance and two years' experience with Ohio National Bank, I am applying for the assistant analyst position advertised in this morning's *Post*.

> My degrees in both marketing and journalism, coupled with strong communication skills, should make me a strong candidate for a copywriter position with your firm.

Mention Meeting or Speaking with Your Reader

If you have met your reader even briefly, you should mention the meeting in the opening of your letter. Even if you only heard him or her speak at a conference, make that contact right away: the personal note will set your letter apart from the others.

> When you spoke to the Balboa Accounting Association last spring, you mentioned that your company is always looking for intelligent and hardworking accounting majors.

If you spoke with the reader, definitely remind him or her of that occasion. If the person recommended that you apply for a job, be especially sure to jog his or her memory.

> Thank you again for taking the time to speak with me about Harrison Corporation at the Marketing Symposium last April. At that time you recommended that I consider a career with your firm when I finished my bachelor's degree. Now that I have graduated from the University of Arizona, I would very much like to apply for a management trainee position with your firm.

Give Personal Recommendations

In a similar vein, if an employee of the firm, preferably someone who knows your reader, has recommended that you apply, then mention him or her in the opening sentence.

> Ms. Patricia Hooper recommended that I apply for an entry-level accounting position with FJI.

Refer to Company's Needs

Another attention-getter is a sentence that reveals your knowledge and interest while also indicating the company's need for your skills.

> The recent *Wall Street Journal* article on your firm's expansion to northern California interested me very much. As the article indicated that you may be looking for computer programmers in the Bay Area, I am enclosing my resume for your consideration.

Refer to the Advertisement

Another approach is to refer to relevant lines of the job description and apply them to yourself.

> Your advertisement for an assistant personnel manager requests that applicants have an undergraduate business degree and at least two years' experience with a retail outlet. I have those qualifications.

Self-Check Test 38-2

Revise the following opening paragraph of a job application letter. You may add detail of your own. (See end of text for sample revision.)

> I am responding to the job description posted in the Placement Office at Ferrier University. I believe I am a good candidate for the management training program you describe. I am a management major at Ferrier and have some experience as assistant manager of the local Burger King.

Provide Concrete Evidence

After getting your reader's attention, you have to keep him or her interested with strong sentences filled with concrete detail concerning your skills and background. Remember, however, to link that experience with the job you are applying for: do not just list items randomly.

Many application letters, for example, catalog the writer's work history like this:

> After graduating from high school, I worked at Hock's Hardware as a salesclerk and then continued there part-time after I started college. I presently work part-time as a cashier and bookkeeper at Toy World and tutor students in algebra in the university Math Laboratory.

This writer actually has some good experience, but she has not developed it successfully in the letter. In fact, she has only repeated information on her resume. Her *interpretation* of that information should depend on the type of job for which she is applying.

If she is applying for a Personnel position, for example, she should highlight her work with people.

> As a bookkeeper/cashier at Toy World, I deal with over a hundred customers a day; I also train new cashiers to work the computerized cash registers and assist the manager with payroll procedures. As a clerk at Hock's Hardware, I received the Employee of the Month Award for maintaining good relations with customers.
>
> While tutoring in the Math Laboratory, I work closely with ten students a semester: since many of them come to me with a "mental block" about algebra, I am happy to say that all of them have finished the course with a B− or better.

In a subsequent paragraph, she should also emphasize that she works at two jobs while attending school full-time.

If the same applicant were applying for an entry-level accounting position, she would interpret her experience differently.

> As a bookkeeper/cashier at Toy World, I work with the manager on payroll procedures and input accounts payable information on the IBM computer system. While a clerk at Hock's Hardware, I helped the manager to choose the best accounting software available for a store of that size and type.
>
> My strong quantitative and personal skills have helped me work effectively with students in the university Math Laboratory. I am happy to say that all my students have received a B− or better in their algebra classes.

Notice that this applicant does not keep saying, "I am a hard worker" or "I am successful." She simply *shows* her success and the trust her employers have put in her.

Most students' application letters will have one or two strong paragraphs on their education and one or two on their experience. Do not write too much, but do make sure you include important information like your degree and where you work at present.

Avoid long lists. Do not mention *every* accounting or computer class you have taken or every duty you had at a certain job. Your sentences, like those in a sales letter, should be crisp and clear—and not too long. Remember, you are constantly in danger of losing your reader's interest. Keep things moving.

Provide Links with Company/Position

Do not assume that your reader can read between the lines of a resume to find your skills. State clearly the connections between your skills and the position. For example, in the preceding application for an accounting position, the applicant should include specific references to the job and the company while detailing her experience.

Avoid general statements like: "I know my skills will be an asset to your company." Instead, try sentences like:

> I know my experience with customers and students will be helpful in a firm like yours, which has such a wide variety of small business clients.

Or:

> Having gone to school full-time while working at Toy World through the Christmas season, I know I will be able to handle the long hours and pressure of the tax season with your firm. In fact, I look forward to the challenge.

As we mentioned earlier, the reader of an application letter is not interested just in *you*: he or she wants to know how you relate to the job and the firm. The more information you have about the company, the better you will be able to provide links between yourself and the job. (This information will become even more important when you get an interview.)

If you are really interested in the position, do some research. Read *The Wall Street Journal*, company newsletters, annual reports, Standard & Poor's industry surveys, and business magazines. If you are applying to small companies, try telephoning for some information. You can at least learn how many employees and offices the company has—and you may pick up some other worthwhile information.

If you are looking for programming work, find out what systems the firm uses. If you are looking for sales work, find out about the products. Concrete details will make your letter stand out from the rest.

> While on the tennis team at Ohio State University, I found Nike tennis shoes to be the most durable and comfortable product on the market. I know I could convince retailers of Nike's superiority and give them useful information to pass on to salespeople and customers.

Of course, if you are writing to a box number in a newspaper ad, you cannot do this type of research; but, in other situations, you should do your homework. A good job is worth some effort!

Conclusion

The beginning and ending are the most important parts of any sales writing, and an application letter is no exception. Many writers become overly assertive or overly formal at the end—many are afraid to get to the point. You should work on being direct and clear: avoid clichés and roundabout expressions.

The point of this letter is to get an interview. Do not avoid the issue with statements like, "May I hear from you soon?" When is soon? "Please contact me at your convenience" is also a poor ending. What do you mean by "contact"? Letter? Telephone? Carrier pigeon? Do not leave things open-ended.

On the other hand, avoid being obnoxious. Most employers will flinch at endings like:

> You need my skills at AMB. Call me at 234-8971 for an
> interview. You'll be glad you did!

A businessperson hoping to set up an appointment with another businessperson will be direct, clear, and polite. If possible, you should follow up your letter with a phone call—you will get much better results. So tell the reader your plan:

> As I would like to discuss this position with you as
> soon as possible, I will call your office next week to set up
> an appointment.

If you have to wait for a response from the reader, let him or her know the best way to reach you.

> If my qualifications interest you, please call me at home
> in the evenings (657-0922) or write me at the above address.

THANK-YOU LETTERS

Every time you have an interview, you should follow up immediately with a letter of thanks—even if you feel relatively certain you will not get the job or would not take the job if it were offered. The thank-you (or "follow-up") letter indicates common politeness on your part; it can also help maintain contact with people and generate their goodwill.

If you are interested in the job, the thank-you letter allows you to reiterate your interest in the position and include any information omitted during the interview. (See Figures 38.7 and 38.8 for examples of good thank-you letters.)

Checklist

The following are some do's and don'ts for thank-you letters:

Do

- Remember your interviewer's name and position; if possible, get his or her card.
- Include, if you can, a particular point from the interview that will remind your reader of the interview and your qualifications.
- Keep the letter short; this is not another application letter. One or two paragraphs are sufficient.

Don't

- Apologize for anything that occurred in the interview.
- Be too chatty or informal, even if the interview was informal.
- Repeat information from your resume or application letter.

Organizing Your Job Search

You may think that you will never forget writing an application or thank-you letter; but, if you are making a concentrated job search, you may soon forget when you wrote, to whom you wrote, and what the responses were.

To save yourself embarrassing omissions or even more embarrassing double applications, you should keep a notebook on your search. Write down the names and addresses of companies you have contacted and the date you called or wrote; note when you get a response of any sort; and even note significant points of the interview.

Checklist for Chapter 38

1. Develop an application letter that indicates you are capable, industrious, loyal, and personable.

2. Make sure your letter contains concrete detail, not vague generalizations.

3. Write letters that sound like you, not like a book.

4. Avoid bragging as well as apologizing. Include nothing negative in the letter.

5. Make sure your application letter gains the attention of the reader in the opening, conveys concrete detail in the middle, and establishes your desire for an interview in the conclusion.

6. Write a thank-you letter every time you have an interview.

7. Keep the thank-you letter short, pleasant, and professional.

8. Keep accurate records throughout your job search so that you know the exact status of each application.

Exercises

1. Write a letter to a firm at which you have held a part-time or summer job. Apply for a full-time career position.

2. Write a letter to accompany your own resume. Exchange the letter with a fellow student for his or her comments.

3. Write an application letter for Rita Dawes (see p. 487) to accompany her application for a summer job at a girls' camp.

4. Revise the following application letter. You may add material if necessary.

Mr. Robert Wagner
Personnel Department
IT Incorporated
2323 L Street
Washington, D.C. 20014

Dear Mr. Wagner:

Your advertisement in the *Baltimore Sun* interested me a lot. I have always wanted to work for a start-up company like yours, and I know quite a bit about the kinds of problems you must be having.

I have worked since I was 15 years old (I'm now 22), so I have extensive on-the-job experience. I have been a waiter, a retail clerk, construction worker, and a cab driver! At present I am a teaching assistant in the Computer Science Department at the University of Maryland, where I am completing my B.S. I will graduate in June, so I could start at IT anytime after that.

I am a very competent programmer in BASIC, C, FORTRAN, and other popular languages. I have also worked in the computer lab here at U.M., so I know I can communicate well with people who aren't familiar with computers. With all the English courses I've taken, too, I am an excellent writer, which should be helpful in the revising of computer manuals you mention in the job description.

I look forward to hearing from you. I'm available for an interview at your convenience.

                                              Sincerely,

                                              Ben Hurd

5. Revise the following thank-you letter.

Mr. Robert Wagner
Personnel Department
IT Incorporated
2323 L Street
Washington, D.C. 20014

Dear Mr. Wagner:

Now that I have talked with you and seen your offices, I am more convinced than ever that I am the perfect programmer for your company. Your company clearly needs someone with strong creative skills like mine to help you compete with larger and more established companies.

Thanks very much for interviewing me last week. I will be home in the evenings all this week if you want to get in touch with me.

Sincerely,

Ben Hurd

Chapter Test 38-1   Write a letter in response to the following advertisement. You may use your own background or a fictional one. (300–350 words)

> WANTED: An outside salesperson to work 30–38 hrs. per week during the summer. You will be selling fine office products to businesses. Must have good personal skills. Do not send a resume. Write a letter outlining your background and why you are interested in working in sales.

Chapter Test 38-2   Write a thank-you letter after an interview with a firm that you are interested in. Tell your interviewer that you are enclosing the references he or she requested.

Exercise for Experts   Write an application letter to accompany the resume in Figure 37.6, 37.7, or 37.9.

Figure 38.1   **POOR APPLICATION LETTER**

```
                                                    2356 Hughes Drive
                                                    Falls Church, VA 22908
                                                    February 4, 19xx


     Mr. Robert Ferrar
     Personnel Manager
     Washington Telephone Company
     237 G Street
     Washington, D.C.  20019

     Dear Mr. Ferrar:

          My college degree, the courses I have taken, plus my sales experience have
     given me valuable knowledge that will make me an asset to your company.  I have
     experience dealing with the public, and I am capable of taking on the responsibil-
     ities required of this position.

          The enclosed resume summarizes details of my coursework and work experience.
     I will be glad to furnish references on request.

          I would very much like to work for your company, and I am available for an
     interview.  I will contact your office in the near future to set up a mutually
     convenient interview.

                                        Sincerely,

                                        Michael Roberts

                                        Michael Roberts
```

Michael's letter has a flaw common to many application letters: vagueness. He never applies for a specific job, nor does he provide any information on himself. Assuming the reader will take time to examine his resume, he does not mention his college major, his former employers, or any reasons why he wants to work for this company. He is equally vague about when or how he will communicate with Mr. Ferrar.

See Figure 38.2 for a revision of Michael's letter.

Figure 38.2   **GOOD APPLICATION LETTER**

opening summarizes qualifications and mentions specific job

paragraph on work mentions specific details of advertising and sales experience

paragraph on education highlights advertising/marketing experience

fourth paragraph mentions specific detail about the company—relates the applicant to the job

ending informs reader when applicant will call

> 2356 Hughes Drive
> Falls Church, VA 22908
> February 4, 19xx
>
> Mr. Robert Ferrar
> Personnel Manager
> Washington Telephone Company
> 237 G Street
> Washington, D.C. 20019
>
> Dear Mr. Ferrar:
>
>   My B.S. in advertising and related work experience qualify me for the advertising/sales position described in the Washington Post.
>
>   Since graduating from St. Stephen's College in June, I have been working on the sales staff of Consumer News, a monthly publication that provides Virginia residents with information on food, drug, and cosmetic products. Through direct sales, I have helped to expand the magazine's advertising by 15 percent, and I have also helped improve the format of the advertising section.
>
>   While working on my degree at St. Stephen's, I took part in several consulting projects for businesses. I assisted in designing a sales campaign for Hagerstown Dairies and wrote mailers for three retail stores. I also took a broad range of classes in management, marketing, graphic art, and sales.
>
>   I am particularly interested in beginning a career with a young company that is growing as quickly as yours. I believe my interest in communications and my experience in sales and advertising would make me an asset to your staff.
>
>   I will call your office on Monday, February 11, to see if we can set up an interview.
>
>   Sincerely,
>
>   Michael Roberts
>
>   Michael Roberts

Michael's revised letter is concrete. He mentions his degree and gives some insights into both his present job and his college experience. By saying that he helped increase sales by 15 percent since June, he provides his reader with definite information.

Figure 38.3   POOR APPLICATION LETTER

---

65 Rose Avenue
Sacramento, CA 95678
June 3, 19xx

Ms. Geraldine Chalmers
Personnel Director
HRW Enterprises
378 Holder Road
Oroville, CA 95735

Dear Ms. Chalmers:

    Is HRW Enterprises looking for an assistant manager with drive, ambition, and a desire for excellence? Look no more.

    Working as an assistant office manager for Harper's Stationery has taught me many things, especially that time is money and good customer relations mean good business. I have always applied the same principles to my work that I do to my private life: strive to succeed and you _will_ succeed. I am sure your acquaintance and my present supervisor, Mr. Robert Fowler, will attest to my success at Harper's.

    While working as a waitress at Small's Cafe, I was known as The Smile because I was always cheerful, even at 6:00 a.m.! I was offered a full-time job at Small's after working the breakfast shift for 3 years while in college, but I wanted to put my knowledge of business to work at Harper's.

    Ms. Chalmers, I am successful at everything I strive for. I maintained a 3.8 average in college and have always been an outstanding employee. I know I can make things happen at HRW. I will call you on Friday for an interview.

        Sincerely,

        Flora McTavey

        Flora McTavey

This letter is both too assertive and too informal. You want your letter to be remembered—but not like this. Most employers do not want applicants charging into them like stampeding buffalo; you will do better to go diplomatically. Avoid implying that things are presently "not happening" at a company. Flora has some good qualifications, but her egotistical tone will probably keep her from getting an interview. Also, like Figure 38.1, this letter lacks concrete detail.

See Figure 38.4 for a revision of her letter.

Figure 38.4   EFFECTIVE APPLICATION LETTER

```
                                              65 Rose Avenue
                                              Sacramento, CA  95678
                                              June 3, 19xx


    Ms. Geraldine Chalmers
    Personnel Director
    HRW Enterprises
    378 Holder Road
    Oroville, CA  95735

    Dear Ms. Chalmers:

        My present supervisor, Mr. Robert Fowler, suggested I write you concerning
    an assistant manager position with your firm.  I will be moving to Oroville in
    July and am looking for a position in a consulting firm such as yours.

        My B.S. in management from Patterson College and 3 years' experience as
    assistant office manager at Harper's Stationery qualify me for the position.

        At Harper's I handle inventory control and supervise six employees when the
    manager is absent.  I also order supplies, hire new clerks, and set up weekly
    staff meetings.  One of my main duties has been researching, buying, and install-
    ing a computerized inventory and accounting system.  With this more efficient sys-
    tem, Harper's profits have increased nearly 12 percent since January.

        My practical business experience has been augmented by my business course-
    work.  At CSUS I maintained a 3.8 average and received an excellent background in
    organizational behavior, finance, and marketing as well as management.  As vice-
    president of the Management Association, I helped to double the number of student
    members and to set up informational meetings with local businesses.

        Mr. Fowler has told me about the diversity of clients and projects at HRW.
    I was very pleased to hear of your ongoing work with small business clients.  My
    jobs at Harper's Stationery, Small's Cafe, and other neighborhood businesses have
    made me particularly interested in their needs and problems.

        As I am very eager to speak with you about your current opening, I will call
    you on Monday, June 12, to discuss setting up an interview.

                                      Sincerely,

                                      Flora McTavey

                                      Flora McTavey
```

This letter is concrete and tactful. Flora mentions immediately that an acquaintance of the reader has recommended she apply for the job. She follows up with some job duties related to those she would have at HRW and mentions an increase in profits. Her G.P.A. and her success as vice-president of a professional organization indicate personal qualities that a prospective employer would like to see.

Also, by mentioning a particular focus at HRW, Flora reinforces her enthusiam and interest in this particular firm.

Figure 38.5   **EFFECTIVE APPLICATION LETTER**

127 Klein Street
Oakland, CA 94765
April 12, 19xx

Ms. Thelma Clarkwell
Personnel Manager
Alan Greene & Company
Los Altos, CA 94567

Dear Ms. Clarkwell:

Ms. Kathryn Wells of your firm suggested I write you concerning an entry-level staff accounting position. I can offer Alan Greene & Company both education and experience. In June I will receive a B.S. in Accounting from California State University, Hayward. I also have over ten years' experience in accounting-related work.

My work experience includes two years with the Bank of Alex Brown and over eight years with Delta Airlines. At the bank, I posted general ledger accounts, audited, prepared period-end statements, handled cash, and dealt with the public. At Delta I processed payroll, prepared management reports, and trained and supervised payroll clerks.

This solid work experience, along with my strong desire for a career as an accounting professional, has contributed to my academic success, evidenced by my 3.8 grade point average.

I first became interested in Alan Greene & Company when I heard of your reputation for excellence and professionalism. I know you have a personal commitment to your clients and work to find innovative solutions to their problems. The extensive education program and dynamic work environment at Alan Greene will provide the challenge and opportunity I am seeking.

I am most interested in meeting you and discussing the position in greater detail. I will call your office on Friday, April 20, to arrange an appointment.

Sincerely,

Georgia McVey

Georgia McVey

This is an effective letter from an applicant with good work experience. She has been careful not to give *too much* detail about herself; she simply presents an interesting outline, expresses her interest in the company, and requests an interview.

See Figure 37.2 for the resume accompanying this letter.

Figure 38.6   **EFFECTIVE APPLICATION LETTER**

2305 Woolsey Street
Seattle, WA 98001
December 2, 19xx

Mr. John Leech
Director of Human Resources
COM-TECH II
209 Yoland Terrace
Miami, FL 33134

Dear Mr. Leech:

Your advertisement in the November issue of <u>Computer Magazine</u> states your need for a programmer analyst who is experienced in COBOL and has worked on IBM PCs. My experience suits your needs.

I will be graduating at the end of this month with a B.S. in Information Systems Management from the University of Washington. As you can see from my resume, I have taken extensive coursework in programming as well as in general business. I have programmed in COBOL on the university mainframe and on my own IBM PC. As owner of a PC, I have also developed both business-related software and games for my own use.

I combine strong technical expertise with good leadership abilities and communication skills. As president of Associated Students, I have learned to speak in front of groups and delegate authority. I have also learned to "translate" computer manuals for fellow students and assist other programmers with technical problems.

I am particularly interested in COM-TECH II, since you are well known for your strong customer support and creative marketing strategies. I was pleased to read in <u>Barron's</u> that you are one of the fastest growing firms in the Southeast.

I will be in Miami for three weeks in January and hope that we can discuss my application at that time. As I look forward to meeting you, I will call your office on December 15 to set up an interview.

Sincerely,

John Zayle

John Zayle

Because this applicant has no related work experience, he must rely on his coursework, school activities, and knowledge of the company. Note that he does not apologize for or even mention his work experience; he appears confident that his background will speak for itself. His letter is direct and to the point.

See Figure 37.8 for the resume corresponding to this letter.

Figure 38.7   **EFFECTIVE THANK-YOU LETTER**

2305 Woolsey Street
Seattle, WA 98001
January 25, 19xx

Mr. John Leech
Director of Human Resources
COM-TECH II
209 Yoland Terrace
Miami, FL 33134

Dear Mr. Leech:

    Thank you for taking the time to speak with me last week. I enjoyed touring the COM-TECH II offices and was particularly interested in the communications software Ms. Hensley demonstrated.

    I was also very happy to return to Miami after many years away. Now that most of my family has moved to Florida, I am looking forward to returning permanently. As I will be moving at the beginning of March, I would be able to start work on March 15.

    Thank you again for considering my application. I look forward to hearing from you.

Sincerely,

John Zayle

John Zayle

This effective thank-you letter briefly mentions two aspects of his interview and tour of the company offices and then reiterates an important fact: when the writer could start work.

Figure 38.8   **EFFECTIVE THANK-YOU LETTER**

```
                                              267 Arroyo Street
                                              Wayne, NM  87457
                                              September 20, 19xx


      Ms. Stephanie Furst
      Director of Personnel
      Bi-County Health Organization
      Tulsa, OK  74648

      Dear Ms. Furst:

          I appreciate your meeting with me last week to discuss the personnel
      assistant position.  I was very impressed by both your enthusiasm for Bi-County
      Health and the excellent work the organization performs.

          If you have any further questions, you may write to the above address or
      call me at (912) 458-0932 in the evenings.

                                      Sincerely,

                                      Celia Wong

                                      Celia Wong
```

Once again, this effective thank-you letter is direct and brief. Note that Celia does not try to "sell" herself in this letter.

PART SEVEN REVIEW TESTS

Now that you have finished Part Seven, look again at the test you worked on at the beginning of the section.

Review Test 7-1

Read the following job application letter and answer the questions given.

Dear Sirs:

I can't tell you how excited I was to see your ad in today's *Bulletin*. I am sure you will be excited, too, when you see how well the qualifications on my resume (enclosed for your consideration) fit with the description in the ad.

I may not have the degree you specify in the ad, but I have the drive and ambition. You can reach me by calling the number on the resume.

Sincerely,

C. Smith

1. Does this letter have any major faults?

2. Is anything wrong with the opening? With the closing?

3. Is any information missing?

4. Is there anything you would delete from this letter?

5. Write your own version of this letter, adding and deleting information as you wish.

Review Test 7-2

I. When you have read the following memo, list problem areas you have spotted in the writer's approach to the situation. Does the memo have any strong points?

To: All Employees

From: Sandra Gorden

Topic: Free Food

Date: July 12, 19xx

It seems to me that there have been some marked discrepancies recently between the gallons of ice cream I have been ordering and the number of scoops you people have been selling. Either ice cream sales are not being properly logged in on the cash register or ice cream is being given away to your friends. Since other problems with the cash register receipts have not appeared, I believe the latter situation is happening. Please understand that "treating" a friend to an ice cream cone is actually stealing from this company. I am not accusing anyone at this point in time, but I am issuing a warning. Anyone found giving away ice cream will be treated in the same way as they would be if they were found stealing money. You will be discharged immediately. On the whole, you are good workers, so don't let "generosity" to your friends get you in trouble.

II. Now revise the memo for tone and organization. Check the grammar, spelling, mechanics, and punctuation of your version.

Review Test 7-3

I. When you have read the following letter, list problem areas you have spotted in the writer's approach. Does the letter have any strong points?

Dr. Harrison Gilroy
Dean, School of Business
Hamlin University
Hamlin, CO 80089

Dear Dr. Gilroy:

I have heard about Hamlin University for many years from several friends in the business world. It seems to have a strong business school, and I hear the graduates are usually able to find pretty good jobs. Now that I am finishing up my B.A. in history at Rochester State, I would really like to talk to you about coming to Hamlin.

Although I have gotten mostly B's at Rochester, I have worked 20 hours a week the whole time I was in school. This business experience should outweigh my grade point average. I have worked as an office clerk for two years now and have acquired many insights into what makes a business profitable. I have also taken some classes in computers and accounting. My knowledge of the history of business through the ages could be worthwhile as well.

As I will be vacationing in Colorado next week, I will give your office a call. Hopefully, we can set up an appointment for Monday afternoon.

Sincerely,

Nathan Jersey

II. Now revise the letter to make it more effective. You may include additional information.

Review Test 7-4

You have applied for a position with an aggressive advertising firm. A committee is seriously considering your application, but the members would like to see a little more of your writing. They have requested that you send them a page "selling" your skills to the company much as you would sell a product. Write 250–350 words reviewing your skills and experience. (You may choose the type of position you are applying for.)

Review Test 7-5

Forty-five employees have been transferred from Dallas to your city. Many of them, arriving over the next two weeks, will be looking for apartments and houses before their families arrive. Meanwhile, the new employees will be staying at local motels. Write a memo to present employees: encourage them to invite these new employees out to lunch or dinner and to offer them advice on their new city and jobs.

Review Test 7-6

You have just completed a market research project for your natural foods company. Among other information, you have discovered that people find the name of your company misleading and associate your products with bland, boring food. Write a memo to the management of your company explaining the data and offering some suggestions on how to resolve some of the problems.

Review Test 7-7

Your small local bank has two drive-up windows that are heavily used in the early morning and late afternoon. As head of operations, you have completed a study evaluating whether the bank should invest in one or more automatic teller machines (ATMs).

Write a memo to the president persuading him that one machine will pay for itself in a short time: include data on costs, projected usage, advantages as well as disadvantages to the machines.

Review Test 7-8

Some employees have been smoking cigarettes in offices where smoking has been forbidden. Other employees have complained. Write a memo reiterating the smoking rules and stating a policy with regard to employees who smoke in the nonsmoking areas.

Review Test 7-9

You are president of a professional campus organization that helps students learn about jobs in their field and sets up events with local businesses. Write a memo to all business students: encourage them to join the organization and point out the many benefits it offers.

FAMOUS FIRST DRAFTS: THE BEATLES
Writing Hint: Use Active Sentences

I wanna hold your hand.

Source: Ford Button

BUSINESS LETTER FORMATS

PARTS OF A BUSINESS LETTER

Heading

The heading usually consists of printed letterhead on business stationery. If you are not using letterhead stationery, the heading consists of your address. Do not type your name over the address.

Date

Type the month, day, and year. Do not abbreviate the month or add *nd*, *st*, or *th* to the day.

> September 2, 19xx

or

> 2 September 19xx

Inside Address

The inside address consists of the name of the person to whom the letter is being sent, that person's official title (Director, Chairman, etc.), the name of the company or organization, and the complete address. You should also include a courtesy title such as Mr., Mrs., Miss, Ms., Dr.

Spell out *Street*, *Boulevard*, and so on. (In fact, most words in business correspondence should be written out, not abbreviated.) You may use the official abbreviations for states in the inside address. Remember to include the zip code after the state.

The official title may appear on the same line as the name (separated by a comma) or on the line below (with no comma).

> Mr. Herbert Tryon   Ms. Helen Brady, Manager
> Director of Personnel   Dartmouth Clothes
> Flare Corporation   2967 D Street
> 2378 Forest Road   Raines, MI 42378
> Bell, TX 78912

Attention Line (optional)

> Attention: Customer Service Department

You may use an attention line to direct your letter to a certain person or department. The attention line appears below the inside address. Usually you will not use a salutation if you use an attention line.

If you use an attention line, the first line of your inside address should be the name of a company or organization, not the name of an individual. When you use an attention line, put it on the envelope as well as on the letter.

Salutation

The salutation should coincide with the first line of the inside address. Thus, if your inside address reads *Mr. George Blake*, your salutation would read *Dear Mr. Blake*. The salutation is usually followed by a colon.

If the first line of your inside address is the name of a company, you will have to decide on a suitable salutation. Traditionally, business writers have used *Dear Sirs* or *Gentlemen* as salutations. Then, in an effort to eliminate sexist language, writers began using *Ladies and Gentlemen*. If you do not have a name to use in the salutation, you might want to use the simplified letter style that does not require a salutation. Or you might use a salutation such as *Dear Editor*.

Subject Line (optional)

Subject: Account Number 234-56-9110

The subject line, which may be capitalized, is an option you may use to indicate the main point of your letter. Usually the subject line opens with *Subject* followed by a colon and a heading or title. The subject line appears between the salutation and the body of the letter.

Body

The message in your letter begins below the salutation or subject line. Single-space the body; double-space between paragraphs.

Complimentary Close

The complimentary close, which appears two lines after the end of the body, is usually followed by a comma. Only the first word is capitalized: *Sincerely yours*.

Company Name (optional)

Some companies include the name of the company under the complimentary close.

Signature

Sign your name above your typed name and title. Do not give yourself a courtesy title.

Writer's Typewritten Name and Title

Your name and title should be typed below the handwritten signature.

Basil Headley

Basil Headley, Director
Research Department

Reference Initials (optional)

Reference initials are those of the writer (capitalized) and the typist (small letters) separated by a colon or slash. Sometimes the typist's initials appear alone in small letters.

BH:ed   BH/ed   ed

Enclosure Line (optional)

If you have included enclosures with your letter, you may write *Enclosure, Enclosures*, or *Enc.* below the reference initials. You may also describe the enclosure: *Enclosure: Resume*.

Copy Line (optional)

cc Dr. Lawrence Kelleher   Copy: Professor Marion
                                        Small
c: Ms. Nancy Ashby
    Mr. David Chatham

If copies of the letter are being sent to other readers, a copy line is used to list readers other than the person to whom the letter is addressed. (Readers are usually listed in alphabetical order.) Nowadays, *c, copy,* or *copies* may be used instead of *cc,* since most copies now are not made with carbon paper. The colon is optional. The notation *bcc* means *blind carbon copy.*

bcc: Mrs. Jane Fredericks

This notation is used on the copy being sent to Mrs. Fredericks, but not on the original letter.

Unless a postscript is used, the copy line is the last line of the business letter page.

Postscript (optional)

If you wish to include a postscript, make it the last item on your page. Begin it at the left margin two lines below the preceding section. You may begin the post-script with *P.S.* or *PS* if you like.

Second Page of Letter

The second page of a business letter should contain the name of the person addressed, the page number, and the date. You may put the information verti-cally or horizontally.

Mr. George Smith   −2−   December 2, 19xx

or

Mr. George Smith
December 2, 19xx
Page 2

FULL-BLOCK LETTER STYLE

printed letterhead	CCC CONSULTING SERVICES 324 Bellson Terrace Merriman, SC 29765
date	May 3, 19xx
inside address	Mr. George Bortz Assistant Manager Nobbley's Department Store 1298 N. Deerfield Avenue Merriman, SC 29766
salutation	Dear Mr. Bortz:
subject line	Subject: Research on Improved Security System
body	During our telephone conversation on Wednesday, April 23, Ms. Charlene Simpson informed me that Nobbley's Department Store has been experiencing increased shop-lifting problems in the last year. She asked me whether CCC Consulting Services could research the problem and provide some recommendations on how Nobbley's could effectively increase security. We are very interested in the project and would like to discuss it with you in more detail. Then we will develop a proposal outlining our methodology, budget, and time frame. I enclose our company brochure. I will call Nobbley's next week to set up a meeting at your convenience.
complimentary close	Sincerely yours,
writer's signature	*Basil Headley*
typewritten name and title	Basil Headley, Director Research Department
reference initials	BH/aj
enclosure line	Enclosure
copy line	cc Mr. John Radner Dr. Laura Turner
postscript	P.S. Congratulations on opening your new store in Bayfair Mall.

With the full block letter style, every line begins at the left margin. Because it is easy to type, this format is gaining in popularity. The subject line may be underlined or printed in capital letters.

This letter shows the standard punctuation for business letters. If you use a first-name salutation, you may follow it with a comma rather than a colon.

SEMIBLOCK LETTER STYLE

```
                         CCC CONSULTING SERVICES

                           324 Bellson Terrace

                           Merriman, SC 29765



                                  May 3, 19xx


Ms. Charlene Simpson, Manager
Nobbley's Department Store
1298 N. Deerfield Avenue
Merriman, SC  29766

Dear Ms. Simpson:

             SUBJECT:  RESEARCH ON IMPROVED SECURITY SYSTEM

        During our telephone conversation on Wednesday, April 23, you informed me
that Nobbley's Department Store has been experiencing increased shoplifting
problems in the last year.  You asked me whether CCC Consulting Services could
research the problem and provide some recommendations on how Nobbley's could
effectively increase security.

        We are very interested in the project and would like to discuss it with you
in more detail.  Then we will develop a proposal outlining our methodology, bud-
get, and time frame.  I enclose our company brochure.

        I will call you next week to set up a meeting at your convenience.

                                  Sincerely yours,

                                  Basil Headley

                                  Basil Headley, Director
                                  Research Department


BH/aj

Enc:  brochure

c:  Mr. John Radner
    Dr. Laura Turner
```

With the semiblock letter style, each paragraph either is indented five spaces, as we see here, or begins at the left margin. The date, complimentary close, and signature begin at the center of page or to the right of the center. The subject line may be indented or, as in this example, centered. The subject line in this example is also capitalized.

You may use the standard punctuation that is used here, or you may use the open style of punctuation. With open punctuation, no colon or comma appears after the salutation, and no comma appears after the complimentary close.

The semiblock letter style is the format most commonly used in business correspondence.

SIMPLIFIED LETTER STYLE

CCC CONSULTING SERVICES

324 Bellson Terrace

Merriman, SC 29765

May 3, 19xx

Ms. Charlene Simpson
Manager
Nobbley's Department Store
1298 N. Deerfield Avenue
Merriman, SC 29766

RESEARCH ON IMPROVED SECURITY SYSTEM

During our telephone conversation on Wednesday, April 23, you informed me that
Nobbley's Department Store has been experiencing increased shoplifting problems in
the last year. You asked me whether CCC Consulting Services could research the
problem and provide some recommendations on how Nobbley's could effectively increase security.

We are very interested in the project and would like to discuss it with you in
more detail. Then we will develop a proposal outlining our methodology, budget,
and time frame. I enclose our company brochure.

I will call you next week to set up a meeting at your convenience.

Basil Headley

BASIL HEADLEY
DIRECTOR
RESEARCH DEPARTMENT

aj

This is the least common format for business letters. Although it is easy to type, it lacks a personal touch. The lines begin at the left margin, as they do with the full block style, but neither a salutation nor a complimentary close is used. The subject line and signature section are capitalized.

PERSONAL BUSINESS LETTER

765 Regency Court
Charles, WI 65478
April 15, 19xx

Ms. Jacqueline Sheerer
Customer Service
Dale's Hardware Store
267 Cherrytown Road
Charles, WI 65479

Dear Ms. Sheerer:

Thank you very much for helping me locate new lawn chairs to replace the two
chairs that were broken in transit. I appreciate the time and personal attention
you gave to a difficult situation.

The new chairs arrived in perfect condition and perfectly match the rest of my
set.

Sincerely,

Thomas Baker

Thomas Baker

Because the writer does not use letterhead, he begins the letter with his address, not his name. He uses standard punctuation and allows about three spaces for his signature.

COMMON EDITING MARKS

I. Common Proofreading Symbols

$\mathring{\mathsf{v}}$	Apostrophe
$\smile$	Close up
$\mathring{\mathsf{ɔ}}$	Comma
$\mathscr{e}$	Delete
$\wedge$	Insert
¶	Begin new paragraph
no ¶	No new paragraph
⊙	Period
$\mathring{\mathsf{v}}\ \mathring{\mathsf{v}}$	Quotation marks
#	Space
$\sim$	Transpose elements

II. Common Correction Marks

Ab	Improper abbreviation
Adj	Improper use of adjective
Adv	Improper use of adverb
Agr	Faulty agreement
Amb	Ambiguous
Awk	Awkward construction
Cap	Improper capitalization
D	Improper word usage
Dgl	Dangling modifier
Frag	Fragment
lc	Lowercase
Num	Incorrect number usage
‖	Not parallel
Punc	Incorrect punctuation
Ref	Unclear pronoun reference
R-O	Run-on sentence
Sp	Spelling error
SS	Poor sentence structure
Tr	Transpose elements
V	Incorrect verb form
Wdy	Wordy

GLOSSARY OF GRAMMATICAL AND EDITING TERMS

ACTIVE VOICE. See VOICE.

ADJECTIVE. A word used to describe or limit a noun or pronoun. (See also MODIFIER.) The most common types of adjectives are the following:

Article: *A, an, the. A* is used before consonant sounds; *an* is used before vowel sounds.

> *A* table is for sale.
> *An* elephant is carrying us.
> *The* report is incomplete.

Common: The *unstable* economy is causing problems.

Demonstrative: *This, that, these, those.* Demonstrative adjectives precede nouns.

> *That* man is an engineer.

Proper: These are formed from proper nouns. (See NOUN.) Proper adjectives are usually capitalized.

> A *European* holiday could be expensive.

ADJECTIVE CLAUSE. See CLAUSE.

ADVERB. A word that describes or limits a verb, an ADJECTIVE, another adverb, a VERBAL, a PHRASE, a CLAUSE, or a SENTENCE. (See also MODIFIER.)

> I ran *quickly.* [adverb modifies verb *ran*]
> The dog is *quite* small. [adverb modifies adjective *small*]
> The company grew *particularly* fast. [adverb modifies adverb *fast*]
> He lost weight by exercising *vigorously.* [adverb modifies verbal *exercising*]
> *Accurately* solving problems is his specialty. [adverb modifies phrase *solving problems*]
> *Therefore,* we will adjourn. [adverb modifies independent clause]

ADVERB CLAUSE. See CLAUSE.

AGREEMENT. The correspondence between SUBJECT and VERB or between NOUN and PRONOUN with regard to PERSON, NUMBER, or GENDER.

Person: If *Pete* works hard, *he* will succeed. [*Pete* and *he* are both third person.]

Number: *Bill and Fred are visiting their* parents. [The plural pronoun *their* agrees with the plural ANTECEDENT, *Bill and Fred; are visiting*, the plural form of the verb, agrees with the plural subject *Bill and Fred*.]

Gender: I gave my *mother her* gift. [*Mother* and *her* are both feminine.]

ANTECEDENT. The noun or group of words to which a PRONOUN refers:

John Schultz bought the hammer before he left the store.

APPOSITIVE. A NOUN or noun substitute set beside a noun or noun substitute to identify or explain it.

My brother, an *accountant*, will speak to us.

ARTICLE. See ADJECTIVE.

AUDIENCE. The person or persons to whom or for whom a piece of writing is created. A writer should remember his or her audience when considering TONE, word choice, and so on.

AUXILIARY VERB. See HELPING VERB.

CASE. The form a noun or pronoun takes to indicate its relationship to other words in a sentence. The three cases in English are subjective (also called *nominative*), objective (also called *accusative*), and possessive (also called *genitive*).

The subjective case is used for SUBJECTS and COMPLEMENTS. The objective case is used for DIRECT OBJECTS, INDIRECT OBJECTS, and objects of PREPOSITIONS. The possessive case is used to show ownership.

He ran the race. [pronoun is in subjective case]
Give *her* the prize. [pronoun is in objective case]
The prize is *ours*. [pronoun is in possessive case]

The possessive is the only case in which nouns change:

Have you checked the *company's* records?

CLAUSE. A group of related words that contains a SUBJECT and a PREDICATE and that functions as part of a SENTENCE. Clauses are either independent (*main*) or dependent (*subordinate*).

A main clause may stand by itself as a sentence.

The company raised wages.

Two or more main clauses may be connected by a coordinate CONJUNCTION and a comma or by a semicolon.

The company raised wages, and the strike ended.
The company raised wages; the strike ended.

A dependent clause must be attached to an independent clause. A dependent clause usually begins with a subordinate CONJUNCTION or a relative PRONOUN.

Because the company raised wages, the strike ended.
We toasted the man *who* bought the building.

Dependent clauses may function as NOUNS, ADJECTIVES, or ADVERBS.

Whoever bought the building is a millionaire. [noun clause acting as SUBJECT of the sentence]

> The building *that we bought* cost a fortune. [adjective clause modifying *building*]
> *Because he wanted a bargain*, Sam bought the building. [adverb clause modifying *bought*]

CLICHÉ. A phrase or sentence that has been overused.

> The room was *clean as a whistle*.

COLLECTIVE NOUN. See NOUN.

COMMA SPLICE. A grammatical error in which a comma is used without a coordinate CONJUNCTION to connect two independent CLAUSES.

> Nancy Hill is studying archaeology, Bill Mason is studying economics.

Revisions:
> Nancy Hill is studying archaeology. Bill Mason is studying economics.
> Nancy Hill is studying archaeology, and Bill Mason is studying economics.
> Nancy Hill is studying archaeology; Bill Mason is studying economics.

COMMON ADJECTIVE. See ADJECTIVE.

COMMON NOUN. See NOUN.

COMPARISON. The forms of an ADJECTIVE or ADVERB to show degree. Forms of comparison are positive, comparative, and superlative.

> The boy is *tall*. [positive: describes without comparing]
> This boy is *taller* than that boy. [comparative: compares two persons or things]
> The boy is the *tallest* in the class. [superlative: compares three or more persons or things]

COMPLEMENT. A NOUN, PRONOUN, or ADJECTIVE that follows a LINKING VERB and renames or describes the SUBJECT.

> Tom is our *manager*. [noun complement]
> This is *he*. [pronoun complement]
> David is *efficient*. [adjective complement]

COMPLEX SENTENCE. See SENTENCE.

COMPOUND SENTENCE. See SENTENCE.

COMPOUND-COMPLEX SENTENCE. See SENTENCE.

CONJUNCTION. A connecting word that joins words, PHRASES, SENTENCES, or CLAUSES. Conjunctions are coordinate, correlative, or subordinate.

Coordinate conjunctions (*and, but, for, nor, or, so, yet*) connect words or groups of words with similar functions in a sentence:

> Jaime *or* Paul went to Spain *and* to France. [conjunctions connecting NOUNS and PHRASES]
> I will go, *but* I may not return. [conjunctions link independent CLAUSES]

Correlative conjunctions are used in pairs: *both . . . and; either . . . or; neither . . . nor; not only . . . but also; whether . . . or*. Like coordinate conjunctions, they connect words or groups with similar functions in a sentence.

> I am *not only* hungry *but also* thirsty. [conjunctions link adjective complements]

Subordinate conjunctions (*because, while, even though, if,* and so on) mark the beginning of a dependent CLAUSE and connect a dependent clause to an independent clause.

> *Because* I was hungry, I ate some sandwiches.
> I was hungry *even though* I ate some sandwiches.

CONNOTATION. The associations related to a word. *Fat* and *overweight* are similar in meaning, for example, but *fat* retains more unpleasant connotations than *overweight.* (Contrast with DENOTATION.)

COORDINATE CONJUNCTION. See CONJUNCTION.

CORRELATIVE CONJUNCTION. See CONJUNCTION.

DANGLING MODIFIER. See MODIFIER.

DECLARATIVE SENTENCE. See SENTENCE.

DEMONSTRATIVE ADJECTIVE. See ADJECTIVE.

DEMONSTRATIVE PRONOUN. See PRONOUN.

DENOTATION. The dictionary definition of a word. (Contrast with CONNOTATION.)

DEPENDENT CLAUSE. See CLAUSE.

DIRECT ADDRESS. A word or phrase naming the person or thing addressed. Commas separate these words or phrases from the rest of the sentence.

> *Rover,* sit!
> Here, *Mrs. Herman,* are the reports.

DIRECT OBJECT. A noun or noun substitute influenced by an action VERB. To locate a direct object, ask WHOM? or WHAT? after the verb.

> The car hit a tree. [Hit WHAT? *tree*]
> Joanne married Fred. [Married WHOM? *Fred*]

A PRONOUN used as a direct object will be in the objective CASE.

> Tanya hit *him.*
> Henry married *her.*

DIRECT QUOTATION. The exact words written or spoken by others. A direct quotation is set off with quotation marks.

> "Please call the meeting to order," said Mrs. Lerner.

An indirect quotation is a paraphrase of words actually spoken or written.

> The manager said he was happy to see us.

EXCLAMATORY SENTENCE. See SENTENCE.

FRAGMENT. A word or group of words, written as a sentence, that is not a sentence.

> *Because of the problem.*
> *Running for help.*

FUSED SENTENCE. See RUN-ON SENTENCE.

GENDER. The aspect of a noun or pronoun that indicates whether it is masculine (*uncle, he*), feminine (*mother, she*), or neuter (*house, it*). (See AGREEMENT.)

GERUND. See VERBAL and PHRASE.

HELPING. (or AUXILIARY) **VERB.** One or more verbs used with a main verb to indicate TENSE, VOICE, MOOD, PERSON, NUMBER. Common helping verbs are formed from *be, do,* and *have.* See VERB.

The helping verbs *be* and *have* indicate the tense and voice of the main verb.

> I *have* eaten.
> He *has* completed the job.
> You *were* running.

The helping verb *do* is used for emphasis, for negative statements, and for questions.

> I *do* have an answer.
> She *does* not have the book.
> *Does* Henry have the report?

Other helping verbs such as *could, can, may, might, must, should,* and *would* indicate necessity, possibility, ability, and so on.

> I *must* finish the report.
> I *might* finish the report.
> I *could* finish the report.

IMPERATIVE MOOD. See MOOD.
IMPERATIVE SENTENCE. See SENTENCE.
INDEFINITE PRONOUN. See PRONOUN.
INDEPENDENT CLAUSE. See CLAUSE.
INDICATIVE MOOD. See MOOD.
INDIRECT OBJECT. A noun or noun substitute that states to whom or for whom the action of the verb is done. Indirect objects must precede direct objects.

> I lent *George* a book.
> Fred owes the *company* $50.
> We sent *Peter* the book.

PRONOUNS that are indirect objects will be in the objective CASE.

> Give *him* the book.

INDIRECT QUOTATION. See DIRECT QUOTATION.
INFINITIVE. See VERBAL and PHRASE.
INTENSIVE PRONOUN. See PRONOUN.
INTERJECTION. A word or words expressing emotion: *Oh, Hurrah!*, and so on. An interjection is followed by a comma or exclamation mark.

> *"Hey!"* cried Dan.
> *"Oh,* that's an error," said Felicia.

INTERROGATIVE PRONOUN. See PRONOUN.
INTERROGATIVE SENTENCE. See SENTENCE.
INTRANSITIVE VERB. See VERB.
IRREGULAR VERB. A verb that does not form its past TENSE and past PARTICIPLE in the standard fashion (by adding *-d* or *-ed*).

> Allen has *run* the race.
> We have *lain* in the sun since noon.

JARGON. Terminology that has grown out of a specialized area.

> Profits are the *bottom line.*

LINKING VERB. A VERB like *be, seem,* and *appear* that expresses a state of being rather than an action. Linking verbs are followed by COMPLEMENTS rather than DIRECT OBJECTS.

He *seems* enthusiastic.
That *is* she at the door.

MAIN CLAUSE. Independent clause. See CLAUSE.
MISPLACED MODIFIER. See MODIFIER.
MODIFIER. A word, PHRASE, or CLAUSE that limits or describes another word or group of words. Modifiers should be placed close to the word or words they are modifying.

A dangling modifier does not clearly modify a word or group of words in the sentence.

> *Going to visit my parents*, the plane crashed.
> Revision: While they were going to visit my parents, the
>   plane crashed.

A misplaced modifier is placed incorrectly in the sentence.

> I gave a speech to the students *using my notes.*
> Revision: Using my notes, I gave a speech to the students.

A squinting modifier may describe either of two items in a sentence.

> Being beaten *thoroughly* disgusted us.
> Revisions: Being thoroughly beaten disgusted us.
>   Being beaten disgusted us thoroughly.

MOOD. The form of a VERB that indicates the attitude of the writer. The three moods are indicative, imperative, and subjunctive.

The indicative mood is used for making statements and asking questions.

> The director *interviews* the candidates.
> *Does* the director *interview* the candidates?

The imperative mood is used for commands or requests. The subject is often understood to be *you*.

> (You) Run!
> Please revise this memo.

The subjunctive mood is used to express wishes and hypothetical conditions.

> I wish I *were* president.
> I request that this matter *be* settled.

NOMINATIVE CASE. Subjective case. See CASE.
NONRESTRICTIVE CLAUSE. A CLAUSE that is not essential to the meaning of the sentence.

> These employees, *who have done exceptionally well this*
> *year*, are being promoted.

NOUN. A part of speech that names a person, place, thing, or idea.

> Common noun: The *man* is carrying a *briefcase.*
> Proper noun: *Caroline* visited *Europe.*
> Collective noun: The *army* is stationed near the
> *university.*

NUMBER. The aspect of a noun, pronoun, or verb that indicates if it is singular or plural. (See AGREEMENT.)
OBJECTIVE CASE. See CASE.

PARTICIPLE. See VERBAL and PHRASE.

PARTS OF SPEECH. The eight basic components of a SENTENCE: NOUNS, VERBS, PRONOUNS, ADJECTIVES, ADVERBS, PREPOSITIONS, CONJUNCTIONS, and INTERJECTIONS.

PASSIVE VOICE. See VOICE.

PERSON. The aspect of a noun, pronoun, or verb that indicates whether one is speaking (first person), spoken to (second person), or spoken about (third person). See also AGREEMENT.

> *I am* a violinist. [first person]
> *You are* a violinist. [second person]
> *He is* a violinist. [third person]

PERSONAL PRONOUN. See PRONOUN.

PHRASE. A group of related words that does not contain both a subject and verb.

> We handed *the new manager* his book. [noun phrase]
> The company *should have negotiated*. [verb phrase]
> *In the morning*, we departed. [prepositional phrase]
> *Climbing mountains* can be dangerous. [gerund phrase]
> *To win this race* requires time and effort. [infinitive phrase]
> The desk *piled with books* is mine. [participial phrase]

POSSESSIVE CASE. See CASE.

PREDICATE. The word or words in a sentence that tell or ask something about the SUBJECT. A predicate always contains a VERB.

> subject   predicate
> The manager *has organized the reception*.

PREFIX. One or more letters in front of the ROOT of a word that alter or modify its meaning.

> *de*-emphasize   *re*-build   *un*-happy

PREPOSITION. A word that links a word or group of words (prepositional PHRASE) to another word or words in the sentence. Common prepositions are *to, for, from, over, near*.

> He spoke *with* excitement *about* the project scheduled
> *for* the autumn.

PRONOUN. A word used in place of a noun.

> Demonstrative pronoun: *This* is outdated.
> Indefinite pronoun: *Each* of us has decided to join.
> Intensive pronoun: I *myself* believe in humanity.
> Interrogative pronoun: *Who* is there?
> Personal pronoun: *He* approves of the speech.
> Reflexive pronoun: She bought *herself* a new scarf.
> Relative pronoun: I bought the house *that* I liked.

PROPER ADJECTIVE. See ADJECTIVE.

PROPER NOUN. See NOUN.

REDUNDANCY. Words that state the same concept two or more times.

> *Past history* can give us the *true facts*.

REFLEXIVE PRONOUN. See PRONOUN.
RELATIVE PRONOUN. See PRONOUN.
RESTRICTIVE CLAUSE. A CLAUSE essential to the meaning of the sentence.

> The pupils *who left school early* were punished.

ROOT. The core of a word to which is added PREFIXES, SUFFIXES, and other modifications.

root + suffix	prefix + root	prefix + root + suffix
add + ed	re + pay	un + bear + able

RUN-ON (or FUSED) **SENTENCE.** Two or more independent CLAUSES that are not separated by appropriate punctuation or a coordinate CONJUNCTION and a comma.

> I saw the proposal it was finished.
> Revisions: I saw the proposal. It was finished.
> I saw the proposal; it was finished.
> I saw the proposal, and it was finished.

SENTENCE. A group of words containing a SUBJECT and PREDICATE that can stand by itself as a complete thought.

Sentences are classified according to their *purpose.*
A declarative sentence makes a statement.

> I like string beans.

An imperative sentence makes a request or command.

> Go to the file cabinet.

An interrogative sentence asks a question.

> Will you assist me?

An exclamatory sentence expresses emotion.

> We're going home!

Sentences are also classified according to their *form.*
A simple sentence contains one independent CLAUSE.

> We won the award.

A compound sentence contains two or more independent clauses.

> We won the award, but they won the publicity.

A complex sentence contains at least one independent clause and at least one dependent clause.

> Although we won the award, they won the publicity.

A compound-complex sentence contains at least two independent clauses and at least one dependent clause.

> Although we won the award, they won the publicity;
> we all went home happy.

SIMPLE SENTENCE. See SENTENCE.
SQUINTING MODIFIER. See MODIFIER.

SUBJECT. The word or words about which something is asserted or asked in a sentence.

> The *man* made a request.
> Are *you* going home?

SUBORDINATE CLAUSE. Dependent clause. See CLAUSE.
SUBORDINATE CONJUNCTION. See CONJUNCTION.
SUFFIX. A letter or letters added to the end of a word that alter or modify it.

> superb + *ly*   ideal + *ize*

TENSE. The aspect of a verb that indicates when an action took place or a condition occurred.

Simple Tenses

> Past: I *rode* home.
> Present: I *ride* home.
> Future: I *will ride* home.

Perfect Tenses

Perfect tenses are formed by combining *have, has, had,* or *will have* with the past PARTICIPLE of the verb.

The past perfect tense shows an action completed by a certain time in the past. The past perfect tense is formed by combining *had* + the past participle of a verb. Past perfect: I *had ridden* home by noon.

The present perfect tense shows an action begun in the past but continuing to the present, being completed in the present, or being completed just before the present.
Present perfect:

> Henry *has realized* the truth since Tuesday.
> I *have written* the proposal.
> Jill *has* just *finished* the book.

The future perfect tense is formed by combining *will have* + the past participle of the verb. The future perfect tense shows that action will have been completed before some time in the future. Future perfect: By September, we *will have finished* the house.

Progressive Tenses

Progressive tenses show ongoing action. Each of the six tenses just described has progressive forms. Progressive tenses are created by combining a form of the verb *be* with the present participle of a verb.
Past progressive: *was* or *were* + present participle

> Jim *was writing* the report.

Present progressive: *is, am,* or *are* + present participle

> Jim *is writing* the report.

Future progressive: *will be* + present participle

> Jim *will be writing* the report tomorrow.

Past perfect progressive: *had been* + present participle

> Jim *had been writing* the report when he got hungry.

Present perfect progressive: *have been* or *has been* + present participle

> Jim *has been* writing the report all day.

Future perfect progressive: *will have been* + present participle

> By noon Jim *will have been writing* the report for six hours.

Emphatic Tenses

Past and present tenses have emphatic forms. These are formed by combining *does, do,* or *did* and the ROOT of the verb.

> I *did finish* the report.
> I *do state* the truth.
> He *does state* the truth.

TONE. The quality of a piece of writing that indicates the writer's attitude, emotions, or sentiments.

TOPIC SENTENCE. A sentence in a paragraph that indicates the main point of the paragraph.

TRANSITION. A word or group of words that helps the reader move from one sentence to the next or from one paragraph to the next.

TRANSITIVE VERB. See VERB.

VERB. A word or group of words that express an action or state of being. Main verbs may be combined with helping verbs to form verb PHRASES.

> I *have* [helping verb] *developed* [main verb] a program.

A transitive verb is an action verb that has a DIRECT OBJECT.

> David *wrote* [transitive verb] the *report* [direct object].

A transitive verb may also have an INDIRECT OBJECT:

> Jim *gave* [transitive verb] *Helen* [indirect object] the *papers* [direct object].

An intransitive verb may be an action verb that does not have a direct object.

> The glass *broke* [intransitive verb].

An intransitive verb may also be a LINKING VERB.

> Jim *seems* [intransitive verb] happy.

VERB PHRASE. See PHRASE.

VERBAL. A word or words derived from a verb that are used as a noun, adjective, or adverb. Gerunds, infinitives, and participles are verbals. Verbals may have COMPLEMENTS, OBJECTS, MODIFIERS, and sometimes SUBJECTS. (See also PHRASE.)

Gerunds end in *-ing* and act as nouns.

> *Training* was essential to the job. [gerund subject]

Infinitives are formed from *to* + the root of a verb.

> *To help* was his goal. [infinitive used as noun/subject]
> This is the car *to buy*. [infinitive used as adjective]
> He plays *to win*. [infinitive used as adverb]

Past infinitives are formed from *to* + *have* + the past participle of a verb:

> *To have finished* the reports this afternoon was our goal.

Present participles are verb forms ending in *-ing* that act as adjectives.

> *Running*, he caught the ball. [present participle acting as adjective]

Past participles of regular verbs end in *-d* or *-ed*.

> *Heated*, the casserole became almost edible.

For a list of irregular past participles, see p. 176.

Combined with HELPING VERBS, participles also function as part of verb PHRASES.

> The car *is stalling*.
> The car *has stalled*.

VOICE. The aspect of a verb that determines whether a subject is doing the action or being acted upon.

Active voice: The subject performs the action.

> Karen *wrote* the book.

Passive voice: The grammatical object becomes the subject of the sentence. The doer of the action either does not appear or appears in a prepositional phrase.

> The book *was written*.
> The book *was written* by Karen.

Passive verbs are created by combining a form of the verb *be* and the past participle of a verb. Writers should use passive verbs only when they serve a clear purpose.

ANSWERS TO PRE-TESTS, SELF-CHECK TESTS, AND REVIEWS

Part One Pre-Test. Nouns: George, job, ARMCO, technician, years, job, hours, pay, work, morale, time, family, situation, years, hours, plant, home, Saturdays. Helping verbs: had, cannot, will. Main verbs: began, worked, requires, keep, spend, says, understand, cut, stay. Adjectives: a, ten, new, more, the, increased, exciting, high, enough, the, two, the. Adverbs: completely. Prepositions: at, as, for, with, In, at, at, on. Conjunctions: after, but, and, but, and. Pronouns: his, he, His, his, I, my, he, they, I, my. Interjections: Oh

SCT 1-1. sits, hoped, wrote, performs, conclude, determines

SCT 1-2. 1) wanted 2) was 3) decided 4) was 5) looked

SCT 1-3. 1) hoping 2) encountered 3) changed 4) deliver 5) ended

SCT 1-4. 1) has begun 2) will orient 3) should have arrived 4) must have taken 5) has played 6) will open 7) could have returned 8) may have discovered 9) did notice 10) should know

SCT 1-5. 1) has sold 2) can be 3) wants 4) must have changed 5) plans

SCT 1-6. 1) Was Patricia hoping 2) Will the Hoppers be arriving 3) Should the committee establish 4) Could Mike know 5) Should Harry Thorne evaluate

SCT 1-7. 1) helped, went 2) Will join, will meet 3) must stay, come 4) disagreed, supported 5) fill, check, give

Verb Review. Helping verbs: have, have, have. Main verbs: addresses, surveyed, found, summarized, listed, outlined

SCT 2-1. surprise, radiator, parade, leader, horse, detail, analysis

SCT 2-2. 1) man, seminar, stress 2) film, radiation 3) radio, lamp 4) index, errors 5) company, hour, regulations 6) partition, privacy, air 7) contracts, information, month 8) message, president 9) Laziness, staff 10) ratio, clerks, managers

SCT 2-3. (Suggested answers) 1) Tom 2) Rome 3) Economics 301 4) IBM 5) Mervyn's

SCT 2-4. 1) secretaries 2) feet 3) men 4) knives 5) teeth

SCT 2-5. (Suggested answers) 1) The doctor examined the bite on the child's arm. 2) The climb up that hill is difficult. 3) The handles on this suitcase are broken. 4) Have you tried a sample of this product? 5) His control of the situation was impressive.

SCT 2-6. 1) hopes, to begin 2) Raising, has been prohibited 3) is, flying, costs 4) is renting, loves, to ski 5) has asked, to transfer

Noun Review. report, problems, contracts, Analysts, customers, reactions, section, report, findings, analysts, section, recommendations, conclusion

SCT 3-1. this, I, it, he, our

SCT 3-2. 1) They 2) It 3) They 4) It 5) He

SCT 3-3. 1) these 2) this 3) these 4) that 5) those

SCT 3-4. 1) Whose 2) Which 3) Who 4) What 5) Whom

SCT 3-5. 1) IND, P 2) INT, P, D 3) IND 4) INT, P 5) INT, P 6) IND, P, P, R/I 7) P, IND, P 8) D, P 9) P, P, P 10) IND, P, P

Pronoun Review. Personal: our, our, I, my. Demonstrative: these. Indefinite: 0. Interrogative: 0

SCT 4-1. handsome, terrible, unhappy, brown, ticklish, random

SCT 4-2. (Suggested answers) 1) successful, wooden 2) slow, unreliable 3) huge, expensive 4) antique 5) dull, thorough

SCT 4-3. 1) the, the 2) a 3) the, the, a 4) that, a 5) that, the

SCT 4-4. enthusiastic, beautiful, refreshing, expensive, tasty, selfish, believable, practical, necessary, perilous

SCT 4-5. 1) This attractive house, the end, a long street 2) the proposition, interesting 3) the heavy paperwork, a temporary clerical worker 4) the new proposal, ready, the executive directors 5) He, temperamental, erratic 6) the flooded basement, an experienced plumber 7) These projections, correct, the older figures 8) This simple command, a second file 9) The well-defined boundaries, the last century 10) a recent graduate, the accounting position

SCT 4-6. 1) A 2) N 3) A 4) A 5) A

SCT 4-7. (Suggested answers) I. 1) more imaginative 2) better 3) less tiring 4) cuter 5) less dangerous. II. 1) best 2) most informative 3) lightest 4) longest 5) loneliest

Adjective Review. Articles: the, the, the, the, the, the. Demonstrative: This. Common: new, simplified, positive, negative, opening, further, second. Proper: 0

SCT 5-1. immediately, attractively, faster, never, often, quickly

SCT 5-2. 1) is running quickly 2) has never seen 3) was heading faithfully, struck viciously 4) are arriving steadily 5) is definitely trying

SCT 5-3. 1) generally low 2) very uncertain 3) highly secret 4) altogether unprepared 5) really good

SCT.5-4. 1) definitely 2) somewhat fast 3) efficiently 4) highly, poorly 5) animatedly

SCT 5-5. 1) differently 2) speaks well 3) quickly 4) directly 5) really 6) bad 7) terrible 8) persuasively 9) awful 10) pretty well, really quickly

SCT 5-6. I. 1) ADV 2) ADJ 3) ADJ 4) ADV 5) ADV. II. 1) clearly 2) well 3) effectively 4) worse 5) randomly

Adverb and Adjective Review. usually, a, simple, more effectively, a, complicated, A, complex, more imposing, impressive, not, very, valuable, easily, carefully, the, unnecessarily, complicated, difficult

SCT 6-1. (Suggested answers) 1) of, for 2) to, by 3) From, of 4) along, to 5) on, on 6) for, at 7) with, after 8) Until, for 9) by, in 10) From until, by

SCT 6-2. 1) across that intersection/to the used car lot 2) with the help/of her two assistants 3) According to real estate analysts, at a later age 4) with us/before April 1 5) to Harry/without Pat's consent

SCT 6-3. 1) to the doctor/for his shots 2) From my experience of the problem 3) about several issues in the conference room 4) with me/ to the symposium 5) except Joe, after the game

SCT 6-4. 1) with, to 2) with, for 3) of, with 4) from 5) for, by

Preposition Review. At noon, on the problems, of small businesses, in today's economy, of 20 small businesses, at the meeting, of GHA Corporation, to us, after Mr. Glover's speech

SCT 7-1. 1) and 2) but 3) so 4) nor 5) and

SCT 7-2. 1) and: nouns 2) but: adjectives 3) or: verbs 4) yet: adverbs 5) or: verbs

SCT 7-3. (Suggested answers) 1) or: nouns 2) so: clauses 3) but: clauses 4) yet: adverbs 5) but: clauses

SCT 7-4. (Suggested answers) 1) either/or: verbs 2) not only/but also: adjectives 3) whether/or: phrases 4) Neither/nor: nouns 5) both/and: clauses

SCT 7-5. I. (Suggested answers) 1) When 2) until 3) As 4) if 5) While. II. 1) but: CRD 2) both/and: COR 3) and: CRD 4) Although: SUB 5) but: CRD; neither/nor: COR 6) Since: SUB; and: CRD 7) so: CRD 8) or: CRD 9) Either/or: COR 10) as long as: SUB

Conjunction Review. and: CRD; but: CRD; both/and: COR; If: SUB; not only/but also: COR; and: CRD; Although: SUB; and: CRD; while: SUB

SCT 8-1. Well, Gee, Hey, No, Drat

Part Two Pre-Test. I. 2, 3, 5. II. 1) 1, 2, 3 2) you 3) (You), speech, (You) 4) yes: 6 (5) yes: 2 (6) idea (7) audience (8) yes: 2

SCT 9-1. 1) My work 2) A new building 3) George and Greg 4) Our chocolate desserts 5) you 6) The incoming administration 7) We 8) Gregory 9) The azaleas 10) anyone

SCT 9-2. 1) Joan 2) checkbook 3) delay 4) question 5) you

SCT 9-3. 1) William Beane, Larry Smith, doctor 2) United States, Soviet Union 3) points, points 4) Max, Lew 5) neighbors, friends

SCT 9-4. 1) Losing 2) bird-watching 3) (You) 4) To succeed 5) Clyde

SCT 9-5. (Suggested answers) 1) Leasing a car 2) Going into debt 3) Landing in New York 4) To sell your shares 5) Buying the restaurant

SCT 9-6. 1) Whoever runs for governor: noun clause 2) Winning: gerund 3) you: pronoun 4) What the report recommends: noun clause 5) Ordering a hundred cases: noun phrase (6) Swimming Lake Tober: noun phrase 7) Whichever set you want: noun clause 8) Memorizing this text: noun phrase 9) Whomever you designate: noun clause 10) Why this door is stuck: noun clause

Subject Review. 1) Jordan Glover 2) Representatives 3) Kathryn Horne, assistant 4) Kathryn 5) implied subject: you

SCT 10-1. 1) supplies 2) imports 3) photographs 4) results 5) terminals

SCT 10-2. I. 1) meeting 2) Bob, Randy 3) to fly west 4) why you are leaving 5) whoever applies. II. (Suggested answers) 1) Bill Rowan 2) to elope 3) delicatessen 4) what you are saying 5) me

SCT 10-3. 1) Poland (IO), message (DO) 2) employees (IO), raise (DO) 3) us (IO), opportunities (DO) 4) him (IO), authority (DO) 5) Phyllis (IO), machine (DO) 6) Jackson (IO), condolences (DO) 7) Hal (IO), typewriter (DO) 8) data (DO) 9) Harriet (IO), job (DO) 10) you (IO), sedan, truck (DO)

SCT 10-4. (Suggested answers) I. 1) Give my congratulations to Molly. 2) This plan increases organization and efficiency. 3) I polished my desk. 4) We will applaud whoever draws the lucky card. 5) She promotes neither clerks nor supervisors. II. 1) They lent Irene and Bill a hundred dollars. 2) Give him my raincoat. 3) Have you tipped the waiters five dollars?

4) The store gave our company a modem. 5) I mailed both Steve and his sisters a Christmas package.

SCT 10-5. I. 1) C 2) DO 3) C 4) IO 5) C II. (Suggested answers) 1) I am insecure about my typing. 2) Sam is the attorney for the case. 3) Harriet seems either careless or unlucky. 4) His opinion sounded accurate. 5) Patsy is a student at the University of Arizona.

Object and Complement Review. Direct objects: speech, refreshments, proceedings, us. Indirect objects: us. Complements: 0

SCT 11-1. 1) Losing a game 2) to win the award/by July 3) Baking cookies, for children 4) To conquer the world, of Alexander the Great 5) stained with mud, for $45.99 6) without a sense of responsibility, at Patton Industries 7) Having finished all the items/on the agenda, for our thoughts/on the investment question 8) To finish this project/on time 9) to the staff 10) Working with the biochemist

SCT 11-2. (Suggested answers) 1) I try to remember names. 2) Developing guidelines is the first item on the agenda. 3) Standing in line for the tickets took three hours. 4) Mr. Jones refuses to consider each person's opinion. 5) Breaking the copier cost Bill his job.

SCT 11-3. 1) with uncertainty (ADV) 2) to win the election (N) 3) Surprised by the rain (ADJ) 4) near the podium (ADV) 5) to avoid bankruptcy (ADV) 6) from a pay telephone (ADV) 7) Just graduated from college (ADJ), for a job (ADV) 8) to the suburbs (ADV) 9) due to the new regulations (ADV) 10) Having stopped (ADJ)

Phrase Review. in sales / within two major lines / To find reasons / for these losses / of researchers / working in the South and Northeast / with selected retailers.

SCT 12-1. 1) Subjects: Randy, Bill; Verbs: Have seen 2) Subject: Jim; Verb: pounded; Phrases: To make his point, on the table 3) Subject: we; Verb: were sitting; Phrases: At dusk, around the conference table 4) Subject: You; Verb: are; Phrase: to bring a portfolio 5) Subject: manager; Verb: is studying 6) Subject: project; Verb: went; Phrase: Despite our planning 7) Subject: change; Verb: came; Phrases: With this technology, in the work force 8) Subject: They; Verb: were stopped; Phrases: by the highway patrol, before getting/to Texas 9) Subject: lettuce; Verb: has been attacked; Phrases: by several types/of insects 10) Subject: you; Verb: will meet; Phrase: in Tijuana

SCT 12-2. I. 1) If you would like the manual 2) After Anna Baines received the message 3) unless you want us to come on Saturday 4) that she knew the truth/because she called me after the meeting 5) — 6) That the tax increases will help the state's school system 7) If we are going to succeed 8) while George ordered breakfast 9) If you give me a week to get a team together 10) before we began the Herley campaign. II. 1) Subjects: you, you; Verbs: would like, should write 2) Subjects:

Anna Baines, she; Verbs: received, made 3) Subjects: I, you; Verbs: will be, want 4) Subjects: I, she, she; Verbs: realized, knew, called 5) Subjects: Being impatient; Verbs: has been 6) Subjects: governor, increases; Verbs: hopes, will help 7) Subjects: we, we; Verbs: are going, must acquire 8) Subjects: we, George; Verbs: met, ordered 9) Subjects: you, project; Verbs: give, will be 10) Subjects: article, we; Verbs: must have been revised, began

SCT 12-3. 1) P 2) I 3) D 4) D 5) P

SCT 12-4. 1) When you are sure/that you know the answers 2) If Carole sees the package/[that] I am waiting for 3) — 4) who are visiting the New York office 5) which has already cost a million dollars. II. 1) DO 2) S 3) DO 4) OP 5) DO

Clause Review. Independent clauses: we need to continue and expand our marketing efforts; The television commercials are being copied by all our competitors; The print ads in local newspapers have lost their appeal; We need to expand our present market and make Humanoid a household word all over America. Dependent clauses: Although our great advertising campaign has doubled demand for our Humanoid dolls; that have been so successful for us; since TarnyToys came out with its Rubberman ads

SCT 13-1. I. 1) F 2) S 3) F 4) F 5) S 6) S 7) F 8) F 9) F 10) S. II. (Suggested answers) 1) We are changing the store name because manual typewriters have virtually disappeared. 2) — 3) Water dripping through the office ceilings stained the carpets. 4) We will not make a plan until we can determine who is responsible. 5) — 6) — 7) Emerging from the meeting, John Bates looked crestfallen. 8) To assess the situation, we are taking a poll. 9) Having taken the easiest route, we arrived early. 10) —

SCT 13-2. (Suggested answers) 1) Katie; she 2) finished, but 3) members because they have been 4) typewriter if it is 5) disaster. We

SCT 13-3. (Suggested answers) 1) wounded; however, 2) fit. Paul 3) month. We are 4) staff, so 5) name; then

Sentence Review. (Suggested answers) Modern technology has led to a large number of specialized areas. Many companies assign highly specialized teams to work on small segments of a project. Deciding how to advertise a product, for example, might necessitate specialists in production, marketing, and finance to coordinate activities. However, one person is usually assigned to supervise the project and coordinate the activities of each specialist.

SCT 14-1. I. 1) S 2) — 3) S 4) S 5) — II. (Suggested answers) 1) I read the report. 2) Without strategic planning, we would have made a terrible error. 3) Henry sent George a letter. 4) Dan and Ellen will host tonight's party. 5) Harry will develop a brochure and coordinate the seminar.

SCT 14-2. 1) S 2) CD 3) S 4) S 5) CD

SCT 14-3. I. 1) CX: Good Foods, Inc. is manufacturing Sno-White Cookies in the gold package. 2) CD: With the rise in interest rates, housing starts have decreased, and banks are advertising more heavily. 3) CX: we will meet at noon in the Madison Hotel. 4) S: Calvin Smith will fly to New York on June 30 in order to set up the meeting with Frozen Foods International. 5) CX: Have you considered. II. (Suggested answers) 1) I was late, so I skipped breakfast. 2) When the meeting begins, ask for a review of last week's agenda. 3) At the beginning of June, we will make the final decision. 4) Having earned a promotion, George began working harder; he always accepts new challenges. 5) When you tour the company that we are studying, please interview the marketing manager.

SCT 14-4. 1) CX: the company will be able to increase salaries and benefits in May. 2) CD: In the following diagram, data flow is indicated by broken lines, and control signals are indicated by solid lines. 3) CX: Zion National Park is being studied by an international team of geologists. 4) CC: Mr. Rowley brings us slices of pizza, and Mr. Kipps brings us potato salad. 5) S: Neither the technicians nor the research staff completely understands the problem.

SCT 14-5. I. 1) P 2) P 3) A 4) A 5) P. II. (Suggested answers) 1) The committee has reached a decision. 2) Did you follow the guidelines? 3) — 4) — 5) If the students have completed the evaluations, you should collect them.

Sentence Review. 1) 4 2) 0 3) 1, 2, 3 4) 0 5) 1, 3, 4 6) 2

Part Three Pre-Test. Each of you realizes . . . One of the two machines is . . . To ease the photocopying problems, we have ordered . . . 2. To save time and money, use the mimeograph machine for more than five copies of any document . . . 3. Put both your name and the number of copies you made . . . 4. Whoever uses the machine at the end of the day should give the sheet to Mel Rose or me. 5. There appear to be coffee stains . . .

SCT 15-1. 1) settles 2) sell 3) know 4) intend 5) manages

SCT 15-2. 1) has 2) does 3) are 4) has, are 5) Am

SCT 15-3. 1) rode 2) was 3) had 4) gave 5) drank

SCT 15-4. I. (Suggested answers) 1) will have 2) hear 3) leave 4) walk 5) will tell 6) take 7) went 8) returned 9) hope 10) will be. II. 1) future 2) present 3) present 4) present 5) future 6) present 7) past 8) past 9) present 10) future

SCT 15-5. I. 1) asked 2) had seen 3) has escaped 4) had noticed 5) had burrowed 6) will have fixed II. 1) past 2) past perfect 3) present perfect 4) past perfect 5) past perfect 6) future perfect

SCT 15-6. 1) has swum 2) has ridden 3) has lain 4) has flown 5) has gone

SCT 15-7. 1) am, leaves, was hurrying, forgot 2) saw, decided, was speaking, learned 3)

was increasing, began 4) burst, sprang, threw, appeared 5) had lain, arrived

Verb Form Review. spoken, brought, began, taken, gone, came

SCT 16-1. I. 1) manager has 2) He is 3) sandwich becomes 4) route has 5) accountant is. II. 1) They are, they do 2) attorneys have 3) heads plan 4) Are secretaries going 5) daisies flourish

SCT 16-2. 1) looks 2) are establishing 3) has 4) C 5) C

SCT 16-3. 1) appears 2) has 3) C 4) are 5) C

SCT 16-4. 1) is 2) have 3) has 4) C 5) comes

SCT 16-5. 1) has 2) C 3) is 4) have 5) is

SCT 16-6. 1) has 2) affects 3) is 4) provides 5) have 6) is 7) C 8) has 9) comes 10) has 11) have 12) has 13) C 14) brings 15) C

Subject-Verb Agreement Review. has studied, has seen, faces, there are, has to make, is intended, Every one of us knows, is unpleasant.

SCT 17-1. (Suggested answers) 1) The employees were shocked because the bank would not cover our payroll checks. 2) After they meet with the accountants, tell the clerks to speak with me. 3) Now that I have finished writing them, please let me know what you think of my reports on taxes and price increases. 4) Maurice Constance's speech on the upcoming woodwind concert will be very interesting. 5) . . . the Canaanites, who were condemned by Hebrew law. 6) Sam's study of management methods in Japanese companies has been very beneficial for our corporation. 7) . . . This double major has delayed her graduation by two years. 8) Phil was wearing a hat when he saw his brother yesterday. 9) The new employees have been meeting every deadline ever since William Snell and Bonnie Grey have begun working with them. 10) . . . many of us felt proud of Philip.

SCT 17-2. 1) about his/her specialty 2) he or she is not feeling well 3) C 4) his or her own choice 5) its offices 6) has decided whether he wants 7) its rules 8) he or she ever decided 9) you would let 10) she still brought me

Pronoun Agreement and Reference Review. (Suggested answers) our products,/ its elegantly decorated,/you, our best customers, can save yourselves

SCT 18-1. 1) Johanna and me 2) Thomas Morel and she 3) Mike and him 4) us council members 5) Carole and they

SCT 18-2. 1) as efficient as she 2) that is he 3) I were she 4) C 5) as careful as he

SCT 18-3. 1) C 2) C 3) C 4) whoever wants 5) who was giving 6) C 7) whom you voted for 8) C 9) whom the instructor trusted 10) C

SCT 18-4. 1) Barbara and I, everyone's 2) its shelf 3) theirs 4) C 5) it's vital

Pronoun Case Review. it's important, 1) . . . give us supervisors 2) Jorge or me 4) your needs

SCT 19-1. 1) in the pinstripe suit, quickly 2) With deliberation, lucky 3) only two 4) To win the debate, quick, her solid, extensive 5) wearing a yellow shirt, that begins two years before his birth

SCT 19-2. (Suggested answers) 1) With a shaking voice, the new accountant 2) just the most essential 3) the pizza covered with pepperoni and sausage 4) he would be victorious within a week 5) to cover only the first three items

SCT 19-3. (Suggested answers) 1) While we were traveling to Arkansas 2) To increase attendance, we will fine absentee members 3) While still haggling over the issues, the politicians are not 4) Although she was unable to finish her education, 5) As I was the youngest person in the room,

Modifier Review. (Suggested answers) Having thoroughly studied the financial and statistical data, the evaluation committee has written this report. We have considered only the most recent information; however, division managers have established a secondary committee that will carefully research the historical background of the problem. When the reports are complete, both committees will make them available to all employees.

SCT 20-1. (Suggested answers) 1) to increase profits, reduce cost overruns, and raise employee morale 2) diversifying, developing 3) and home ownership 4) experience and goals 5) and (3) fewer hourly employees

SCT 20-2. (Suggested answers) I. 1) major either in accounting or in economics 2) but also she is a good writer 3) can neither type accurately nor program computers 4) but also made several personal comments 5) and in computers. II. 1) I am neither a supervisor nor a manager. 2) Frances plans either to retire or to work part-time. 3) We looked not only in the office but also in the corridor. 4) Either Ray will win this contract or he will resign. 5) Neither renting a house nor buying a condominium appeals to us.

Parallelism Review. (Suggested answers) with both the staff's enthusiasm and its productivity . . . either a memorable office party or bonuses . . . but it also wants to let you know that your work is being recognized.

Part Four Pre-Test. Tom Carpenter, who works as an executive with Towne Company, makes an excellent salary and has always been satisfied with his job. His boss says, "Tom is one of this company's best managers. He is intelligent, thorough, and conscientious." Management considers Tom a practical man with skills and adaptability that give him a maturity beyond his years.

Now that Tom has been with the company for over twenty-three years, he is being seriously considered for the position of vice-president. Tom, however, is not certain he wants to make the move to New York that the promotion would entail, so he is evaluating his options and discussing them with his family and with his friends in the company.

SCT 21-1. 1) project. We 2) 3:00 p.m. 3) typing if you have 4) Mr. Howard. He is a well-known 5) meeting is over.

SCT 21-2. 1) well. 2) asked, "to Brazil?" 3) Frank. "Therefore, 4) potential if Carstairs 5) next week?

SCT 21-3. 1) lawsuit? 2) "No!" shouted the crowd. "We won't take it anymore!" 3) merger. 4) "Oklahoma!" 5) improving. Sales

Punctuation Review. . . . Approaching a professor on campus, the student asked, "Excuse me, where's the cafeteria at?"

The professor looked sourly at the student. "Young man, never end a sentence with a preposition."

SCT 22-1. 1) negotiations, call 2) morale, and they 3) sweeteners, but the new 4) overcrowded; we should 5) lunch is not

SCT 22-2. 1) park, Tim headed 2) sales, we should 3) report, Klein 4) today, Fred Rivera 5) notes, the speaker

SCT 22-3. 1) Kentucky, the bluegrass state, 2) project, in our opinion, 3) "Well, 4) No, 5) Katrina, the Austrian violinist,

SCT 22-4. 1) This small, elegant Swiss watch has cost us a large amount, but not 2) me, Mr. Barkeley, 3) small electronics 4) As you can see, our portable, efficient home computer 5) C

SCT 22-5. I. 1) Albany, which is the capital of New York, 2) Paris, France, but he has always wanted to live in Bar Harbor, Maine 3) C 4) January 12, 1984, and 5) man who was recommended II. 1) comma sets off appositive 2) commas set off negatives or contrasts 3) comma precedes coordinate conjunction between two independent clauses 4) comma sets off introductory modifying phrase and precedes coordinate conjunction separating two independent clauses 5) comma sets off introductory prepositional phrases 6) comma sets off interjection and separates introductory dependent clause from independent clause 7) comma separates date from year and separates introductory dependent clause from independent clause 8) commas set off appositive 9) comma follows introductory modifying phrase 10) comma precedes coordinate conjunction separating two independent clauses

SCT 22-6. 1) business and 2) Henry and his sister Maude waited 3) vacation for two weeks 4) Green Bay to Chicago 5) promotion in April, I

Comma Review. Working closely with Sam Brown, the manager of the restaurant, was the head chef, Henry Plante. Henry, who often attended meetings with Sam Brown and the restaurant's owner, was considered as good a manager as he was a cook. With the approval of Sam Brown, Henry allowed the restaurant employees the most freedom possible.

As one of the waitresses explained, "Everyone here knows one another, and working here is really a joy."

On several occasions when well-known customers complimented him, Henry relayed the compliments to the rest of the kitchen staff. This courtesy was well received and gave the employees great pride in their work. Said one employee about Henry, "I've worked in restaurants all my life, but here it's more than just a job; it's a pleasure."

Both the customers and the owner believed it was Henry who made the restaurant such a success.

SCT 23-1. 1) twig: 2) Florida; New York, New York; and 3) Prices are right, 4) Sherlock Holmes: 5) computer; however,

SCT 23-2. 1) downtown Baltimore 2) twenty-two, streamlined, operating procedures 3) extracurricular, employees—many 4) eighty-pound bags, backyard 5) re-sign

Semicolon, Colon, Dash, and Hyphen Review. twenty-five/include:/more paperwork/obvious;/600 percent/situa-tion/from all of you, we will be meeting in the Red Room at 4:30 p.m.

SCT 24-1. 1) "In the spring," said Henrietta, "we 2) agreement," said 3) facts"; 4) that she should be given . . . reports. 5) mentions "leadership," he

SCT 24-2. 1) lawsuit? Mr. Harrison asked himself. 2) (in the Rose Hill Mall). 3) *gigot d'agneau,* the 4) share?" 5) understand.) 6) poem 'Into the Twilight.'" 7) *Newsweek* 8) *a* 9) supervisor) is 10) C

Punctuation Review. . . . Friday?" . . . impatient), . . . "Two weeks!" . . . *Romance in Moscow* if I don't . . . chapter entitled 'Kiss in the Snow.'"

SCT 25-1. I. 1) authors' 2) goose's 3) patio's 4) corporation's 5) lease's II. 1) men's 2) arteries' 3) oxen's 4) banners' 5) actresses' III. 1) doctor's instructions 2) street artists' antics, fellow businesmen's protests 3) That popular novelist's book 4) my colleagues' attitudes, our project's secrecy 5) the restaurants' proprietor, company's staff

SCT 25-2. 1) C.P.A.'s, Kathryn James' house 2) Napoleon's strategies 3) shouldn't, movie's 4) Bentley's, 1960's, their 5) Let's

Apostrophe Review. 1) manager's, employees 2) Conrad's 3) country's 4) men's, customers 5) employees' 6) their itineraries 7) faculty's 8) Jane and George's, Bill Taylor's 9) C.P.A.s or C.P.A.'s 10) apartments, doctor's

Part Five Pre-Test. Standford Office Supplies / 3467 Hoover Blvd. / Dear Mr. Glassman: / Tuesday / received / 155 boxes / stationery / $600 / accommodating / please refer / Thanksgiving / Sincerely

SCT 26-1. I. (Suggested answers) 1) Three circuses are performing this weekend. 2) The elegies were written by Thomas Rowe. 3) These industries thrive on competition. 4) Our ranches have been sold. 5) Theresa's analyses seem thorough. 6) Harry's speeches last only six minutes. 7) As a child, she attended many rodeos. 8) Four calves were born here in May. 9) Pete baked five loaves of rye bread. 10) Their larynxes have been damaged. II. variety, patients, believe, weird,

weight, diets, hygiene, receive, grief, clients, conceited, achieved, efficient

SCT 26-2. 1) We have not accepted the proposal. 2) I never regretted that decision. 3) His betrayal was unexpected. 4) The insulation business is growing. 5) The corporation is debating a change in marketing techniques. 6) The car has been stalling. 7) This is preferred stock. 8) Roland will be controlling this division. 9) Have you acknowledged their presence at the meeting? 10) Peter was stretching the truth in this report.

SCT 26-3. Employees / February / thoroughly / embarrassed / errors / customer / forgotten / omitted / relevant / piece / hurriedly / written / data / guarantee / liable / forgetfulness / jeopardize / business / courteous / conscious

SCT 26-4. I. (Sample answers) 1a) This pear is ripe. 1b) The pair of socks is missing. 2a) He looks hale and hearty. 2b) The hail damaged my plants. 3a) Steve will bare his soul to anyone. 3b) I can't bear this tedious meeting. 4a) The scene was emotional. 4b) Have you seen the Marx Brothers' last film? 5a) The Arabs consider this a holy place. 5b) She was wholly unaware of the situation. 6a) We try to play fair with our customers. 6b) The fare is a quarter. 7a) Bail was set at a thousand dollars. 7b) A bale of hay had landed on the road. 8a) There is a lien on the building. 8b) Jack looks lean and healthy. 9a) I bowled a perfect game. 9b) The decision was bold but risky. 10a) He paid off his car loan. 10b) Mr. Matthews played a lone hand in the deal. II. (Sample homophones) hear/here, pain/pane, lie/lye, our/hour, do/due

Spelling Review. 1) erasable, questionnaires 2) susceptible, innocuous, develop 3) tallied, mileage, accommodation, receipts 4) privileged, receive, certain, jeopardize, schedule 5) bookkeeper, skillful (or skilful), business

SCT 27-1. 1) "to leave 2) (or noon 3) she is 4) "We need 5) (it is

SCT 27-2. 1) Berlin, Germany, July 2) Hancock Corporation, Tokyo 3) Pete, Lutheran 4) Republican 5) Pepsi, Safeway 6) United States Treasury Department 7) Mother's Day 8) Wednesday, March 9) Cornell University, Sears 10) Avon

SCT 27-3. 1) Harry, ROTC 2) — 3) MBA, September 4) Montgomery County, April 5) Mr. Green, Dr. Smithe, (They were

Capitalization Review. Employees / Friday, / May 4, / Dr. / Research and Development Department / Ph.D. / University of Michigan / Kotell, Inc. / *The Industrial World* / French / countries / Dr. Hart / she / Research and Development staff.

SCT 28-1. 1) three o'clock, 230 19th Avenue 2) Three hundred forty-six 3) March 4, $4,500 4) 40 feet long, 20 feet deep, 156 feet wide. 5) 6 to 0 in the first quarter.

Number Review. 25th anniversary / year 2000 / 13 inches by 18 inches / 350 pages / hundreds / five employees / $10,000

Part Six Pre-Test. (Suggested revisions) 1) I have summarized the essentials of this report. 2) In the future, please write to Francis Deering. 3) We were astonished by the sudden changes in plans. 4) Maureen Hammond has reviewed your letter. 5) As we agreed on March 21, we have sent you the new terminal. 6) If we do not hear from you by May 2, your membership will be canceled. 7) The Board reached an agreement. 8) I enclose the report with June statistics. 9) The meeting between employees and management last week did not resolve the problems. 10) Philip Tremaine is unsure about the facts.

SCT 29-1. (Suggested outline) I. Congratulate her on the promotion. II. Tell her we will celebrate at the picnic. III. Provide details on picnic. IV. Repeat congratulations and offer good luck for the future.

SCT 29-2. (Sample answers) I. Gerri might use order of increasing importance to move the reader toward the main reason for choosing one machine over the others. II. Heriot would probably choose an order of time that would show employees each step one at a time. III. Peggy might use a problem to solution order. If she presents problems with the current system, the president might want to read her solutions. As the president's time is short, she might start with her most compelling point in favor of flextime and then move to less important points.

SCT 30-1. (Sample answers) 1) pro- = onward, on behalf of, for 1a) We will *proceed* with the meeting. 1b) We are in charge of company *procurements.* 2) hyper- = over 2a) The child is *hyperactive.* 2b) Holly is *hypersensitive* about the issue. 3) super- = situated over 3a) Hal is our *supervisor.* 3b) They have *superimposed* the photographs on each other. 4) dis- = not 4a) He is a *disinterested* observer. 4b) I am *disappointed* in the results. 5) de- = opposite, reversal 5a) Ted was *dehydrated.* 5b) I was *deflated* by the news.

SCT 30-2. 1) would have 2) alludes 3) stationery, elicited 4) principles 5) fewer people 6) apprised 7) accept, a lot 8) eminent, already 9) number 10) than

SCT 30-3. I. 1) We will go to the meeting all together. I am altogether delighted with this result. 2) This budget is purely imaginary. You were extremely imaginative to develop it. 3) The incidence of disease is decreasing in this area. The incidents described in the paper are exaggerated. 4) I am not conscious of any errors here. Joe has no conscience about money. 5) This coat will envelop you in mink. The envelope does not match the letter. 6) The incredible story was not believed by our listeners. I am always incredulous about advertising. 7) I will condole with the widow. I cannot condone his behavior. 8) The color of this shirt will detract from the tie. I hope the wallpaper will not distract you from your work. 9) This elemental principle was described by Plato. Police have arrested six elementary schoolchildren. 10) The populace has grown by three hundred thousand. New York is one of the most populous cities in the world. II. 1) sat, set 2) lain, lying, laid 3) rose, raising, rising 4) sit, setting 5) lying, laid

Word Usage Review. we had lain / continuously / so we proceeded / number of people / was rising quickly / to go sit / fewer than ten people

SCT 31-1. (Suggested revision) In your October 12 letter, you suggested purchasing the new Honeywell XZ by paying installments every two months.

Although we have carefully reviewed your request, we will not be able to accept the arrangement. I hope you will consider the monthly installment plan summarized in the enclosed brochure. We believe that the Honeywell XZ is the best microcomputer on the market today and that you will find our terms reasonable.

We will reserve a Honeywell XZ for you until the end of the week. I look forward to your order.

SCT 31-2. (Suggested revisions) 1) I am applying for the technical writer position you advertised in the *Sun-Times* as I have both the education and experience you require. 2) I have a B.S. in accounting and have held a summer internship with Coopers & Lybrand. While working full-time and attending school part-time, I graduated in the top tenth of my class. 3) Come to the exciting annual sale at Simpson's Clothing where all Ralph Lauren and Calvin Klein sportswear will be half price. 4) I am sure you will be interested in our new office furniture lease-buy program. This program enables you to lease desks, chairs, and filing cabinets for under $249 per month and to apply your payments to the purchase price, if you like, after only six months. 5) This restaurant, which seats 200 people, serves French and German dinners for under $10 apiece.

SCT 31-3. (Suggested revisions) 1) Our store was robbed last April by a man wearing a mask. 2) The whole staff was wasting time on Friday afternoon until the supervisor told us to start working. 3) The new manager seems to enjoy giving orders to everyone. 4) The project is a failure even though we labored over it for weeks. 5) The new employee is going to inform the manager if we leave work early.

SCT 31-4. (Suggested revisions) 1) Please let me know when you receive the brochure I am sending separately. 2) Please give this matter some thought so we can discover what measures we should take. 3) This department is going to change its sales policy. 4) After the meeting, we included sick leave in the company benefit plan. 5) If you are uncertain about this situation, please understand that we will try to pay you for your work.

SCT 31-5. (Suggested revision) Thank you for the bank and credit card references you gave us. We are happy to raise your credit limit to $2,000. We look forward to serving you.

Word Choice Review. (Suggested revision) Several of you have suggested that employees working on Christmas Day should receive double pay rather than the standard time and a half. Company managers are presently considering this proposal, and I will tell you as soon as they make a decision.

SCT 32-1. (Suggested revisions) 1) To improve the appearance of our salespeople, I am requesting that, starting Friday, May 3, all male employees wear a coat and tie while on the sales floor. All female employees should wear dresses or skirts. 2) As we agreed, you must get your check in the mail to us by August 4. 3) As the new health insurance does not cover dental bills, employees are responsible for obtaining their own dental coverage or paying their individual dental bills. 4) If you send us the enclosed card and a check $12.50 by June 1, we will renew your subscription to *New Ideas* for another year. 5) Please smoke only in the lounge areas, not in the offices or rest rooms of this building.

SCT 33-1. (Suggested revisions) 1) The new accounting technique is the first item on our agenda. 2) The two departments have combined to discuss the outcome of the project. 3) After careful consideration, I have listed the following requisites for the marketing survey. 4) He is now eliminating redundancies in his application letter. 5) The stocks have been depreciating throughout the year.

SCT 33-2. (Suggested reivisions) 1) Our Alaskan correspondent wrote the report on training sled dogs for television commercials. 2) A vast number of misinformed voters elected the superior court judge. 3) The driver did not see the curve in the road. 4) I stamped and addressed 50 envelopes before midnight. 5) Our company started negotiations to end the price war.

SCT 33-3. (Suggested revisions) 1) decide 2) used 3) talked 4) appreciates 5) seriously considered, I perceive

SCT 33-4. (Suggested revisions) I. 1) Seven people were waiting in the hallway. 2) The rain ruined the parade. 3) I am pleased to meet you. 4) The author is saying that life is a continuum. 5) "The union wage is inflationary," claimed Herman Fenwick. II. I find a problem with our cataloging system in the company library. We should always keep the most recent issue of a periodical in the periodical rack. So, even if a periodical has been in the office for over two weeks, it should not be shelved with old periodicals until a more recent issue arrives.

SCT 33-5. (Suggested revisions) 1) The woman wearing a clown suit ordered buttered toast. 2) Mr. Framley will consult an advertising expert. 3) The freckled boy delivers the most fragile packages to this office. 4) The completed employee evaluation is very favorable. 5) Even liberal arts majors have enjoyed this new text on management principles.

SCT 33-6. (Suggested revisions) As some of our customers have complained about slow service at the cash registers, I propose we have six, not four, registers working simultaneously. When necessary, moreover, we can open up the seventh register at the back of the store.

When I spoke to the checkout clerks about this plan, they responded enthusiastically. Let's discuss this idea at our meeting next week.

SCT 34-1. (Suggested revisions) 1) Although I plan to visit Des Moines for Christmas, the snow may keep my plane from leaving Chicago. 2) While the highway runs along the river, it does not go as far south as the river does. 3) The corporate records are incomplete because of last year's fire in the document library. 4) Before Theo meets with union delegates in Boston, he will meet with me and Ford Guthrie in Philadelphia. 5) Since Mrs. Leeman works on Saturdays, she cannot work on Tuesdays.

SCT 34-2. (Some suggested revisions) 1) When the earthquake hit, everyone panicked, buildings trembled, and some trees fell. Although tremors continued for an hour, no one was seriously injured. 2) Nearly fifty parents attended the noon meeting in the library. The high school principal addressed their concerns about a possible teachers' strike. 3) Computer security is such a problem that no computer is completely protected; even children have broken into some computers. 4) As an eighth-grade teacher, Maurice Young, age 37, has developed patience and a strong sense of humor while also learning the names of 55 rock bands. 5) The new fifteen-story office building on the corner of Third and South Streets contains ten stores, three restaurants, and four software companies.

SCT 34-3. (Suggested revisions) 1) The gala event will be a night to remember. Beginning at 7:00 p.m. in the Chandelier Room of the Holter Hotel, you will dine on lobster and champagne and listen to the amusing tales of guest speaker Rob Johnson. Then you will move to the PomPom Room for music and dancing. 2) The reporters are uncertain about the details of the situation. 3) Mr. Ganley is retiring for reasons known only to himself, his administrative assistant, and a dozen others. He may simply be tired of administrative controversy. 4) Whether her employers agree or not, Marion has planned a series of lunchtime concerts; she is a good pianist who enjoys playing jazz as much as classical music. 5) The Mayfield, Massachusetts university that is sponsoring a daily newspaper is popular with a new breed of liberal arts graduate students interested in business careers with a humanistic touch.

SCT 34-4. (Suggested revisions) 1) Concordia Home Supply not only has increased its profits by 30 percent annually over the past three years but also is still growing rapidly. To keep pace with the growth of the business, management is going to consider opening a new branch in Stockton, Modesto, or Bakersfield. 2) Of these three cities, Bakersfield was considered the best choice because it met the five criteria for determining the ideal location: number of homeowners, average income level, number of home supply stores, transportation costs, and number of construction firms in the area. Moreover, an excellent site for the store had been found in Bakersfield. 3) To attract customers to the new store, Concordia planned a grand opening celebration. Management offered customers a 20 percent discount on all items during the first two days, handed out discount coupons for special items if they were purchased within the next month, and offered professional services in gardening, plumbing, and carpentry. 4) Research showed that potential Bakersfield customers did not like to carry large amounts of cash and preferred using a special store credit card rather than their bank credit card. As a result, Concordia introduced Concordia credit cards in Bakersfield. 5) The Bakersfield Concordia Home Supply Store has prospered for three major reasons: (1) it has won several contracts from major local construction firms which currently contribute 30 percent of the store's earnings; (2) the store has effectively used the media, particularly newspapers, to advertise its products, special sales, convenient locations, and helpful personnel; and (3) management and staff have worked very hard to make every customer a steady customer.

SCT 34-5. (Suggested revisions) 1) The city needs public transportation since highways are crowded, gasoline prices are soaring, many people cannot afford cars, and young people and senior citizens find it difficult to get around without cars. 2) Currently senior economic adviser at Northeast Research Institute, Martina Deloreth is an economist who became interested in interest rate fluctuations while working for several banks. 3) My experience, as well as my B.S. in business administration, qualifies me. As a personnel assistant with Darth Enterprises, I was in charge of reviewing files and handled correspondence with prospective employees. 4) Our company's trial agreement with Elmer Corporation entails sharing production facilities. We will review the success of this arrangement in three months. 5) The report examines morale problems in five Tulsa companies that experience high turnover of clerical employees.

SCT 35-1. (Suggested supporting sentences) 1) In fact, it is more alive than it has been in decades. Decreasing fuel prices and an aging population have contributed to major upswings in sales of big cars. Some forecasters predict that someday soon the Japanese will produce a Toyota the size of a Lincoln. 2) They believe that a well-rounded background can be useful in today's multidimensional business world. Moreover, liberal arts students are often good communicators. Combined with the quantitative skills and specialized information of a business major, a liberal arts minor can be a valuable asset to a recent graduate. 3) While maintaining excellent relationships with his co-workers and staff, he has produced noticeable increases in efficiency and production. He impresses his fellow workers with his knowledge of and enthusiasm for the product. And he makes sure his staff is equally informed and enthusiastic. 4) First, they are constantly out of order. Second, the food is dull, fattening, and unappetizing. And, third, the food is more expensive than it is in the convenience store down the street. 5) We do far

more business on the West Coast than we do in the Southwest, so an office in Washington, Oregon, or California would be more useful than one in Oklahoma. Operating a Tulsa office would preclude our opening on the West Coast for the next two or three years. Furthermore, we might lose enough money in Tulsa to prevent us from opening the Florida office we need so badly.

SCT 35-2. (Sample revision) Although John Matthews has worked for GMC Inc. for 30 years, he is young at heart. Since he loves coordinating events, we put him in charge of the yearly company picnic. He doesn't play softball anymore, but he enjoys watching the game and is particularly good at choosing the teams as he knows who will be most effective in each position.

Paragraph Review. (Suggested revision) People are listening carefully to the weather broadcasts as the clouds are so dark and ominous. Since it rarely rains in this part of the country in July, we are probably just in for a muggy afternoon. People know, however, that there is always a chance of a tornado.

Part Seven Pre-Test. (Suggestions for revision) In the opening sentence, the writer should apply for a particular job. Central parts should include specific details about the writer's background and experience. The writer should not mention anything about the degree. The ending should include the telephone number.

SCT 36-1. (Suggested reordering) III, I, II, VI, V, IV

SCT 36-2. (Suggested draft) The three applications attached to this memo seem suitable for our current opening. As you know, we need a programmer with an undergraduate accounting degree who has also worked for a small company for at least a year and has some good communication skills.

Please interview these applicants by July 1. If any of them seem to fit our needs, have them set up a second interview with me.

SCT 36-3. (Suggested title) Programmer Data

SCT 36-4. (Suggested reorganization) 2, 5, 4, 3, 1 (order of decreasing importance makes major point quickly)

SCT 37-1. (Suggested items) 1, 2, 6, 7, 8, 9 (items that show leadership and skills useful in a summer camp)

SCT 37-2. (Suggested revisions) 1) Developed new personnel manual 2) Illustrated company's newspaper advertisements 3) Trained clerical employees to operate new computer hardware 4) Screened job applicants before scheduling their interviews with department managers 5) Handled office operations in the absence of the supervisor

SCT 37-3. (Suggested skills) 1) leadership skills (president of sorority, swimming coach, sales manager) 2) athletic skills (hockey, swimming, lifeguarding) 3) musical skills (guitar playing)

SCT 38-1. (Sample revision) As administrative assistant, I can contribute significantly to your company. My coursework as an accounting major at Derby College, combined with my experience as a bookkeeper, has given me a solid background in bookkeeping and accounting methods. The courses I have taken at Grace's Business College have provided me with a strong understanding of office procedures.

SCT 38-2. (Sample revision) My education and experience qualify me for the management training program described in the Ferrier University Placement Office. I will be graduating in June with a bachelor of science degree in management, and I am presently working as assistant manager of the Concord Burger King.

INDEX